THE JEWISH LAW ANNUAL

VOLUME TWENTY

Volume 20 of *The Jewish Law Annual* features six detailed studies — three on questions that fall under the rubric of halakhic methodology, and three that address substantive questions (privacy, cohabitation, medical triage) — and a book review. All three 'methodological' articles discuss creative interpretation of legal sources. Two consider the positive and forward-thinking aspects of such halakhic creativity, the third examines tendentious invocation of new halakhic arguments to advance an extraneous interest. The first exploration of positive creativity surveys the innovative midrashic exegeses of R. Meir Simha of Dvinsk, demonstrating his willingness to base rulings intended for implementation on such exegesis. The second examines exegetical creativity as to the laws of capital offenses. Midrashic argumentation enables the rabbinical authorities to set aside the literal sense of the harsh biblical laws, and apply more suitable penologial policies. On the other hand, the article on tendentious innovation focuses on a situation where novel arguments are advanced in the context of a power struggle, namely, Israeli rabbinical court efforts to preserve jurisdiction.

Two articles discuss contemporary dilemmas. One considers the hypothetical scenario of triage of an HIV vaccine, analyzing both the talmudic sources for resolving issues related to allocating scarce resources, and recent responsa. The second discusses the status of civil marriage and cohabitation vis-à-vis payment of spousal maintenance: can rabbinical courts order such payment? Another article explores whether privacy is a core value in talmudic law, as recent scholars have claimed. Does Jewish law indeed uphold a 'right to privacy?' The volume concludes with a review of Yuval Sinai's *Application of Jewish Law in the Israeli Courts* (Hebrew).

The Institute for Research in Jewish Law
Faculty of Law, The Hebrew University of Jerusalem

THE JEWISH LAW ANNUAL

VOLUME TWENTY

THE INSTITUTE FOR RESEARCH IN JEWISH LAW
FACULTY OF LAW
THE HEBREW UNIVERSITY OF JERUSALEM

Routledge
Taylor & Francis Group
LONDON AND NEW YORK

First published 2013
by Routledge
2 Park Square, Milton Park, Abingdon, Oxon OX14 4RN

Simultaneously published in the USA and Canada
by Routledge
71 Third Ave, New York NY 10017

Routledge is an imprint of the Taylor & Francis Group, an informa business

British Library Cataloguing in Publication Data
A catalogue record for this book is available from the British Library

Library of Congress Cataloging in Publication Data
A catalog record for this book has been requested

ISSN 0169-8354
HB ISBN13: 978-0-415-52625-8
HB ISBN10: 0-415-52625-0

eISBN13: 978-0-203-71420-1
eISBN10: 0-203-71420-0

Typeset in Palatino by RefineCatch Limited, Bungay, Suffolk

The Jewish Law Annual is published under the auspices of
The Institute for Research in Jewish Law
Faculty of Law, The Hebrew University of Jerusalem

Editorial communications should be addressed to Dr. Benjamin Porat, Institute for Research in Jewish Law, Faculty of Law, The Hebrew University of Jerusalem, Mount Scopus, Jerusalem 91905, Israel. All communications should be clearly marked "Attention: Editor, Jewish Law Annual." Contributors should consult the style sheet that appears at the end of the volume; it is also available from the editor upon request. Submissions are welcome from all. Neither the editor nor members of the Board of Editors are to be associated with the views expressed by contributors.

This book is part of a series. The publisher will accept continuation orders, which may be cancelled at any time, and which provide for automatic billing and shipping of each title in the series upon publication. Please write for details.

CONTENTS

The Jewish Law Annual, Vol. XX

Midrashic Exegesis and Legal Creativity in the *Meshekh Hokhma*

Yitshak Cohen*

* Faculty of Law, Ono Academic College; adjunct instructor, Hebrew University of Jerusalem and Bar Ilan University

1 RMS and the use of midrashic exegesis to develop the law

i Introduction

R. Meir Simha Hakohen (henceforth RMS) was born in 1843 in the village of Butrimonys, in the Vilnius district. Having gained renown as one of his generation's leading scholars, in 1888 he was appointed rabbi of Daugavpils (Dvinsk), a post he held until his death in 1926.[1] RMS's lifetime coincided with the period in which Lithuanian yeshivot were ascendant in Eastern Europe.[2] His literary output was quite varied, as his writings fall into several genres. He spent most of his life writing a book on Maimonides' *Mishne Torah* (henceforth, *Code*), *Or Sameiah*.[3] In the introduction to another of his works, *Meshekh Hokhma*, he characterized it as "elucidations and interpretations, insights and homilies, comments and novellae on the Pentateuch."[4] R. Meir Simha also wrote novellae on the Babylonian and Jerusalem Talmuds, and a volume of responsa.

Elsewhere, I demonstrated that many decisors regarded *Or Sameiah* not only as a collection of novellae, but also as a halakhic work, containing legal rulings.[5] Should this also prove true of *Meshekh Hokhma*, RMS's commentary on the Torah, this would be an even more significant discovery, as RMS does not so characterize the work, and it is extremely unusual for halakhists to base normative rulings on midrashic exegesis of biblical verses.[6] Thus the question of whether RMS did so,

1 Benzion Eisenstadt, *Dor Rabanav Vesofrav*, vol. 6 (NY: 1904), 39.

2 S. Stampfer, *The Formation of the Lithuanian Yeshiva* (Hebrew), rev. edition (Jerusalem: 2005), 12.

3 This work is generally classified as a commentary on Maimonides' *Code*; see, e.g., M. Elon, *Jewish Law: History, Sources, Principles* (Hebrew), (Jerusalem: 1992), 930.

4 First published in Riga about a year after his death, it has since come out in over sixteen different editions, including those of A. Abraham, S.H. Domb, Z. Metzger, and Y. Cooperman.

5 See Y. Cohen, "R. Meir Simcha HaKohen ('Or Sameah') of Dvinsk and his Halakhic-Juristic Method" (Hebrew), (PhD dissertation, Bar Ilan University, 2005), 247ff.

6 *Responsa Maharik*, root 139, p. 156; R. Elijah Mizrahi, in his commentary on the Torah, beginning of the Torah portion 'Matot' s.v. *vayedaber*, notes that the authority to do so was only granted to the Sages of the Mishnah; *Sdei Hemed*, Klalei Haposkim 16:50; *Responsa Beit Avraham* states that this approach is not adopted by any rabbinical decisor, neither early nor late. For an academic perspective, see Z. Frankel, *Darkhei Hamishna* (Berlin: 1923), 18.

and whether the decisors accepted these rulings as normative law, merits examination. In this article, I will survey RMS's unique midrashic exegeses in *Meshekh Hokhma*, exploring their legal status and the extent of their influence on subsequent decisors. Did these decisors indeed consider *Meshekh Hokhma* a work that had actual legal import, or did they relegate it to the genres of biblical commentary and novellae? Did they accept RMS's midrashic exegesis even when the laws he deduced from it did not fit within the accepted boundaries of the normative halakha? And did they rely on his novel rulings even with respect to issues that had serious legal consequences, such as prohibited marriages, the release of *agunot*, and so on? This article will present some of the creative rulings RMS reached via his midrashic exegesis, and discuss the extent of their impact on subsequent decisors. Building on this analysis, it will examine why RMS's midrashic exegesis had such a formidable impact.

ii Traditional reluctance to use midrashic exegesis to develop the law

Gilat asserts that in the post-talmudic period, there is almost no evidence of law being created through midrashic exegesis, not in the period of the Early Authorities, and certainly not in the period of the Later Authorities.[7] Thus in the main, legal creativity arising from the original scriptural source — the Torah — atrophied.[8] The scriptural source was used only to provide a basis for laws that had already been laid down in the Talmud. For a decisor to 'skip over' the talmudic and Geonic literature, and the works of the Early Authorities, and go directly to the scriptural source itself for the purpose of creating new legal precedents, required tremendous judicial boldness and courage. Over time, as the 'source' grew increasingly distant, fewer and fewer were willing to bypass the received views and instead render new rulings via exegesis of that distant source.

7 Y.D. Gilat, *Studies in the Development of the Halakhah* (Hebrew), (Ramat-Gan: 1992), 389.

8 See B. Lifshitz, "Aggada and its role in the unwritten law" (Hebrew), 22 *Shenaton Hamishpat Haivri* (2004), 233, 295, on the Written Law's role as a canonical work that does not itself create new law, but serves as the source of the authority to do so.

Urbach engages in a lengthy discussion of the problematics of accepting midrashic exegesis as the basis for halakhic rulings.[9] He quotes the opinion of R. Y.I. Halevy, who contends that the sole source of law is the masoretic tradition, and the Rabbis never relied on midrashic exegesis as a source for legal innovation.[10] Epstein also holds this view.[11] On the other hand, Albeck argues that when a case on a point of law regarding which there was no extant tradition reached the High Court (*beit din hagadol*), the judges engaged in midrashic exegesis of the scriptural text, deriving the ruling from it alone.[12] Epstein and Albeck do agree that laws from the period of the "Pairs" (*zugot*) and the Tannaim derived only from: decrees, enactments (which were rooted in the authority of the established institutions), actual cases, testimony, and tradition (transmitted in the form of custom). This historical background highlights the boldness of deriving innovative law by way of midrashic exegesis.

The decisors' reluctance to generate new law directly from the Scriptures stems from several concerns. Firstly, the stories in the Pentateuch and even more so in the Prophets are narrated with a wealth of detail; they mention certain modes of behavior or actions that the biblical 'narrator' may not have sought to present as worthy of emulation, but simply recounted in the course of describing an incident and its historical background, with no normative intent. Second, and more problematic, even if the biblical 'narrator' intended to impart halakhic rulings, decisors will have difficulty deciding which of the myriad details recounted in the biblical text are relevant and essential to the halakhic determination — meaning, without them, the law in question would be different — and which are merely background information,

9 E.E. Urbach, *The World of the Sages — Collected Studies* (Hebrew), (Jerusalem: 2002), 50; idem, "The derasha as a basis of the halakha and the problem of the Soferim" (Hebrew), *Tarbiz* 27 (1958), 166.

10 Y.I. Halevy (Rabinowitz), *Dorot Rishonim* (Berlin: 1923), part 1, 3:292; 5:467.

11 J.N. Epstein, *Prolegomena ad Litteras Tannaiticas* (Hebrew), (Jerusalem: 1957), 511; see too M. Halbertal, *Interpretative Revolutions in the Making* (Hebrew), (Jerusalem: 1997), 14.

12 H. Albeck, "The laws and the exegeses" (Hebrew), *Alexander Marx Jubilee Volume* (NY: 1950), Hebrew section, 1–8. Shamma Friedman appears to adopt a similar approach in *Tosefta Atiqta: Synoptic Parallels of Mishna and Tosefta Analyzed with Methodological Introduction (Pesah Rishon)* (Hebrew), (Ramat-Gan: 2002), 77.

and not crucial to the law.[13] In light of these problems, RMS's midrashic exegesis calls for examination in and of itself, and all the more so if it influenced subsequent decisors.

iii RMS's pioneering adoption of midrashic exegesis as a means of developing the law

Gilat cites four examples where Later Authorities use midrashic exegesis as a basis for new halakhic determinations, despite the traditional opposition to doing so. Surprisingly, three of the four examples were taken from the works of RMS. A thorough examination of RMS's writings reveals that these are not the only instances. Due to their unexpectedness and originality, several such instances are widely cited in subsequent halakhic works and in scholarly analysis of Jewish law. RMS's *Meshekh Hokhma*, an unusual undertaking for a halakhist, provides ample material to explore this phenomenon. To underscore the complexity involved in creating new law via midrashic exegesis, I have chosen to begin with cases where the decisors reject laws RMS derives via midrashic exegesis. Against the background of this rejection, RMS's boldness is thrown into sharp relief.

2 Rejection of RMS's exegesis-based rulings

(1) One who kills someone in the throes of death

After the Israelites' defeat in their war against the Philistines, a fugitive reaches David and relates the following tale:

> I happened to be at Mount Gilboa and I saw Saul leaning on his spear, and the chariots and horsemen closing in on him. . . . Then he said to me, 'Stand over me, and finish me off, for I am in agony and am barely alive.' So I stood over him and finished him off, for I knew that he would never rise from where he was lying. (2 Samuel 1:6–10)

After David laments, the following dialogue ensues:

13 A. Grossman, *The Early Sages of Ashkenaz* (Hebrew), (Jerusalem: 1988), 157, asserts: "Needless to say, usually such descriptive details are not needed to convey the plain sense of the scriptural text, and often are not even needed for its interpretation by the methods used by the halakhic midrashim; they are considered mere supportive allusion (*asmakhta*)."

> David said to the young man who had brought him the news, 'Where are you from?' He replied, 'I am the son of a resident alien (*ger*), an Amalekite.' 'How did you dare,' David said to him, 'to lift your hand and kill the Lord's anointed?' Thereupon David called upon one of the attendants and said to him, 'Come over and strike him!' He struck him down and he died. And David said to him, 'Your blood be on your own head! Your own mouth testified against you when you said, 'I put the Lord's anointed to death.' ' (2 Samuel 1:13–16)

According to Maimonides:

> Whether one kills a healthy person or a dying invalid or even a person in his death throes (*goses*), he must be put to death on this account. But if the death throes are humanly-caused, for example, if one who has been beaten to the point of death is in his throes (*goses*), the court may not put his slayer to death.[14]

Commenting on this passage, RMS deduces a halakhic norm from the story about King David:

> And note, in the case of [the killing of] someone whose death throes were humanly-caused (*goses bidei adam*), there was a dispute regarding whether the murderer is liable [to punishment by death]. And our Teacher [Maimonides] ruled in accordance with the Rabbis that he is exempt. It seems that in this case as well, he is liable by the law of the king of Israel, and the king may put him to death. And proof for this may be adduced from the case of David, who killed the Amalekite proselyte on the basis of his admission [of guilt]; and this was on the strength of the king's law . . . even though he [King Saul] had fallen on the spear and [the Amalekite] stated, 'for I knew that he would never rise. . . .' And so we see that where the death throes are humanly-caused, the one who kills him is liable to punishment by death, by the king's law.

RMS agrees that the court cannot put to death the killer of someone in his death throes; however, he puts forward the novel position that the king has the authority to do so. This refines the Maimonidean position by adding a halakhic component grounded in midrashic exegesis.[15]

14 *Code*, Laws concerning Murder and the Preservation of Life 2:7.

15 In my "The *Or Sameiah*'s objectives and their halakhic and jurisprudential implications" (Hebrew), 25 *Shenaton Hamishpat Haivri* (2008), 97–138, I showed that RMS's primary goal in the *Or Sameiah* was to improve Maimonides' *Code* and expand it to cover additional cases; I also discussed the methods he used to achieve those ends. Here, we see yet another means — midrashic exegesis — by which the RMS seeks to develop and refine the law.

RMS makes every effort to prove that Maimonides would agree with this ruling:

> And our Teacher manifested sensitivity to this point in his holy words: "But if the death throes are humanly-caused . . . the court may not put his slayer to death." He specified "the court," but by the king's law, [the slayer] is liable to punishment by death. And therefore our Teacher rules that a Noahide who killed a dying invalid (*treifa*) is killed on the strength of an a fortiori argument, as that is the king's law.

It would be interesting to examine whether the fact that RMS seeks to reconcile his innovative ruling with Maimonides' language is what led subsequent decisors to accept it. What did RMS hope to achieve by drawing attention to its consistency with Maimonides' wording of the law?

In his *Tzitz Eliezer*, R. Eliezer Waldenburg (1917–2006) disputes the law RMS derives by midrashic exegesis:

> And so, apparently, we must study the source adduced by the *Or Sameiah* [to derive the law] in the case of [one who kills] someone whose death throes are humanly-caused from the case of the Amalekite proselyte, on the basis of the scriptural language . . . and this implies that David judged that he was to be put to death on the strength of the special law applicable to one who maims and kills the Lord's anointed one. So he invoked the law of the king in this case of one who kills the Lord's anointed one, though his death throes were humanly-caused. And this being so, it does not constitute proof that the king's law would apply in a similar case involving an ordinary person.[16]

R. Waldenburg argues that a crucial element of the Amalekite proselyte's transgression, an element that was crucial to David's decision to execute him, was the fact that the victim was "the Lord's anointed one." In his opinion, only on this condition was the perpetrator liable to punishment by death on the strength of the king's law. RMS apparently did not consider this detail a crucial element of the transgression, but took it as just another detail that set out the narrative's historical background. He therefore concluded that one who kills someone who is already in his death throes — no matter what the dying person's status may be — is liable to punishment by death on the strength of the king's law. This discussion highlights the problematics that arise in seeking to

16 *Responsa Tzitz Eliezer*, 18:66.

derive legal rulings directly from the scriptural text, the principal reason for the Later Authorities' reluctance to do so. It thus also demonstrates RMS's daring in utilizing midrashic exegesis as a legitimate tool for developing Jewish law or rendering innovative rulings.

Yet reading between the lines of R. Waldenburg's ruling, an interesting phenomenon comes to light: although R. Waldenburg rejects the halakhic ruling arrived at via midrashic exegesis, he himself has recourse to this very methodology. That is, he himself engages in midrashic exegesis, but draws a different legal conclusion than did RMS. RMS's use of midrashic exegesis as a legitimate tool for developing the halakha seems to have made an impression on the Tzitz Eliezer, who in turn used midrashic exegesis to dispute RMS's conclusion and limit the ruling to the killer of the Lord's anointed one. The Tzitz Eliezer could have rejected RMS's argumentation as categorically unacceptable in principle, as other halakhic authorities indeed did, as we will see below. That the Tzitz Eliezer did not do so is thus significant.

(2) The Amalekite proselyte

The transgressor's identity as an Amalekite proselyte is an important element with legal import. Commenting on the Torah portion 'Ki Teitze,' RMS adduces the Mekhilta's assertion that God swears that no Amalekite will ever be accepted as a convert.[17] Hence there can never be an Amalekite proselyte, and the individual mentioned in the verse must be an ordinary Noahide. King David ordered that he be put to death, as he would have for any Noahide, as Noahides may be put to death on the strength of self-incrimination. This differs from the legal rule that applies to Jews, who cannot be put to death on the strength of their own testimony: "no one may incriminate himself."[18] The law set down by RMS is by no means obvious, and in fact, is quite innovative.

17 See M.I. Kahana, *The Two Mekhiltot on the Amalek Portion* (Hebrew), (Jerusalem: 1999), 102.

18 See bSanhedrin 9b; Maimonides, *Code*, Laws concerning Evidence 12:2; A. Kirschenbaum, *The Criminal Confession in Jewish Law* (Hebrew), (Jerusalem: 2004).

The Tzitz Eliezer objects to this midrashic exegesis.[19] In his opinion, Maimonides himself did not read the verse this way. In fact, the opposite seems to be true: Maimonides seems to explicitly state that an Amalekite proselyte is a righteous convert, whose conversion to Judaism is acceptable.[20] This is corroborated by the fact that Maimonides finds it necessary to justify David's decision to execute the proselyte on the basis of his self-incrimination (since Jews cannot be put to death on the strength of their own testimony) by explaining that it was either a temporary ruling (*horaat shaa*) or it was carried out on the strength of the king's law. Had the Amalekite proselyte been considered a Noahide, as RMS declares, there would have been no need to invoke the idea that his execution was carried out on the strength of a temporary ruling, since a Noahide can be put to death on the basis of self-incrimination.

(3) Exhuming and moving a corpse

The prohibitions against exhuming and moving the dead provide another example of the complexity involved in deriving innovative legal rulings through midrashic exegesis. Here too, it is difficult to determine whether details mentioned in the scriptural text are essential to the law's formulation or merely provide historical background. RMS adduces the verse: "You shall not remove your countryman's landmarks, set up by previous generations, in the property that will be allotted to you" (Deut. 19:14), as the source for the prohibition against exhumation.[21] RMS struggles with the question of whether this derivation suffices to endow the law with biblical status or merely serves as an *asmakhta*, a supportive allusion that bolsters a Rabbinically-mandated law.[22] R. Ovadia Yosef, the Sefardic Chief Rabbi of the State of Israel in the 1970s, maintained that RMS considered the prohibition to be

19 *Responsa Tzitz Eliezer*, 13:71.

20 Maimonides, *Code*, Laws concerning Kings and Wars 6:1–4. *Kesef Mishne* comments that if such converts agree to observe the seven Noahide laws, they are no longer classified as Amalekites, but rather as Noahides.

21 *Or Sameiah* (*OS*), Laws concerning Mourning 14:15.

22 This is one of the central questions arising from creation of law through midrashic exegesis: does attaching a law to a biblical verse endow it with the status of biblical law or is the said law deemed to have only Rabbinic status? On this distinction, see J. Levinger, *Maimonides' Techniques of Codification* (Hebrew), (Jerusalem: 1965), 34; *OS*, Laws concerning Rebels 1:1; Haim H. Cohn, *The Law* (Hebrew), (Jerusalem: 1991), 214.

biblically mandated.[23] Another authority disagreed, arguing that there is no determination of the prohibition's normative status in *Or Sameiah*.[24] If the prohibition forbidding exhumation is indeed considered to be of biblical status, then RMS's halakhic creativity is even more daring than it first appears.

In his *Shulhan Arukh*, R. Joseph Caro forbids the moving of a corpse from a town that has a graveyard to another town. This is permitted only when the remains are being taken to the land of Israel.[25] R. Moses Isserles, the Rema (Krakow, 1525–1572), adds another instance of permitted moving of remains: "or if he is moved to the place where his ancestors are buried."[26] R. Shabetai Meir Hakohen, the Shakh (Lithuania, 1621–1662), provides the rationale for the *Shulhan Arukh*'s ruling: "it is to uphold the honor of deceased persons who are buried in that town, for it would disgrace them were he not to rest among them."[27] Thus, there are two prohibitions: a prohibition against disinterment for the purpose of reburial anywhere other than the cemetery where the ancestors of the deceased are buried, and a prohibition against moving remains to another site.

Invoking his midrashic exegesis, RMS proffers a ruling on disinterment and moving of a corpse, a ruling that is contrary to the law as set down by the *Shulhan Arukh* and the Rema:

> In the case of Eleazar, we see that at the end of the book of Joshua, it is written: "and they buried him on the hill of his son Phinehas in the hill country of Ephraim . . ." (Josh. 24:33), and undoubtedly, Eleazar was the High Priest, so that when Shiloh was consecrated the same laws applied to it as [later applied to] to Jerusalem, and he would have been required to always reside in Shiloh. . . . So when they carried him to his grave, they carried him to the hill country of Ephraim, and not to the graveyard in Shilo, for [the burial ground in Ephraim] belonged to his family, belonged to Phinehas, his son; for even though Phinehas was still alive, it was considered his family's [burial place]. This proves that [the dispensation] to move [the deceased] to his grave applies even to the family [burial place] when his family are still among the living. And this being so, this is the law with respect to exhumation — it is considered his and his family's even if they are still alive, and this is clear. . . . This is the [correct] interpretation of

23 *Responsa Yabia Omer*, vol. 7, YD #35.

24 R. Pinhas Zevihi, *Responsa Ateret Paz*, part 1, vol. 2, YD 18:1.

25 *SA*, YD 363:2.

26 *Rema* ad loc.

27 *Shakh* ad loc.

the biblical text, for if not, what does it teach us? Hence the biblical verses seem to indicate that the burial ground belonging to his living family is tantamount to his own grave and that of his ancestors, and it is thus permitted to move the deceased from there [i.e., where the corpse is] to his family burial place.

RMS's exegesis, claiming that the text would otherwise make no point, derives from it — though it is speaking of prophets and not people in general — that it is permissible to relocate a corpse even if the destination is a family burial ground (and the family is still alive), and not an ancestral burial ground.[28] To prove this, he adduces the case of Eleazar, who was moved to the burial ground of his son Phinehas, rather than to an ancestral plot. While it might be argued that the innovation is actually explicit in the verse, other commentators did not draw this inference. It seems clear that one's orientation has a pronounced impact on one's interpretation of the scriptural text.

R. Moses Feinstein (Russia 1895–U.S. 1986), one of the greatest recent decisors, addresses the substance of RMS's innovative ruling, rejecting it as normative law:

But the eminent sage R. Meir Simha Hakohen, author of *Or Sameiah*, set down the innovative ruling that if one purchases a large plot for a family burial ground, this too is considered an ancestral burial ground with respect to the permissibility of exhuming remains and reinterring them there, notwithstanding both the prohibition against exhumation and the prohibition against moving the corpse from a town with a cemetery to another town. And his proof — derived from the fact that Eleazar the priest, who had to reside in Shilo permanently, and therefore must have died in Shilo, was nonetheless buried on the hill of his son Phinehas in the hill country of Ephraim, even though there was a cemetery in Shilo — should be rejected, since it can be argued that when Eleazar the priest died, no one else had died yet in Shilo, and therefore [the basis for] his innovation is unclear.[29]

R. Feinstein claims, then, that Eleazar's being taken to Phinehas' plot for burial cannot be considered a precedent for permitting a corpse to be moved from a town with a cemetery to another town, since when

28 This innovative ruling may indicate that RMS's approach is essentialist rather than formalistic, insofar as it focuses on underlying principles, and therefore, in this case, permits the removal of remains even to a site that is not actually the deceased's ancestral burial ground.

29 *Responsa Igrot Moshe*, YD 1:236.

Eleazar died there may not have been any graves in Shilo, and hence there would have been no need for apprehensiveness about disgrace to those buried in the town from which the deceased would be moved.

In another responsum, R. Feinstein examines RMS's proof and declares that it applies only to the case mentioned in the biblical text. In his opinion, what is recounted in the biblical account was applicable only to Eleazar, and cannot be invoked as a precedent applicable to other burials.

> And aside from this, it is only logical that since the reason we may not move a corpse from a town with a cemetery to another town is so as not to disgrace those buried there . . . this is not applicable to the case of Eleazar the priest, for he was greater than all Israel, and not everyone would merit being buried near him, and therefore it would by no means disgrace those who were buried there [in Shilo] if Eleazar the priest was not buried there, since they were not akin to him . . . and therefore the proof adduced by R. Meir Simha from Eleazar the priest does not constitute proof.[30]

In a third responsum, R. Feinstein not only attacks the specific proof adduced by RMS vis-à-vis burial, but also his very boldness in taking such authority upon himself:

> And his proof does not necessarily follow . . . and from the fact that it was necessary for it to be written in the verse where he was buried, the Gemara infers that "the husband is not entitled to receive a share of [his wife's] prospective [property] to the same extent as of [property] in her possession [at the time of her death]." And even ignoring this point, we cannot engage in midrashic exegesis on our own [cognizance]. And it is surprising that he [RMS] wrote: "for if not, what does it teach us?" And therefore we cannot act in accordance with his proof, because it is not a proof that follows necessarily.[31]

In the first two responsa, R. Feinstein rejects RMS's midrashic exegesis, but he nonetheless appeals to this same methodology, though he reaches a different conclusion. Only in the third responsum does R. Feinstein object to the methodology itself. Here too, as in the case of R. Waldenburg, we can see RMS's influence, for even though R. Feinstein rejects RMS's halakhic conclusion, he adopts his methodology in two of the three responsa.

30 Ibid., OH 2:107.
31 Ibid., YD 1:238.

Yet though Feinstein rejected RMS's innovative ruling, both because he believed the specific midrashic exegesis on which it was based to be flawed and because he felt that RMS was arrogating to himself too much authority, he nonetheless decided to be lenient and decide the law in accordance with RMS's innovative ruling, in light of RMS's authoritative stature:

> And therefore, as to the law in practice, if there is something you can do to dissuade them from exhuming their father, you should certainly try and do so, and tell them that this causes the deceased much anguish. . . . However, if there is nothing you can do, you can rely on [the ruling of] the eminent sage R. Meir Simha–an eminent sage of the previous generation — and not protest; however, they should at least wait until the flesh has rotted. . . . And this is only if they have already purchased a family plot, and not if they have not yet done so, but just wish to exhume the body so that it will be buried next to their mother, who was his wife; for the eminent sage, the Or Sameiah, would also certainly forbid this.[32]

In another responsum, R. Feinstein again accepts RMS's ruling as the law to be put into practice on the strength of his authority as a decisor:

> The venerable sage (*zaken*), the author of *Or Sameiah*, has already issued his ruling that it is permitted, and the Taz seems to adopt a similar position, for he wrote, "to a place that is his [means,] where his family members lie [buried]," wording that implies that even [moving him] to a place where his other relatives are [buried] is permitted.[33]

Let us now take a closer look at RMS's midrashic exegesis regarding the exhumation and moving of remains, and R. Feinstein's attitude to it. The exegesis, and the innovative ruling derived from it, differ from the exegesis and ruling regarding the Amalekite proselyte in two fundamental ways. Firstly, the latter exegesis addressed the king's authority to execute transgressors, and the law in question was purely theoretical; neither in our day, nor in RMS's, could it have been put into practice. Presumably, this would have made it easier for RMS to issue an innovative ruling. Secondly, and more importantly, in the case of the Amalekite proselyte, RMS's ruling did not contradict any received law, and he even attempted to demonstrate that Maimonides' choice of wording supported his exegesis. In contrast, the case of the prohibition

32 *Responsa Igrot Moshe*, YD 1:236.
33 *Responsa Igrot Moshe*, YD 2:161 and 158.

against exhumation has practical ramifications, and RMS's intent was to issue a ruling that was to be implemented in practice. Furthermore, his ruling is contrary to the rulings of R. Joseph Caro and R. Moses Isserles, and adduces no Maimonidean support.

I have shown that R. Feinstein's mode of argumentation, if not the substance of his view, was influenced by RMS. Why did R. Feinstein accept RMS's ruling even though it conflicted with the halakhic consensus? In his responsum, he notes that RMS "was an eminent sage of the previous generation." It would seem that R. Feinstein accepted RMS's ruling because of his reputation as an eminent Torah scholar (*gaon*), a reputation garnered in the competitive milieu of the great Lithuanian sages of that era. We must ask ourselves, what is meant by the accolade "*gaon*," and why should such scholarly genius be a legitimate consideration in deciding the law? Alternatively, might it be the case that R. Feinstein is merely employing a rhetorical device aimed at reinforcing RMS's status, so as to render reliance on his view, as a matter of law to be implemented in practice, more credible?

(4) Self-endangerment to save the nation

According to Maimonides, "An exiled person may never (*leolam*) leave his city of refuge. . . . Indeed, not even if all Israel needs his help . . . may he leave the city until the High Priest dies. If he does leave, he surrenders himself to death."[34]

In *Or Sameiah*, RMS suggests an explanation for this law, an explanation based on logical reasoning (*svara*):

> Our Teacher specified a reason why [the manslayer] cannot leave — for [it would stand to reason that since] the commandment that life be saved (*pikuah nefesh*) overrides all the other commandments in the Torah, should it not certainly [override all else] when it is a matter of saving the entire Israelite nation? . . . However, against [human] nature, we need add nothing to [the measures put in place by] the commandments given by the Creator of nature, who knows what lies in the hearts and minds of men. He declared that if a blood avenger kills the manslayer in hot anger, he does not incur the penalty of death, and further, the court cannot put him to death, and since the blood avenger is permitted to slay him, [the manslayer] cannot, in order to save someone else's life from certain danger, put himself in a situation where he may be in mortal danger. So it would seem.[35]

34 *Code*, Laws concerning Murder and the Preservation of Life 7:8.
35 *OS* ad loc.

Surprisingly, when RMS addressed the same law in *Meshekh Hokhma*, he gave a different, and original, rationale:

> I already raised the difficulty in my [other] work: why did they declare "not even if all Israel needs his help": the king and the High Court should decree that anyone who kills him will be executed. However, the concern was that perhaps when he left [the city of refuge] he would scheme to cause the death of the anointed priest so that he would not have to return to his city of refuge, and [thus] he would put the High Priest's life at risk.[36]

The third mention of this law, which is also in *Meshekh Hokhma*, is even more surprising, for instead of offering an explanation based on logic (*svara*), it invokes midrashic exegesis of the verse: "Go back to Egypt, for all the men who sought to kill you are dead" (Exod. 4:19):

> This proves that if those who sought to kill Moses had still been alive, he would not have been obligated to go and take the children of Israel out of Egypt. Even though the entire nation of Israel needs him, he does not have to put himself in a situation where he may be in mortal danger. And this led our holy Teacher to conclude in the *Code* that one who is exiled to a city of refuge, even if all Israel needs him . . . may never (*leolam*) leave there.[37]

It is illuminating to compare the rationales offered in RMS's two works, *Or Sameiah* and *Meshekh Hokhma*, for the law that one is not required to put himself in a situation where he may be in mortal danger, in order to save the entire nation of Israel. In *Or Sameiah*, RMS suggests an original rationale. In *Meshekh Hokhma*, in one place he proposes a different rationale, and in another, he argues that this law is derived via midrashic exegesis: "And this led our holy Teacher to conclude that. . . ." Note the wording used by RMS — "this led" — he is saying that midrashic exegesis led to the law, not logical reasoning (*svara*). In offering these various rationales, RMS seems to be inconsistent, at least with respect to his methodology. If we assume that midrashic exegesis provides a sturdier foundation for the Maimonidean law than that provided by logical reasoning, RMS's proposed midrashic exegesis in *Meshekh Hokhma* would seem to prove that it was written after *Or Sameiah*, for otherwise RMS would have adduced that exegesis in *Or Sameiah*.

36 See Numbers 35:28.

37 *Meshekh Hokhma*, Exodus 4:19.

RMS's choice of words seems to imply that in his view, the midrashic exegesis here only plays a supporting role, providing proof for an innovative ruling that is Maimonides', not his. However, as will be shown below, subsequent decisors contended that the legal conclusion drawn from the exegesis is RMS's own creation; this must be the case, they maintained, because Maimonides ruled elsewhere — so they claim — that an individual must endanger his life to save the entire nation.[38] If so, RMS has indeed put forward a creative midrashic exegesis.

Some decisors objected to RMS's innovative reading of Maimonides, and the legal conclusion he draws from it. R. Isaac Herzog (1887–1959), the State of Israel's first Ashkenazic Chief Rabbi, maintained that there is no doubt that an individual must place himself in mortal danger to save the entire nation of Israel. He first criticizes only the inference RMS draws from Maimonides' language, not the methodology of midrashic exegesis itself:

> And I was astonished when I saw that in *Or Sameiah*, the illustrious sage, R. Meir Simha, had concluded that not only does an individual not have to put himself in a situation where he may be in mortal danger in order to save a single life, but [he does not have to do so] even to save the entire nation of Israel. And he adduces proof from Maimonides' language, "and if he does leave, he surrenders himself to death." . . . And I am astonished: when the entire nation of Israel requires his assistance, this would come under the category of an obligatory war, and how could it be that the king and the High Court could not force him to leave? Even if it was only a question of saving one Jew, the Jerusalem Talmud maintains that . . . an individual must put himself in a situation where he may be in mortal danger. Is it possible that everyone erred in understanding black letter law?[39]

He then criticizes RMS's midrashic exegesis, first calling its methodology into question as a matter of principle, and then disputing the specifics of the exegesis at hand:

> And as to the fact that the Gaon from Dvinsk adduced a proof for this law from the verse, "Go back to Egypt, for all the men who sought to kill you

38 Neria Guttel claims that according to R. Pines, Maimonides held that an individual is obligated to put his life in danger to serve the collective, see his *Innovation in Tradition: the Halakhic-Philosophical Teachings of Rabbi Kook* (Hebrew), (Jerusalem: 2005), 137.

39 *Responsa Heikhal Yitzhak*, OH #39.

are dead" — deducing that had those who sought to take Moses' life been alive, he would not have been obligated to go to Egypt to save Israel — it is certain that this does not provide a foundation on which the law can be built.

And our Rabbis, of blessed memory, already put forward an exegesis [of this verse], declaring that they [Moses' enemies] did not die, but rather, they contracted leprosy and lost their wealth. But even according to the literal reading [of the verse], no proof can be adduced from it. The simple meaning of the verse is that had they still been alive, you [Moses] would have been afraid that they might inform on you to Pharaoh and he would have killed you, so in any event you would not have been able to even begin the process of saving [the nation of] Israel.

R. Israel Meir Lau, the Ashkenazic Chief Rabbi of the State of Israel in the 1990s, also rejects RMS's exegesis of the scriptural text. He maintains that the verse only places the story in its appropriate historical framework, but does not impart a legal precedent:

> However, this proof, too, does not necessarily follow, for perhaps the Holy One, blessed be He, was merely telling Moses not to worry about succeeding at his mission, since they might turn him over to Pharaoh. He therefore told him that they had died. But this has nothing to do with the obligation to put oneself in a situation where one may be in mortal danger in order to save someone else.[40]

Some decisors dispute RMS's ruling because they question his reading of Maimonides, without even raising the issue of the midrashic exegesis. R. Yehiel Jacob Weinberg (Lithuania 1884–Switzerland 1966) contends that one need not read Maimonides as RMS does. In one responsum, he writes that an exile may leave the city of refuge in order to save another Jew's life without forfeiting his own[41]; in another, he expressed surprise at RMS's ruling, as the law dictates that an inadvertent killer who leaves his city of refuge risks exile, not death.[42] R. Weinberg quotes decisors who rejected RMS's reading of Maimonides, explaining that the word *leolam* (translated above as "never") does not imply that he may never leave the city of refuge, just that when he is permitted to do so, he may not leave for good, but must return as soon as he has completed his mission.

40 *Responsa Yahel Yisrael*, #73.

41 *Responsa Sridei Esh*, 2:101.

42 *Responsa Sridei Esh*, 2:34.

R. Herzog, in his second argument, and R. Lau, address the specific issue of the midrashic exegesis. In contrast to other decisors discussed above, rabbis Herzog and Lau do not adopt RMS's methodology and apply it to derive a different ruling; instead, they reject RMS's exegesis, and seek to interpret the scriptural text without drawing any legal conclusions. R. Weinberg, and R. Herzog's first argument, do not address the issue of midrashic exegesis, they just question RMS's interpretation of Maimonides. I would argue that RMS's interpretation seems the best fit with Maimonides' language: RMS explains Maimonides' assertion that "an exiled person may never leave his city of refuge" quite literally. However, the decisors in question clearly found the halakhic conclusions RMS drew from his reading to be implausible, and I can understand their view. Nevertheless, this does not invalidate the exegesis, even if this means that we must accept its legal import. R. Weinberg's interpretation of "never leave" as meaning that the manslayer cannot leave "for good" is no more plausible than RMS's exegesis.

Taking into account Maimonides' well-known penchant for linguistic precision, I contend that the reading advanced by RMS reflects Maimonides' own opinion on the question of self-endangerment. Perhaps the said decisors were uncomfortable attacking Maimonides, and so instead of criticizing his ruling directly, chose to do so by proxy, attacking its interpreter, RMS. For his treatment of the issue of self-endangerment highlights RMS's fidelity to interpreting Maimonides in accordance with the straightforward meaning of the text, even if the halakhic conclusions that follow from this reading seem implausible and conflict with positions taken by post-Maimonidean decisors. It is possible that this very tenacity led some decisors to rely on RMS's readings of Maimonides in cases where Maimonides' views were not entirely clear.

RMS's novel ruling has also been noted by researchers.[43] Rakover characterizes it as too far-reaching, supporting this stance by adducing R. Meir Dan Plotzki (Poland, 1826–1928)[44] as having disputed RMS's view, at least when it was a matter of saving "the entire nation of Israel." In my opinion, RMS did not put forward his conclusion because he took the principle of the importance of "the entire nation of Israel"

43 N. Rakover, *Sacrificing One to Save Many* (Hebrew), (Jerusalem: 2000), 144; idem, "*Klal Yisrael* — philosophy and law" (Hebrew), *Tehumin* 16 (1995), 211.

44 *Kli Hemda*, Torah portian 'Pinhas,' at the beginning.

lightly, for in other places he ascribes great value to it.[45] But RMS drew the legal conclusion that followed from his midrashic exegesis, and believed that it reflected Maimonides' intent.

RMS's far-reaching minority opinion led various decisors to decide the law in a manner contrary to his innovative ruling. Some opposed it because they favored a different exegesis of the scriptural text, others because they felt that the Maimonidean law in question should be interpreted differently. It is possible that they rejected it, ultimately, due to the radical substance of RMS's ruling: how could it be argued that an individual should stand idly by when "the entire nation of Israel" might be in mortal danger? Does RMS indeed maintain that the law cannot impose on the individual an obligation to endanger himself for the good of the collective, or is he simply espousing the position that follows from his midrashic exegesis? That is, might it be the case that RMS's reasoning and halakhic outlook indeed mandate individual self-endangerment for the good of the community, but since his midrashic exegesis implies that the scriptural text instructs us that this is not so, he decided the law in a manner that was contrary to his own reasoning? If so, this would indicate that he ascribes great weight to midrashic exegesis.[46]

(5) Concluding remarks

I have analyzed three examples of RMS's exegesis-based rulings that were rejected by subsequent decisors. They can be ranked by degree of boldness, and, perhaps corresponding to this, by the strength of the opposition they aroused. The first case, that of the king's law, has no contemporary ramifications and does not challenge the halakhic consensus. RMS may have taken the exegesis to have no practical

45 E.g., in *Meshekh Hokhma*, Deuteronomy 34:8, he writes that a Noahide may allow himself to be killed rather than transgress the commandments, whereas an Israelite who does so commits a heinous sin, for his death would harm others, who would be impacted by his absence.

46 It is interesting to compare this law to another that is conceptually similar: whether an individual is required to cut off a limb in order to save his fellow's life. The Radbaz takes this to be obligatory; see *Responsa Radbaz*, 3:1052. However, RMS takes a surprising position in this case too, arguing that an individual should not endanger (even) one of his limbs in order to save someone else from death (*OS*, Laws concerning Murder and the Preservation of Life 7:8).

ramifications, and therefore he was not conflicted about proposing it, and the response of the decisors was fairly subdued. The second case, that concerning exhumation and moving of remains, dealt with an issue of contemporary relevance, not a matter of merely theoretical concern. Moreover, the conclusion RMS drew from it contradicts the law explicitly set forth in the *Shulhan Arukh*. The third example, concerning self-endangerment, also addressed an issue with contemporary bearing; in this case, RMS's conclusion flew in the face of common sense. These factors may explain why the latter two rulings garnered fierce criticism from subsequent decisors. To summarize my findings up to this point, those of RMS's midrashic exegeses that gave rise to rulings that were contrary to rulings of the preeminent decisors, especially on practical matters, or seemed unreasonable, were rejected by subsequent decisors. Nevertheless, these same decisors were clearly influenced by the methodological possibilities opened up by RMS: they too engaged in midrashic exegesis of these verses to reach normative conclusions, but their conclusions differed from RMS's.

3 Acceptance of RMS's exegesis-based rulings

(1) The prohibition against rebuilding Jericho

I will now examine a series of instances in which RMS's midrashic exegesis generated law that was accepted as normative, and attempt to ascertain why some decisors accepted the laws derived by exegesis in these instances, but not those discussed above. The first law to be examined is the prohibition against rebuilding Jericho.

> And in [the passage mandating destruction of] the idolatrous city (*ir nidahat*) it is written, "it shall not be built again"; apparently, because if Jericho, were it to be rebuilt, were again to be destroyed, it would be permissible to rebuild it. But an idolatrous city, even if were to be rebuilt and destroyed again, would not be [permitted to be] rebuild again afterwards. So it seems; and consult the Jerusalem Talmud. Since it can be rebuilt — one may settle there.[47]

RMS derives from the scriptural text a legal inference that is even bolder than that put forward in the Jerusalem Talmud.[48] In his opinion, after Jericho has been rebuilt once, not only may one live there, one may

47 *Meshekh Hokhma*, Deuteronomy 13:17.

48 jBerakhot 9:5.

even rebuild it again. He reaches this conclusion by comparing the ban imposed on it by Joshua and the commandment that an idolatrous city is to be destroyed. In the passage discussing the idolatrous city, the ruling is: "it shall not be built again." By contrast, Joshua decreed: "Cursed of the Lord be the man who shall rise up and build this city of Jericho" (Josh. 6:26). Joshua does not include the word "again" in his ban; from this, RMS deduces that should Jericho be rebuilt once (and then destroyed), it would be permissible to rebuild it again.

To derive a law by midrashic exegesis from a dictum uttered by Joshua is innovative in itself, especially since the law in question is not stated in the Pentateuch. Perhaps this was why RMS sought to examine the validity and normative status of Joshua's ban. He first cites the Jerusalem Talmud, which asserts that Joshua's ban was one of three things to which the heavenly court assented. RMS has difficulty adducing the Jerusalem Talmud as proof, but grants that Joshua's ban has a normative status equivalent to that of a biblical injunction. He adduces his own proof for this and concludes that Joshua's ban is "like the word of the Lord, which He spoke by way of Joshua the son of Nun" (1 Kings 16:34).

R. Eliezer Waldenburg, the Tzitz Eliezer, has difficulty comprehending how Maimonides could have completely overlooked the prohibition against rebuilding Jericho, which does not appear in the *Code*, and how over the generations many Jews have evinced total disregard for Joshua's ban by settling there and calling the city by the same name.[49] He overcomes his bewilderment by invoking RMS's midrashic exegesis:

> Behold what a wonderful discovery I have made in the book *Meshekh Hokhma* by the eminent sage, the author of *Or Sameiah*, of blessed memory, which sheds light on this mystery. And in [commenting on] the Torah portion 'Ree,' the law is expressed in his clear remarks there, that in the case of the idolatrous city (*ir nidahat*), of which it is written, "it shall not be built again" — even if the city is rebuilt and destroyed [again], it is forbidden to rebuild it after this as well, but Jericho, since it has [already] been rebuilt, if it is destroyed [again], it is permitted to rebuilt it. Thus, we have learned from this renowned sage (*gaon olam*) a most important law (*hilkheta gevirta*), that the prohibition against the rebuilding of Jericho applied only to the one who would arise and rebuild it the first time, obscuring the visible face of its destruction. But after that, if it has already been rebuilt and destroyed again — it is permitted to rebuild it.

49 *Responsa Tzitz Eliezer*, 10:1.

We see, then, that RMS's halakhic creativity, reflected in his midrashic exegesis of seemingly redundancies or omissions in the scriptural text, leads R. Waldenburg to endorse the normative conclusion that Jericho can be rebuilt. It is interesting that whereas RMS's ruling was accompanied by the words "So it seems to me," R. Waldenburg accepts it as law without hesitation. In other words, upon discovering a lacuna in Maimonides' *Code*, RMS utilized midrashic exegesis as a legitimate tool to develop the law, and R. Waldenburg in turn adduced RMS's innovative analysis to fill the lacuna in Maimonides' *Code*.

RMS deduces a second law from the wording of Joshua's ban:

> And it appears that when he declared "cursed . . . be the man," Joshua was careful to specify "the man," and not the collective, meaning that if the collective, all of Israel, [were to do this], it would not be subject to this rule, as it is stated in the Sifra regarding those liable to divine extirpation (*karet*): "'that person shall be cut off" (Lev. 7:21) — not the collective.' So too here, the collective is not subject to this rule; indeed, perhaps they were permitted to do it [rebuild Jericho] *ab initio*.

R. Waldenburg accepts this exegesis and rules that the addressee of the prohibition against the rebuilding of Jericho is indeed the individual, not the collective.[50]

It is not easy to distinguish between these exegeses and those offered in the previous section, and determine why the former gained normative force and the latter did not. It is all the more difficult when we consider that these exegeses deal with matters that are of contemporary relevance, and not just theoretical. I would like to suggest two possible reasons why these innovative rulings were accepted as normative law: first, they did not contradict any existing law; indeed, as we said, Maimonides does not even mention the ban on rebuilding Jericho in his *Code*. Thus, RMS merely utilized midrashic exegesis to enhance the *Code* by filling in a legal lacuna. Second, the laws in question accord with customary practice. While these suggested reasons may explain the decisors' decisions to accept or reject RMS's innovations, it is important to remember that RMS himself was not guided by them. He adduced midrashic exegesis as the basis for innovative legal rulings even when they conflicted with existing law.

50 *Responsa Tzitz Eliezer*, 11:12.

(2) Inheriting property from a relative one has murdered

RMS sometimes derived a new law directly from the plain meaning of the scriptural narrative, without any recourse to midrashic inferences from textual redundancies and so on, which, as we saw, had often been rejected. In these cases, the question is no longer that of RMS's authority or exegetical prowess. Rather, the question is whether the Bible can be used as an authoritative source of law. An example is the issue of a murderer's inheriting the possessions of a relative he has murdered. Maimonides rules that the father of a stubborn and rebellious son can inherit from his son even though he caused him to be stoned to death.[51] RMS ad loc. comments:

> So it is explained in 2 Samuel, in the verse, "Then the whole clan . . . even though we wipe out the heir" (14:7). And consult the Radak,[52] [who suggests] that they did not intend to avenge the blood of the victim, just to inherit from them; thus a blood avenger who kills his nephew is his heir if he has no sons, as proven by the verse there, since the murderer is his brother's heir.

At first glance, RMS seems to be simply adducing an episode from the Prophets in support of Maimonides' ruling, as the classic commentators on Maimonides are wont to do. RMS recounts the story that the Tekoan woman told King David after Absalom had Amnon slain. She stated that after her husband's death, one of her sons murdered his brother. Members of the family sought to avenge the death of slain brother by killing the perpetrator: "Hand over the one who killed his brother, that we may put him to death for the slaying of his brother, even though we wipe out the heir" (2 Sam. 14:7). The Radak explains that the family members wished to kill the heir so that they would inherit the husband's assets. RMS adduces the Radak's interpretation, takes it to have normative legal status, and from the text of the biblical story itself arrives at the ruling that murdering someone from whom one will inherit does not bar the perpetrator from inheriting from the victim.

The Tzitz Eliezer deliberated over whether to accept the argument of a woman who had blinded her husband and then, claiming "[he is] repulsive to me," demanded that he give her a bill of divorce.[53] First he

51 Maimonides, *Code*, Laws concerning Rebels 7:14.

52 R. David Kimchi (Narbonne, 1160–1235).

53 *Responsa Tzitz Eliezer*, 17:18.

compared this case to Maimonides' ruling on the stubborn and rebellious son: just as the father is his son's heir even though he caused him to be stoned to death, so too the woman should be able to get a bill of divorce even though she caused her husband's injury. But he goes on to withdraw this analogy, drawing a distinction between the two cases: in the case of the stubborn and rebellious son, the father caused his son's death, this being the punishment mandated by biblical law; therefore, the father should not be penalized. The woman, on the other hand, maliciously committed an act that certainly deviated from biblical law; hence she should be penalized, and not allowed to benefit from her deplorable deeds.

Further on in the responsum, R. Waldenburg turns his attention to RMS's exegesis regarding the murderer who inherits. In making some general remarks about RMS's methodology, he seems to hint at why he has chosen to adduce it:

> For this purpose I will cite what the eminent sage R. Meir Simha of Dvinsk wrote in providing a scriptural basis for his remarks, and in quoting the Radak. . . . thus, it becomes clear from his remarks that he had no doubt that even a murderer, as long as he is his victim's heir by biblical law, inherits from him; and the fact that he caused his death, killing him with malicious intent, does not change the law [of inheritance]. He learns this from 2 Samuel in the Holy Scriptures.

This midrashic exegesis, according to the Tzitz Eliezer, expands the law set out in Maimonides' *Code* to include not only the stubborn and rebellious son's father, who acted as mandated by biblical law, but also an heir who acted without any biblical mandate. Employing the putatively 'interpretive' technique of adducing a biblical source, RMS expands Maimonides' ruling to cover a more complicated case that does not fall under it directly.[54] This 'straightforward' biblical interpretation, which does not entail glossing textual redundancies or omissions, becomes another means for enhancing the Maimonidean code and expanding it to cover a broader spectrum of cases, making it easier for subsequent decisors to incorporate still more cases into the rubric of the law. RMS's halakhic innovativeness becomes a vital link in the process of expanding the *Code* to cover new cases brought before the contemporary decisor. Moreover, it seems that we can explain why

54 See Y. Rivlin, *Inheritance and Wills in Jewish Law* (Hebrew), (Ramat-Gan: 1999), 122.

R. Waldenburg decided to ground his halakhic conclusion in RMS's novel ruling. He notes that RMS bases his view on the scriptural text; presumably, this confers additional legitimacy on it, facilitating its acceptance.

(3) Bathsheba and Uriah the Hittite — conditional divorce

Another issue where an innovative ruling by RMS was accepted as normative had to do with conditional divorce. Here too, he based the law on a straightforward reading of the biblical narrative, employing no exegetical techniques. R. Waldenburg was asked whether a woman who had received a conditional bill of divorce was permitted to engage in mourning for her husband.[55] In King David's time, the practice of giving one's wife a conditional bill of divorce before going off to war was commonplace, as the Talmud relates in bKetubot 9b: "Anyone who goes out [to fight] in the wars of the House of David writes his wife a bill of divorce." Rashi comments: "so that if he dies in battle, the bills of divorce will take effect retroactively, from the day it was written." This legal mechanism was designed to preempt the marital limbo (*aginut*) of the wife whose husband had absented himself without granting her a divorce. The soldiers in David's army would write their wives conditional bills of divorce so that if they did not return from battle, the bills of divorce would go into effect and their wives would be retroactively divorced. R. Waldenburg cites *Responsa Beer Sheva*, which rules that a woman who has received a conditional divorce is forbidden to mourn her husband and take part in the funeral procession, as this might make a mockery of the conditional bill of divorce, suggesting that it was ineffectual, and the rabbis might permit her to marry a man of priestly lineage, erroneously assuming that she should be treated like a widow, not like a divorcee.[56]

In the continuation of the responsum, R. Waldenburg cites RMS's position, which is diametrically opposed to that taken in *Responsa Beer Sheva*. RMS had stated his position in a letter to R. Shalom Shakhna Chernik:

55 *Responsa Tzitz Eliezer*, 15:56.

56 *Responsa Beer Sheva* #79, cited in *Pithei Teshuva*, EH 145:7.

> I will tell him (to copy into his book in my name) what is written on the pages of my [*SA*], EH 145:9 in the Rema's gloss, concerning a woman who received a conditional bill of divorce: "but there is nothing prohibited about it (if she wishes to conduct herself with severity, and weep for him, etc.)." And see *Pithei Teshuva* ad loc., which cites [*Responsa*] *Beer Sheva* (which rules with absolute stringency that she is forbidden to eulogize him or weep for him), and regarding this, I have written that [the case of] Bathsheba can be adduced as proof (that the law is not in accordance with the view in [*Responsa*] *Beer Sheva*).[57]

In contrast to the examples adduced above, where the decisors deduced on their own that RMS sought to decide the law through his midrashic exegesis, here RMS himself turns to one of his generation's greatest halakhic authorities and explicitly asks him to issue a ruling (permitting women granted conditional divorces to weep for their husbands) in RMS's name. RMS bases the law, which is to be applied in practice, on Scriptures, and not derive it exegetically. He perceives himself as having the authority to issue normative rulings, and tells other halakhic authorities to decide the law and rule in his name. R. Waldenburg thus need not make a great intellectual leap to accept RMS's ruling as normative (and to extend this conclusion to RMS's other rulings too).

(4) The "if two do it" exemption

Occasionally, a decisor accepted RMS's midrashic exegesis, but in light of the positions upheld by other decisors, did not rule in accordance with it. This is the case regarding the "if two do it" exemption in the context of labors prohibited on the Sabbath. R. Ovadia Yosef permits a Jewish doctor to treat a non-Jewish patient on the Sabbath, even if he must carry out biblically-prohibited labor.[58] There are two reasons for this dispensation: to preempt animosity toward Jews (*mishum eiva*), and to preempt reciprocity, viz., non-Jewish doctors in the Diaspora declining to treat Jewish patients. Despite this dispensation, R. Yosef advises Jewish doctors to perform any biblically-prohibited labor together with another doctor. This recommendation is based on the "if two do it" exemption: any labor that could have been carried out by one person, but is done by two together, is not deemed to be prohibited as a matter of biblical law, but only Rabbinically prohibited. Now it is

57 R. Shalom Shakhna Chernik, *Mishmeret Shalom Vehaim Uverakha*.
58 *Responsa Yabia Omer* 8, OH #38.

preferable that, if a prohibition must be violated, it be a Rabbinic prohibition and not a biblical one. The "if two do it" exemption thus enables physicians to minimize the severity of their unavoidable Sabbath transgressions. Despite his recommendation, R. Yosef quotes a number of Later Authorities, including RMS, who contend that when two persons carry out a labor together though it could have been done by one alone, this constitutes transgression of a biblical prohibition. R. Yosef adduces RMS's midrashic exegesis of the verse "You shall observe (*tishmoru*) My Sabbaths" (Lev. 26:2):

> It may be that in the Ten Commandments, the biblical text reads "observe" (*shamor*) [Deut. 5:12; in the sing. imperative] with regard to the Sabbath to refer to the commandments transgression of which incurs the punishment of death, implying that only when a lone individual does this is punishment incurred, but if two do it, they are exempt from divine extirpation (*karet*) and from having to offer a sacrifice, for it is written, "If any person . . . in doing" (Lev. 4:27). But in any event, to make it clear that two are not allowed [to carry out a forbidden labor together] *ab initio*, He wrote, "You shall observe" (*tishmoru*), in the plural.[59]

R. Yosef rejects this midrash, since he believes that a close reading of Maimonides' *Code* may lead to the opposite conclusion, namely, that when two carry out a prohibited labor together, this only transgresses a Rabbinic prohibition. Maimonides writes: "and wherever it is stated that one who does such a thing is 'exempt,' this means exempt from divine extirpation (*karet*) and from having to bring a sacrifice; however, it is prohibited to do [the labor in question] on the Sabbath, a prohibition that is Rabbinic."[60] Elsewhere, Maimonides writes: "any labor which an individual can carry out by himself, and two did it together . . . they are exempt."[61] R. Yosef does not reject RMS's midrashic exegesis in and of itself or object to its methodology in principle. This is also true of R. Yosef's approach to the exegeses discussed above. The most surprising element in R. Yosef's stance is that even when RMS's position contradicts that of Maimonides — for instance, when he claims that those who rely on the "if two do it" exemption have nonetheless transgressed a biblical prohibition — R. Yosef still does not reject RMS's view: though he rules in accordance with Maimonides' view, he presents both views as legitimate.

59 *Meshekh Hokhma*, Torah portion 'Behar.'
60 Maimonides, *Code*, Laws concerning the Sabbath 1:3.
61 Ibid., 1:15.

4 The normative intent of RMS's exegesis-based legal creativity

(1) The prohibition against abortion: biblical or Rabbinic?

I have examined both cases where subsequent decisors tended to reject RMS's exegesis-based rulings, and cases where they accepted them as law. But with respect to all the cases examined above, it is clear that RMS indeed intended to determine the law to be applied in practice, and was not merely engaging in theoretical exegesis. However, there are instances in which RMS's intent is less clear. Turning to these cases, I will seek to ascertain how subsequent decisors distinguish between midrashic exegesis that was intended to determine the law and midrashic exegesis that was merely theoretical. One such unclear case is the status of the prohibition against abortion: is it biblical or Rabbinic? This determination has bearing on the permissibility of abortion where the mother's life is in danger.

In *Meshekh Hokhma*, RMS interprets the verse "a Sabbath of complete rest, holy to the Lord; whoever does any work on it shall be put to death" (Exod. 35:2) as follows:

> In every place in the Bible where it says "death" (*mita*), it is written "shall surely be put to death" (*mot yumat*), except for extraordinary cases. And it is written, "the ox shall be stoned and its owner shall also die (*yumat*)" (Exod. 21:29) and this refers to death at the hand of heaven. . . . and it may be that [the phrase] "one who kills a human being [shall be put to death] (*yumat*)" (Lev. 24:21) applies to fetuses, for it is written, "whoever sheds the blood of man in man (*dam haadam baadam*) — that is, a fetus — by man shall his blood be shed" (Gen. 9:6); for a Noahide is slain on their account, and as for an Israelite, his death is consigned to the laws of heaven.[62]

RMS deduces that the verse "one who kills a human being" refers to abortion, and deduces from the fact that the biblical text reads, "one who kills a human being shall be put to death (*yumat*)" and not "shall surely be put to death" (*mot yumat*), that one who kills a fetus is liable to be slain by the laws of heaven, not by the laws of man.

R. Yosef enumerates the halakhic authorities who maintain that the prohibition against abortion is Rabbinic, and, citing the aforementioned exegesis, includes RMS in this list.[63] Adducing this opinion, R. Yosef tends to be lenient, permitting abortion in cases of medical necessity

62 *Meshekh Hokhma*, Exodus 35:2.

63 *Responsa Yabia Omer* 4, EH #1.

and where the woman is suffering greatly. By contrast, R. Eliezer Waldenburg dismisses RMS's exegesis and rules that the prohibition is biblical:

> And the author of the *Meshekh Hokhma*, apart from the fact that he did not write this as the law to be put into practice, but was merely giving an interpretation of the biblical passage, also prefaced it with the words "and it may be that." Moreover, he was also careful with his words, and did not use wording such that it could be said in his name that the Israelite was liable to be punished by death at the hand of heaven. Rather, he uses the wording "his death is consigned to the laws of heaven"; it is possible that by this he only meant that the verdict as to the Israelite's deed is up to the heavenly court, which will decide, in light of the circumstances, whether he is liable to be punished for his deed by death.[64]

R. Yosef assumes that RMS indeed intends to derive the law to be put into practice from his midrashic exegesis, and makes the determination that the prohibition against abortion is of Rabbinic status. R. Waldenburg, on the other hand, maintains that RMS's midrashic exegesis is purely theoretical, and devoid of normative import vis-à-vis the prohibition. This invites the following question. Why did R. Waldenburg conclude in this case — unlike all the other cases discussed above — that RMS did not intend to set down the law to be applied in practice? On what basis did he distinguish between midrashic exegesis the conclusions of which are intended as rulings to be implemented, and midrashic exegesis that is only intended as interpretation of the biblical text? Was it because RMS used the phrase "it may be that," or was it because the exegesis conflicts with that offered in the Sifre? Note that in this instance too, as in the previous examples, R. Waldenburg grapples with RMS's exegesis, seeking to adapt it to fit in with his halakhic approach, and by no means rejects RMS's methodology outright.

(2) Acts carried out by one who is inebriated

Some of RMS's innovative halakhic rulings were dismissed because they were perceived to be based on midrashic exegeses that were purely theoretical. An example is RMS's ruling concerning the status of acts

64 *Responsa Tzitz Eliezer*, 13:102.

carried out by someone who is inebriated or asleep. The Talmud discusses a scenario that may have bearing on this question:

> If he says, write a bill of divorce for my wife, and is then seized with delirium (*kordiakos*) and retracts and says, do not write. . . . Resh Lakish said, the bill of divorce may be written at once, R. Johanan said, it is not to be written until he comes to himself again. . . . Resh Lakish compares him to one who is sleeping; R. Johanan compares him to one who is mentally unsound (*shote*).[65]

R. Johanan believes that one who is seized with delirium is not considered competent to conduct his legal affairs.[66] Hence an agent he appointed when he was healthy cannot complete his mission. Resh Lakish disagrees and permits the agent to complete his mission, even though his principal is no longer legally competent. In the ensuing talmudic discussion, it is asserted that if the deficit that imparts legal incompetence clears up of its own accord, and there is no need to undertake special measures to restore the afflicted individual's competence, then it can be overlooked, and the individual can be considered legally competent.

In *Meshekh Hokhma*, RMS explains that the biblical verse "and they [Joseph's brothers] drank their fill [and became inebriated] with him" (Gen. 43:34) teaches that when someone is severely inebriated, the passage of time, that is, sleep alone, does not alleviate his condition. Joseph wanted Benjamin to stay in Egypt as his household servant, and decided to achieve this with the pretext that he stole his goblet (Gen. 44:2). However, he was afraid people would question his decision to keep a known thief as a servant. So Joseph planned to tell his servants that it was because Benjamin was drunk that he was overcome with greed and stole the goblet; he would not have acted that way had he been sober. RMS asks: since Joseph's brothers went to sleep after the feast, wouldn't the effects of the wine have worn off by morning? If so, Benjamin would not have been drunk when he was caught stealing. To ensure that Benjamin would still be drunk in the morning, Joseph made sure that "they drank their fill with him"; that is to say, he made sure that they each drank a quarter of a *log* of wine in his presence, an

65 bGitin 70b.

66 Y. Levi, "What is '*qordiakos*'?" (Hebrew), *Assia* 6 (1989), 59–60, claims that this is a hypoglycemic condition that may follow eating. The low brain glucose level leads to confusion.

amount sufficient to ensure that the effect would not wear off while they slept. Since severe inebriation does not clear up on its own merely by the passage of time (sleeping it off overnight), someone who is very drunk is not deemed legally competent.

R. Ovadia Yosef was asked whether, to spare a convert or an adult Jew who was not circumcised as an infant the pain of circumcision, it could be performed under general anesthesia.[67] At first, he considered forbidding this, since Jewish law requires that one have the intent to observe the commandment when doing (or, in this case, undergoing) the prescribed act, and one who is sleeping cannot have intent.[68] He then quotes RMS's exegesis, according to which one who drinks more than a quarter of a *log* of wine is considered legally incompetent.[69] Therefore, for instance, a scribe may not write a bill of divorce when the husband is inebriated (contra R. Johanan's approach in the talmudic *sugya* quoted above), and by extension, someone under a general anesthetic cannot form legal intent. However, R. Yosef does not accept RMS's ruling as law to be applied in practice, categorically declaring that "one need not respond to midrashic exegesis," and that RMS's remarks do not undermine the law set down by the Beit Shmuel,[70] who rules that those who are asleep or inebriated are legally competent, as their deficit is only temporary — with the passage of time their condition will clear up without any special measures being taken.[71]

The disparity between the views of the Beit Shmuel and of RMS led R. Yosef to construe RMS's creative ruling as purely theoretical exegesis, and deny it legal import. But it is not clear how R. Yosef differentiates between those of RMS's exegesis-based rulings to which he ascribes normative weight (for instance, the ruling re therapeutic abortion) and those which he dismisses as merely theoretical. Is the determining factor RMS's writing style, or the fact that RMS's view conflicts with accepted rulings? It seems, and I say this guardedly, that the decisors in question are inconsistent in this regard. In my opinion, once a decisor

67 *Responsa Yabia Omer* 5, YD #22.

68 *SA*, OH 60:4.

69 E. Shochetman, "The legal competence of one who is intoxicated in Jewish law" (Hebrew), *Sinai* 70 (1972), 212, notes that imbibing a quarter of a *log* is the criterion for inebriation instituted by the Sages of the Jerusalem Talmud; in contrast, the Sages of the Babylonian Talmud maintained that the criterion was "inability to speak before the king."

70 R. Samuel b. Uri Shraga Phoebus (Feivish), (Poland, 17th c.).

71 *Beit Shmuel*, EH 121:2.

has accepted RMS as a halakhic authority, it is hard to accept any subsequent discounting of his rulings, especially when there appears to be no consistent basis for it.

5 Gilat's assessment of RMS's intent

(1) Marrying a "beautiful captive"

The biblical laws of war permit an Israelite soldier to marry a beautiful prisoner of war (*eshet yefat toar*) even though she is not an Israelite: "When you take the field against your enemies, and the Lord your God delivers them into your power and you take some of them captive, and you see among the captives a beautiful woman and you desire her and would take her to wife" (Deut. 21:10–11). RMS deduces from the scriptural text that the dispensation to take the beautiful captive as one's wife only applies in the case where "the Lord your God delivers them into your power," that is, the Israelites are completely victorious. However, if both sides have taken prisoners, and there is a possibility that a prisoner exchange will be carried out, it is not permitted to marry the woman. In RMS's opinion, the Torah would never allow an Israelite to marry a captive woman when the hostilities were ongoing, and the enemy might keep an Israelite soldier in captivity until her return. RMS reads the clause "and the Lord your God delivers them into your power," as stipulating an important condition, and not merely as part of the background narrative: it defines when an Israelite may marry a beautiful captive. Y.D. Gilat argues that, inasmuch as the Sifre does not view this clause as having any halakhic weight,[72] this is an innovative conclusion on RMS's part.[73] According to the Sifre, the clause is only a promise: if the Israelites observe all the laws of war, including that of the beautiful captive, then they will triumph in battle. This willingness to put forward a view that runs counter to the Sifre attests to RMS's interpretive boldness.

(2) Stealing from outside the owner's domain

> If the thief is seized while tunneling, and he is beaten to death, there is no bloodguilt in his case. If the sun has risen on him, there is bloodguilt in that

72 Sifre Deuteronomy, 211 (Finkelstein edition, p. 245).
73 Gilat, n. 7 above.

> case. He must make restitution; if he lacks the means, he shall be sold for his theft. But if what he stole — whether ox or ass or sheep — is found alive in his possession, he shall pay double. (Exod. 22:1–3)

According to RMS, these verses refer to two different laws: the first addresses the case of a thief who takes something from its owner's domain; the second addresses the case of a thief who steals something that happens to be in his own domain, for example, a thief who locks the gate behind an animal that has wandered into his field. RMS infers that only in the former case does the Torah mandate the harsh punishment "he shall be sold for his theft"; in the latter case, the thief must make restitution, but should not be sold if he cannot do so. RMS notes that this seems to be the verses' plain meaning and the Sages say nothing that contradicts this interpretation. Gilat takes this comment to imply that the goal of RMS's midrashic exegesis was indeed to derive innovative laws, even when they had contemporary application, but only if they did not contradict accepted laws that were explicitly stated in the Talmuds.

I did not find any references in the halakhic literature to the two innovative rulings discussed by Gilat. This may be due to the fact that these laws have no contemporary application. I nonetheless find it necessary to disagree with Gilat's conclusion. From my analysis of RMS's various midrashic exegeses, it seems clear that not only did RMS propound exegetically-based laws that conflicted with accepted laws, but in some cases, these rulings were invoked by subsequent decisors as law to be applied in practice. Furthermore, if Gilat is right, then it is difficult to explain why some of RMS's exegesis-based rulings were rejected by subsequent decisors.

6 Supportive midrashic exegesis

RMS's midrashic exegeses are invoked mainly as supportive exegesis (*midrash tomekh*), that is, to provide scriptural grounding for known and accepted laws. It remains to be seen whether this supportive role 'raises' the status of the laws in question from Rabbinic to biblical. Presumably, decisors adduced RMS's conclusions more freely, and with fewer misgivings, when they perceived them simply as supportive midrashic exegeses, and not innovative interpretations with concrete legal import. I will give only two examples of RMS's supportive exegesis, since neither its formulation nor its acceptance by subsequent authorities involved normative innovativeness.

(1) Children of a convert

R. Waldenburg, the Tzitz Eliezer, addresses the question of whether children born to a convert before his conversion fulfill the precept of procreation ("be fruitful and multiply").[74] A talmudic dictum states that a convert who converted is like a newborn child,[75] as conversion severs the convert from his pre-conversion past. Does it not follow that any children born to him prior to his conversion are not considered his children, and ipso facto he has not fulfilled the precept "be fruitful and multiply"?[76] As we will see, however, neither the source of the teaching regarding the convert's newborn status, nor its normative weight, are clear. The Tzitz Eliezer cites RMS as elucidating the halakhic source of the teaching. In his commentary on the verse "return to your tents" (Deut. 5:27), RMS claims that the source can be found in the instructions in the Torah after the revelation at Mount Sinai. His exegesis is quite original:

> For presumably those who left Egypt had many wives . . . women whom Noahides are not admonished against marrying, and Amram constitutes proof of this, for he was the leading figure in his generation, and he married his aunt . . . so how could the Merciful One have said, after the giving of the Torah, "return to your tents," since one's "tent" means his wife, and those who had married their relatives [marriage to whom was now forbidden] would have to separate from them? We are thus compelled to say that a convert who converted is like a newborn child.

RMS contends that, in essence, the people of Israel underwent conversion at Mount Sinai. Afterwards, the Torah allows, and even commands, these 're-born' Jews to go back to their wives. RMS expresses surprise at this directive, since wives who were also related to their husbands should have been forbidden to them. He infers from this that the conversion process severs the convert from his previous life and family ties; ipso facto, these men were no longer related to their wives (other than by marriage) and hence could be married to them. R. Waldenburg had trouble accepting this exegesis.[77] He quotes R. Ezekiel

74 *Responsa Tzitz Eliezer*, 4:16.

75 bBekhorot 47a.

76 See *Talmudic Encyclopedia* (Hebrew) s.v. *ger*, §3: *yahaso likrovav*, 6:259; R. Akiva Eger, EH 1:17.

77 *Responsa Tzitz Eliezer*, 16:24.

Abramsky, the Hazon Yehezkel, who argues that the Torah was given to the forefathers of the Jewish people long before it was given at Sinai.[78] If so, the Israelites never married their close relatives, even before the revelation at Sinai. The "convert who converted" exegetical solution was thus unnecessary, because there would have been no halakhic objection to the Israelites returning to their wives after the giving of the Torah.[79]

(2) Sanctity of the Temple Mount

A second example where RMS's midrashic exegesis is invoked only as 'supportive' exegesis, and not 'creative' exegesis, is the debate over the sanctity of the Temple Mount. R. Waldenburg was asked about the sanctity of the Temple Mount's southern wall.[80] He adduced RMS's commentary on the Haftorah (reading from the Prophets) for the Torah portion 'Pikudei,' in which RMS expounds his view on the basis of the Zohar. Since David did not actually build the Temple, but only contemplated doing so, the sanctity continues to be sustained in perpetuity even in the Temple's "utmost absence," that is, though the Temple is no longer standing. RMS takes the verb "*hetivota*" (lit., "you did well") in the verses, "[As regards your intention to build a House for My name,] you did well (*hetivota*) to have that intention. However, you shall not build the House" (1 Kings 8:18–19) to be transitive, and have as its implicit object the word "sanctity." That is, he takes the verse to read: David, you did well regarding the sanctity, which will exist forever since you only had the intention, in your heart and in your mind, to build the Temple, but did not actually do so. On this interpretation, the Temple Mount remains sanctified to this very day, and therefore it is forbidden to go there or to offer sacrifices on altars outside the Temple area proper (*bamot*).

Immediately after the Six Day War, when the Temple Mount came under Israeli sovereignty, the Tzitz Eliezer was asked whether sacrifices could be offered in the present day.[81] He first notes that the law

78 R. Ezekiel Abramsky (Lithuania 1886–Israel 1976), *Tosefta Hazon Yehezkel*, bZevahim, Responsa section, #6.

79 He also expresses discomfort with RMS's interpretation in another responsum, see *Responsa Tzitz Eliezer*, 18:52.

80 *Responsa Tzitz Eliezer*, 10:7.

81 *Responsa Tzitz Eliezer*, 10:5.

had already been decided by the majority of the decisors, who had ruled that it was not permitted. Then he attempts to decide the controversy between Maimonides and R. Abraham b. David (Rabad) of Posquières. The Rabad maintained that it was forbidden to offer sacrifices after the destruction of the Temple, since the sanctity of the Temple was not extant. Maimonides contended that the Temple's sanctity remains in perpetuity. The Tzitz Eliezer availed himself of a halakhic-philosophical ruling in the *Meshekh Hokhma*. Commenting on the Torah portion 'Vayikra,' RMS recounts the controversy between Maimonides and Nahmanides over the rationale for the institution of sacrifices, using kabbalistic concepts to arrive at a novel way to decide the issue.

> The *Guide* [*for the Perplexed*] states that [sacrifices were instituted] to distance people from the desire to practice idolatry. Nahmanides and his camp declared that [sacrifices were instituted] to unite all the forces of the worlds, this being an electric–spiritual matter, wherein the priest's actions, as is well-known, have a sublime impact on the various worlds. And perhaps we should conclude that sacrifices offered outside the Temple were only designed to distance the desire to practice idolatry from the people of Israel, and therefore He commanded that they make offerings for the sake of Heaven. But this was not the case with regard to the Temple sacrifices, which were definitely offered in order to bring the worlds together. . . . and concerning this a secret (*sod*) was revealed to me regarding Rabbenu Haim Kohen's[82] innovative ruling: according to those who maintain that [the Temple area] was not sanctified in perpetuity, in any event it is forbidden to bring sacrifices on the altars outside the Temple, because the Men of the Great Assembly quashed the desire to practice idolatry.[83] Hence there is no longer any need to offer sacrifices on outside altars in order to safeguard the nation from idolatry.

Thus, RMS declared that in our time we do not offer sacrifices on altars outside the Temple, because the urge to engage in idolatry has been quelled. R. Waldenburg accepted this account and ruled accordingly. At the end of his discussion, he characterizes RMS's interpretation as follows: "and all this is just peripheral to the primary and fundamental rationales set out by the great decisors as to the impossibility of bringing sacrifices in these [post-Temple] times." It is unclear why R. Waldenburg regards RMS's remarks on this matter as

82 R. Haim b. Hananel Hakohen, a twelfth-century Tosafist who lived in Paris.

83 See bYoma 69b; bSanhedrin 64a.

merely peripheral, unlike the cases discussed above, where he accepted RMS's rulings as law. Let me suggest two possible explanations. First, perhaps in cases where R. Waldenburg relies on one of the great decisors, like the Rabad, RMS's commentary is deemed to merely provide peripheral embellishment, whereas in cases where R. Waldenburg has no other sources to rely on except for RMS, he presents RMS's exegesis as a legal ruling, and proceeds to rely on it. Second, it may be that when — as in the case at hand — RMS addresses an issue that is of no concrete contemporary relevance to him, and study of which simply constitutes fulfillment of the precept to study Torah for its own sake, R. Waldenburg is unwilling to rely on his ruling if the issue subsequently acquires practical import.

7 Exegesis-based halakhic creativity — concluding remarks

This article has addressed halakhic issues that fall under all four parts of the *Shulhan Arukh*, almost all concerning non-ritual matters: capital cases, civil law, the law of evidence, the king's law, inheritance law, personal status, conversion, legal competence, and more. I have argued that several decisors took *Meshekh Hokhma* to be more than just a commentary on Scriptures: they took RMS's midrashic exegeses to have legal import, and understood that RMS's intent was indeed to set down legal rulings intended for implementation; he was not just engaging in theoretics. RMS's letter to R. Shalom Shakhna Chernik, expressly instructing him to decide the law in practice in accordance with his innovative ruling, in his name, attests that this was his intent.

I also argued that RMS's rendering of innovative legal rulings via midrashic exegesis was not a minor, incidental element of his work, comprising no more than a handful of instances, but fundamental and central to his scholarly pursuits. This enterprise attests to RMS's courageousness in seeking to draw innovative legal conclusions from midrashic exegesis in our day, especially in light of the reluctance to do so evinced by other decisors.

We saw that although these decisors sometimes claimed that RMS's midrashic creativity was purely theoretical, there are nonetheless many instances in which it was clear to them that RMS had gone beyond theoretical interpretation and entered the normative halakhic realm. This can be demonstrated in two ways: from the fact that his novel rulings are quoted in several subsequent decisors' responsa concerning concrete cases; and from the fact that when his midrashic exegeses are quoted in these responsa, they are invoked in terms of legal rubrics: "the most important law" (*hilkheta gevirta*); "raised as a point of law" (*heela ledina*), and so on.

From the manner in which RMS's rulings are cited by certain subsequent decisors, I have concluded that RMS issued exegesis-based rulings even where they rendered permissible that which biblical law prohibited, or were contrary to the established law as set out in the *Shulhan Arukh* and the *Mapa*. These findings run counter to Gilat's assertion that RMS advanced exegesis-based legal conclusions only when they were consistent with existing law.

Although the decisors in question believed that RMS intended his midrashic exegeses to have normative weight, they did not necessarily rule in accordance with his view. Let me attempt to articulate the rule of thumb that seems to guide them in choosing which exegeses to accept as the basis for normative law, and which to reject. Where the ruling ensuing from RMS's midrashic exegesis contradicts black-letter law, subsequent decisors tend to reject it. When it serves to fill a lacuna in the existing law, or to confirm an existing custom, they tend to accept it, notwithstanding their instinctive tendency to reject this method of reaching legal determinations. I must admit, however, that the decisors in question are somewhat inconsistent in this regard. I must also stress that RMS himself did not subscribe to this rule, for he drew halakhic conclusions from midrashic exegesis regardless of whether they were consistent with accepted law. When the decisors in question rejected RMS's exegesis-based rulings, this was generally because their own understandings and exegeses of the verses differed from RMS's. I found only two cases in which rejection of RMS's rulings reflected opposition in principle to either the exegetical method itself or to RMS's having arrogated the authority to draw legal conclusions from midrashic exegesis. In some cases, though the decisors rejected RMS's halakhic conclusions, they did not — surprisingly — reject the methodology used to arrive at them, and were indeed so influenced by this method that they adopted it themselves. We must therefore conclude that they disputed RMS's interpretations, but did not call into question the legitimacy of midrashic exegesis itself.

Two phenomena that may explain the acceptance of RMS's innovative rulings are the accolades — references to his genius and brilliance — routinely attached to RMS's name by both those who accept his rulings, and those who do not, and the praise for the clear and straightforward manner in which he expresses himself. Perhaps these commendations were deemed necessary if his legal methodology was to be accepted. It is not certain whether the said decisors' characterization of RMS's writing style as clear and straightforward played a role in persuading them to rule in his favor, but in several responsa, they explicitly mention this clarity right before accepting his innovative rulings as law.

Proffering midrashic exegesis to which normative import is ascribed meshes well with RMS's pragmatism and his general approach to legal decision-making, which I discussed elsewhere,[84] and also endows RMS's development of the halakha with a fresh and distinctive character.

84 See Cohen, n. 15 above.

The Jewish Law Annual, Vol. XX

Exegetical Creativity in Interpreting the Biblical Laws on Capital Offenses

Israel Zvi Gilat*

1. **Biblical exegesis (*midrash hatora*) as a distinctive source of the law**
2. **Between "putting away the evil from your midst" and "the congregation will judge . . . the congregation will save"**
3. **Exegetical interdependence of murder and rape**
4. **"Zealotry for My sake" — punishment by volunteers**
5. **"Thou shalt not kill–nor kill oneself": suicide as an act of murder**
6. **"Thou shalt surely smite the inhabitants of that city" — exegesis on collective punishment**

1. Biblical exegesis (*midrash hatora*) as a distinctive source of the law

Eminent talmudic scholars have invested much effort in seeking to understand the phenomenon of legal midrashic exegesis (*midreshei halakha*), where the law is explained by adducing a biblical verse, the relationships between biblical verses, or specific words or phrases within the verses, which are interpreted by means of the exegetical rules. These rules were applied systematically, and reflect specific Tannaim and their approaches. Which came first? Is an existing law derived exegetically from a given verse, which is invoked to buttress the law? Or might it be the case that the exegetical derivation is not merely a literary device for associating a law with a given biblical verse, but much more than that? Perhaps the verse which is intertwined with a given law does not simply support the law in question, but is also its source, meaning that the law was generated through meticulous

* Law School, Netanya Academic College; School of Education, Bar-Ilan University

study of the biblical verse, and without this exegetical study of the verse, would not have existed. From the very inception of the Jüdische Wissenschaft approach to Judaism, the relationship between halakhic midrash — that is, legal midrashic exegesis — and the halakha itself, was the subject of an ongoing controversy between Isaac Halevi, the author of *Dorot Rishonim*, and Isaac Hirsch Weiss, the author of *Dor Dor Vedorshav*.[1] And in later generations too, scholars such as Jacob N. Epstein,[2] Hanoch Albeck,[3] Yekutiel Neubauer,[4] and Ephraim E. Urbach[5] were unable to agree about the role and orientation of legal midrashic exegesis. To contemporary students of Jewish law and lore, the very notion of legal exegesis is rather peculiar: given the many other kinds of legal sources — laws, enactments and decrees, custom, reasoning (*svara*) — why did the Sages even need to utilize midrashic exegesis as a source of law? For even if used to 'create' law (as opposed to merely 'supporting' law), midrashic exegesis seems to resemble legal wizardry and gymnastics much more than it resembles a sincere effort to probe the true meaning of the biblical text. And if it is intended only as 'supportive' exegesis, that is, if its purpose is simply to supply a basis for an ancient law already known to the Sages, by attaching it to a verse or a string of words within a verse — that is, if the verse does not create the law — then what is the purpose of the whole exercise? Why invest so much effort to create the impression of harmony between the law and the scriptural text, the impression that the verse was the source for the law, when that is not the case?[6]

1 Weiss contended that the Oral Law was partly generated by halakhic midrash, i.e., by exegesis of biblical verses, whereas Halevi maintained that all of the Oral Law originated in the ancient oral tradition originating at Sinai, and that halakhic midrash reflects the Sages' efforts to reconcile the oral tradition with the scriptural text. See n. 8 below.

2 E. Z. Melamed, *Introduction to Tannaitic Literature* (Hebrew), (Jerusalem: 1957), 511.

3 *Introduction to the Mishna* (Hebrew), (Jerusalem and Tel-Aviv: 1961), 42.

4 "*Halakha* and *midrash halakha*" (Hebrew), *Sinai* 22 (1948), 49–86; idem, *Maimonides on Rabbinic Enactments* (Hebrew), (Jerusalem: 1957), appendix 2, 101–150.

5 "The *derasha* as a basis of the halakha and the problem of the *Soferim*" (Hebrew), *Tarbiz* 27 (1958), 166–82; idem, *The Halakha — Its Sources and Developments* (Hebrew), (Givatayim: 1984), 69–78.

6 See also M. Elon, *Jewish Law: History, Sources, Principles* (Philadelphia and Jerusalem: 1994), 286–90.

If we take the approach endorsed by the Sages themselves, namely, that exegesis indeed 'creates' law, then we must consider another question, that of the limits of this 'creative' exegesis. In comparison with other sources of law, exegesis seems to be completely limitless — anything goes. This contrasts with custom, which is constrained by what people actually do[7]; reasoning, which is limited by the rules of logic; and enactments and decrees, which are, as is well known, constrained by rules that place restrictions on rabbinical authority to issue directives not to carry out prescribed acts ('sit and do nothing,' *shev veal taase*), or to act in contravention of an existing law ('rise and act,' *kum vease*), either temporarily due to an exigency situation, or permanently, by invoking the court's authority to declare property ownerless (i.e., to confiscate property), and so on. But with regard to midrashic exegesis, there do not appear to be obvious constraints on the laws that are created. Did the Sages not recognize any 'default rule' in Scriptures that enjoined them not to change, via exegesis, anything that was expressly stated in the Torah, or was long-standing practice?[8] It is not my intention to address the theological question of the Bible's divine origin: the source of rabbinical authority is one thing, the rabbinical authorities' conduct in practice vis-à-vis using exegesis to generate law is quite another.[9] It is the latter question that will be addressed in this article.

7 Berachyahu Lifshitz, "'*Minhag*' and its place on the scale of the norms of the Oral Law" (Hebrew), 24 *Shenaton Hamishpat Haivri* (2006/2007), 123.

8 In *Die Geschichte und Literatur Israels*, part 1, vol. 3 (Berlin: 1923), 467–544; vol. 5 (Berlin: 1920), 242–92, R. Isaac Halevi critiques J. Hirsch Weiss, *Zur Geschichte der Jüdischen Tradition* [*Dor Dor Vedorshav*] as to the relationship between halakhic midrash and the law itself. See also Zacharias Frankel, *Introduction to the Mishnah* (Hebrew), (Warsaw: 1923), 7, 92 n. 7; and see the critical survey by H. Tchernowitz-Rav Tzair and his theories as to the dispute over the role of halakhic midrash in *History of Hebrew Law* (Hebrew), vol. 1 (NY: 1945), 37–61. In my view, all the scholars quoted in the works adduced in this and the preceding notes, except for Elon, did not maintain that the Sages viewed 'creative' exegesis as a means of introducing laws through the back door, so to speak, but rather saw it as a tool for arriving at a better understanding of the scriptural text.

9 In this article I will not address the question of the rabbinical authorities' jurisdiction to issue enactments that conflict with express scriptural law, which is discussed at length by Elon. On the development of halakhic rules governing this jurisdiction, see I.D. Gilat, *Studies in the Development of the Halakha* (Hebrew), (Ramat-Gan: 1992), 191–204.

In addition to the 'which came first?' debate (i.e., does exegesis of a verse create law, or does it connect an existing law to a verse?) represented by the controversy between those who take Weiss's view, and those who side with Halevi, and the question as to the limits of halakhic midrashic creativity, there is another no less interesting question: what is the purpose of exegesis? What is the significance of the gap between the plain meaning of a biblical verse and the law that is derived from it? Is this, perhaps, a case of "the integrity of the upright shall guide them" (Prov. 11:3)? Or is it more plausible that the sages who engage in exegesis are engaged in what present-day legal discourse would call 'pragmatic interpretation'? Is it the case that Menachem Elon's daring thesis that halakhic midrashic exegesis serves as the preferred means of implementing the spirit of biblical law when a problem arises as to its application in practice, a problem that cannot be satisfactorily resolved without recourse to new enactments or decrees (which must somehow be anchored in Scriptures, mandating exegesis), is itself agenda-driven and possibly anachronistic, in seeking to present the halakhic authorities as present-day judges?[10]

In this article, I will seek to substantiate the thesis that the Sages used biblical exegesis as a tool for shaping legal policy by examining recourse to exegesis of the scriptural verses pertaining to capital offenses, especially those incurring the punishment of death imposed by the court. We will examine the verses themselves, the manner in which they were exegetically expounded by the talmudic Sages, and interpretations of these exegeses that have been offered by commentators from the early Middle Ages to the present day, an exploration that will reveal the labyrinthian interpretive process by which the plain meaning of scriptural verses has increasingly been distorted.[11]

10 Another account that addresses this point is M. Halbertal, *Interpretative Revolutions in the Making — Values as Interpretative Considerations in Midrashei Halakha* (Hebrew), (Jerusalem: 1997), 15.

11 See D. Daube, "Rabbinic methods of interpretation," *HUCA* 22 (1949), 239; B.S. Jackson, *Essays in Jewish and Comparative Legal History* (Leiden: 1975), 1–24. On the tension between literal interpretation of the scriptural text and Rabbinic exegesis thereof, see A. Kirshenbaum, *The Criminal Confession in Jewish Law* (Hebrew), (Jerusalem: 2005), 123–27.

2. Between "putting away the evil from your midst" and "the congregation will judge . . . the congregation will save"

The biblical obligation to punish one who transgresses Torah law, and even to put him to death, is set out in the verses "and you shall put away the evil from Israel" (Deut. 17:12; 22:22); "so you shall put away the evil from your midst" (Deut. 13:6; 17:7; 19:19; 21:21; 22:21; 24:7); and "but you shall put away the guilt of innocent blood from Israel" (Deut. 19:13). However, it was interpreted by the Sages in a manner that severely limited the authorities' freedom to execute this directive.

These limitations were set out in tSanhedrin 11:1 (Zuckermandel, 431) and in bSanhedrin 8b: "All who are liable to the various punishments of death [set out] in the Torah, are not put to death except in the presence of a congregation, and with witnesses and due forewarning (*hatraa*)." The meaning of this dictum is as follows:

1. An offender cannot be punished, according to Torah law, except on the basis of a ruling handed down in the presence of a "congregation," that is, a duly-authorized court, viz., one whose members have been duly ordained. Capital cases are to be heard by a 'small Sanhedrin,' that is, a court of twenty-three elders[12]; offenses punishable by flogging are tried by a court of three. Adjudication of extremely serious transgressions requires a court of seventy-one elders.[13]
2. No one can be punished on the basis of self-incrimination.[14] Only upon the testimony of two witnesses deemed by the law to be fit to testify, can guilt be established and punishment imposed.[15] The

12 See mSanhedrin 1:6, where the size of the small Sanhedrin is deduced from the verses "and the congregation will judge . . . and the congregation will save" (Num. 34:24–25). But in *Code,* Laws concerning the Sanhedrin 5:3, Maimonides rules that this was known by tradition, and the verse is only a prooftext.

13 For a historical account of judicial practices with respect to capital offenses, including the question of whether they were tried in every town or only in Jerusalem by a special court of 71, see G. Alon, "Studies in Philonian halacha" (Hebrew), *Tarbiz* 5 (1934), 241; Urbach 1984, n. 5 above, 47–57.

14 See Maimonides, *Code*, Laws concerning the Sanhedrin 18:6, where he rules that this is mandated by biblical decree (*gzeirat hakatuv*). The Radbaz ad loc. explains that one's soul is not his own property, but belongs to God. Even so, Akhan was put to death on the basis of his own admission, as a temporary ruling, see jSanhedrin 6:3; Numbers Rabbah, Torah portion 'Masei,' 23.

15 Deuteronomy 17:6; *Rashi*, bMakot 5a s.v. *mai taama*; *Responsa Maharatz Chajes*, 3.

testimony itself is an essential part of the process, and not solely a means of ascertaining the truth of the matter. Circumstantial evidence is not acceptable for the purpose of determining culpability. The Babylonian Talmud tells of R. Shimon b. Shetah, who saw "someone pursuing his fellow with a sword in his hand, and he went into a ruin [to elude him], and he ran after him." R. Shimon b. Shetah ran in "and the sword was in [the murderer's] hand, and it was dripping blood, and the slain man was in his death-throes," but it was impossible to bring the murderer before the court, as there were no witnesses to the murder itself.[16]

3. One cannot be punished for a transgression, unless it has been proved definitively that he had criminal intent. The criminal intent must be confirmed by the witnesses, who testify that he was forewarned, in their presence, not to commit the act, but he carried out the prohibited act nonetheless. This intention cannot be established by making a reasonable presumption, as is done in various other contexts. According to biblical law, the principle that "it can be assumed that one intends to achieve the outcome that is the natural result of her actions" is not valid.[17]

The Sages do not view forewarning as simply a cautionary warning to a potential offender, as is the case in contemporary legal systems, of the consequences of his acts. Nor is it just an example of the talmudic saying, 'there can be no punishment unless there has been a prior admonition,' often quoted by learned judges and legal scholars in speaking of the Western democratic tradition that no punishment is to be meted out unless there is an explicit directive in the law forbidding the act and defining it as a crime.[18] The precise talmudic statement — "the scriptural text does not punish without having issued an admonition" — has a different intention: no punishment should be imposed unless the offense in question is mentioned in two different verses in the

16 bSanhedrin 37b.

17 Judgment on the basis of reasonable presumptions is acceptable for Noahides, but this is unusual. See *Hidushei Haramban*, bMakot 9a; *Rashi*, bJebamot 47b s.v. *umodiin oto; Tosafot Yeshanim* ad loc.; *Responsa Shoel Umeshiv* (2nd edition), 1:84; *Responsa Maharatz Chajes*, ch. 3.

18 On the *nulla poena sine lege praevia* principle, see *Eshed v. Attorney General*, CA 53/54 8 PD 785, 819; S.Z. Feller, *Elements of Criminal Law* (Jerusalem: 1984) 1:4–10, 47–49.

Pentateuch.[19] The first verse admonishes against committing the act, but generally does not provide a detailed definition of the proscribed conduct; the second verse sets out the punishment for the forbidden act, thereby completing the definition of the forbidden act. But in addition to this, Torah law, as interpreted by the Sages, requires that the transgressor be warned, prior to his committing the transgression, with a forewarning, which he must acknowledge prior to commission of the transgression, and in addition, "he must surrender himself to death." In other words, he must literally say that he is going to do the deed on the basis of knowledge that he will be liable to punishment by death. Furthermore, the transgression has to be carried out immediately after the forewarning, "within the time needed for an utterance."[20]

The forewarning process is explained by R. Menahem Hameiri:

> And as to the forewarning, he is told to desist and not to commit the transgression, for if he does it, he will be liable on that account to [the punishment of] death administered by the court, or to a flogging. Even if he was forewarned, if he desisted and did not commit the transgression immediately, but rather after the time needed for an utterance had elapsed, he is exempt, since he may have forgotten the warning, and it would have been necessary to forewarn him again immediately prior to his action, [i.e.,] within the time needed for an utterance. And even if he was forewarned immediately prior to his action [lit., within the time needed for an utterance], if he did not respond, he is exempt. And even if he lowered his head as if to say, I know that it is so [he is exempt]. And not only that, but [he is liable only if] he accepted the forewarning, by explicitly saying, I know that it is so, and on that very basis I will do it.[21]

It is obvious that, given the detailed conditions stipulated for the forewarning, it will be difficult to find an offender who can be punished,

19 The dictum is found in the following places: bZevahim 106b; bYoma 81a; bKeritot 3b; bSanhedrin 56b. And see bSanhedrin 54a; Sifra Leviticus (Weiss edition), 'Kedoshim' 10:10, 12; tMakot 4:1 (Zukermandel edition, 441); bMakot 16a; Maimonides, *Book of Percepts*, Root 8; Maimonides, *Commentary on the Mishnah*, mMakot 3:1 (Kafih edition, 158).

20 On the talmudic requirements, see my "On the validity of the duty of *hatraa* in Jewish criminal law" (Hebrew), 6 *Bar Ilan Law Studies* (1988), 119–22, which also discusses the controversy over the precise wording of the forewarning, the formula that has to be articulated by the forewarner, and the form and extent of the warning formula for a learned person, an enemy, and so on.

21 *Beit Habehira*, bSanhedrin 40b s.v. *hayavei mitot* (Sofer edition, 175–76).

who will surrender himself to the punishment of death and will transgress immediately after the admonition–forewarning.

Various Tannaim and Amoraim tried to find supportive textual anchors for the forewarning requirement in scriptural verses. Thus, for example, jSanhedrin 5:1 states:

> From whence do we infer the forewarning requirement? . . . It was taught: R. Shimon b. Yohai says: "At the mouth of two witnesses or three witnesses shall he that is to die [lit., the dead one] be put to death" (Deut. 17:6) — the dead one is already dead, but rather, one should inform him of the type of death he will die.

The *Pnei Moshe* commentary explains:

> It is written in Scripture "shall he that is to die [lit., the dead one] be put to death," but can a dead person die? Rather, it is to teach you that he must be forewarned and informed of the type of death that he will die if he transgresses and does the deed.[22]

And in bSanhedrin 41a, when the Talmud asks about the source for the claim that the offender is not liable unless he surrenders himself to death, Rava replies: "Scripture states, "shall he that is to die [lit., the dead one] be put to death" (Deut. 17:6). [He is not put to death] unless he surrenders himself to death." Rashi explains: "He is, as it were, already dead when he appears before the court, since his own mouth consigned him to death."

The *sugya* in bSanhedrin 41a states that some schools invoked other verses in support of the forewarning requirement:

> The school of Hezekiah taught: "And if a man come presumptuously upon his fellow, to slay him with guile" (Exod. 21:14) — this implies that they forewarned him, yet he acted with deliberate malice. The school of R. Ishmael taught: "And they that found him gathering sticks [on the Sabbath]" (Num. 15:33) — this implies that they forewarned him, yet he continued gathering. The school of Rabbi taught: "On account of the fact [lit., of the word] that he violated [his fellow's wife']" (Deut. 22:24), which teaches that [it is] on account of 'the word' [that the punishment is imposed].[23]

22 *Pnei Moshe*, Deuteronomy 17:6.

23 For a list of all the verses used as a basis for the forewarning requirement, see Gilat 1988, n. 20 above, 223.

Scrutiny of these exegeses reveals that not only are the Sages not in agreement as to the source of the forewarning requirement, but the scriptural verses adduced in both Talmuds as the basis for the requirement are also given very different explanations, and invoked with respect to other matters, matters that are likewise unrelated to the verses' plain meanings.[24]

On the other hand, there are two verses that mention a forewarning requirement fairly explicitly, and are so interpreted by the Talmud. Ultimately, however, these verses are the exceptions with respect to derivation of the forewarning requirement.

i) In the case of the wife suspected of adultery (*sota*), Scripture states: "And the spirit of jealousy come upon him, and he be jealous of his wife, and she be defiled: or if the spirit of jealousy come upon him, and he be jealous of his wife, and she be not defiled" (Num. 5:14).[25] According to the plain sense of the verse, it would seem that the jealousy follows a specific warning to the wife that she not closet herself with a specific man, and this was R. Nahman b. Isaac's opinion: "the invocation of jealousy is nothing but a reference to forewarning (*hatraa*), as Scripture also states, 'Then will the Lord be jealous for His land' (Joel 2:18)."[26]

ii) In the case of the rebellious son, Scripture states: "Then shall his father and his mother lay hold on him, and bring him out unto the elders of his city, and unto the gate of his place; And they shall say unto the elders of his city, This our son is stubborn and rebellious, he will not obey our voice; he is a glutton, and a drunkard" (Deut. 21:19–20). Once again, it would seem that failure to heed one's parents and ignoring their earlier admonitions is central to the "stubborn and rebellious" son's transgression, and the Talmud indeed interprets it thus: "'This our son' (Deut. 21:20) — [implies] forewarning (*hatraa*) before two witnesses."[27]

24 In bMakot 6b, the verse about "two witnesses" is expounded as meaning "the Sanhedrin may not hear testimony through an interpreter."

25 On the historical and textual sources pertaining to the ordeal of the wife suspected of adultery, see I. Rosen-Zvi, *The Rite that Was Not — Temple, Midrash and Gender in Tractate Sotah* (Hebrew), (Jerusalem: 2008), 152–79.

26 bSota 3a.

27 bSanhedrin 71a–b.

These cases are thought-provoking. Moreover, the term 'forewarning' (*hatraa*) does not appear in the Bible at all, but only in the talmudic literature. In several other biblical contexts, a different word that similarly connotes warning (though it is variously translated into English) — *haeid* — is used. In Genesis, for instance: "And Judah spake unto him, saying, The man did earnestly forewarn us (*haeid heiid banu haish*), saying, Ye shall not see my face, except your brother be with you" (Gen. 43:3).[28] Similarly in Exodus: "And the Lord said unto Moses, Go down, charge the people (*haeid baam*), lest they break through unto the Lord to gaze, and many of them perish" (Exod. 19:21); "for Thou did charge us (*haeidota banu*) saying, Set bounds about the mount, and sanctify it" (Exod. 19:23). In Deuteronomy: "I forewarn you (*haidoti bakhem*) this day that you shall surely perish" (Deut. 8:19).

The aim of the forewarning is to prove criminal intent with the help of witnesses, and this in effect restricts it to humanly-administered punishments, as opposed to punishments at the hand of heaven.[29] This is corroborated by a passage in Song of Solomon Rabbah: King Solomon sought to administer justice "just as God's throne judges without witnesses and warning."[30] This is also apparent from the Sages' answer to a query posed to R. Eliezer — "Since, with regard to the offense of the golden calf, all were equal, why are the punishments of death [imposed by the court] not all equal?" — by a "wise woman" in tractate Yoma. The answer was that "[where there were] witnesses and forewarning (*hatraa*) — death by sword, [where there were] witnesses without forewarning (*hatraa*) — death, [where there were] neither witnesses nor forewarning (*hatraa*) — death by dropsy."[31]

Indeed, scholars of the early halakha were aware of the oddity of the warning requirement within the framework of the laws of capital

28 *Rashi* ad loc. explains that the verse expresses a forewarning.

29 This article deals neither with the question of the degree of criminal intent necessary to establish homicide, nor the degree of criminal intent mandated by the Sages of the Talmud. On these questions, see B S. Jackson, *Wisdom-Laws: A Study of the Mishpatim of Exodus 21:1–22:16* (NY: 2006), 120–71; J. Habba, "Actus reus in the crime of homicide under Jewish law" (Hebrew), 20–21 *Dine Israel* (2001), 475–84.

30 Song of Songs Rabbah 1:10; bRosh Hashana 21b; *Maharsha* ad loc. s.v. *bikesh kohelet*; *Rashash* ad loc. s.v. *gemara besof hainyan*.

31 bYoma 66b. See also *Nahmanides*, Exodus 32:27 s.v. *simu ish harbo* (Chavel edition, 513–14).

offenses, and advanced many theories regarding its purpose. Some saw it as a means to "confirm the offender's criminal intent beyond any doubt,"[32] and argue that Jewish law construes this verification of intent as called for since the offender "is punished for the severity of his sin against God and not for the damage he caused to society . . . . this is only the case where the transgressor transgressed as an attack on God and a desecration of His name,"[33] or because "the central purpose of Torah law is educational and mystical, to refine the Israelite soul, 'to burnish and purify the individual.'"[34] A different explanation was put forward by Shemesh, who, comparing Rabbinic law to that of the Dead Sea sects at the close of the Second Temple period, reached the

32 As A. Shemesh puts it in "Rebuke, warning and the obligation to testify in the Judean Desert writings and Rabbinic halakha" (Hebrew), *Tarbiz* 66 (1997), 149, 161. This article responds to, among others, my article, n. 20 above; it is, however, insufficiently precise. S. Albeck addresses the subject in *Principles of Talmudic Criminal Law* (Hebrew), (Ramat-Gan: 1997), 100–106 and sees this as a key rationale. In the present context, I will not discuss the many insightful comments in the halakhic literature regarding the peculiarity of the forewarning requirement; a short summary can be found in *Tzofnat Paneiah* on *Code,* Laws concerning Forbidden Intercourse 1:3, which takes forewarning to have two aspects: one evidentiary, the other epistemic. With respect to the former, R. Meir Simha takes forewarnings to constitute evidence; with respect to the latter, he takes the requirement that the offender be aware that he is about to commit a transgression to be mandated by biblical decree (*gzeirat hakatuv*); see also R. B.J. Zolty, *Mishnat Yaavetz* (Jerusalem: 1963), HM, 16.

33 A. Enker, *Fundamentals of Jewish Criminal Law* (Hebrew), (Ramat-Gan: 2007), 23–74. S. Albeck suggests a third explanation for the forewarning requirement, adopting an even more extreme stance. In Albeck's opinion, in support of which he adduces many sources, any punishment administered by the Torah is meant "solely for atonement, and has no other purpose" and hence "a transgressor should not be punished for a transgression unless it is well established that he transgressed and needs atonement, which will be achieved via punishment. While an inadvertent transgressor also needs atonement, it is impossible to compel him to accept punishment, for he can say that he transgressed intentionally, and since there are no witnesses to show he acted intentionally, nor was he forewarned, the court is unable to punish him" (Albeck, ibid., 125, 127–28).

34 A. Kirschenbaum, "The role of punishment in Jewish criminal law: a chapter in rabbinical penological thought" (Hebrew), 12 *Iyunei Mishpat — Tel-Aviv University Law Review* (1987) 253, 256; idem, *The Criminal Confession in Jewish Law* (Hebrew), (Jerusalem: 2004).

conclusion that it was "in order to make it possible for witnesses to discharge their obligation to forewarn that the Sages instituted the forewarning procedure."[35] It has even been suggested that the Sages had a general policy of maximizing the number of people found innocent, and that they supported it by invoking the verse cited in mSanhedrin 1:6, "'the congregation will judge . . . and the congregation will save' (Num. 35:24–25) — a congregation judges and a congregation saves." In other words, according to this theory, "more than the court ["congregation"]'s role is to judge someone accused of a capital offense, the role of the court ["congregation"] is to seek to save him (by handing down an acquittal) from the punishment of death."[36]

However, these general explanations do not accord with known details of the laws in question as elucidated in the talmudic and rabbinical literature. For the obligation to forewarn a potential transgressor does not apply to all transgressions. Some of the transgressions that are explicitly stated in the Torah, such as those of the 'rebellious elder,' 'blood avenger,' and 'conspiring witnesses," do not, according to the Sages, require forewarning the transgressor as a necessary condition for punishment.

There are also situations where someone has not yet transgressed, but is nonetheless "sentenced on account of his ultimate destiny," such as the 'stubborn and rebellious son'; the 'stealth [lit., tunneling] burglar,' that is, the burglar who enters a dwelling stealthily [lit., by digging an opening underneath it] with the intention of killing anyone who interferes; and the 'pursuer' — and in these cases no forewarning is required for punishment to be imposed, as, say, in the case of the perfect murder. In addition, there are punishments that are not stated explicitly in Scriptures and which the Sages do not deem to fall under the rubric of biblical law, but rather are imposed as a matter of 'a temporary ruling' (*horaat shaa*); 'the king's law'; 'confinement in a cell' (*onesh hakipa*);

35 See Shemesh, n. 32 above, 160.

36 Y. Lorberbaum, "On murder, capital punishment, and *imago dei* in Rabbinic literature" (Hebrew), 7 *Plilim–Israel Journal of Criminal Justice* (1998), 223, 236; idem, *Image of God — Halakha and Aggada* (Tel Aviv: 2004), 308. At the beginning of that paragraph, Lorberbaum asserts: "I do not claim that this is the purpose of all the laws that were referred to above [as forewarnings — IZG]; it is possible that some were designed (*ab initio*) to protect innocent suspects, and others had their own specific justification."

'zealots kill him'; 'lashes for rebellion against the Sages' (*makat mardut*); and 'informing.' In these cases, the Sages are of the opinion that transgressors need not be forewarned for punishment to be imposed.

None of the theories we have advanced can explain why, "the native is on earth and the stranger is in the highest sky" (bEruvin 9a), that is, why those who commit explicit and grave transgressions such as murder, idolatry, and incest, transgressions that are indisputable and egregious, cannot be punished unless the perpetrator has been forewarned in a way that almost completely precludes the possibility of punishment, whereas less serious transgressions, which may even be of Rabbinic origin, do not require forewarning.[37] The Sages do not generally give their reasons for 'exempting' the former — that is, the egregious — transgressions from the forewarning requirement. The main exception is 'conspiring witnesses,' which are the subject of an extensive discussion in the Talmud, which attempts to account for the 'exemption.' However, here too, there is no consensus as to the explanation.[38]

37 Enker, n. 33 above, 199ff., discusses the four exceptions: enticement to engage in idolatry, conspiring witnesses, the 'rebellious elder,' and the 'stubborn and rebellious son.' However, there are additional cases, and it is thus necessary to find a broader common denominator than that which is common to these four crimes, namely, the fact that Scripture says, vis-à-vis these cases, "and all the people shall hear and fear" (Deut. 17:13). S. Albeck, n. 32 above, 106–40 discusses the objective of punishment mandated in the Torah at length, trying to assess why punishment is sometimes imposed as a 'temporary ruling' and 'to safeguard the law': "we can therefore deduce that punishment mandated in the Torah is intended for the atonement of the individual who has sinned, to cleanse the sin away and to purify her moral failing, so that she may repent and rectify the flaw in her character; whereas the extra-legal punishments are not addressed to the individual but are for communal rectification, to impose safeguards for the law in accordance with what is temporarily required. The community's need to protect itself from a proliferation of transgressors changes from generation to generation and from place to place." In Albeck's opinion, since the punishment is for the public good, there is no need for forewarning. However, Albeck does not offer an account of the reasons for exempting from the forewarning requirement conspiring witnesses, the 'stubborn and rebellious son,' one who incites others to engage in idolatry, the blood-avenger, and the wife suspected of adultery, all of which are transgressions according to biblical law, and not extra-legal.

38 This issue is the subject of a controversy between Abbaye and Rava in bKetubot 33a. Maimonides offers a rather different explanation of the

In my opinion, the correct explanation is that which I put forward in my "On the validity of the duty of *hatraa* in Jewish criminal law,"[39] and I will not refer to it again except to highlight the halakhic authorities' use of midrashic exegesis to facilitate a pragmatic interpretation of the scriptural text that would allow them to implement a suitable punishment policy, as suggested by Menachem Elon. Such a policy can explain the apparent contradictions in their approach. On the one hand, they said of themselves: "Had we been members of the Sanhedrin, no one would ever have been put to death,"[40] and on the other, "If a person kills another and there is no clear evidence, or if no forewarning has been given him . . . the king may, if the exigency of the hour demands it, put him to death in order to ensure the stability of the social order. He may put to death many offenders in one day."[41] Would it not be fitting to save the offender from the clutches of the king, just as he would have been saved from the clutches of the Sanhedrin, which is empowered by Torah law?

It seems that, according to Torah law, the verses, "you shall put away the evil from your midst" and "you shall put away the evil from Israel"[42] are absolute commandments. Along with the obligation of administering justice, biblical law commands the court to eliminate evildoers from the midst of Israel, and the court does not have the authority to implement penological policies, such as punishment reduction, or deciding to ignore certain offenses and not bring their perpetrators to justice, possibilities available to present-day legal

exemption in *Code*, Laws concerning Evidence 20:4, and both the Raavad and the Radbaz object to Maimonides' 'independent' approach, which the Radbaz sees as a solution "of convenience." Let me note that whereas the Sages of the Babylonian Talmud, and afterwards, the Earlier and Later Authorities, take the case of conspiring witnesses to be exempted from the forewarning requirement, Saul Lieberman has pointed out that the Sages in the land of Israel did require forewarning prior to punishment in the case of conspiring witnesses; see *Hayerushalmi Kiphshuto, A Commentary Based on Manuscripts of the Yerushalmi* . . . edited by Menachem Katz (NY and Jerusalem: 2008), 14.

39 N. 20 above, 217–59.

40 mMakot 1:10.

41 Maimonides, *Code*, Laws concerning Kings and Wars 3:10; see also *Beer Hagola*, HM 2:6; R. Meir S. Hakohen of Dvinsk, *Or Sameiah*, Laws concerning Kings and Wars 3:10.

42 See above at the beginning of this section.

systems. In other words, if two fit witnesses appear before the court and testify as to a capital offense, the court is obliged to impose the punishment of death. It has no discretion to reduce the maximum punishment set down in the Torah, and all the more so has no authority to decide that a suspect need not stand trial.

Unlike Torah law, in contemporary legal systems it is accepted that an authorized judicial instance has, in most cases, discretion to consider imposing a reduced penalty, a penalty that is considerably lighter than the maximum sentence specified by the law on the books. Furthermore, the state can in any event pardon offenders or reduce their punishment. The state is also sovereign with respect to deciding, through its administrators and institutions, not to try an offender. All these means are established features of the contemporary administration of justice. But as we said, they are alien to biblical law.

Since a Sanhedrin is not empowered to consider mitigating circumstances in order to lighten an offender's punishment or to exercise the discretion to refrain from trying her, the Sages introduced the constraints noted above: trial by "congregation," that is, by a duly-authorized court, witnesses, and forewarning. The forewarning requirement, with all its onerous pre-conditions, in fact reflects a penological policy that serves to preclude excessive punishment and seeks to reduce capital punishment to an absolute minimum. At the same time, the Sages purposely instituted an extensive framework that would allow for the punishment of transgressions not deemed to mandate forewarning, or in other cases, witnesses and an authorized court.

What, precisely, was this 'penological policy,' that on the one hand seems intended to undermine a commandment expressly stated in the Torah — "you shall put away the evil from your midst" — yet on the other, identifies novel transgressions whose perpetrators are subject to being punished by death, though there is no mention of these transgressions in the Bible?

The Torah contain many positive and negative commandments. These commandments are generally accompanied by punitive sanctions, some at the hand of heaven, and others imposed by the courts.[43] The courts' obligation to administer justice and ensure the purging "of evil from your midst" is apparently a positive commandment like any other positive commandment, with respect to which the operative

43 "Four death sentences are administered by the court" (mSanhedrin 7:1).

principle is 'the more one does, the more praiseworthy it is,'[44] but the Sages did not see their judicial role that way, and tried to keep punishment by human hands to an absolute minimum. Their desire to limit their jurisdiction vis-à-vis punishment reflected the following premises.

i. In light of divine providence, human punishment is superfluous

There are two different biblical verses that address the offender who has committed murder, and is therefore subject to the punishment of death. A verse in Genesis states: "Whoever sheds man's blood, by man shall his blood be shed" (Gen. 9:6), while a verse in Exodus states: "But if a man come presumptuously upon his neighbor, to slay him with guile; thou shalt take him from Mine altar, that he may die" (Exod. 21:14). In the former, there is no hint of an obligation to ascertain the offender's criminal intent, and the transgression, that is, the murder, is regarded as an absolute crime, but in the second verse, intent to kill is a condition for punishing the murderer.

The clear difference between the verses was already noted, with puzzlement, by Isi b. Akiva in the Mekhilta: "Before the giving of the Torah, we were warned against shedding blood. After the giving of the Torah, [is it conceivable that] instead of being made stricter, the laws were made lighter?!" The Mekhilta suggests the following resolution: "Indeed, the Sages said: he is exempt from judgment by the human court, but his judgment is left to heaven."[45] This approach, where man limits his role and consigns it to heaven, is also found in the midrashic comment on the biblical rubric "he shall surely be put to death": "if he was not forewarned by the earthly court, he will be put to death by the heavenly court."[46] This belief is also reflected in the words of R. Shimon

44 Maimonides, *Code,* Laws concerning the Sanhedrin 14:2–3.

45 Mekhilta de-Rabbi Ishmael, Torah portion 'Mishpatim,' para. 4 (Horowitz-Rabin edition, 263).

46 The midrash on the verse "he shall surely be put to death" is in the Albihani collection; see R. M. Kasher, *Tora Shleima,* Exodus 21:12:244. See also R. Haim Atar, *Or Hahaim* ad loc.: "Know that judgment is God's, He judges the whole world, putting to death those who do evil. But He chose to give some [jurisdiction] to earthly judges, to put to death those whose punishment is set down in God's Torah . . . and in this context, our Sages said that even if the courts have become defunct, their judgments have not been cancelled, and the [heavenly] judge will judge the [evildoers] forever."

b. Shetah, cited above.[47] He saw someone pursuing someone else, sword in hand, and upon running after the pair, found the pursuer with his sword dripping blood, while the pursuee was on the ground, in his death throes. Aware that the perpetrator could not be brought to justice due to the lack of witnesses, he stated: "But what can I do, for your life is not consigned to my hands; He who knows [our] thoughts will exact vengeance from whichever man [killed his fellow]."[48] The Midrash puts it in this way: "When you kill somebody secretly and nobody knows about it except for the murderer himself, even though the court does not know about it so that [the slayer] cannot be killed, I will demand [that he pay the price for spilling] the victim's blood."[49]

This assumption that divine providence is also involved in matters that were entrusted to man led to the conclusion that the court should not utilize all its power with respect to imposing the punishment of death, and that this reluctance does not constitute dereliction of the duty to do justice and purge evil, since in every case that the court will not utilize its authority to punish, the punishment will be imposed by God. This attitude is apparent in the dictum: "Although the Sanhedrin was disbanded [the import of which was that the Sages explicitly refrained from trying cases involving capital offenses], the laws of the four types of court-imposed death were not nullified."[50] Indeed, in some cases the Sages took afflictions, illnesses, and natural disasters to be heavenly punishment for certain transgressions,[51] punishment visited upon people in lieu of the punishment mandated by Torah law that was not imposed out by the court.[52]

47 See text at n. 16 above.

48 bSanhedrin 37b.

49 Aggadic midrashic exegesis on the verse "And surely your blood of your lives will I require" (Gen. 9:5), quoted in *Torah Shleima,* Genesis 9:34. The same idea is referred to in Sifre Numbers 117 (Horowitz edition, 134): "What is your source for the statement that one who burns his neighbor's crop on the Day of Atonement, even though the courts do not exact punishment from him, will be found liable to the punishment of death?"

50 bSanhedrin 37b; bKetubot 30a; bSota 8b.

51 bShabat 32a; Deuteronomy Rabbah 2:512; *Avot de-Rabbi Nathan*, ARN1 38, ARN2 41 (Schechter edition, 113–15).

52 For a detailed discussion of Jewish and other ancient Near Eastern conceptions of divine punishment, see Peretz Segal, "Liability under Divine Jurisdiction: The Punishment of Death by a Human Court and at the Hand of God" (PhD dissertation, Hebrew University of Jerusalem, 1986);

ii. Punishment reflects divine providence, and it is inappropriate for mortals to enter into partnership with the Creator

Many of the Sages' exegetical interpretations of scripture address the existence and nature of man qua man: the fact that all people are equal,[53] and equal before God,[54] and that only by carrying out God's will as embodied in the Torah and its commandments are the righteous, who are rewarded, distinguished from the evil, who are punished. Reward and punishment are conferred by God, and from the human perspective, seem to be random. Good things are seen as rewards and bad things as punishment.[55]

This approach also led to the conclusion that a mortal should not assume the role of the Creator and take a fellow human's life in the name of divine providence, even if such intervention is legally justified. This is expressed in the following talmudic passage. "R. Joshua b. Korha sent the following message: Vinegar, the son of wine, how long will you continue handing the people of our God over to be slain?! [R. Eliezer b. Shimon] sent the reply: I am weeding thorns from the vineyard. He sent a reply to him: Let the owner of the vineyard come and weed out his thorns."[56] We find a similar outlook in bGitin:

---

idem, "Postbiblical Jewish law and theology," 9 *Jewish Law Annual* (1988), 107. In Segal's opinion, divine punishment was an integral part of the religious outlook, and was connected to the notion of maintaining the purity of places of worship. He contends that punishment by man was administered according to different principles than punishment by priests; the latter was rejected by the Sages.

53 See E.E. Urbach, *The Sages — Their Concept and Beliefs*, trans. I. Abrahams (Jerusalem: 1987), 1:216–17; *Avot de-Rabbi Nathan*, ARN1 31 (Schechter edition, 91): "A single individual is as important as the whole of creation."

54 See Urbach, ibid., 255–85, and the sources cited there.

55 Albeck, n. 32 above, 106–21, addresses the subjective aspect of punishment, whereby only God can know the exact punishment that a transgressor deserves. He concludes that "the law punishes one who perpetrates deeds that are considered evil in the eyes of man and are deserving of punishment, but legal punishment is imposed for mediocre acts committed by mediocre individuals" (121). Divine law, in his opinion, is intended "not only to punish one whose guilt was not suitably punished by human law, but also to rectify and supplement human punishment, in accordance with the measure and character of each individual."

56 bBaba Metzia 83b.

> Mar Ukba sent a message to R. Eleazar: there are people who are harassing me, and I can hand them over to the governmental authorities; what should be done? . . . [R. Eleazar] replied: "Rest in the Lord, and wait patiently for Him" (Ps. 37:7) — that is to say, wait for the Lord, and He will bring them down prostrate before you.[57]

It is true that these dicta speak of those who left the task of punishing wrongdoers to outsiders, but in essence they are applicable to any punishment meted out by humans. This is the case not only with regard to informers, whose punishment is not set out in the Torah, and who the Sages were leery of having punished by the rabbinical court, but also cases that the Sanhedrin was obligated to judge by Torah law. Above, I quoted the assertion of R. Tarfon and R. Akiva: "Had we been members of the Sanhedrin, no one would ever have been put to death."[58] R. Shimon's dictum about the rebellious son and the idolatrous city can be interpreted in this same vein: "it never happened and never will happen. Why then was this law written? That you may study it and be rewarded."[59] For the stubborn and rebellious son is not condemned for his acts, but rather, "he is sentenced on account of his ultimate destiny,"[60] and the Sages find the punishment for the idolatrous city, which is collective, far too sweeping.[61]

iii Sin kills: punishment as a means of educating

Sifre offers the following interpretation of the verse: "'you shall put away the evil from your midst' — eliminate evildoers from Israel,"[62] but this still leaves room to inquire into the Sages' views on the purpose

57 bGitin 7a. The idea of not intervening in judgment also reflects the weightiness of the punishment for murder, which is not exhausted by the court's putting the murderer to death. See *Avot de-Rabbi Nathan*, n. 53 above: "'The voice of your brother's blood [plural] is crying out to me' — this teaches that his sons' and his grandsons' blood and the blood of all his descendants until the end of time . . . cried out before God."

58 mMakot 1:10. In reply, they were told: "Because of you, bloodshed proliferates among Israel," meaning that when courts were lenient, murderers who were acquitted re-offended, giving rise to increasing societal problems and violence.

59 bSanhedrin 71a.

60 mSanhedrin 8:5.

61 On the punishment for an idolatrous city, see bSanhedrin 111b.

62 Sifre Deuteronomy, 151 (Finkelstein edition, 205).

of punishment: was it retribution and vengeance, or was it, perhaps, education, by which I mean, was it to forcibly deter the potential sinner and threaten him, so that he does not sin, or to deter the perpetrator so that he does not re-offend?[63]

There are halakhic sources that support both explanations. In bEruvin, the verse: "and repays those that hate Him to their {His} face, to destroy them" (Deut. 7:10) is explained as follows: "R. Joshua the son of Levi said, were it not written, it would be impossible to say, It is like one who carries a burden and seeks to rid himself of it."[64] Sifre is clearer: "It is a source of joy for the Omnipresent when those who anger Him are eliminated from the world: . . . 'and when the wicked perish, there is joy' (Prov. 11:10)."[65] On this approach, the aim of punishment is to purge transgressors, to do away with them, harm them, and remove them from the world.[66] There is, however, a more compassionate approach, on which one must distinguish between the sin and the sinner. The sinner's soul needs refining and purification, not retribution and vengeance. Commenting on the verse: "May sinners disappear away from the earth" (Ps. 104:35), Bruria, R. Meir's wife, asserts: "It is not written 'sinners,' but rather, "sins" is written"[67]; and on the second half of the verse, "and may the wicked be no more," R. Nehemiah explains: "they

63 Arye Edrei discusses punishment in Torah law and its relevance to guilt in "'If any one shall sin through error': on the culpability of the unwilling transgressor in biblical and Rabbinic literature" (Hebrew), 24 *Shenaton Hamishpat Haivri* (2006/2007), 1. Edrei addresses the question of punishment from a novel perspective, considering the obligation devolving on one who has sinned intentionally to atone for his sin. He maintains that one who is devout should always be aware of her actions, and attend to her obligations to God. Sin indicates that one has not paid attention to her acts, and she is therefore liable to bring a sin-offering. On Edrei's account, it seems that the Sages regarded punishment as educational rather than retributive.

64 bEruvin 22a.

65 Sifre Numbers, 117 (Horowitz edition, 13); bSanhedrin 113b; tSota 10:3 (Lieberman edition, 214). This approach is also found in Ecclesiasticus (ben Sira) 16:6–7; 38:22–24, and in Genesis Rabbah 49:1 (Theodor–Albeck edition, 496).

66 See the interpretation of Psalms 104:35 in bBerakhot 10a.

67 This interpretation may allude to the fact that the Hebrew word here for "sinners" can be read as "sins." To reconcile the conflicting attitudes to sinners, some claim that they reflect the stages of the legal process: during the legal proceeding, there is room for leniency, but not afterwards; see Tanhuma, Numbers (Eshkol edition), 96:8; see also bNida 70b.

are not wicked at that time."[68] If one sees punishment as a means of purging the sin rather than the sinner — using force to prevent the sinner from transgressing — then there is no point in punishment if it has no deterrent effect, even if it physically destroys the transgressors.

This explains why the Sanhedrin suspended imposition of the punishment of death prior to the destruction of the Second Temple. The Talmud connects it to the Sanhedrin's voluntary exile, forty years before the destruction, from its fixed location on the Temple Mount to the 'Hanuyot' (shops) area: "What was the reason? They saw that because there were so many murderers, they were incapable of judging them. They said: it is preferable to transfer the Sanhedrin to a place where they could not hold someone liable [to be put to death]."[69] Similarly, they abolished the ritual of the beheaded heifer, as well as the ordeal of the wife suspected of adultery (*sota*). As R. Johanan b. Zakai tells us:

> When the number of murderers multiplied, the beheaded heifer was abolished[70] . . . when the number of adulterers multiplied, the [ordeal of] the bitter waters was abolished.[71]

~ ~ ~ ~ ~ ~ ~ ~

68 See Midrash on Psalms 104:27 (Buber edition, 448) and Genesis Rabbah 98 (Theodor–Albeck edition, 1257): "it intended to curse them but only cursed their anger"; 1 Enoch ch. 1, where punishment is described as humanity's cure for sin.

69 bAvoda Zara 8b; *Midrash Hagadol* (Margoliot edition, 472), on the verse "you shall take him from My altar to die" (Exod. 21:14); Mekhilta de-Rabbi Ishmael, Torah portion 'Mishpatim,' para. 4 (Horowitz–Rabin, 264) on the same verse; jMakot 2:6; *Sefer Mitzvot Gadol,* positive commandment 99; Maimonides, *Code,* Laws concerning the Sanhedrin 3:2. All these sources attempt to find a connection between the Sanhedrin and the altar. See too *Tosafot,* bAvoda Zara 8b s.v *ela,* which states that before the destruction of the Temple, the Sanhedrin would occasionally return to its place on the Temple Mount, when they felt it was necessary. This illustrates that the Sages had a penological policy and applied it as warranted.

70 On the "beheaded heifer," see Deuteronomy 21:1–10; on the ordeal of the bitter waters for the suspected adulteress, see tSota 14:1 (Lieberman edition, 235); bSota 47b; Numbers Rabbah 9:43.

71 bSota 47a. Some argue that there were 'external' historical reasons why the Sanhedrin was unable to punish transgressors, and the general cessation of punishment was due to the Roman authorities, although occasionally, an exceptional case would be tried; see G. Alon, *History of the Jews in Palestine in the Period of the Mishnah and the Talmud* (Hebrew), (Tel-Aviv: 1966), 129–92.

Let me now turn to the shaping of the law through exegesis. The commandments "you shall put away the evil from your midst" and "you shall put away the evil from Israel" require the courts to judge and punish transgressors of Torah law. The courts have no discretion about whether to conduct a legal proceeding or not, and whether to punish or to refrain from punishing a transgressor. If the preliminary requirements and conditions that enable punishment to be imposed have been satisfied, the law mandates that the prescribed punishment — of which there is only one for any given transgression — be fully imposed. In many cases, this punishment is death, and the judges have no discretion to be lenient, to reduce or change the punishment in any way.[72] Under these circumstances, the impossibility of formulating a clear penological policy to guide the judges in their deliberations, but yet would leave them some judicial discretion, as is the case in modern legal systems, led the Sages to strengthen, via midrashic exegesis of biblical verses, the requirements and pre-conditions that rendered an offense punishable. The forewarning requirement — which is not found in the Torah, and in essence, falls under the laws of evidence, serving as an effective and convenient tool for assessing an offender's criminal intent — evolved, as a consequence of the Sages' outlook on punishment, and their desire to limit human penal jurisdiction, into a rigid and substantive constraint on punishment. Indeed, it almost completely blocked any possibility of punishment in practice, since it was obviously difficult to find a transgressor who would "surrender himself to death" as per the exegesis-based requirement.[73]

72 See, e.g., Maimonides, *Code*, Laws concerning the Sanhedrin 14:2–3; this is also the conclusion in jSanhedrin 6:3.

73 This policy also influenced the forms of punishment that were mandated, which differed from the ancient biblical prescriptions. E.g., the burning described in bSanhedrin 52a (carried out by pouring molten lead down the condemned person's throat) was adopted in place of the biblical form of death by burning, viz., actual burning. The Talmud explains the change as follow: "'Love thy neighbor as thyself' — choose an aesthetic death for him." In recent years a number of works have been published on the relationship between specific punishments and both concrete historical traditions, and philosophical ideas popular among the Sages during the Second Temple period; see A. Shemesh, *Punishments and Sins–From Scripture to the Rabbis* (Hebrew), (Jerusalem: 2003), parts 1 and 2, 127–49; Y. Lorberbaum, n. 36 above, 140–277.

This penological policy is rooted in the legitimate and humane idea of saving a convicted offender from the Sanhedrin's penal jurisdiction. The verses "the congregation will judge . . . the congregation will save" (Num. 35:24–25) are the halakhic source for limiting the Sanhedrin's penal jurisdiction. Over time, these verses, which address the obligation to differentiate between an inadvertent manslaughterer, who was to be exiled to a city of refuge, as stated in the Bible, and a deliberate murderer, who is punished by death, came to be seen as positing a broad legal mandate for the institution of punishment in general, and the Sanhedrin's role in particular, especially vis-à-vis the laws of evidence and criminal procedure, on the one hand, and the criminal code, on the other hand.[74]

In my opinion, the development of a penological policy based on midrashic derivations from the verses "the congregation will judge . . . the congregation will save" led to invocation of the forewarning requirement in cases where the Sages thought it reasonable to 'save' the perpetrator from punishment. The 'saving' is therefore shorthand for a penological policy that, as the Sages conceived it, was expressed in a reduction of the Sanhedrin's authority to punish transgressors.[75] The biblical obligation to save ("the congregation will save") is deemed to apply only to judicial proceedings — that is, it must be carried out by the Sanhedrin, and for the Sanhedrin, it is obligatory. In other words,

74 A few examples must suffice. In bSanhedrin 69a, these verses are used to deduce that a simple majority is insufficient for conviction in capital cases. In bRosh Hashana 26a, we learn that, should a Sanhedrin witness a murder, "R. Akiva says that they are all witnesses, and a witness cannot serve as a judge. . . . R. Akiva says this only with regard to capital offenses, since the verse states, 'the congregation will judge . . . the congregation will save,' and as they all saw him kill someone, nobody can speak in his favor." In jSanhedrin 3:9, the verses are adduced to derive the conclusion that "the congregation [court] should not be related to the assailant or to the victim." See A. Kirschenbaum, "Aspects of criminal defense in Jewish law" (Hebrew), 22 *Dine Israel* (2003), 9–48.

75 Perhaps one can find some support for this novel idea in the words of R. Joseph Engel, *Gilyonei Hashas*, bSanhedrin 8b s.v. *baeida*: "One must say that the whole issue of forewarning pertains to saving . . . . the forewarning is not required to actually render him liable, for in cases where he did something that would not render him liable today, he nonetheless did do something for which he was liable, but because he was saved [by the forewarning requirement], he was exempted from liability."

no considerations other than proof of the transgression can be introduced, and the offender is entitled to be saved by the Sanhedrin. This is why the Sages 'exempted' from the forewarning requirement cases where the punishment was not a legal procedure, but rather voluntary, such as 'zealots kill him' and 'the blood avenger.' As to the former, it is stated apropos Phinehas' zealotry that "if the zealot comes to take counsel,[76] [it is the law, but] we do not instruct him to so act."[77] As to the latter, the Sages regarded blood vengeance as an unworthy precept,[78] and in cases of inadvertent killing, the manslaughterer going into exile was escorted by two learned men in case he was in danger of pursuit by a blood-avenger. If they encountered the blood-avenger, they would persuade him not to shed blood, since the killing was inadvertent.[79] The Sages therefore saw no reason to warn the blood-avenger, since the situation was under control.[80]

76 Regarding the question of whether to punish certain transgressors.

77 bSanhedrin 82a, see section 4 below.

78 Views differ as to the role of the blood-avenger in the judicial system in light of the talmudic sources. According to Maimonides, *Code,* Laws concerning Murder and the Preservation of Life 6:8, in the case of a deliberate murderer who was not forewarned as well as that where the killing was "inadvertent but close to deliberate," the blood-avenger acts in place of the judicial system; this is the view of *Ketzot Hahoshen,* HM 20:1, and it seems to follow from the plain meaning of the verses. According to *Pesikta Zutrata,* Torah portion 'Shoftim,' 15 (Venice edition 77b), and *Hidushei Haran,* bSanhedrin 48b, the blood-avenger simply executes the ruling that holds the murderer liable to be put to death. However, according to Sifre Zuta, Numbers 38:12–19 (Horowitz edition, 332); Nahmanides, addenda to the *Book of Precepts,* commandment 13; and *Beit Habehira,* bSanhedrin 48b (Sofer edition, 193), the blood-avenger plays neither of these roles, but rather, his role is merely to bring the murderer before the court and to present the case against him. Whatever his role, the blood-avenger is certainly not a court in the regular sense, since, even if his role is quasi-legal, the blood-avenger acts voluntarily, and his act is not always desirable.

79 bMakot 10b, and see also *Talmudic Encyclopedia* (Hebrew), "Blood avenger," 5:224.

80 With regard to the question of the witnesses required to punish a blood avenger, see the dispute between R. Meir Simha of Dvinsk, *Or Sameiah, Code,* Laws concerning Kings and Wars 3:10, and R. I.Z. Meltzer, *Even Haezel, Code,* Laws concerning Murder and the Preservation of Life 6:8. *Hidushei Haritba,* bMakot 10b, ponders the verse: "whereas he was not deserving of death, inasmuch as he hated him not in times past" (Deut. 19:6)" — who is the subject of the verse, the blood avenger or the murderer?

Some of the Early Authorities claimed that in the same way, the Sages 'exempted' the case of the 'stubborn and rebellious son' from the forewarning requirement, even though the rebellious son is subject to a legal proceeding before the community, that is, the city's elders, viz., the court, and it would seem imperative to save him because he is not judged by his actions but "on account of his ultimate destiny," that is, possible future actions. Why is this so? It would seem that the answer is to be found in a statement by R. Josiah in the name of Zeira who testified in the name of the men of Jerusalem: "if the father and mother wished to pardon a 'stubborn and rebellious son,' they pardon him"[81] — that is, the legal proceeding is subject to the consent of the father and mother. Thus the Sages' penological policy of reducing punishment is sustained through the parents' empowerment to retract their incrimination of their son.[82] Similarly, they did not require forewarning for the suspected adulteress since, "if the husband renounced his warnings [to his wife whom he suspected of adulterous conduct], his warnings are renounced," and there is therefore no need to escalate the warning from the level of empirical suspicions to that of essences.[83]

81 bSanhedrin 88a–b; Maimonides, *Code*, Laws concerning Rebels 7:8.

82 Indeed, the Torah verses themselves support the notion that the parents are partners in the process, since, according to the biblical text, the conditions that give rise to a 'stubborn and rebellious son' specifically involve both parents: "they chasten him," "they should lay hold on him," "they should bring him out unto the elders," "they shall say unto the elders," "he does not listen to our voice" (Deut. 18–20). See also Halbertal, n. 10 above, 53–67.

83 bSanhedrin 88a. This is not incompatible with the view that the ordeal of the bitter waters is not a legal procedure, but rather an examination carried out by priests, see bYoma 66a. Another approach is that of Rosen-Zvi, n. 25 above, 152–80. He argues that the procedures prescribed in the talmudic account diverge from the ordeal as set down in the Bible, and that there is no evidence that the ordeal as presented in the Talmud was in fact carried out in the Temple. He also claims that the ordeal as described by D.Z. Hoffman and J.N. Epstein, and their identification of the relevant Mishnah as dating back to the Second Temple period, is problematic. In Rosen-Zvi's opinion, the talmudic account was invented in the study-hall, and should be treated accordingly. He also adduces Menahem Kahana's work on differences between the descriptions of the ordeal in various Tannaitic sources: "the mishnaic ceremony has a very specific character, and any source that was not in harmony with this ceremony was omitted or set aside." He points out that only the mishnaic form of the ceremony was retained in the two Talmuds. Rosen-Zvi's account strengthens the claim that the sinner need not be warned in advance.

Since the forewarning requirement seeks to save the offender from the Sanhedrin's lack of discretion vis-à-vis which cases were to be tried, and which transgressions punished, it was superfluous in cases where the biblical laws of capital offenses were not applicable. This was the situation with respect to all punishments imposed on the strength of "temporary rulings" necessitated by exigency circumstances, for example: "and it happened that a man rode a horse on the Sabbath during the time of the Greeks, and they brought him to the court and stoned him to death, not because he deserved it, but because it was an exigency of the times."[84] In other words, since the court had the discretion not to stone the transgressor, forewarning was not necessary. This discretion is even more salient in the case of the special laws of the king. As Maimonides rules: "The king may, if the exigency of the hour demands it, put him to death in order to ensure the stability of the social order."[85] Here too, therefore, the Sages did not require forewarning. So too with regard to the punishment of "confinement in a cell," which according to the Amora Mar Samuel was used in cases where there was evidence of the murder but no evidence as to criminal intent from forewarning.[86] However, this was not an obligatory, biblically-mandated punishment, but was imposed at the Sages' discretion, hence there was no need for forewarning.[87]

84 bSanhedrin 46a; bJebamot 90b.

85 Maimonides, *Code*, Laws concerning Kings and Wars 3:10.

86 bSanhedrin 81a.

87 On another aspect of the situation where there is an urgent need to punish using non-biblically-mandated measures, thereby avoiding the need to forewarn offenders, see Albeck, n. 32 above, 127–40. But Albeck adds a condition limiting the power to impose punishments if the situation necessitated a temporary ruling: "These were not enactments enacted by the sages or the court as temporary rulings proscribing specific acts and specifying what the punishments would be, before the acts were carried out. These were punishments that the court imposed on transgressors without explaining — before the acts were carried out — that the acts would incur these punishments. But these were not punishments for new transgressions invented by the judges that punished people for acts that they did not know were forbidden, and thus when they carried out the acts they were not transgressing at all, but rather, they were for transgressions that were known before commission of the acts [that prompted the punishment], since they were forbidden by Torah law or by a decree that had been decreed previously, or because they were acts that only people who endanger the public would commit."

A similar distinction can be drawn between the punishment of flogging imposed on one who transgressed a negative commandment, and that imposed on one who transgressed a positive commandment. The former had to be forewarned if the punishment of flogging (thirty-nine lashes) was to be carried out, and moreover, the convicted offender had to be examined to be sure that he was capable of enduring the beating; if there was any doubt, the number of lashes would be reduced lest the beating prove fatal.[88] The Talmud states that "had there had been no forewarning in the case of [a transgressor of] negative commandments, offenders would be flogged without a fixed number of lashes or an assessment of their ability to bear suffering."[89] On the other hand, with regard to one who transgressed a positive commandment, the punishment is administered differently. As the baraita states: "But in the case of a positive commandment, for example, when they tell somebody to build a booth (*suka*) and he does not do it, or to ritually 'take' a palm frond (*lulav*) and he does not do it — he is lashed until his soul expires."[90] Why is this so? With regard to the punishment of flogging, the judges had no discretion, hence the Sages were very cautious about its imposition. But lashes imposed for rebelling against the Sages' directives (*makat mardut*) is not a biblical punishment, hence the Sages can exercise discretion as to its imposition. For this reason, those sentenced to flogging had to have been forewarned, whereas no forewarning was necessary in the case of lashes imposed for rebelliousness.

Let us consider further examples of the development of the Sages' penological policy. Forewarning is only appropriate in cases where there is a 'duty to save,' in other words, where the offender who has been sentenced to punishment is entitled to some empathy from the

88 With regard to the flogging, Deuteronomy 25:3 states: "Forty stripes he may give him, he shall not exceed; lest, if he should exceed, and beat him above these with many stripes, then thy brother should be dishonored before thine eyes." The Sages deduced from the latter clause that "when the lashes are applied, they must be applied to the back of a living person," hence it was necessary to assess the offender's ability to withstand punishment, lest he die while being flogged. *Rashi,* bSanhedrin 10a s.v. *venikla* states: "Even while he is being flogged, he should still be 'your brother.' You should beat him while he is alive and not dead, and since it is possible that he may die in the middle of the punishment, he should only be flogged according to what he is able to withstand."

89 *Nimukei Yosef,* Makot, last Mishnah, s.v. *kol hayavei kritot lokin.*

90 bKetubot 86a; bHulin 132b.

court even though he has committed a serious transgression of Torah law. However, in cases where 'saving' him might endanger another person's life, the Sages saw no reason to impose the draconian forewarning requirement. Consider the law of "one who pursues his fellow to slay him, [or pursues] a male [to rape him], [or pursues] a betrothed maiden [to rape her]."[91] In each of these cases, the pursued person could be harmed due to the pursuit, and it is therefore permissible to kill the pursuer, "saving them with his life." An even stronger case is that of the householder who may, without issuing any forewarning, kill a 'stealth burglar' who breaks into his home, on the strength of the legal fiction that "tunneling is his forewarning" — his mode of entry into the house serves as the burglar's warning.[92] The reason for the exemption from the forewarning requirement is apprehensiveness lest the householder lose his advantage — the element of surprise — and there is no reason to save the 'stealth burglar' at the householder's expense.[93]

Another case is that of one who incites others to worship idols. In this case, unlike that of the pursuer, what is at stake is not physically saving the pursuee but rather, saving souls. The reason for exempting the case of one who incites to idolatry from the forewarning requirement is apprehensiveness that if we warn him, this will save him from punishment and he will, on another occasion, incite others to engage in idol worship, rendering them liable to be punished by death. This is why one who incites others to engage in idol worship, unlike the murderer, need not be forewarned. The murderer's punishment is not intended to be preventative, but is imposed after the transgression, that is, the killing, has been committed, and not before, whereas in the case of incitement to engage in idol worship, the transgression — the incitement — has already been committed, but no idol worship has yet taken place, and even if no one had been convinced by the incitement to actually worship idols, the inciter is liable to be put to death.[94]

91 mSanhedrin 8:7.

92 bSanhedrin 72b.

93 Self-defense and defense of the party being pursued are discussed in the next section.

94 bSanhedrin 67a. This case differs from that of the rebellious elder, whose rebelliousness, according to the Talmud in bSanhedrin 88b, consists in the fact that "he hands down a ruling [that conflicts with the majority view] to others and they follow his ruling."

Granted, in the Mishnah on incitement to engage in idolatry there is a sort of warning: "How could we forsake our God in heaven and go and worship wood and stone?"[95] but it is immediately apparent that this utterance is merely a ruse to enable witnesses to attain evidence regarding the attempt to incite them to idolatry,[96] or perhaps, as the Hazon Ish explains, it is pronounced in order to solicit atonement for the attempted incitement.[97]

The difference between the punishment for one who incites others to engage in idolatry and that of the murderer is based on biblical verses, and it would seem that the Sages' teachings in this regard are based on these verses. Regarding the inciter, Scripture states: "Thou shalt not consent unto him, nor hearken unto him; neither shall thine eye pity him, neither shalt thou spare, neither shalt thou conceal him. . . . And thou shalt stone him with stones, that he die; because he hath sought to thrust thee away from the Lord thy God" (Deut. 13:9–10). The type of punishment demonstrates that the sole intention here is to save the nation from the spread of apostasy, by killing the inciter. This was the textual source for the Sages' deduction that no attempt should be made to save the inciter by imposing a forewarning requirement.[98] The opposite is true in the case of a deliberate murderer, who is put to death in order to gain atonement. As Scripture states: "So ye shall not pollute the land wherein ye are, for blood pollutes the land, and no atonement can be made for the land for the blood that is shed therein, but by the blood of him that shed it" (Num. 35:33). The Sages thus see no contradiction between punishing a murderer and trying to save him, just as there is no contradiction between the foregoing verse and the verses "the community shall judge" and "the community shall save," which are near it in the Book of Numbers,

95 mSanhedrin 7:10.

96 There is a controversy between Maimonides (*Code,* Laws concerning the Sanhedrin 11:5) and Rashi (bSanhedrin 8b s.v. *ushear kol hayavei mitot*), who both think that this inciter does not need to be forewarned, and can be punished even if he was not forewarned, and R. Jonah Gerondi, *Hidushei Rabeinu Yona,* bSanhedrin 8b, who seeks to deduce the forewarning requirement from the words, "How could we forsake our God in heaven?"

97 *Hazon Ish,* HM, Sanhedrin, 24:9.

98 This Rabbinic teaching is not explicit, as it does not appear in bSanhedrin 36b in R. Abbahu's list, where he states, "and it is the opposite in the case of the inciter."

indeed, in the same Torah portion, as if to declare, atonement (by being put to death) and being saved are not opposites, but two sides of the same coin.

Inquiry into the rationale for the punishment is not a matter of "interpreting biblical laws on the basis of their reasons," something the Sages do not usually endorse,[99] but serves to guide the Sages in deciding when it is necessary to be stringent about the evidentiary requirements for a specific offense, and when it is not; when the forewarning requirement is warranted, and when it is not.

Let us now examine the differences between two transgressions that pertain to very similar matters: the rebellious elder and the false prophet. Why, in the case of the rebellious elder, who rebels against the High Court in Jerusalem and instructs others to act in accordance with his opinions, is there no need for forewarning in order to punish him,[100] whereas by contrast, the false prophet who prophesies in the name of an idol and says, as Maimonides puts it, "a certain idol or a certain star told me that we are commanded to do such-and-such or not to do such-and-such"[101] — has to be forewarned in order to be punishable? If the punishment is imposed due to the gravity of the offense, namely, undermining the spiritual authorities, why is it that one who prophesies "that which he did not hear and that which was not said to him"[102] is not punished without the appropriate forewarning, yet in the case of the rebellious elder, who disputes a ruling of the High Court, there is a duty to pursue and punish him without any forewarning? After all, both are serious offenders, who incite and entice the people to rebel.

We have no choice but to conclude that it is not the severity of the offense that determines whether there is an obligation to forewarn the offender, but rather, the degree to which it is influential. The rebellious elder is the most outstanding member of the court in his town, who was ordained to issue laws and judgments to the public, yet he dissents from the High Court's ruling on an offense the penalty for which is,

99 bSanhedrin 21b; bBaba Metzia 115a.

100 Maimonides, *Code,* Laws concerning Rebels 3:8; *Beit Habehira,* bSanhedrin 88b (Sofer edition, 318).

101 Maimonides, *Code,* Laws concerning Idolatry 5:6. I use the terms 'rebellious elder' and 'false prophet' as they are understood in the Talmud and by the decisors; for other understandings, see Shemesh, n. 73 above, 150–65, which offers an original interpretation.

102 mSanhedrin 11:8.

when committed deliberately, divine extirpation (*karet*), and when committed inadvertently, a sin-offering. When he returns to his own town, he defies the High Court and instructs others to act in accordance with his dissenting view, or himself acts in accordance with that view. Because of the elder's status, it would be dangerous to save him from the death penalty, because were he to be saved by the imposition of a forewarning requirement, others would act in accordance with his dissenting opinion — he is, after all, the town's outstanding sage — and become liable to the punishment of divine extirpation. And even if he did not issue rulings for others, but only himself acted in accordance with his dissenting view, one might say that there is no point in saving him from the punishment of court-imposed death, since either way, he is liable to the punishment of divine extirpation for the actions performed in accordance with his dissenting view. Furthermore, people are also likely to learn from his deeds. The Sages therefore refrained from making punishment of the rebellious elder conditional on his being convicted in a legal proceeding, because he might thereby be saved from judgment and punishment, and continue his rebelliousness. To allow forewarning, with all its specific conditions and details, would be very dangerous, because he is highly influential. And were the court to appoint someone to forewarn him, he too might be influenced, and follow the rebellious elder. A false prophet, on the other hand, is not a sage who serves as a judge and issues rulings on matters of Jewish law. He is thus less dangerous than a rebellious elder. The Sages therefore treated him like any other transgressor, and required that he be forewarned, and not punished unless he accepts the forewarning and 'surrenders himself to death.'[103]

This is also the case vis-à-vis conspiring witnesses (*zomemim*). The Talmud offers two rather weak reasons for exempting conspiring witnesses from the forewarning requirement, and Maimonides offers a third. And very recent decisors have also put forward various suggestions to account for the fact that Maimonides felt impelled to add his own reason.

It would seem to me, therefore, that if the conspiring witnesses were only liable for punishment if they were warned prior to giving their testimony, the result would be that in most cases, there would be

103 See Maharatz Chajes, *Torat Haneviim*, Maamar 'Divrei Neviim, Divrei Kabala,' ch. 1, 137–39.

no prior warning, and if their testimony was found to be false, the biblically-mandated punishment — "And you shall do to him as he conspired to do to his brother" (Deut. 19:19) — could not be imposed. Furthermore, witnesses whose testimony is contradicted by that of other witnesses are not relied on in the case in question, but are not deemed to be tainted by any sort of unfitness, and their testimony about others would be acceptable. In addition, their testimony about other matters — even concerning the same people about whom they gave false testimony — will not be deemed unreliable. Clearly, the law of conspiring witnesses indirectly saves those who would be victims of such false testimony. Hence the Sages were not interested in undermining this sophisticated protective mechanism for testimony by introducing the forewarning requirement.

We have seen that the forewarning requirement is not only the product of a meta-halakhic outlook on the nature of biblical punishment, nor is it only a method of revealing the truth. Nor was it devised *ab initio* to protect innocent suspects. But ultimately it did become a means of preventing conviction of suspected offenders, and almost completely blocking the legal process, as Lorberbaum claims. However, the forewarning requirement was, at its inception, conceived as a means of affording the court discretion with regard to convicting offenders. Where it was necessary to recognize considerations against punishing an offender, the court would be stringent in its application of the forewarning requirement, and where it was not, the requirement was waived.[104]

3. Exegetical interdependence of murder and rape

Deuteronomy 22:25–27, which presents the law of the 'betrothed maiden' (the halakhic meaning of which is 'married woman'), contrasts the punishment meted out to the rapist and the blamelessness of the victim of the rape.

104 Another goal of forewarning is discussed in A. Radzyner, "Witnesses' *hatra'ah* (warning) and the beginning of their testimony" (Hebrew), 20–21 *Dine Israel* (2001), 515. In Radzyner's opinion, which is based on his reading of mMakot 1:5, the aim of forewarning in monetary matters is not to prove illegal intent, and certainly not to protect witnesses from being declared perjurers, but to procure witnesses to the act.

> Then the man only that lay with her shall die. But unto the maiden thou shalt do nothing; there is in the maiden no sin worthy of death: for as when a man riseth against his neighbor, and slayeth him, even so is this matter. For he found her in the field, and the betrothed maiden cried out, and there was no one to save her.

It would seem that these verses are no more than an explanation of something that is evident to those with contemporary sensibilities, but in many ancient societies, it was not generally accepted that there is no culpability absent criminal intent. The Bible explains the raped woman's exemption from punishment on the basis of a comparison with murder, and just as in the case of murder, only the murderer has sinned and incurs punishment, so too only the rapist of the betrothed maiden incurs punishment. Comparing the case of the betrothed maiden to that of murder is only intended for interpretive purposes, and is comparable to the biblical interpretations of the precept of the *suka* (sitting in a booth on the festival of Tabernacles), the obligation to allow a slave to rest on the Sabbath, the prohibition against eating the sinew of the thigh, the prohibition against a king's having many wives, and so on. The additional explanation, that the maiden cried out but "there was no one to save her," was only inserted to distinguish between the biblical law as to rape in an isolated place and the preceding law, in Deuteronomy 22:23, as to rape in an urban setting ("if there be a maiden that is a virgin betrothed unto a man, and a man find her in the city, and lie with her"). In the latter case, the maiden is also stoned, because she did not cry out.

However, from the beginning of the Tannaitic period, the Sages interpreted this verse in a manner that departed from its plain meaning, using the putative 'reason for the verse' as raw material, so to speak, from which to deduce halakhic principles. In many other instances as well, this was indeed the Sages' practice: to construe a verse in a manner that goes beyond its plain meaning and context, to interpretively create new laws. The particular verses we are discussing here, Deuteronomy 22:25–27, are exceptional in that they have become the basis for the principles of halakhic criminal law. How so?

First, it was established that whoever raped a betrothed maiden (meaning, let me again note, a married woman) was not only liable to the punishment of death as per biblical law, but furthermore could be killed in order to save the married woman. In other words, any bystander was permitted and even obligated to kill a would-be rapist to prevent him from carrying out his objective. The derivation of this principle from the verse, "the betrothed maiden cried out, and there was no one to save her"[105] is an exegetical tour de force, transforming the explanation into a normative directive permitting anyone to kill someone attempting rape before he does so, or as the Sages put it: "'and there was no one to save her' — but if there is someone who can save her, he must save her by any means possible."[106]

The Sages went a step further and decided that the dispensation to kill a 'pursuer' was not restricted to the case of the betrothed maiden, but was broader in scope, encompassing other transgressions. This position has absolutely no biblical support, but the Sages arrived at it by using the exegetical rule they called, "it is invoked to shed light, and is itself illuminated" (lit., came to teach, but also learned), which, as formulated in several places in the Talmud, is a bi-directional inference:

> The School of Rabbi [Judah the Prince] taught, It is derived by analogy: "for as when a man riseth against his neighbor, and slayeth him, even so is this matter" (Deut. 22:26). But what do we learn from [this analogy with] a murderer? It is invoked to shed light, and is itself illuminated. The [case of the] murderer is compared to [the case of] a betrothed maiden; just as a betrothed maiden can be saved [from dishonor] by [taking the rapist's] life, so in the case of a murderer, he can be saved by [taking] his life.[107]

Additional Tannaitic exegeses that use this exegetical rule compare the betrothed maiden's ability to defend herself with that of the householder encountering a stealth burglar.[108] The author of the Mekhilta of the School of R. Ishmael invokes bi-directional inference to expand the comparison between the laws of the stealth burglar (*haba bemahteret*) and those of the betrothed maiden (*naara meurasa*), asserting:

105 On the Jerusalem Talmud's inferences from these verses, see jKetubot 3:9, jSanhedrin 7:11.

106 bSanhedrin 73a.

107 bSanhedrin 73a, 74a; bPesahim 28b; bYoma 82b. The version in Sifre Deuteronomy, 243 (Finkelstein edition, 273) is different: "'for as when a man riseth against his neighbor, and slayeth him' means that all the coerced victims in the Torah are exempt [from punishment], and they are to be saved by taking their [attackers'] lives. I only have this one case, how can I derive the law as to the] cases of one who pursues his fellow to kill him or a male [for sexual relations]? The verse states: 'even so is this matter.'"

108 Although the 'stealth burglar' appears to be a particular case of the law of "he who pursues his fellow to slay him," namely, the case where the pursuee himself, and not a third party, is involved in the rescue, the two

> R. Ishmael says: You say that the intent is [or, is only] to distinguish between day and night, do you want to say that if he killed by day he is liable, and if he killed by night he is exempt [from punishment]? Therefore Scripture teaches, "but unto the maiden thou shalt do nothing . . ." — just as here there is no distinction between day and night, so also in this case there is no distinction between day and night.[109] Just as, in this case, if the householder killed the attacker before [he could carry out his purpose] he is exempt [from punishment], so there, if she acted first and killed him — she is exempt. Just as there, if there was someone who could save her from [the rapist] and she [nonetheless] killed [the rapist], she would be liable, so too, in this case, if there was someone capable of saving the householder from [the stealth burglar], and he [nonetheless] killed him, he would be liable.[110]

---

cases must not be confused. A bystander is permitted to kill a pursuer only if the pursuit is unambiguous and is taking place openly. In the case of the 'stealth burglar,' the perpetrator's intent is evident from the very nature of his action — "tunneling is his forewarning." The pursuer can be killed only if the rescuer has forewarned him, admonishing him to desist, and only if "he cannot be saved by [the maiming of] one of his limbs," i.e., if the pursuer cannot be stopped by merely wounding him. The householder, who is defending himself and his property, does not need to forewarn the burglar or try to merely wound him, either because he is frantic about saving himself, or because he will lose the advantage of surprising the stealth burglar. See A. Enker, *Duress and Necessity in the Criminal Law* (Hebrew), (Ramat-Gan: 1978), ch. 8, "The line dividing necessity from self-defense in Jewish law" (with D. Frimer), 212–34, and idem, n. 33 above, 234–35, 251–53. See also D. Henshke, "The thief who steals in a house: the relationship between exegesis (*midrash*) and plain meaning (*pshat*)" (Hebrew), *Megadim* 7 (1989), 9, which not only provides a critical examination of the commentators' views, but also offers an original analysis of its own.

109 Whereas the Torah distinguishes between a householder's finding a burglar who has entered the house stealthily and his finding a thief upon whom "the sun be risen" (Exod. 22:1), which, taken literally, denotes a distinction between day and night, the Sages used the sun as a metaphor for 'peace':

> Is it only on him that the sun has shone? Has it not shone on the entire world? Rather, just as the sun [represents] peace in the world, so, too, if it is known that this burglar comes in peace [viz., intends no violent harm] and [the householder nonetheless] kills him, he is liable. (Mekhilta de-Rabbi Ishmael, 13 [Horowitz-Rabin edition, 293]).

That is to say, as long as there is no certainty that the stealth burglar's intentions are not criminal, he may be pursued and killed. See also bSanhedrin 72b.

110 Mekhilta de-Rabbi Ishmael, ibid., also quoted in Midrash Tannaim, Deuteronomy 22:26 (Hoffman edition, 143).

The Mekhilta of R. Shimon b. Yohai asserts: "and [Scripture] also states: 'for as when a man riseth against his neighbor, and slayeth him,' and so on, and this is a similar case. Just as the one is a case of possible mortal danger, so too the other is a case of possible mortal danger."[111] I would suggest that this inference is not merely interpretive — that is, does not merely seek to offer a rationale for the betrothed maiden's exemption from punishment for murdering her assailant — but also serves to create doctrines of 'self defense' and 'constructive intent' that apply both to the case of the betrothed maiden and to that of murder.

In addition to the connections explicitly discussed in the talmudic literature, it seems to me that the exegetical interdependence of the verses in question gives rise to concealed connections between the case of the murderous pursuer and that of the rape of the betrothed maiden. Consider, for example, the scope of the law of the pursuer. The Mishnah states:

> The following are saved by [taking] their lives: he who pursues his fellow to slay him, [or pursues] a male [to rape him], [or pursues] a betrothed maiden [to rape her].
>
> But he who pursues an animal [to engage in bestiality], or who desecrates the Sabbath, or commits idolatry, is not be saved by [taking] his life.[112]

This distinction is not self-evident. If the aim of the attack on the pursuer is to save the perpetrator himself from a grave religious transgression, why is it not permitted to kill someone who is about to do work on the Sabbath, or commit idolatry or bestiality, since all these transgressions incur the punishment of court-imposed death? On the other hand, if the reason the attack on the perpetrator is permitted is to save the pursuee from the pursuer, why is it permissible to kill one who pursues a betrothed maiden in order to rape her, given that she herself will not be punished? And not only that, but in the Tosefta, R. Judah asserts that "if she says 'leave him be' — he is not saved by [taking] his life,"[113] even though she thereby (in choosing to let him rape her rather than kill him) attests that she is about to transgress the prohibition against adultery, and cause the pursuer to sin.[114] I would therefore

111 Epstein-Melamed edition, 192.

112 mSanhedrin 8:7.

113 tSanhedrin 11:1 (Zuckermandel edition, 432).

114 A similar question is posed, but not resolved, in *Tosafot*, bSanhedrin 74a s.v. *lehatzilo benafsho*.

argue that the difference between pursuing someone in order to kill him, pursuing a betrothed maiden in order to rape her, and pursuing a man in order to rape him, on the one hand, and pursuing those intending to commit other serious religious transgressions, is **not** related to the severity of the transgression in question, but rather, to the potential danger to the pursuee. While in the case of one who pursues someone in order to kill him, the danger that the potential victim will lose his life is clear, in the case of the betrothed maiden, the dispensation to kill the pursuer is due to apprehensiveness that the maiden might prefer death over rape and "might give up her life because of modesty" (as it is said in another context[115]). The Sages therefore extrapolated from the dispensation to kill one who pursues his fellow with murderous intent to the dispensation to kill one who pursues a betrothed maiden intending to rape her, or pursues a male intending to rape him.[116]

115 See bKetubot 3b.

116 For the same reason, tSanhedrin 11:11 (Zukermandel edition, 432) rules that "if she was a widow about to be married to the High Priest, or a divorcee or *haluza* about to be married to a priest — the husband-to-be is not saved by taking his life." jSanhedrin 8:9 adds to these examples, "a bastard or a descendant of the Gibeonites (*netina*) about to marry a Jew, a Jewess about to marry a descendant of the Gibeonites or a bastard — the husband- or wife-to-be is not saved by taking his/her life." In all these cases the perpetrators do not see the acts they are about to carry out as serious offenses, and there is no danger to their partner-to-be. This same explanation applies to the fact that "after the act has been carried out, the perpetrator is not saved by taking his life. . . . R. Judah says: if she said 'leave him be' — he is not saved by [taking] his life, for if the victim lets him [rape her, rather than be killed by him], bloodshed is unnecessary," since in each of these cases there is no danger that the raped woman will kill herself rather than be raped.

Note also that bSanhedrin 73a-b cites a Stamaitic tradition, which is not attributed to any Tanna, that describes the range of application of the law of the pursuer by exegesis of the verse: "But unto the maiden (*naar{a}*) thou shalt do nothing; there is in the maiden no sin (*het*) worthy of death (*mavet*)" (Deut. 22:26):

> '*naar*' refers to the male [being pursued with intent to rape], '*naara*' to the betrothed maiden [being pursued with intent to rape], '*het*' refers to those sexual unions that incur divine excision, '*mavet*' to those that incur death imposed by the court. Why do we need all these terms? We need them. Since if the Torah said [lit., God had written] '*naar*' [it might be inferred that the pursuee could be saved because rape of a

The best-known exegetical inference from this verse is that one who is about to suffer incestuous rape[117] should "be killed rather than transgress." In tractate Sanhedrin of the Babylonian Talmud, the Amora R. Johanan from the land of Israel says, in the name of R. Shimon b. Jehozadak: "They took a vote and decided, in the loft of the house of Nitza in Lod: regarding every [other] law of the Torah, if someone is told, 'Transgress and you will not be killed,' he may transgress and not be killed, with the exception of idolatry, sexual transgressions (*gilui arayot*), and bloodshed."[118] The phrasing of the tradition suggests, though not decisively, that the source is Tannaitic[119] and dates back to

male] is unusual, and that since *'naara'* [rape of a woman] is usual [it might be inferred that the woman could not be saved]. And if the Torah had said *'naara'* [it might be inferred that] the concern is injury to her [honor, i.e., her virginity], and [a male being pursued with intent to rape] would not be included [in the directive to save the pursuee]. . . . And the Torah said "sin worthy of death," and was it asking about the male and the maiden? Yes, both [one who rapes a woman and one who rapes a man are subject to court-imposed death]. But why are the male and the maiden adduced in the context of divine excision [since the punishment applicable to a rapist is court-imposed death]? The first, to exclude idolatry, the second, to exclude bestiality and [desecration of] the Sabbath.

This approach is not consistent with the opinions of various Tannaim as to the scope of the law of the pursuer. In *Yalkut Shimoni*, Likutei Derashot, Deuteronomy, §247, 933 and *Midrash Hagadol*, Deuteronomy 22:26 (Margaliot edition, 507) this explanation is attributed to Mar Samuel. See Maimonides, *Commentary on the Mishnah*, mSanhedrin 8:7 (Kafih edition, 130) on reconciling this approach with that in Tanna Devei Rabbi. See also Enker, n. 108 above, 212–34; Halbertal, n. 10 above, 50 n. 15.

117 *"gilui arayot,"* often translated as 'incest' or 'sexual transgressions'; it encompasses various biblically-prohibited sexual unions.

118 bSanhedrin 74a.

119 A comparison of the different sources reveals that the decision reached in the loft of the house of Nitza in Lod merits meticulous investigation. In jSanhedrin 3:5, the tradition is adduced as follows: "Zeira and R. Johanan said in the name of R. Yanai, R. Yirmiya and R. Johanan said in the name of R. Shimon b. Jehozadak: they took a vote in the loft of the house of Nitza in Lod, with regard to the Torah. What is the source for the statement: if an idolater told a Jew to transgress any one of the commandments in the Torah, with the exception of idolatry, sexual transgressions, and bloodshed, he should transgress and not be killed?" Furthermore, whereas the

the days when controversies between the Sages were resolved by invoking the phrase " they took a vote and decided," but it would seem that the editors of the Talmud had no clear tradition as to why this phrase was used in deciding about these three transgressions, and they adduce various explanations to substantiate the house of Nitza decision. With regard to idolatry, the Sages preferred a tradition from a baraita ascribed to R. Eleazar over the opposed tradition in a baraita ascribed to R. Ishmael, which rules that one should "transgress and not be killed." As to bloodshed, they adduced Rabbah's reply in the following incident: "The governor of my town said to me, Go kill so-and-so, and if you don't, I will kill you. Rava [some MS read 'Rabbah'] said to him, Let him slay you rather than you slay someone else, [for] who says that your blood is redder? Perhaps the other person's blood is redder?" And as to sexual transgressions (*gilui arayot*), they quoted the Tanna Devei Rabbi, which interpreted this dictum by applying the exegetical rule, 'it is invoked to shed light, and is itself illuminated,' as follows: "And the betrothed maiden is compared to [one ordered to be] a murderer: just as one should be killed rather than transgress [by submitting to the order to kill someone], so also should the betrothed maiden be killed rather than transgress [the prohibition against sexual transgressions (*gilui arayot*) by submitting to the rape]." Not only is this derivation partial, referring only to the case of the betrothed maiden and not to all categories classed as 'sexual transgressions' (*gilui arayot*), but it is also weak in terms of logic, and has to rely on a late — that is, Amoraic — opinion, that of Rava, an opinion of which there is no trace in the Tannaitic sources.[120]

Tannaitic provenance of the versions in tractate Sanhedrin in both Talmuds is not explicit, the house of Nitza decision as adduced in bKidushin 40b has an explicitly Tannaitic context: "and when R. Tarfon and the elders were reclining in the loft of the house of Nitza in Lod, this question came before them: is study more important, or is action more important?" Similarly in tShabat 2:5 (Lieberman, 7): "R. Judah said, when we were in session in the loft in Beit Nitza in Lod, they would pierce an egg shell with a tube. . . . There were elders present and none of them said anything." On the location of the house of Nitza in Lod, see Lieberman, *Tosefta Kifshuta* ad loc., p. 29, n. 35; B.Z. Rosenfeld, "Sages and householders in Lod during the Yavne period" (Hebrew), *Sinai* 103 (1988), 60, 83–88.

120 Note that the exegesis ascribed to Tanna Devei Rabbi is cited only in the Babylonian Talmud; there are several versions of it (bSanhedrin 73a, 74a; bPesahim 25a-b; bYoma 82a). It is instructive to compare the version cited

The Early Authorities took exegesis of the said verses on the basis of bi-directional inference even further, extending the exegetical interdependence of murder and rape to reach the conclusion that the "be killed and do not transgress" imperative applies only when action is required, and does not apply where the victim is passive. This extension was apparently urgently required in the Tosafist era, when rape of married women occurred frequently due to the pervasive oppression. Among the questions posed to rabbinical authorities during that period was whether the women had transgressed by not committing suicide.[121] In responsa, the authorities marshaled the precedent of Queen Esther. According to several traditions in bMegila, she was not living with Mordecai as his adopted daughter (*bat*), but rather, his wife (*bayit*), and as Rabbah b. Lima says, "she would leave Ahasuerus' embrace, immerse herself in a ritual bath, and settle back into Mordecai's embrace" (according to Rashi, the immersion was for hygienic purposes, so that the righteous man would not be repelled by her having lain with Ahasuerus).[122] The Tosafists ask: why did Esther not consign herself to death, that is, commit suicide, since her relations with Ahasuerus were 'sexual transgressions' (*gilui arayot*), and fall under the rubric "be killed and do not transgress"?[123]

> It is strange, shouldn't the Talmud have asked, didn't Esther commit a sexual transgression? For everyone agrees that the murderer and the

in *Rif*, bYoma 82b (printed edition, 4a) with the text of bYoma itself. I have already noted the Jerusalem Talmud's account of the house of Nitza decision. In bPesahim 25a–b, jShabat 14:4, and jAvoda Zara 2:2, R. Johanan presents an additional ruling, in the name of R. Jacob: "anything may be used for healing except [if it involves] idolatry, sexual transgressions, and bloodshed." On these two traditions adduced by R. Johanan, and their interconnections, see D. [Weiss-] Halivni, *Sources and Traditions* (Hebrew), *Pesahim*, 343–44. In the continuation of the *sugya*, R. Johanan states: "that he said 'kill so-and-so' is not the sole criterion, but even if he said 'use violence against so-and-so.'" On the surface, this would suggest the addition of another transgression to the class of acts that fall under the "be killed and do not transgress" rubric, but see the commentators ad loc. See also Halevi, n. 8 above, part 2, vol. 8, 156–58.

121 See, e.g., *Mordekhai*, bKetubot, 286.

122 bMegila 13b; see also the statement by R. Abba in bMegila 15a: "if I perish, I will perish; just as I am lost to my father's house, so I will be lost to you," and the *Tosafot*'s comments thereon.

123 bSanhedrin 74b s.v *veha ester*.

> betrothed maiden should kill themselves and not transgress. . . . They maintain that Esther can claim that she was completely passive [lit., like the ground of the earth], and thus was not obligated to consign herself [to death] for having committed a sexual transgression, for we learned this from the case of the murderer, who is only obligated to consign himself to death before carrying out the act with his own hands, but where he does not carry out an action, as, for instance, when they throw him onto a baby and he crushes it, it would seem that he is not obligated to consign himself to death. For he can say, 'on the contrary, why do you say that my friend's blood is redder, perhaps my blood is redder?', for he has not carried out any act.

In another context, the Tosafists elaborate on the case further, and invoke the exegetical interdependence of murder and the betrothed maiden to claim that Esther's passivity is not restricted to her gender, nor is it a retrospective dispensation applicable solely in the case of Queen Esther, but rather, it is an egalitarian principle of criminal law applicable to all women who are raped and all men who are forced to have prohibited sexual intercourse on pain of death. Rava's statement in bJebamot 53b that "rape differs from other prohibited sexual relations since an erection cannot be involuntary," which would seem to differentiate between men and women, is explained as follows:

> When idol worshipers place him on a naked woman and it is impossible for him to escape except by being killed, it is as Rava said, he should allow himself to be killed if he knows that he cannot avoid an erection, since an erection cannot be involuntary, and he is considered to be carrying out an action. However, if he has an involuntary erection or he already had an erection or he knows that he will not have an erection, he is not obligated to consign himself [to death], since he is not carrying out an action, but is like the ground of the earth [i.e., completely passive].[124]

But the opposite is the case regarding the betrothed woman. R. Isaac the Elder, the Tosafist, interprets "just as the murderer should be killed and not transgress, so the betrothed maiden should be killed and not transgress" as follows: "what it says is that she should allow herself to be killed prior to carrying out the act and bringing upon herself a sexual transgression." According to the Tosafists, there is exegetical symmetry between the "be killed and do not transgress" law in the case of the murderer and the "be killed and do not transgress" law in the

124 *Tosafot*, bJebamot 53b s.v *ein ones*. And see *Beit Habehira* ad loc. (Dickman edition, 210–211).

case of the betrothed maiden whose life is threatened if she does not engage in forbidden intercourse.[125]

4. "Zealotry for My sake" — punishment by volunteers

Numbers 25:6–8 relates the story of Phinehas' act of zealotry:

> And, behold, one of the children of Israel came and brought unto his brethren a Midianitish woman in the sight of Moses, and in the sight of all the congregation of the children of Israel, who were weeping at the door of the tent of meeting. And when Phinehas, the son of Eleazar, the son of Aaron the priest, saw it, he rose from the midst of the congregation, and took a spear in his hand; And he went after the man of Israel into the chamber, and thrust both of them through, the man of Israel, and the woman through her belly.

We learn in the next Torah portion that the man of Israel who was stabbed was "Zimri, the son of Salu, a prince of a father's house among the Simeonites" (Num. 25:14) As a reward for his act of zealotry, Phinehas was endowed with "everlasting priesthood" (Num. 25:13). The Bible does not explain why Phinehas came forward and acted publicly, "in the sight of Moses, and in the sight of all the congregation of the children of Israel." And why did Moses not instruct Phinehas to take the couple outside the camp and kill them there, as he had directed all the Israelites in the episodes of the man who cursed God (Lev. 24:10–14), the man who chopped wood on the Sabbath (Num. 15:32–36), and those who worshipped the golden calf? (Exod. 32)

125 But see *Beit Habehira*, bSanhedrin 74b s.v. *yesh gorsin* (Sofer edition, 277), which explains the phrase, "be killed and do not transgress" in the case of the betrothed maiden as follows: "our statement only applies to the case when the woman is told, 'go on your own to have intercourse with so-and-so, and if you do not, we will kill you.' But one who is taken against her will does not fall into that category . . . and I see this as exemplifying what it says 'like the ground of the earth.' . . But in the case of a man, even if he is taken against his will, since the act is up to him, he should be killed and not transgress." Thus, according to the Meiri, "Esther was completely passive" is a question of gender. The two approaches may reflect Maimonides *Code,* Laws concerning Forbidden Intercourse 1:9 and *Hasagot Haraavad* ad loc.; the commentaries thereon rebut the Raavad's critique of Maimonides. On Esther's passivity, see *Yam Shel Shlomo,* Jebamot 6:3; R. Isaac Elhanan Spector, *Responsa Ein Yitzhak,* #33d.

The Sages, who discussed Phinehas' zealotry at length, mentioned Moses' "silence" and that of "all the congregation of the children of Israel."[126] According to the talmudic and midrashic sources, Phinehas was not acting at the behest of Moses or the children of Israel, but on his own initiative. Zimri, according to the Sages, was not satisfied with bringing the Midianite woman into "the sight of Moses and the sight of all the children of Israel," but also insolently told Moses that what he was doing was permissible: "And if you say, 'forbidden' — who permitted Jethro's daughter to you?!" Moses did not answer, for at that moment he did not remember the law, "which he had received on Mount Sinai," that "whoever has intercourse with a Cuthean woman is killed by zealots," and only Phinehas "saw the act and remembered the law." There are two different opinions as to Phinehas' subsequent actions. According to the Amora Mar Samuel, Phinehas immediately went and acted on his own initiative, since he believed that "wherever God's name is being desecrated, honor is not paid one's teacher"–in this case, Moses. However, according to Rav, Phinehas turned to Moses and said, "did you not teach us this on your descent from Mount Sinai: He who has intercourse with a Cuthean woman is killed by zealots?" Moses admitted that Phinehas was right and said, "He who reads the letter, let him be the agent [for carrying out its instructions]." But both Rav and Samuel consider Moses to be less zealous than Phinehas, since Moses forgot the law, and . . . became powerless at that time.' It was said of Moses: "because he was indolent — 'no man knows his burial place' (Deut. 34:6), to teach you that one should be strong as a panther, light as an eagle, swift as a deer, and heroic as a lion, to do his Maker's will. From this we learn that God judges the righteous punctiliously."[127]

From various comments by Amoraim in the Babylonian Talmud, it appears that Moses' silence is not interpreted literally and is certainly not seen as weakness in knowledge of the law. R. Dimi brought a tradition to Babylon from the land of Israel that the "court of the Hasmoneans" decreed that consorting with Gentile women promiscuously was forbidden.[128] We can thus infer that previously, to flog or put someone

126 bSanhedrin 82a; jSanhedrin 9:7; Midrash Tanhuma, Torah portion 'Balak,' 29 (Buber edition, 148); Exodus Rabbah 33:5, among others.

127 Numbers Rabbah 20:24.

128 bAvoda Zara 36b; bSanhedrin 82a.

to death for promiscuous intercourse with a Cuthean would have been unwarranted.

The biblical prohibition against marrying non-Jews does not apply to non-marital relations, and even one who violates it not liable to flogging, according to some opinions, unless the woman is from one of the seven nations who lived in Canaan.[129] Furthermore, according to a ruling attributed to R. Johanan,[130] the zealot has no right to act unless he acts at his own initiative, but "if he comes to take counsel, we do not instruct him to so act." Morover, an act of zealotry is permissible only while the couple are engaged in intercourse, thus "if Zimri had desisted and Phinehas had then killed him, Phinehas would have been killed for doing so." That is, the judgment meted out to him would have been no different from that of any other murderer. It would seem, therefore, that Moses' silence may not have been due to his forgetting the law, but because he was not able to issue a ruling to Phinehas and the other Israelites when Zimri claimed that his act was permissible.

The weakness of the justification for Phinehas' zealotry is reinforced by the fact that both Talmuds list six miracles that occurred when Phinehas carried out his act, including "Zimri should have desisted but did not desist" (had he desisted, it would no longer have been possible to kill him — Rashi).[131] In the light of the many miracles that saved Phinehas from harm, we can deduce that his act was exceptional, and could not be an appropriate norm for most people, and thus differed from the episodes of the man who cursed God, the man who chopped wood on the Sabbath, and those who worshipped the golden calf.

We can conclude, therefore, that according to R. Johanan, Phinehas could easily have been considered a murderer had Zimri desisted in mid-act. Indeed, had Zimri not desisted, but "turned around and killed Phinehas — he would not have been liable to be put to death, since Phinehas was a pursuer." Through his zealous act, the zealot "surrenders himself to death," since he "pursues his fellow to slay him" and the pursuee is entitled to save himself by taking the pursuer's life.

The situation where an obligatory deed (*mitzva*) coincides with a transgression is not addressed in either of the Talmuds. How can

129 See Deuteronomy 7:3; bAvoda Zara 36b. See *Tur*, EH 16 and *Bah* ad loc. s.v. *derekh ishut*.

130 bSanhedrin 82b.

131 Ibid.; jSanhedrin 9:7.

Phinehas' zealous act, which was rewarded with "everlasting priesthood," at the same time be classified as falling under the law of the pursuer, where the pursuee may take the pursuer's life in order to save himself? Why is Phinehas' act not seen as an obligatory act, like the act of a bystander who comes to the aid of someone being pursued? In the latter situation, the pursuer is not entitled to turn around and kill the rescuer.

The Early Authorities offer two explanations. *Yad Rama* asserts: "There is no duty to kill [under the circumstances in question], but in general, it is permitted. Nobody would instruct him to do so. Just as Phinehas was permitted to kill Zimri, so Zimri was permitted to save his life by taking Phinehas' life."[132] In other words, had Zimri been about to commit a serious transgression, such as killing someone, he would have been forbidden to save himself from Phinehas' impending zealous act by taking Phinehas' life, since Phinehas would have been intervening to save a victim from a pursuer, in fulfillment of a Torah commandment exegetically derived from biblical verses. Zimri, on the other hand, was not about to commit such a serious transgression, but only to have intercourse with a Cuthean woman, and it is not at all clear that the Torah prohibits such an act. Hence the zealot — Phinehas — was permitted to act as he did, but not commanded to do so, and therefore Zimri was allowed to save himself from Phinehas, his pursuer, by killing Phinehas.

In his novellae on bSanhedrin, R. Nissim Gerondi (Ran) offers a different explanation:

> And [Phinehas' act] is not like that of the pursuer . . . and the reason is that in the case of one who pursues his fellow in order to kill him, he [the pursuee] may be saved by [taking] his life, and when the other person [i.e., a rescuer] came to kill him, he [the pursuer] could have decided himself to cease pursuing his fellow in order to kill him. He has no right to turn around and kill the person coming to kill him [i.e., the pursuer] in order to save the pursuee, and why should he be exempt [from the punishment of court-imposed death] if he succeeds in killing the pursuee—he could have done nothing [lit., sat down] and not committed the transgression. But in the case of intercourse with the Cuthean woman, the zealots are not killing him to save him from transgression, since he has already transgressed, but this is an act of vengeance, and [the operative principle is]: "if someone

132 R. Meir b. Todros Halevi Abulafia, *Yad Rama*, bSanhedrin 82a s.v. *amar rav hisda*.

> comes to kill you, preempt this by killing him"[133] in any way that does not incur court-imposed death.[134]

In other words, the rationale for preventing a pursuer from saving himself by killing a rescuer is because it is pointless, since, whether he continues to pursue the pursuee, and kills him, or turns around and kills the rescuer, in any event he has committed murder. He should therefore desist altogether. The situation in the case of Phinehas' pursuit of Zimri, which is motivated by zeal, is different. Zimri is permitted to turn around and kill Phinehas, since he himself has not committed an offense that renders him liable to the punishment of court-imposed death.

It appears that the Sages' exegeses almost negate the value of Phinehas' zeal. The Early and Later Authorities differentiate between Zimri, who can turn around and kill Phinehas, and bystanders who may see that Phinehas is about to kill Zimri, but are not allowed to kill Phinehas.[135] This idea is dubious, since the talmudic Sages saw acts of zealotry as voluntary, and not a matter of religious obligation, so not only should Zimri have been allowed to kill Phinehas in self-defense without being considered a murderer, but any bystander should also be permitted to kill Phinehas without being liable for murder.

5. "Thou shalt not kill–nor kill oneself": suicide as an act of murder

In addition to the plain meaning of the commandment: "Thou shalt not kill" — the prohibition against taking someone else's life — the Sages exegetically derived an additional hidden meaning: the prohibition against suicide. The following is said in a baraita quoted in the Babylonian Talmud: "we have learned, 'And surely your blood of your lives will I require' (Gen. 9:5). R. Eleazar says: your soul will have to answer to Me for your blood."[136] This is also stated more directly: "Thou shalt not kill — nor kill oneself,"[137] which is in turn explicated as "you shall not be murdered by the one whose blood you have shed."[138] These

133 bSanhedrin 72a.
134 *Hidushei Haran*, bSanhedrin 82a s.v. *mai taama*.
135 See Enker, n. 108 above, 228–29.
136 bBaba Kama 91b.
137 *Pesikta Rabbati*, Exodus, §24.
138 M. Ish-Shalom, *Meir Ayin*, ad loc.

exegeses make clear that not only is it not permitted to take someone else's life, but that all killing, even of oneself, is prohibited, whether directly, by intentional suicide intended to bring one's life to an end, or indirectly, by endangering oneself unnecessarily, in the hope of extricating oneself successfully.

Invoking the idea that one is not allowed to impose death on herself, the author of the Mekhilta de-Rashbi[139] solves a problem that has long troubled criminal law scholars: does the legal prohibition against murder have any independent value beyond instilling fear of punishment? If so, what about the case where someone, wishing to 'surrender himself to death,' willingly commits a crime that renders him liable for the death penalty: is this permissible? The Mekhilta de-Rashbi addresses this very point:

> Whence do we know that if someone said, I am going to commit murder so that I will be executed, he is considered forewarned? Therefore Scripture teaches, 'Thou shalt not kill.' . . . Whence do we know that if someone is going to be executed, and said, I am going to commit murder, he is considered forewarned? Therefore Scripture teaches, 'Thou shalt not kill.' . . . Whence do we know that if someone said, I am going commit adultery so that I will be executed, he is considered forewarned? Therefore Scripture teaches, 'Thou shalt not commit adultery.'

In other words, the murderer and the adulterer are being punished in accordance with Torah law for the harm that they did to others, but at the same time they have transgressed the religious prohibition against suicide. This outlook is undoubtedly based on the assumption that the soul is not one's own property, and one has no right to decide what to do with his body.[140] This solution to the aforementioned dilemma is thus opposed to the secular liberal worldview that enshrines freedom of the individual, and the individual's sovereignty over his or her body.[141]

Yet the halakhic exegeses that prohibit self-harm are not without problems. On the one hand, there are examples in the Bible, the Apocrypha, and even the writings of those who documented the

139 Mekhilta de-Rabbi Shimon b. Yohai, 20:13 (Epstein-Melamed edition, 152).

140 See *Radbaz, Code*, Laws concerning the Sanhedrin 18:6.

141 L. Shalaf, "Between the sanctity of life and human dignity: bodily suffering, advances in medicine, human sensitivity, and the criminal law" (Hebrew), 4 *Mishpatim* (1994), 207–40, discusses how the question is approached in secular law.

destruction of the Second Temple and the rebellions that followed in its wake, of esteemed figures who voluntarily chose to end their lives either by suicide or by dying in 'elective' wars: Samson, King Saul, Hannah and her seven sons, the defenders of Masada, and so on.[142] Moreover, some of the Sages even praised these actions. On the other hand, the sweeping prohibition against self-harm gave rise to an important and long-running debate, beginning with the Early Authorities, over the question of whether suicide was prohibited even in the case of one who is being forced to commit a transgression falling under the category of 'be killed and do not transgress.' Is one who finds himself in such a situation permitted to avoid the evil by committing suicide, "if he fears he will be unable to withstand the temptation [to transgress]," as the Tosafists put it? Or might it even be a religious obligation for someone in that situation to kill himself, a view ascribed to Rabbenu Tam?[143] Or is neither view correct, the decision being left to the individual who faces the terrible dilemma?[144]

It is important to point out that, with respect to the law intended for implementation, such questions have no clear-cut answers, and that the examples of biblical and post-biblical figures who chose to take their own lives rather than transgress have been adduced in support of different positions, and are the subject of much deliberation in the literature.[145] King Saul, who is described in the Bible as "him whom the

142 There are also examples in the legends of the Sages, including Bruria, the wife of R. Meir, who strangled herself, see bAvoda Zara 18b, *Rashi* ad loc. s.v. *veika deamri*; and Yakim of Tzrurot, the nephew of R. Jose b. Yoezer of Tzreida, who "imposed on himself all four modes of execution by the court" (Gen. Rabbah 65:22 [Theodor–Albeck edition, 722–23]). There is no clear tradition regarding Hanania, Mishael and Azaria. It is argued in *Tosafot*, bPesahim 53b s.v. *ma rau* that they "were handed over to die," i.e., that others threw them into the furnace, and they did not do so on their own.

143 *Tosafot*, bAvoda Zara 18a s.v. *veal yahbol azmo*.

144 *Tosafot*, bBaba Kama 91b s.v. *hahovel beatzmo*; Nahmanides, *Torat Haadam*; see also *Yam Shel Shlomo*, Baba Kama 8:59.

145 See Y. Lichtenshtein, "Suicide as an act of atonement in Jewish law," 16 *Jewish Law Annual* (2006), 51–91; on the prohibition against suicide in the context of martyrdom in medieval Germany, see H. Soloveitchik, "Religious law and change: the medieval Ashkenazic example," *AJS Review* 12 (1987), 205; E. Kanarfogel, "Halakha and *metziut* (realia) in medieval Ashkenaz: surveying the parameters and defining the limits," 14 *Jewish Law Annual* (2003), 201–16; A. Grossman, "The cultural and social background of Jewish

Lord has chosen" (1 Sam. 10:24), used a necromancer to call up the spirit of the prophet Samuel. Samuel reprimands Saul for this action, concluding his remarks with: "Moreover the Lord will also deliver Israel with thee into the hand of the Philistines: and tomorrow shalt thou and thy sons be with me" (1 Sam. 28:19). On the following day,

> the battle went sore against Saul, and the archers hit him; and he was sore wounded of the archers. Then said Saul unto his armor-bearer, Draw thy sword, and thrust me through therewith; lest these uncircumcised come and thrust me through, and torment me. But his armor-bearer would not; for he was sore afraid. Therefore Saul took a sword, and fell upon it. (31:3–4)

How could Saul end his own life? One traditional interpretation is that in so doing, Saul did not sin, "since Saul knew that his fate was to die in battle—Samuel had told him."[146] Saul's action was based on his certain knowledge that he was fated to die in that battle. But someone else, who would not have such knowledge, would not be permitted to take his own life. This opinion is based on the following Midrash: "Samuel prophesied in his lifetime and after his death. For Samuel said to Saul: if you take my advice and fall by the sword, your death will atone for your deeds, and your destiny will be in the place where I am in repose. And Saul heeded his advice and was killed together with his sons."[147] We learn indirectly, then, that Saul's glorious action is not the basis for an enduring halakhic norm but only for a temporary ruling — in order to atone for his sins, and in accordance with a prophecy he had received.

Another explanation put forward by the commentators is that Saul's act was not defined as suicide, "since the archers had found him and he could not escape from them, it was better that he kill himself than that the uncircumcised torment him." This explanation is also, like the previous one, based on the exceptional nature of Saul as king of Israel, since Saul "thought that if he was captured alive, and they would

---

martyrdom in 1096" (Hebrew) in Y. Assis et al. (eds.), *Facing the Cross: The Persecutions of 1096 in History and Historiography* (Jerusalem: 2001), 55; I.J. Yuval, "Vengeance and damnation, blood and defamation: from Jewish martyrdom to libel accusations" (Hebrew), *Zion* 58 (1993), 33; and responses to this article in *Zion* 59 (1994), 59.

146 As explained by R. David Kimhi, 1 Samuel 31:5.

147 *Yalkut Shimoni*, 1 Samuel, §141.

torment him and torture him, it was very possible that the children of Israel would be unable to stand the sight and sound of their king's suffering, and they would strive to avenge him or save him, and it would costs tens of thousands of lives." Or, as the Maharshal, R. Solomon Luria, puts it: "possibly because of the respect for a king who is the Lord's anointed, it would not be fitting for him to be killed by the uncircumcised, who would torture him to death and mutilate his body, which would be a desecration of God's name according to the tenets of our religion."[148] These commentators teach us that Saul's hasty action cannot serve as a precedent for others.

By contrast, some commentators maintain that Saul was fully subject to halakhic norms and that his special status did not except him in any way from the prohibition against suicide. Both Nahmanides and R. Asher b. Jehiel (Rosh) ruled that Saul's action was permissible because he was being pursued, and "therefore what he did was not classified as suicide."[149] In his *Beit Yosef,* R. Joseph Caro adopts an even more extreme approach.[150] He assesses Saul's action in light of the debate among the medieval rabbinical authorities as to whether, when Jews feared that non-Jews "might force them, by inflicting unbearable torture, to transgress," it was obligatory for them to harm themselves, in accordance with Rabbenu Tam's ruling,[151] or not. He states:

> The explanation is that during a period of forcible conversions (*shmad*), one may surrender oneself to death or kill oneself if one knows that he will not be able to withstand the temptation [to transgress] . . . and proof for this can be brought from the cases where children were killed during periods of forcible conversions. Others forbid the act and explain . . . that one cannot kill oneself, and that Hanania, Mishael, and Azaria

148 *Yam Shel Shlomo,* bBaba Kama 8:59, from which all the quotations in this paragraph are taken.

149 Nahmanides, *Torat Haadam,* Shaar Hahesped (Chavel edition, 84); *Rosh,* bMoed Katan 3:94. Both are elucidating Genesis Rabbah 34:13: "'And surely your blood of your lives will I require' (Gen. 9:5) — your soul will have to answer to Me for your life blood. Could this apply even to one who was being pursued, like Saul? Therefore Scripture teaches: 'And surely' (*akh*) [which indicates exceptions]." Note that the word 'pursued' does not appear in the midrash, but was added by the Early Authorities to explain the circumstances.

150 YD 157 s.v. *veharambam.*

151 *Tosafot,* bAvoda Zara 18a.

> gave themselves up to others but did not harm themselves. **And Saul b. Kish acted contrary to the Sages' wishes.**[152]

In his opinion too, then, Saul's conduct was subject to the halakhic norms, and did not escape criticism by the rabbinical authorities.

However, in later generations, Saul's conduct was regarded by the halakhic authorities as exemplary, and this shift in attitude is discernible in the responsa literature. For example, the following question was posed to R. Haim Joseph David Azoulay, the Hida: "the case of a Jew, who, due to our many iniquities, was caught and was to stand trial, and he was imprisoned in the king's prison, but was in a room by himself. And some days later, the prison guards said they found him strangled with a scarf around his neck. We are uncertain as to whether he should be considered a suicide, who should not be mourned, or whether he should be mourned."

He answered as follows:

> We have to say that in this case, since it was widely known that he was the murderer, the unfortunate man feared they would torment him and sentence him to torture and death. And because of that, he chose to die on his own, without torment. And the author of *Beit Lehem Yehuda* wrote: '. . . if one kills himself out of fear that he will be subjected to the severe torture that typically is part of non-Jewish trials, which are usually preceded by torture, he is certainly not considered a suicide.[153] . . . And it is as was stated in Genesis Rabbah, 'And surely your blood of your

152 He continues: "it is told of a certain rabbi that he killed many children during a period of forcible conversions, to prevent them from being converted, and there was another rabbi with him who became angry and called him a murderer, and the first rabbi ignored what he said. The rabbi who sought to stop him said: if it is as I say, the rabbi will die an unnatural death. And so it was, the non-Jews caught him and flayed him and put sand between his skin and his flesh. Afterwards, they ceased the persecution and it is possible that, had he not killed the children, they might have been saved and they might not have been harmed." These remarks, written by R. Caro, were copied from earlier commentators; see the *Daat Zekenim* commentary (Gellis), *Tosafot Hashalem: Otzar Peirushei Baalei Hatosafot*, vol. 1 (Jerusalem: 1982), 262. See also *Yam Shel Shlomo*, n. 148 above.

153 R. Zvi Hirsh b. Azriel of Vilna, *Sefer Beit Lehem Yehuda Veshaar Efraim*, YD 345:3. The author presents numerous rulings on the following issue: "if somebody stole and because of this was killed by the laws of the realm, one may mourn him . . . he is not considered a suicide . . . if someone took upon himself, as a means of repentance, the four court-imposed types of death, and drowned himself in a river — he is not considered a suicide. In my

> lives' (Gen. 9:5) — could this apply even to Saul? Therefore Scripture teaches: 'And surely' (*akh*) [which indicates exceptions]. In the case of Saul, Scripture tells us that he feared lest the Amalekites torment him. And we have learned that one who kills himself because he fears torment is not considered a suicide.[154]

We can conclude that on the Hida's approach, fear of torment and torture is a special case, where self-harm is permissible even though it does not involve a transgression that falls under the category of 'be killed and do not transgress.'[155]

R. Abraham Isaac Kook's approach differs. In *Mishpat Kohen*, he explains Saul's conduct, and the conduct of the other esteemed figures who voluntarily chose to end their lives either by suicide or by dying in battles where death was inevitable, as follows. Saul was not worried about being tortured because of his status as king, but rather "he was apprehensive lest the uncircumcised Philistines would torment him sexually . . . and one who fears being forcibly sexually defiled may commit suicide pre-emptively." This would seem to imply that there is no dispensation to commit suicide where one fears he will suffer physical torture, but not be forced to engage in prohibited acts.[156]

---

opinion, this is also the case for one who kills himself out of fear that he will be subjected to the severe torture that typically is part of non-Jewish trials, which are usually preceded by severe torture; he is certainly not considered a suicide. This seems straightforward in light of what is written in the *Tosafot* [bGitin 57b s.v. *kaftzu*]: "they jumped and fell into the sea because they feared torment."

154 *Responsa Haim Shaal*, #144.

155 It could be argued that this is no more than post facto justification of a suicide, and indeed the case of Saul was deliberated on after the fact, to decide whether or not, given his deed, it was appropriate to eulogize him. Some of the decisors rule that Saul's falling on his sword did not warrant denying him a eulogy.

156 R. Kook's approach is based on interpreting the same verse, "And surely your blood of your lives" (Gen. 9:5), but the careful reader may see that his reading is a creative one. Genesis Rabbah 34:13 states: "'And surely your blood of your lives' (Gen. 9:5) — could this apply even to Saul? Therefore Scripture teaches: 'And surely' (*akh*) [which indicates exceptions]." The Rosh explains: "because they abandoned him," which R. Kook explains as "they treated him in an unrestrained manner." Similarly, in support of his assertion that Saul was afraid of sexual assault rather than physical torture, he adduces the case of the concubine in Gibeah (Judg. 19:22–29), which, he says, "also speaks of sexual abuse." His intention is to

The debate over Saul's act was revisited in our day in a concrete context, in a polemic between two prominent contemporary rabbinic authorities. Most of the discussion focused on the question of whether or not the heroism of the defenders of Masada was normative and in accordance with halakhic rulings.[157] R. Shlomo Goren, at the time the chief rabbi of the Israel Defense Forces, and later Chief Rabbi and president of the Rabbinical High Court, handed down the following ruling: "the heroic acts of the defenders of Masada were in accordance with the normative halakha rulings."[158] He justified this ruling as follows:

> (a) One who falls into the hands of a cruel enemy that is about to kill him during a war, and he fears that they will compel him, by means of torture, to commit the kinds of transgressions regarding which we were commanded to [let ourselves] be killed and not transgress, such as idolatry, sexual transgressions, and the shedding of blood — [under such circumstances], it is obligatory to die a self-imposed death rather than fall into the hands of the enemy. . .(c) When his capture by the enemy will lead to a desecration of God's name, and provide the enemy with something to pride itself on and boast about, and in the end he will be killed, it is also obligatory to die a self-imposed death rather than fall into the hands of the enemy, like what happened to King Saul and the people of Masada.

In support of his ruling that the suicide of the defenders of Masada was in accordance with the law, R. Goren invoked the case of Saul:

> Saul's act was not based on his own decision, for we find in *Yalkut Shimoni* . . . that Samuel said to Saul, 'if you take my advice and fall on your sword, your death will atone for your deeds.' . . . It is specified explicitly that it was Samuel's advice that he fall on his sword, and Samuel gave that advice as a prophecy in God's name.

---

reconcile Maimonides' ruling in *Code,* Laws concerning the Fundamental Principles of the Torah 5:4 — "Wherever one is enjoined to transgress rather than be killed, and chooses to be killed rather than transgress, he is himself responsible for his death" — with Saul's precipitation of his death. Further on, he hints at another possible resolution: "the dispensation to subject oneself to danger in the context of [fighting] wars, though in my opinion that is a special case connected with the laws of kings."

157 On other present-day issues regarding which the decisors have invoked Saul's act, such as disconnecting life-preserving machines, see N. Guttel, "Saul's suicide–halakhic perspectives" (Hebrew), *Netivei Merhavim* 4 (2006) 43, 52–54.

158 "A responsum on the heroes of Masada" (Hebrew), *Or Hamizrah Quarterly* 20 (1960), 22–27.

R. Goren thus concurs with Rabbenu Tam's view, arguing that in the context of war, when there is fear that the enemy will force the prisoner into transgressing the dictates of his religion, by making him transgress one of the commandments for which he should 'be killed and not transgress' — or even where there is no apprehensiveness that the prisoner will be forced to transgress his religion, if the captivity will "lead to a desecration of God's name . . . and in the end he will be killed" — suicide is not merely retroactively permissible, but obligatory a priori.[159] R. Goren also adds an innovative element to the discussion, in stating that "King Saul's act of falling on his sword was carried out in accordance with a prophetic command."

This ruling, and the sources it adduced, was vigorously attacked by R. Moses Z. Neria. He asserts: "Indeed, this commentary is very strange: where have we found in the words of Samuel — quoted in the *Yalkut* — that he told Saul to fall on his sword? For what it says there is that he will fall by the sword, the explanation being that he will go out to war and fall there."[160] R. Neria raises a second objection: if Samuel commanded Saul to fall on his sword, why does Saul ask of his armor-bearer: "draw thy sword and thrust me through therewith"?

159 R. Goren words his ruling very carefully. Where it is feared that there will be "unbearable torture if he is captured by the enemy," but the torture would not be accompanied by attempts to induce the captive to convert, or desecration of God's name, but "the enemy is cruel and will undoubtedly kill him in the end, by way of unbearable torture," R. Goren states that "some authorities permit one, in this case, to kill himself rather than fall into the enemy's hands." That is, in this case it is permissible, but not obligatory. R. Goren also rules:

> When there is apprehensiveness that prior to his death, while he is being tortured, the enemy will try to elicit from him important military information — and we are also commanded not to give such information to the enemy, to protect lives, for anybody who hands over such information is deemed to be like one who pursues his fellow in order to kill him, and like one who hands over a fellow Jew to Gentiles [to be persecuted], **and all are obligated to kill him** — avoiding this situation is also obligatory, **and to achieve this, one is obligated to kill himself** and not transgress.

160 "The suicide of the people of Masada–halakhic perspectives" (Hebrew pamphlet, summer 1961), reprinted in Moses Z. Neria, *Tznif Melukha* (Kfar Haroe: 1992), 196–98.

Thirdly, if Saul's act of falling on his sword was "in accordance with a prophetic command," then this constitutes a counterexample to the alleged normativity of the suicide by the fighters at Masada, since "there is a general principle that 'a prophet is not permitted to introduce anything law'[161]; his instructions are nothing but temporary rulings, and cannot be invoked by future generations."

R. Neria goes further, claiming that R. Goren's ruling regarding the fighters at Masada is not in accordance with the approach adopted by most of the Early Authorities and the Later Authorities until recently, and that Rabbenu Tam's opinion is even quoted from a different perspective in various sources, namely, as permitting suicide but not regarding it as obligatory, and he discusses the subject at length.

It is not only the substance of the controversy between these two contemporary halakhic luminaries that is of interest, but also R. Neria's wariness about drawing halakhic conclusions from early halakhic sources themselves, without attending to their interpretations by the halakhic sages:

> The ancient event on the heights of Masada still requires study and clarification, regarding the conditions of imprisonment under the Romans, and what would actually have been in store for the defenders had they surrendered .... even if we assume that the circumstances warranted their actions, we still must explicitly take issue with the rationales put forward by their commander Eleazar b. Yair. In his opinion, committing suicide was imperative not only for the heroes of Masada, but for the entire nation, 'since from ancient times God executed this judgment on all Jews for posterity — and we have no way to save ourselves from it' and furthermore, 'God imposed this decree upon us' and 'so our Torah commanded us.'... No proof is needed that these statements have no substance, and the laws of our Torah commanded us to preserve our existence and our lives, even in circumstances of surrender and captivity, and so on, "and He planted eternal life in our midst."
>
> ... And our brethren who were subjected to tribulations and captivity in the ghettos and concentration camps, and could expect torture and torment and attempts to convert them — had they acted in accordance with this [R. Goren's] ruling, no trace or remnant of them would have survived.

161 bShabat 104a.

6. "Thou shalt surely smite the inhabitants of that city" — exegesis on collective punishment

The laws governing a city whose inhabitants were incited to engage in idol worship are unclear, and many of the details have been controversial from the mishnaic period until the present. It would seem that the author of the Tosefta had his reasons for saying: "there has never been an idolatrous city, and there never will be. Why, then, was this law written? That you may study it and be rewarded."[162] As is well known, this same rubric is used vis-à-vis the law of the 'stubborn and rebellious son,' the detailed provisions of which the halakhic authorities have always found to be problematic. Both the Tosefta and the two Talmuds state: "there never has been a stubborn and rebellious son, and never will be. Why then was the law written? That you may study it and be rewarded."[163]

I will demonstrate the problematic nature of the 'idolatrous city' by analyzing two controversies regarding punishment of its inhabitants.

i The Bible points out the extent of the punishment that is peculiar to the inhabitants of an idolatrous city: "Thou shalt surely smite the inhabitants of that city with the edge of the sword, destroying it utterly, and all that is therein, and the cattle thereof, with the edge of the sword. And thou shalt gather all the spoil of it . . . and burn with fire the city . . . ." (Deut. 13:16–17). Two separate discussions about the scope of these verses are found in the halakhic literature. In the Mishnah, the explanation for "all that is therein" is that it only applies to movable property, and "the property of righteous people within [the city] is destroyed, and outside [the city] is saved, but that of evil people, whether it is within or outside [the city], is destroyed."[164] In the Tosefta, there is discussion about imposing the punishment of death on additional people in the city, besides those who were incited to engage in idol worship.[165] "Minor children of people in the idolatrous city who were incited together with the city, are not killed. R. Eliezer says, they are killed." The Sages' discussion reveals that the minors are liable even if they themselves did not engage in idol-worship. They are punished because they are being cared for by their parents, who were incited to

162 tSanhedrin 14:1 (Zuckermandel edition, 436).
163 tSanhedrin 11:6 (Zuckermandel edition, 431); bSanhedrin 71a.
164 mSanhedrin 10:2.
165 tSanhedrin 14:3 (Zuckermandel edition, 436).

engage in idol-worship. Sifre Deuteronomy puts forward a similar idea, anchoring it in the biblical verse: "'Thou shalt surely smite the inhabitants of that city' — from this we deduce that their dependents are not left alive. Abba Hanan says, 'The fathers shall not be put to death for the children' (Deut. 24:16) — Scripture is referring to the idolatrous city."[166]

Examination of the views of the Early Authorities also reveals an unresolved controversy. Maimonides is of the opinion that one should distinguish the situation where those who were incited to idolatry are a minority, in which case "they are stoned and the rest of the city is saved." If those who were incited are the majority, or the entire city, "they are brought before the high court, and their sentence is decided, and all those who worshiped idols are killed by the sword. And every human being that is in the city is struck by the sword, [including] children and women, if the whole city was incited. If the majority worship idols, all the children and women of those who worshipped idols are struck by the sword."[167] Maimonides thus accepts the view that the children are only killed because they are dependent. R. Meir Halevi of Toledo found this Maimonidean law puzzling, and asked the sages of Lunel, "why should women and children be punished, since they are not obliged [to observe all the precepts]?" They answered:

> Because it says in Sifre, 'Thou shalt surely smite (*hakei take*) {*et*}[168] the inhabitants of that city'—from this the Sages deduced that their dependents are not left alive at all, as they are to be killed, deriving this from the word '*et*,' which amplifies the scope [of the direct object, "the inhabitants of that city"] . . . and also, since we should learn from what happened to Korah's congregation and to the people of Jabesh-Gilead, where in both cases they killed the women and the children. Even though they had not sinned, they were punished with [lit., for] the adults, for two reasons. First, because they were the cause, as they impelled the adults to settle [in the city to raise a family], and second, to distress the adults by their being killed, because the adults loved them.[169]

166 Section 94 (Finkelstein edition, 155).

167 Maimonides, *Code*, Laws concerning Idolatry 4:6.

168 The particle "*et*" is used to mark the accusative case, and precedes a direct object.

169 Quoted in *Migdal Oz*, ad loc.

In his *Kesef Mishne* commentary on Maimonides, R. Joseph Caro hinted that the explanations of the sages of Lunel were unsatisfactory. It seems that Maimonides himself sought to clarify his opinion on the matter: "There are certain sins for which justice requires that repayment be exacted in this world; through the sinner's person, through her possessions, or through her small children. For one's small children, who lack understanding and have not reached the age of precept observance, are considered to be like one's property, as it is written, 'A man will die because of his own sins" (Deut. 24:16) — [the law applies] only after one has become a man (viz., an adult).'[170] Maimonides' comments can generally be taken as reflecting a metaphysical attempt to defend the world order put in place by heaven. However, in the case of the idolatrous city, they have normative significance vis-à-vis the high court.[171]

ii The Early Authorities also differ on the question of whether the inhabitants of the idolatrous city need be forewarned in order to be punished. There would seem to be no obvious difference between an individual who engages in idol worship, who must be forewarned if he is to be punished, and the inhabitants of an idolatrous city, who have been incited to engage in idolatry, and have done so. Yet in setting down the laws of the idolatrous city, Maimonides states:

> The high court sends its representatives to carry out an inquiry and examination until they know, on the basis of clear evidence, that all or most of the city has become idolatrous, and has gone back to idol worship. They then send two Torah scholars (*talmidei hakhamim*) to warn them and induce them to return [to God]. If they return and repent, it is well; if they persist in their folly, the court commands all Israel to go up to them as an army, and they besiege the city, and wage war against it until [its defenses are] breached. And after they break through, many courts are set up to try them. Anyone about whom two witnesses testify that he engaged in idol worship after they forewarned him is set apart [from the rest]. If all the idolaters make up a minority, they are stoned and the rest of the city is saved. If they make up a majority, they are brought before the high court, and their sentence is decided, and all those who worshiped idols are killed by the sword.[172]

170 *Code*, Laws concerning Repentance 6:1.

171 The problem of group punishment is addressed in Moshe Greenberg, "Some postulates of biblical criminal law," in A. Shapira and M. Greenberg (eds.), *Torah Nidreshet* (Hebrew), (Tel-Aviv: 1981), 13–83.

172 *Code*, Laws concerning Idolatry 4:6.

The mishnaic commentary on the verses

> If thou shalt hear tell concerning one of thy cities . . . saying: 'Certain base fellows [lit., children of Beliyaal (worthlessness)] are gone out from the midst of thee, and have drawn away the inhabitants of their city, saying: Let us go and serve other gods, which ye have not known,' then shalt thou inquire, and make search, and ask diligently; and, behold, if it be truth, and the thing certain . . . thou shalt surely smite the inhabitants of that city. (Deut. 13:13–16)

requires that a majority of the inhabitants have been incited to idolatry. Maimonides, as we saw, suggests a legal process that has no basis whatsoever in Rabbinic sources.

The Raavad disagreed with Maimonides, pointing out that Maimonides did not seem to have a talmudic source for the two Torah scholars sent to forewarn the idolaters. How, he asks, could Maimonides write, "If they return and repent, it is well"? He continues: "I have not found any case where repentance has been efficacious after someone has been forewarned and has transgressed nonetheless." He asks in what way the case of an individual who engaged in idol worship, was forewarned, and persisted in his transgression, whose sin cannot be absolved by repentance, differs from that of those who were incited to engage in idolatry together with other residents of their city, who are — according to Maimonides' account — permitted to repent after having transgressed. Various explanations were offered by other commentators on Maimonides, including R. Joseph Caro in *Kesef Mishne*. R. Caro asserts that Maimonides thinks "that the forewarning was not completely satisfactory since it was not given to each [transgressor] individually," and therefore the inhabitants of the idolatrous city are given an opportunity to repent of their folly, and if they repent, are not punished at all. But this defense of Maimonides is problematic. Why is it not necessary to forewarn the inhabitants of the idolatrous city **before** they transgress? Why are they punished if they do not repent, since they were not forewarned before their transgression? Furthermore, since when does a forewarning have to be relayed by Torah scholars?

It seems, therefore, that Maimonides does indeed require that the inhabitants of the idolatrous city be forewarned if they are to be punished, as is the case for individual idolaters, but he divides their punishment into two separate stages:

At the **first stage,** the townspeople are tried individually, hence each one has to be forewarned of the consequences of his actions, so that if they persist, testimony can be given in each case as to both commission of the offense and the transgressor's criminal intent, as is the case with respect to individual idolaters. The forewarning must be complete, that is, each inhabitant should be forewarned before witnesses, and the admonition must detail the punishment for the offense in question. The offender must 'surrender himself to death.' This warning, which the Torah requires for most transgressions, serves not only to differentiate between inadvertent and deliberate transgressions, but also to save transgressors from punishment by the court, as discussed above, since few transgressors will 'surrender themselves to death.'

The **second stage** occurs after the residents of the idolatrous city have been individually tried for idolatry. If it becomes evident that most of the inhabitants of the city engage in idol worship, the idolaters are brought to Jerusalem and tried as inhabitants of an idolatrous city. At this stage, forewarning is not required, for they can no longer be saved, because, as individuals, they have already been tried and convicted as idolaters. The warning by Torah scholars is not a full forewarning, but is intended so that the high court can be apprised, on the basis of clear evidence, that all or most of the city has become idolatrous. The high court need not be given specific details, just information about the scope of the idolatry, that is, how many of the inhabitants persist in their folly — the majority or a minority. The warning by the Torah scholars is also intended to decrease the number of those who persist in their rebelliousness. Repentance on the part of those who were incited to idolatry will not save them from the punishment meted out to idolaters, but will keep them from being subject to the law of the idolatrous city, which, in the opinion of some of the rabbinical authorities, mandates the burning of idolaters' possessions and killing of their young children. Hence this warning must be carried out by Torah scholars who have the moral status to influence those who have been convicted to repent, even if it will not save them from punishment by the court.

Maimonides' innovation was to institute punishment in stages, allowing the sages to influence the process and partly rehabilitate those subject to collective punishment, by first trying and sentencing them as individuals. However, the Raavad and other commentators who discuss the ruling do not accept Maimonides' interpretation of the procedures for dealing with the inhabitants of an idolatrous city.[173]

~ ~ ~ ~ ~ ~ ~ ~ ~

In this article, I have attempted to elucidate the halakhic authorities' approach to midrashic exegesis of biblical verses. Their exegeses are pragmatic, seeking to present the biblical verses relating to capital cases in a moderate light and thereby, in essence, neutralize their substance.

173 See also Halbertal, n. 10 above, 122–44. He notes that Maimonides' novel approach describes "a complicated and strange procedure" (129), but does not explain the significance of Maimonides' divergence from the talmudic sources. Other explanations are suggested in *Arukh Laner*, bSanhedrin 111b; N. Rakover, "The effect of repentance on punishment" (Hebrew), in M. Beer (ed.) *Studies in Halakha and Jewish Thought Presented to Rabbi Emanuel Rackman* (Hebrew), (Ramat-Gan: 1994), 183–86.

The Jewish Law Annual, Vol. XX

Problematic Halakhic 'Creativity' in Israeli Rabbinical Court Rulings

Amihai Radzyner*

1 Introduction

As historians and scholars of nineteenth-century Jewish law have pointed out, when Orthodox Judaism emerged in response to sociocultural developments in modern Jewish history, and specifically, the tendency to abandon religious observance, some decisors, notably those from Hungary, invoked unconventional and innovative halakhic

* Faculty of Law, Bar-Ilan University; editor of *The Law and Its Decisor (HaDin Ve'haDayan)*

sources and rulings to protect and fortify the authority of what they took to be the halakhic tradition. These sources had not been adduced previously. There is no doubt that the innovative rulings emerged against the background of the struggle to preserve halakhic authority, as perceived by the said decisors.[1]

In this article, I intend to show that a similar phenomenon is taking place today in the State of Israel: recourse to problematic halakhic positions in order to protect halakhic authority.

It is no exaggeration to say that the official rabbinical courts in Israel are the most significant halakhic institutions in the Jewish world today. This is true both with regard to the scope of their authority, which extends over the largest Jewish population, and with regard to their influence on the lives of Jews and Jewish communities in Israel and abroad. The system of official rabbinical courts was established in the land of Israel at the beginning of the British Mandate period, with the creation of the Chief Rabbinate of Israel in 1921 and the delineation of its jurisdiction in Mandatory legislation in 1922.[2] Since then, the system has been embedded in Israeli law as an official judicial system of the state, with special authority to adjudicate matters of marriage and divorce for all Jewish citizens and residents of Israel. Moreover, this adjudication is to be carried out solely in accordance with Orthodox

1 See, e.g., J. Katz, *Halacha in Straits: Obstacles to Orthodoxy at Its Inception* (Hebrew), (Jerusalem: 1992), 7–20, 18–9, 150–83, 181–83; Benjamin Brown, "Stringency: five modern types" (Hebrew), 20–21 *Dine Israel* (2000/2001), 123, 154–77; M.K. Silber, "The emergence of ultra-Orthodoxy: the invention of a tradition" (Hebrew), in Y. Salmon et al. (eds.), *Orthodox Judaism: New Perspectives* (Hebrew), (Jerusalem: 2006), 297. According to Silber, "Paradoxically, in order to preserve the tradition without compromises, these conservative figures adopted, in their halakhic decision-making, methods that diverged from the accepted norms not only of traditional pre-modern Judaism, but also of the central stream of post-traditional Orthodoxy" (299). The works listed here explore the tendency to be stringent manifested by decisors in the midst of confrontation, but at times, confrontation brought about lenient positions that were based on unusual halakhic considerations, unconventional sources, or innovative interpretation of the sources, with a view to protecting traditional society. See I. Brown (Hoizman), "'The violation of the Torah is its true fulfillment' . . . R. Hayim of Sanz as a case study" (Hebrew), *Tarbiz* 78 (2009), 555, 590.

2 *Palestine Order in Council*, 1922, Art. 51, 53.

halakha.[3] In recent years, the rabbinical court system has also been granted authority (subject to various conditions) to handle divorce suits involving Jews who are not citizens or residents of Israel. The reason for this is the understanding that only a rabbinical institution that operates by virtue of state law can resolve situations of refusal to grant a divorce and exercise pressure on recalcitrant husbands using means placed at its disposal by the state.[4] To a significant degree, Orthodox rabbinical courts abroad are subject to the halakhic policy of Israeli rabbinical courts regarding matters of divorce and conversion.[5]

This reality, in which a halakhic institution operates by virtue of civil law, has far-reaching operational consequences for the rabbinical courts. In addition to clear advantages, there are also complex problems. In the early years of the official rabbinical courts, during the British Mandate, they had to cope with various demands made by the British authorities, demands inconsistent with accepted halakhic norms. The first confrontation involved the demand that the rabbinical courts establish an appellate instance. The founder of the Chief Rabbinate and the first Ashkenazic Chief Rabbi, R. Abraham I. Kook, gave in to this demand despite ultra-Orthodox opposition, which claimed that it was an unacceptable halakhic reform. This was the genesis of the institution referred to as the "Rabbinical High Court of Appeal" (also known as the "Supreme Rabbinical Court"); it still exists today.[6] R. Kook, and his successors, R. Isaac Halevi Herzog and

3 *Rabbinical Court Jurisdiction (Marriage and Divorce) Law 5713–1953* [henceforth, *RC Jurisdiction Law*], §1, 2; M. Chigier, *Husband and Wife in Israeli law* (Jerusalem: 1985), 12–22, 66; T. Einhorn, *Private International Law in Israel* (Austin TX: 2009), 168–70, 212–13.

4 *RC Jurisdiction Law*, ibid., §4a; Einhorn, ibid., 214–15, 218–20.

5 Not all rabbinical courts that grant divorces and perform conversions are recognized in Israel. There is a list of authorized courts, and to be listed, courts are required to follow the policies of Israel's state rabbinical courts. Those who wish their divorce or conversion to be recognized in Israel must submit a request to Israel's official rabbinical court system, which does not approve such requests automatically, but rather investigates each procedure to ascertain its conformity with the aforementioned policies.

6 On the establishment of the Rabbinical High Court of Appeal (henceforth RHC), its halakhic innovativeness, and the controversy it engendered, see my "Rabbi Uziel, the Tel-Aviv-Jaffa Rabbinate and the Rabbinical Court of Appeal: A play in four acts" (Hebrew), 21 *Bar-Ilan Law Studies (Mehkarei Mishpat)* (2004), 129.

R. Benzion Uziel, struggled against additional Mandatory demands that entailed changing traditional halakhic procedures and adapting them to modern judicial norms. But they gave in to the demands, because the Mandatory authorities warned that the powers that had been granted to the rabbinical courts by law were contingent on their leaders' willingness to adopt these procedural reforms.[7]

The Mandatory authorities' interference with the operation of the rabbinical courts went beyond procedural matters. The mere fact that the law specified the areas the rabbinical courts could adjudicate — "matters of marriage and divorce" — left outside its jurisdiction most of the legal issues that rabbinical courts everywhere had adjudicated since time immemorial, namely, civil law cases (*dinei mamonot*). These matters were deemed within the rabbinical courts' jurisdiction only where both sides agreed to accept their authority, that is, to adjudicate their matter in accordance with the state's arbitration law (*Arbitration Law, 5728–1968*), a law that allows the civil courts to interfere with the arbitrator's ruling.[8] Moreover, the rabbinical courts were not given exclusive jurisdiction over many of the issues related to family law unless both parties agreed to accept their authority.

The State of Israel inherited this situation from the Mandatory government,[9] and — from the point of view of the rabbinical courts — even made things worse. Although the law made it possible for the rabbinical courts to exercise jurisdiction over matters related to divorce (property, maintenance, etc.), it specified that this authority was contingent on the claim's being filed with the rabbinical court before its submission to a civil court, as civil courts also had jurisdiction

7 On R. Kook, see my "The origins of procedural regulations for rabbinical courts: '*Sidrei Ha-Mishpatim*' 1921" (Hebrew), 25 *Bar-Ilan Law Studies* (2009), 37; on R. Herzog and R. Uziel, see idem, "The origins of procedural regulations for rabbinical courts: '*Takanot Hadiun*' 1943" (Hebrew), 25 *Dine Israel* (2008), 185.

8 And even this possibility of adjudication by agreement of the sides was later eliminated, as we will see below. On the rabbinical courts' authority to adjudicate beyond "matters of marriage and divorce," see my "The halakhic status of the Israeli official rabbinical courts . . ." (Hebrew), 13 *Mishpat Umimshal* (2011), 271–355.

9 Chigier, n. 3 above, 12–28.

over such matters.[10] According to many rabbinical judges, it is halakhically problematic for a divorce proceeding to be conducted in parallel by a rabbinical court and a civil court, as they represent very different legal systems. In other words, it is problematic that divorce proceedings in their entirety are not under the exclusive jurisdiction of the rabbinical courts, and thus not necessarily conducted entirely in accordance with Jewish law. Furthermore, the State of Israel has determined, legislatively and through Supreme Court rulings, that matters pertaining to property are not to be adjudicated in accordance with Jewish law even in the rabbinical courts, unless both sides explicitly agree to it.[11] This is clearly problematic, as it means that the rabbinical court judge is required to divide the parties' property in a manner that does not accord with the rules of Jewish law.[12]

It is not just legislation that has reduced the rabbinical courts' jurisdiction. Over the years, the Supreme Court, in its capacity as High Court of Justice, has handed down various rulings that narrowed the rabbinical courts' powers and directed them to act contrary to what they perceived as binding halakha.[13] This trend culminated in an April 2006 ruling that rabbinical courts are not authorized to engage in arbitration. The import of this ruling is that rabbinical courts have no authority at all to adjudicate monetary issues, including conflicts

10 *RC Jurisdiction Law*, n. 3 above, §3; Chigier, n. 3 above, 66–7; Einhorn, n. 3 above, 188–89.

11 See Einhorn, n. 3 above, 201–12.

12 R. A. Sherman, a senior rabbinical court judge, contends that it is not possible to divide a divorcing couple's property according to the rules of Israeli law, as they run counter to those of Jewish law, see A. Sherman, "The principle of common ownership in light of Torah law" (Hebrew), *Tehumin* 18 (1998), 32; idem, "The community property system is not anchored in Jewish law" (Hebrew), *Tehumin* 19 (1999), 205.

13 For a critical summary of this move, see R. Halperin-Kaddari, "Towards concluding civil family law — Israel style" (Hebrew), 17 *Bar-Ilan Law Studies* (2001), 105; S. Dichovsky, "Rabbinical and civil courts: insights on the friction between them in family law matters" (Hebrew), 4 *Moznei Mishpat* (Netanya Academic College L. Rev.) (2005), 261; B. Lifshitz, "The garden of illusions in matters of marriage and divorce" (Hebrew), 2 *Family in Law Review* (Hebrew), (2009), 107.

arising from the execution of divorce agreements after the bill of divorce (*get*) has been granted.[14]

The foregoing remarks are intended to provide necessary background for the central argument that I will make in this article, namely, that since the end of the 1990s, there has been a backlash on the part of the rabbinical courts. In the past too, and indeed, the present, some rabbinical court judges[15] ignored various civil court rulings and legal ordinances they believed to be contrary to Jewish law, even though these ordinances were explicitly addressed to the rabbinical courts as well as the civil.[16] But it appears that in recent years a backlash of a new type has developed, one that is of great interest to legal and halakhic scholars as well as students of the evolving relationship between religion and state in Israel. Some of the rabbinical court judges are adopting problematic halakhic positions that were rarely if ever upheld in the past, in order to restore to the rabbinical courts the authority these judges take to have been misappropriated (or to be in danger of being misappropriated) by Israeli law and the civil courts. In other words, Jewish law is being used as a weapon to restore authority to the rabbinical courts, or to protect it from further erosion. Decisors are adopting

14 HCJ 8638/03, *Amir v. Rabbinical High Court of Appeal* (2006), http://elyon2.court.gov.il/files/03/380/086/R08/03086380.R08.htm. In Radzyner 2011, n. 8 above, I discuss the significance of this ruling, and explain why it is perceived by the rabbinical courts as the worst blow to its status by far. There is no doubt that the effect of this ruling is to accelerate the rabbinical courts' growing tendencies toward stringency, as I show in "From Lvov to Tel-Aviv: 'wrongful divorce' judgments in the Israeli rabbinical courts" (Hebrew), 39 *Mishpatim* (2009), 155.

15 I say "some" rabbinical court judges, because the phenomena I address are manifested by some panels, not all. But it is clear that there is opposition to them, and under no circumstances can the positions in question be ascribed to all Israel's rabbinical court judges. It is well known that, with regard to many substantive issues, there is no consensus among the rabbinical courts, and it happens that different panels hand down very different rulings in cases that are quite similar. The main reason for this is that despite the existence of the RHC, it cannot create precedents, because Jewish law as a whole opposes the principle of legal precedent; see Z. Warhaftig, "Precedent in Jewish law," in H. Ben-Menahem and N. Hecht (eds.), *Authority, Process and Method; Studies in Jewish Law* (Amsterdam: 1998), 1–32.

16 See, e.g., HCJ 8214/07, *Plonit v. Ploni* (2010), http://elyon1.court.gov.il/files/07/140/082/b16/07082140.b16.htm.

halakhic positions that, under different circumstances, they would in all likelihood not even consider, and are doing so only out of a desire to maintain their legal authority and not relinquish it to the civil courts, whose adjudication will undoubtedly not be in accordance with Jewish law.[17]

Elsewhere[18] I discussed a recent phenomenon that has no precedent in the rulings of rabbinical courts before the last decade: the retroactive annulment of a divorce because the wife breached the divorce agreement, especially by bringing a civil-court action for child support. I showed that analysis of the rulings and the halakhic sources on which they are based indicates that this is a genuine halakhic innovation, and it is highly doubtful that it is indeed warranted on the strength of the sources adduced in support of it. I argued that we must understand the genesis of this halakhic weapon against the background of the rabbinical courts' desire to prevent women from taking the agreements that are approved by rabbinical courts as the basis for the granting of the divorce for further litigation in civil courts, and, if they nonetheless turn to the civil courts, to force these women back to rabbinical court to debate the validity of their divorce. Clearly, for women who are considering turning to the civil courts, this constitutes a significant deterrent. This creates a new and problematic halakhic tool intended to serve the rabbinical courts in the struggle to retain their authority.

In this article, I continue the critical examination of three halakhic tools of this type, which in my opinion are being used by certain panels of rabbinical court judges to preserve their authority. These tools, which have been adduced in halakhic rulings only in recent years, are based on 'creative' analysis of halakhic sources. They include: increasing the

17 Quite apart from the religious desideratum of protecting judgment that accords with Jewish law, the rabbinical courts' wish to retain their authority (and even expand it, as I show in Radzyner 2011, n. 8 above), is understandable. In recent years, analysis of judicial systems using sociological research methods, e.g. organizational sociology, has developed considerably. Contemporary research tends to regard legal systems as seeking, like other political entities, to amass power, see, e.g., P. Bourdieu, "The force of law: toward a sociology of the juridical field," 38 *Hastings Law Journal* (1987), 805–53. On the use of sociological research methods to analyze the rabbinical courts' power struggles, see A. Westreich, "The 'gatekeepers' of Jewish family law: marriage annulment as a test case," 27 *Journal of Law and Religion* (2012), 101–29.

18 See Radzyner 2009, n. 14 above, 155.

husband's ability to impose conditions at the time the divorce is granted; deeming a civil court action brought by the wife to render her 'obligated' to be divorced; a new halakhic definition of civil marriage and its dissolution.[19]

2 Limits on imposition of conditions for granting a divorce

In 2008, R. Ariel Yanai of the Netanya District Rabbinical Court addressed the issue of whether a husband deemed by the court to be obliged to divorce his wife on various grounds, can make the granting of the divorce (*get*) conditional on his wife's paying back to him monies that he claims are his.[20] This is a question of principle, which R. Yanai formulated as follows: "The question of principle that must be clarified is whether a husband who was obligated [by the court] to grant a divorce is entitled to impose preconditions for his agreement to do that which was imposed on him." R. Yanai answers in the negative; he also claims that even those who contend that the imposition of such conditions is allowable — a view we will soon examine — would agree that in the specific case R. Yanai was addressing, the husband cannot make the granting of the divorce conditional on satisfaction of his monetary demands.

With respect to the issues discussed in this paper, the remarks made by R. Yanai at the beginning of his deliberations, after he presented the question just cited, are crucial:

> This matter originates in the famous responsum by the Maharashdam (EH end of #41), which issued the innovative ruling that even if the husband is compelled [by the court] to divorce his wife, if he made the divorce contingent on a condition that the wife can readily fulfill, the court need not compel him to divorce her unconditionally — and one that does so, "contributes to the proliferation of *mamzerim* [children born to a woman married to someone other than the father] — because the bill of divorce (*get*) is invalid, for it is a coerced *get* (*get meuse*). Much has been written

19 The first two are indicative of increased stringency on the part of the rabbinical courts, whereas the third appears (see n. 206 below) indicative of leniency, but in my opinion it is clear that the motivation in all three cases is similar.

20 Netanya District Rabbinical Court, case 9707-21-1 [12.5.2008], http://www.daat.ac.il/daat/psk/psk.asp?id=309. The court rejected the husband's demand.

> about this statement by the Maharashdam, and it was discussed extensively **for the first time** by the Tel-Aviv District Rabbinical Court headed by R. Prover (case 5082-27-1 [9.07.2000]).[21] . . . This ruling was appealed in the Rabbinical High Court and was heard by an expanded panel of five judges (RHC, case 5082-64-1 [29.5.2002]; see also RHC, case 1390-21-1 [11.01.2006]), **and since then**, the issue has arisen from time to time in the rabbinical courts. (emphasis added)

But when R. Yanai's ruling was made public in *Shurat Hadin*, a periodical published by the rabbinical court directorate,[22] someone, presumably seeking to conceal the ruling's novelty, eliminated two significant terms from the above paragraph: the highlighted expressions "for the first time" and "and since then." It is difficult to assume that this was done to correct a putative slip of the tongue. Although the panel that heard case 5082 had already handed down a very similar ruling in the mid-1990s,[23] a simple survey reveals that reliance on the Maharashdam's opinion[24] in rabbinical court rulings in order to preclude 'coerced divorce' has only occurred in recent years. Remarks by a senior rabbinical court judge, R. Solomon Dichovsky, provide firm evidence of this:

> Let me note that use of the Maharashdam['s view] to prevent coerced divorce, where the husband makes his agreement contingent on [fulfillment of] certain conditions, is something that has come up only in recent years. In all twelve years that I sat on the district rabbinical court, and in the twenty years that I have sat on the Rabbinical High Court — except until relatively recently — the greatest of the rabbinical court judges did not rely on this method. When they reached the point where coercion was needed, they did not take account of conditions that recalcitrant husbands sought to impose. The reason for this was certainly that they did not consider it appropriate to base their rulings on this opinion.[25]

21 This reference is incorrect; the ruling was published in 21 *PDR* (2005), 176.

22 Ariel Yanai, "A husband who is obliged to grant a divorce can impose conditions" (Hebrew), 15 *Shurat Hadin* (2009), 361.

23 S. Bibi, Y. Goldberg, N. Prover, "A husband who is obliged to grant a divorce — can he delay it because of a monetary claim?" (Hebrew), 2 *Divrei Mishpat* (1996), 153–57.

24 R. Samuel b. Moses di Medina (Salonika, 1506–1589).

25 S. Dichovsky, "The proper mode of adjudication in rabbinical courts" (Hebrew), *Tehumin* 28 (2008), 19, 26–7. R. Dichovsky elaborated on this in other rulings, which will be discussed below; see n. 54 below.

This statement asserts the two fundamental points that I will make in this article, namely, that rabbinical courts have been relying on the Maharashdam's view only in recent years,[26] and that this reliance is highly problematic in view of this opinion's status in the annals of Jewish law. I begin by examining how the Maharashdam's opinion is being used, then attempt to explain why recourse to it by some Israeli rabbinical court panels has been so popular of late. Lastly, I indicate the considerable difficulties that recourse to this opinion involves.

2.1 Reliance on the Maharashdam's opinion

Rabbinical courts that have recourse to this opinion generally quote the end of the responsum:

> And I said to myself that there is no doubt that even those Sages in the Mishnah who said that they compel . . . did not say that they compel him to grant a divorce unless he does not want to grant a divorce at all. But if he wants to grant a divorce, but wants to impose some condition for granting the divorce, as to this, they certainly did not say that they compel him to grant a divorce unconditionally. And whoever compels [the husband] in this manner, I would almost say that he has tripped over the stumbling block of coercion. But until now I have not found a source for this, and in searching the laws of [stipulating] conditions, I found in *Beit Yosef*, EH 143 . . . the following:
>
>> I found written at the end of the book *Haze Hatenufa* that even in the case of one who grants a bill of divorce to his wife with the intent (*al menat*) that she not go to her father's home, the divorce is effective and the condition stands. Yet no one should allow the granting of a divorce on such a condition, for there is no doubt that this condition cannot be fulfilled, as it is impossible that she should not go to her father's home, and the divorce would thus be invalid, and her children *mamzerim* retroactively. If the husband granting the divorce is one of those who was compelled [by the court] to do so, and does not want to grant the divorce except on this condition, we do not listen to him, and he is compelled to grant the divorce without this condition.
>
> I saw and was happy, for from this statement, his intention regarding this has been made clear, for he wrote the word "this" twice, and it was proper

26 The Maharashdam's opinion was considered by the RHC in case 84/1963, 5 *PDR* (1965) 68, 79, but the court did not rule in accordance with it. See R. Lavi's discussion of this ruling, n. 54 below, 648–49.

> for him to make his statement only conditionally and no more than that, but certainly, only regarding this condition, which is almost impossible to fulfill, did he rule that it is possible to compel him to grant a divorce unconditionally, but in the case of another condition, which is easy to fulfill, there is no doubt that compelling him to grant an unconditional divorce contributes to the proliferation of *mamzerim*.[27]

Clearly, according to the Maharashdam, even those who can, by law, be compelled by the court to grant a divorce, can say that they are interested in granting the divorce of their own free will if certain satisfiable conditions are met. In such cases, compelling the husband to grant the divorce produces an invalid divorce, and the children of a woman who remarries on the basis of such a divorce will be deemed *mamzerim*, children born to a woman married to someone other than the father. The Maharashdam admits that he arrived at this view on the basis of his own reasoning, and had difficulty finding a halakhic source for it, other than an argument based on the specific wording of a quotation from the book *Haze Hatenufa* adduced by R. Joseph Caro. Below, I will examine the Maharashdam's remarks, and the source he quotes, but I will first discuss the manner in which this opinion has been used in recent years.

I cannot review all the rabbinical court decisions that invoke the Maharashdam's opinion for the purpose of ruling that the husband has a right to impose conditions for granting a divorce even in cases where the law allows the court to compel him to grant the divorce, but in all of them, the use made of the Maharashdam's view is quite similar. I will begin with the opinion of the panel that first invoked the Maharashdam's view, namely, rabbinical court judges Prover, Goldberg, and Bibi of the Tel-Aviv District Rabbinical Court. This panel handed down two rulings on a similar matter: in both cases, the husband demanded that the authority to adjudicate the property, spousal maintenance (*mezonot*), and child support issues be transferred from the civil courts to the rabbinical.[28] He demanded not only that future litigation on these matters be

27 *Responsa Maharashdam*, EH #41. On the circumstances of the case discussed in this responsum, see below, §2.3.1.

28 First ruling: n. 23 above; second ruling: n. 21 above. In the first case, the court has no qualms about stating that the husband was responsible for the situation that resulted in his being obliged by the court to grant the divorce. The second case involved a separation of nearly twenty years, in the course of which the husband also filed for divorce. See the beginning of the ruling handed down when the case was appealed: RHC, case 5082-64-1 [29.5.2002], http://www.daat.ac.il/daat/psk/psk.asp?id=91. In a later case, the same

conducted by the rabbinical court (which the wife had already agreed to), but also that a new hearing be held by the rabbinical court regarding monetary obligations to the wife already imposed by the civil court. In other words, as a condition for granting the divorce, the husband demanded that the wife commit herself to paying back monies she was awarded by the civil court, should the rabbinical court rule that these monies were awarded to her contrary to Torah law. In both cases, the rabbinical court determined that the demand had to be fulfilled, adding that even in cases where the law allows the court to compel the husband to grant the divorce, the Maharashdam's opinion could be relied on as a basis for ruling that there was no room for such compulsion if the husband stipulates conditions[29] that the woman can easily fulfill.[30]

---

panel, except that R. Goldberg was replaced by R. Attias, based its ruling on the Maharashdam's opinion as a matter of course, and saw no need to make more than a reference to the ruling mentioned in n. 21; see RHC, case 1665-21-1 [3.7.2008], 22 *HaDin Ve'haDayan* (2009), 6–7. This was also a case in which the husband had left his wife for another woman, and the court was persuaded that he should be obliged to divorce his wife, but the husband made the granting of the divorce conditional on his wife's renouncing the rights due her by Israeli law. These rights, in the rabbinical court's opinion, were not due her by Torah law, and consequently it ruled that the husband need not be obliged to grant a divorce. There is a ruling by the same panel (Tel-Aviv District Rabbinical Court, case 7479-21-1 [18.11.2007]; http://www.daat.ac.il/daat/psk/psk.asp?id=334), in which the situation was the reverse: the court obliged the wife to accept a divorce, but after she demanded that the property-related issues be adjudicated by the rabbinical court according to Torah law, whereas the husband demanded civil-law adjudication (in accordance with which the rabbinical court is indeed obligated to rule), and proved that a civil-court hearing on the property issues had already been held, the court withdrew its directive that the wife was obliged to accept a divorce, and determined that the husband was "chaining himself." The panel's arguments for so ruling were similar to those adduced in its other rulings.

29 N. 23 above, 156: "We see from the Maharashdam [that] even in cases where the law is that the husband can be compelled to grant the divorce, he can impose a condition as to the divorce"; "And from the Maharashdam it follows that he can impose any condition" (157).

30 N. 21 above, 181: "The conclusion from the responsum by the Maharashdam is that all those [husbands] who are compelled [by the court to grant a divorce] . . . can impose a condition as to the divorce, **a condition that is easy to fulfill**" (emphasis added). This is indeed the way the Maharashdam formulated his view, quoted above. There is an apparent contradiction

With respect to its willingness to accept the Maharashdam's view, it appears that the court's decisions reflect an increasing stringency that is consistent with the general trend of increasing stringency in the rabbinical courts: whereas in the first ruling it was stated, regarding a husband who imposes conditions, "if they compel him, even ex post facto **there is apprehensiveness about the validity of the divorce**,"[31] in the second case what was previously a matter warranting apprehensiveness has become certainty: "Obligating the husband to grant the divorce must be deferred, and there should not even be imposition of Rabbenu Tam's sanctions,[32] and ex post facto, if they compelled the husband to grant the divorce, **the divorce is annulled**."[33]

A similar approach can be found in the rulings of other rabbinical court judges, even if the Maharashdam is not mentioned explicitly, as, for example, in a Jerusalem District Rabbinical Court case involving a violent husband who had even been convicted of violence.[34] In this case, the Rabbinical High Court determined that the husband could be coerced to grant a divorce, but when the case returned to the district rabbinical court, the latter ruled as follows:

> The husband is willing to grant the divorce, which will be handed to the wife after it has been ensured that his children will be educated in religious institutions and will receive [at least] a minimal religious education, which the court sees as a reasonable request, especially as it

between the Maharashdam's view as stated in the previous note (implying that any condition can be imposed) and as stated here; this has been pointed out by critics of reliance on the Maharashdam's view. See, e.g., R. David Bass, "Imposition of conditions by a husband who has been obliged to grant a divorce" (Hebrew), *Tehumin* 25 (2005), 149, 151–52.

31 N. 23 above, 157, emphasis added.

32 These measures of religious and social ostracism, imposed in order to persuade the recalcitrant husband to grant the divorce, are not considered coercion.

33 N. 21 above, 186, emphasis added.

34 Case 2353-21-1 [20.9.2006], 19 *HaDin Ve'haDayan* (2008), 5. In a previous case, in which a husband made monetary demands of his wife, the rabbinical court in Jerusalem rejected the husband's demand for payment, and rejected the Maharashdam's view as a matter of theoretical law, but in practice was wary of the stricter view, and did not compel the husband to grant the divorce even though it maintained that there was ample basis for doing so. See R. Jacob Eliezrov, "Can someone who is obliged to grant a divorce impose conditions?" (Hebrew), 12 *Shurat Hadin* (2007), 381–83.

> does not appear that the wife would refuse to give her children a religious education. And there is no reason to compel him to grant the divorce.

A different panel from the same rabbinical court ruled as follows:

> In the course of the hearings that were held about the wife's demand that the husband be obliged and even compelled to release her with a divorce, she revealed to us the broad swath of suffering, and continuous abuse and severe violence — especially emotional — perpetrated by the defendant toward the claimant and her children. Indeed, from the beginning of the hearings on this matter, the court reached the clear-cut conclusion that it must separate the two through divorce. Moreover, the husband himself agreed and wanted a divorce, but he imposed several conditions for granting the divorce. Upon scrutiny, the court found that the conditions were decidedly reasonable and unexceptional, and ought not be rejected out of hand.
>
> As a result, we were prevented from issuing a clear and decisive ruling obliging and compelling him to grant the divorce, in light of what the Maharashdam, of blessed memory, said in his responsa, whereby even in severe cases in which it is clear to all that the husband should be compelled to grant his wife a divorce, if the husband is willing to grant the divorce and agrees to do it, but demands [fulfillment of] certain conditions, to which he is entitled by the fundaments of the law, and there is no reason to deny him their fulfillment, we do not compel him to grant the divorce.[35]

And R. Abraham Sheinfeld, Head of the Tel-Aviv District Rabbinical Court, ruled as follows:

> When a violent husband is willing to be divorced, but requests that, in arranging for the divorce, he receive what he is entitled to by law — in such a case, even if it is proven that the husband is violent and obliged to grant the divorce, we cannot obligate him to do so without also arranging the monetary matters. Because in such a situation, the wife can save herself by way of the monetary arrangements, and there is no longer any danger.[36]

35 Case 7178-25-2 [31.8.2004], 8 *HaDin Ve'haDayan* (2005), 6–7.

36 R. Abraham Sheinfeld, "Violence as grounds for divorce" (Hebrew), 15 *Shurat Hadin* (2009), 319. R. Sheinfeld does not explicitly mention the Maharashdam's view, but it serves as the central source in the three rulings he mentions. By contrast, he claims that his opinion follows from a responsum by the Rosh (*Responsa Rosh*, 43:3) and from the RHC ruling published in 12 *PDR* (1980), 12. But this ruling appears to indicate both that the court mandates that every effort be made to save a woman who is endangered by her husband (14), and that the court recommends restrictive readings of the Rosh's responsum (10–14), and states that it is possible

It appears that this position penetrated the Rabbinical High Court as well, though it does not seem to have been uniformly adopted. In 2002, the Rabbinical High Court determined that it was clear that the [Petach Tikva] District Rabbinical Court's strict position should not be accepted. The District Rabbinical Court had ruled that a husband could not be obliged to grant a divorce if he demanded payment for doing so, as the court held that demand to be reasonable, and that if a divorce was arranged without fulfilling the husband's justified demand, it generated "apprehensiveness about an unlawful divorce."[37] But two years earlier, the Rabbinical High Court had already stated, in a majority ruling by judges Bar-Shalom and Nadav (against the opinion of R. Dichovsky), that, in light of the Maharashdam's view, there was reason for apprehensiveness when the husband imposed conditions. In this case, the majority opinion even had doubts as to the validity of a divorce that had already been granted without the conditions having been fulfilled.[38]

It appears that, over time, most Rabbinical High Court judges have shown increased willingness to accept the stringent position that evinces apprehensiveness in light of the Maharashdam's view. This is evident from the appeal and further hearing regarding the Tel-Aviv District Rabbinical Court ruling discussed above.[39] In this case there was disagreement between the judges at both hearings. At the first hearing, the position of Chief Rabbi Bakshi-Doron was unambiguous: "Whoever is obligated to grant a divorce must grant a divorce, even

---

to rely on decisors who disagreed with the Rosh. The Rosh's opinion cannot serve as an earlier source for the opinion of the Maharashdam, and this is demonstrated by the fact that the Maharashdam does not rely on the Rosh; see text below at n. 74.

37 For the ruling of the Petach Tikva District Rabbinical Court and the RHC's response to it, see case 3252-21-1 [14.7.2002], 2 *HaDin Ve'haDayan* (2003), 10–1. The district court relied on R. Prover's ruling, n. 21 above, and openly refused to accept the ruling addressed to it by the RHC.

38 RHC, case 4273-21-1 [18.12.2000]. The ruling is quoted in Bass, n. 30 above, 155. Bass shows that former Chief Rabbi R. Mordechai Eliyahu, and the Rabbi of Jerusalem, R. Shalom Messas, disputed this ruling, following which the RHC changed its stance.

39 Case 5082-64-1, n. 28 above. This is the ruling in the further hearing conducted by an expanded panel of five; it mentions the outcome of the initial appeal heard by a panel of three.

if he has monetary demands, and one should not perpetuate a wife's being 'chained' because of his demands." But R. Tufik claimed that the District Court's ruling was correct, and R. Ben-Shimon maintained that the matter should not be decided, and the case should be returned to the District Court for reconsideration. Because there was no consensus, an expanded panel of judges was convened. R. Sherman concurred with R. Bakshi-Doron, and in a long ruling explained why the District Court ruling, and its reliance on the Maharashdam's view, should not be accepted. By contrast, the three additional judges, Goldberg, Ben-Shimon, and Tufik, supported the idea of returning the case to the District Court to reconsider, as R. Tufik put it, "the wife's possibilities, what amounts she can return to him, if [the court] ultimately rules that she must do so. . . . or they should try to get the sides to accept a compromise whereby the wife pays the husband a one-time amount for his claim." In other words, the court evinced willingness to accept the demands of a husband who conditioned the granting of a divorce on his being paid back some or all of the monies awarded his wife by the civil courts.[40]

40 In another RHC ruling (case 7041-21-1 [11.3.2008]; http://www.daat.ac.il/daat/psk/psk.asp?id=252), R. Menahem Hashai invokes the Maharashdam's view to establish that it is the husband's right to make granting of the divorce contingent on the wife's paying him back compensation monies the civil court had ordered him to pay her for refusing to grant her a divorce. It should be noted that another opinion was also expressed by some RHC judges, led by R. Dichovsky, who maintained that the Maharashdam's view was not to be relied on. This opinion is expressed in two rulings mentioned in n. 54 below, cases 1390 and 3847. But it is apparent that, at least in case 1390, even if R. Dichovsky's opinion was ultimately accepted, some on the panel did not agree with it in its entirely. See also the majority opinions of rabbis Sherman and Izirer in case 1702-21-2 [26.2.2007], unpublished. In their opinion, the husband's appeal of the ruling obligating him to grant a divorce regardless of his property claims should be accepted because "the delay in granting the divorce in this case is a genuine need on the husband's part, because after the court ruled that he also has rights, and given that he has no way of legally ensuring the realization of these rights except [by steps taken] prior to granting the divorce, there is, here, an element of taking the law into his own hands [self-help]. And also from the perspective that one who grants a divorce can, according to the Maharashdam, impose conditions to realize his rights before granting the divorce." The court does not add anything to this statement. In other words, reliance on the Maharashdam's view is

It appears that the broadest and most extreme position on this matter was voiced in a Rabbinical High Court ruling.[41] In 2004, it discussed an appeal by a wife who had asked the local district rabbinical court to obligate her husband to grant her a divorce on the grounds of unfaithfulness and violence. In parallel, she was awarded NIS 2,400 per month in child support in civil court. The district rabbinical court rejected her suit because the husband demanded that the child-support be reduced to NIS 2,000, which he felt was a reasonable request. Relying on the Maharashdam's view, the Rabbinical High Court rejected the wife's appeal, and declared, in the words of R. Izirer:

> Although today it is not customary to arrange conditional divorces, the husband's right to impose a condition has not lapsed, and therefore, given that his original right is to impose a condition, and he imposes it as a precondition for the divorce, the demand is valid by virtue of his right to make the divorce conditional on it. . . .
>
> Let us further make clear that the right to impose a condition does not exist only in monetary matters, but also in the realm of conduct, for instance, [stipulating] that she should not eat certain foods or wear certain clothes. The rabbinical court cannot obligate the wife to accept these demands, but they apply as part of the conditions for the divorce, and are binding, even in cases where the husband has been obligated to grant the divorce or compelled to grant the divorce. All these are conditions that the wife can fulfill, despite the fact that she has no legal obligation vis-à-vis her husband to fulfill them.

This ruling, and especially the last paragraph, caused a public outcry, and it was appealed to the Supreme Court. As a result, a few months later R. Izirer took the unusual step of issuing a clarification of the ruling.[42] In the clarification, he refines and restricts his original determination. Though continuing to rely on the Maharashdam's view, he states that "if the conditions are such that it is clear to the court that the wife cannot fulfill them . . . the husband who has been obligated to

---

already seen as self-evident, requiring no further explanation. We can see here, as in other cases, the increased stringency reflected in R. Sherman's opinion in case 5082-64-1.

41 RHC, case 0027-21-1 [29.08.2004], rabbis Izirer, Tufik, and Ben-Shimon, http://www.daat.ac.il/daat/psk/psk.asp?id=92. For the facts of the case, see Bass, n. 30 above, 157.

42 The clarification, issued on 1.2.2005, was published in 9 *HaDin Ve'haDayan* (2005), 6–7 and online together with the original ruling, see n. 41 above.

grant a divorce or compelled to grant a divorce will not be able to impose such conditions." He explains that his ruling was not properly understood, and asserts:

> It appears that the husband who has been obligated to grant a divorce or compelled to grant a divorce will not be able to impose conditions on the wife's conduct with respect to food and clothing, even where such conditions are justified, such as [the condition] that she not eat foods that are harmful and would make her sick (and unable to care for the children), or that she wear modest clothing.

What, then, is the scope of the Maharashdam's rule? R. Izirer's answer suggests a personal test for each case: "Only the rabbinical court that hears the case can determine, regarding each case, based on its acquaintance with the parties, whether the condition can be satisfied." In the case in question, this is exactly what the court did:

> The court checked the monetary condition [that had been stipulated] and found it to be very reasonable both with regard to the children's needs . . . and with regard to the husband's ability to carry out his commitment. And also, the condition is not imposed for an extensive period (which would make us apprehensive that due to the lengthy period, the wife would forget and breach the condition), but fulfilling it will be a one-time agreement before the divorce, with guarantors, as required, so that there is no apprehensiveness that the condition will not be fulfilled, and the wife will not have to go through annulment of the divorce. Therefore the husband can impose conditions.

Nevertheless, the meaning of this test, as R. David Bass observed,[43] is that in every case, the husband can make the granting of the divorce contingent on various matters, and claim that questions of maintenance, property, or child custody that were already decided in civil court need to be revisited by the rabbinical court. In cases of this sort, the rabbinical court will have no choice but to accept the husband's claim, and perhaps even reach the conclusion that the wife can indeed fulfill his monetary or other demands, and thus cannot be divorced without doing so. The court will have to give serious consideration to the husband's demands, because otherwise it is liable to unlawfully obligate him to grant a divorce, because "the Maharashdam states that whoever acts contrary to his opinion and compels the granting of a

43 N. 30 above, 159.

divorce, and does not attend to the condition, will contribute to the proliferation of *mamzerim* among [the people of] Israel. That is, the divorce is invalid. It is clear, therefore, that this is a rule in halakhic divorce law, though not civil divorce law."[44]

By the latter statement, R. Izirer means that it is not right to assess the husband's claims on their own without also considering the question of whether the husband is obligated to grant the divorce.[45] Even if matters of maintenance, property, and child custody can be settled in accordance with Israeli law in civil court, if they are raised again as conditions for granting the divorce, they must be discussed in the rabbinical court that is adjudicating the granting of the divorce or imposition of the obligation to grant it, because these matters affect the divorce's validity.

2.2 The significance of reliance on the Maharashdam

The reason for the increased reliance on the Maharashdam's opinion in recent years is simple: it serves as a tool that rabbinical courts can use in their struggle with the civil courts to regain the authority they take to have been stolen from them. It is, in effect, a way of forcing women to have their cases adjudicated in accordance with the rabbinical court's halakhic outlook.

According to Israeli law, various matters related to the divorce process, especially the division of property and child custody, can be settled in either the civil courts or the rabbinical. Adjudication takes place in the court where suit is first filed.[46] In the cases discussed here, the wife filed suit before her husband did, and did so in family court, which is considered more sympathetic to women, in most cases awarding them higher maintenance, and being more careful to ensure

44 R. Izirer's decision in case 0027, n. 41 above. R. Izirer claims that R. Joseph Caro, in both *Beit Yosef* and *SA*, EH 143, takes positions that are consistent with the Maharashdam's view, but bases this claim on details of R. Caro's wording, not explicit statements. In fact, R. Caro's view appears to be different, see R. Uriel Lavi, n. 54 below, 652.

45 Contrary to the arguments of R. Bakshi-Doron, text at n. 39 above, and R. Dichovsky, n. 47 below, 157, and the rulings there cited.

46 See text at n. 10 above.

an equitable division of the property.[47] By contrast, adjudication of the divorce itself, including determination that there is a obligation to grant a divorce, or that it is compulsory to do so, is solely within the authority of the rabbinical courts, and civil courts have no jurisdiction.[48]

Examination of court rulings shows that the rabbinical courts generally invoke the Maharashdam's view in cases where the husband has been ordered by the civil courts to make payments to the wife, especially maintenance. In these cases, the husband demands that the wife transfer her claim for maintenance (for the children) from family court to the rabbinical courts, or agree to a new hearing in a rabbinical court, which could change awards made in the civil court judgment. At times, these cases involve a demand that monies previously awarded by the civil court, which the rabbinical court maintains that the wife does not — according to Jewish law — deserve, be repaid. Less common, but no less significant, demands have to do with child custody. In one of the cases discussed above, the rabbinical court ruled that a violent husband who imposes the condition that his children be given religious education cannot be compelled to grant a divorce.[49]

The rabbinical courts' motivation is therefore clear. It was expressed explicitly by R. Izirer: reliance on the Maharashdam's view enables the court to argue that the validity of the divorce is tied to fulfilling the husband's demands, which usually involve accepting the authority of the rabbinical courts and Torah law. If the wife does not consent to these demands, she will not be able to obtain a divorce, because any divorce granted under these circumstances will be deemed invalid, and the court that arranges it will be deemed to contribute to the proliferation of *mamzerim*. In his opinion, this enables the rabbinical courts, and Jewish law, to regain their power and authority.

This move obviously generates uneasiness, especially when it is clear that the husband who demands that adjudication be transferred to the rabbinical courts does not do so because of the halakhic prohibition

47 For data on support payments and the number of cases settled in civil vs. rabbinical courts, see R. Halperin-Kaddari and I. Karo, *Women and Family in Israel: Statistical Bi-annual Report* (Hebrew), (Ramat-Gan: 2009), 87–93. See also S. Dichovsky, "A husband who makes the granting of a divorce contingent on cancellation of his previous obligations" (Hebrew), *Tehumin* 26 (2006), 156–57.

48 See text at n. 2 above.

49 N. 35 above.

against litigation in Gentile courts (*arkhaot shel goyim*) (the civil courts in Israel being perceived as such by the rabbinical courts and most if not all the decisors[50]), but out of economic considerations: the rabbinical court will impose smaller support payments on him than the civil court imposed, or he may recover payments mandated by a civil court ruling. R. Dichovsky describes this uneasiness:

> It appears to me that a husband cannot demand of his wife that their divorce be adjudicated in accordance with Torah law when he himself is not particular about doing so vis-à-vis his relations with others, and whenever it is beneficial to him, he turns to the civil courts. It is not possible to punish the wife by denying her the divorce because she turns to the civil court, when her husband transgresses the law both out of irrepressible lust, and to flout the law. . . .
>
> . . . Going along with the husband's demand is in some ways a desecration of God's name. Many of those who demand adjudication by Torah law do not really seek [to comply with] Torah law, but rather, material benefits. They use the Torah as a source of personal gain [lit., a spade for digging], to advance an obvious interest. This is true of our case too, when the husband cynically embraces Torah law to force his wife to obtain the divorce in a manner that accords with his interests, even when he is obligated to grant the divorce.[51]

The panel of judges that pioneered this recourse to the Maharashdam's view is entirely aware of the husband's motives, but does not consider them a problem:

> Let me add and clarify that, according to what has been explained, since the wife must obey Torah law, she is not considered to be 'chained' (*aguna*), but to be chaining herself; or, according to another innovative ruling by the Maharashdam, because she can easily fulfill the condition, she is not considered to be 'chained,' and therefore it makes no difference whether the husband who demands that the wife transfer all the authority from the civil court to the rabbinical is religious and indeed wants the matter adjudicated according to Torah law, or is secular and wants to exploit adjudication by the rabbinical court for his own benefit, since the reason for obligating a husband to grant a divorce arises from the wife's 'chained' state, and in the case at hand, where we consider the wife to be 'chaining' herself, it makes no difference if the husband's demand follows from a wish to uphold Torah law, or a wish to benefit himself via recourse to the

50 See E. Shochetman, "The halakhic status of the courts in the State of Israel" (Hebrew), *Tehumin* 13 (1992/93), 337.

51 See Dichovsky 2006, n. 47 above, 158–59, and see his remarks quoted near n. 125 below.

rabbinical court. In any case, the reason for the obligation does not exist, for in practice she is not considered to be 'chained,' and therefore the husband's obligation to grant the divorce collapses.[52]

Elsewhere, I showed that when, in cases where the wife files suit in civil court, the rabbinical court casts doubt on the validity of a divorce, its actions are motivated by a desire to adjudicate the matters that were adjudicated by the civil court.[53] This seems to be the situation here too, and in what follows, I will demonstrate that this motivation is disclosed by the fact that there are serious problems in the halakhic process followed by the rabbinical court.

2.3 Difficulties raised by the Maharashdam's position

In addition to the uneasiness just mentioned, the main reason that the Maharashdam's view has not played an important role in rabbinical rulings until recently appears to be the simple fact that reliance on it is problematic. The difficulties have been raised both within the rabbinical courts, by judges who refuse to accept it,[54] and outside

52 21 *PDR* (2005), n. 21 above, 182.

53 See Radzyner 2009, n. 14 above.

54 R. Abraham Sherman, in case 5082-64-1, n. 28 above. Later, however, R. Sherman changed his stance, see n. 40 above; R. Dichovsky in case 1390-21-1 [11.1.2006], 12 *HaDin Ve'haDayan* (2006), 3, and idem 2006, n. 47 above; R. Dichovsky, in case 3847-53-4 [30.10.2007], 19 *HaDin Ve'haDayan* (2008), 4; R. Ariel Yanai, n. 22 above; R. Uriel Lavi (Head of the Safed-Tiberias Rabbinical Court), "Can someone who is obligated to grant a divorce impose conditions on granting the divorce? Clarification of the Maharashdam's method" (Hebrew), in idem, *Ateret Devora* (Tiberias: 2008), 2:647–62.

Thus, e.g., in case 1390, R. Dichovsky rejected the district court's reliance on the Maharashdam's view in not obliging a husband accused of severe acts of violence and rape to grant a divorce because he had 'only' demanded that all matters associated with the divorce that had been adjudicated in civil court be transferred to the rabbinical court. R. Dichovsky sharply criticized such rulings, and termed a demand made by a husband who refuses to grant a divorce a "judgment-day weapon," because it helps the husband continue to avoid granting the divorce and make demands in exchange for granting it. He argued that this move, whereby the court facilitates the recalcitrant husband, was "the result of the rabbinical and civil courts vying for power." He voices the same sentiment in case 3847, where he annulled a district court ruling that was based on the

them.[55] These difficulties are discernible in the Maharashdam's stance in itself, and when it is viewed against the background of various statements by previous decisors, especially the Early Authorities.

2.3.1 *Original context of the Maharashdam's opinion, and its interpretation by contemporary courts*

What is the context of the Maharashdam's ruling? Those who rely on it quote the statement at the end of the responsum (EH #41). The paragraph quoted above[56] appears after the following introduction:

> After I wrote and signed my name to the written and signed ruling above, I constantly wondered whether I would find support for what I had written, namely, that given that the levir wants to grant the levirate release (*halitza*), but with the intention that his brother's widow who is subject to levirate marriage (*yevama*) [to him] not [if released] marry her uncle, who is married to his aunt, if so, it is impossible to compel him grant the levirate release under any circumstances, and I said to myself. . . .

From this passage, which is appended to the responsum (as the first sentence indicates), and the responsum as a whole, it is clear that it was written in answer to a question about a specific case that does not involve divorce at all. The Maharashdam is discussing a case in which a levir was afraid that after granting his brother's widow levirate release, she would marry his aunt's husband; the couple [the aunt and her husband] were married and had children.[57] He therefore demanded that the levirate release be conditional on the widow's undertaking

---

Maharashdam's view. This ruling held that no restrictive orders were to be imposed on a husband who had been obliged by the rabbinical court to grant a divorce, but agreed to grant it voluntarily if his demand for child custody was met. R. Dichovsky showed that the Maharashdam's position is controversial, and that it would be difficult to establish that it could be relied on in the case in question, or similar cases, to enable someone obligated to grant a divorce to make its granting conditional.

55 R. David Bass, n. 30 above; P. Shifman, "Jewish halacha in a changing reality: what delays the *get*-delayed woman?" (Hebrew), 6 *Alei Mishpat* (2007), 27, 39–40.

56 Text at n. 27 above.

57 The inquirer presents two scenarios for such a marriage: the aunt's husband could marry the widow as a second wife (this being legal in the community in question), or divorce his wife and then marry the widow.

the obligation not to marry the levir's aunt's husband. In other words, this was a case of conditional *halitza*, and it had an important goal: preventing the destruction of a family. The Maharashdam considered this element crucial, and at the end of his ruling, before the appended remarks, he stated:

> And especially because they told me that the levir is a decent man, and his sole intention is that his brother's widow not marry her uncle . . . and the intention of her uncle is to divorce his wife, who is the levir's aunt, and marry this young woman. To this I say, because this matter depends on this, that it is proper for her [the widow] to make herself unavailable to this man by every stringent means possible, and the same goes for the husband of his aunt, so as to bring the matter to a satisfactory conclusion, that is not contested or doubted, and inspires confidence so that the levir can grant the levirate release, and we will not need to resort to any sort of compulsion. This is the straight and clear path, in my opinion, so as not to engage in compulsion.

Still, the Maharashdam does not entirely rule out pressuring the levir. He adds an important qualification: "But if the sages of the city find that it is necessary to impose social sanctions on him . . . they should do so only if their intent is to do so for the sake of heaven."

Only further on, as a kind of addendum, but not as a ruling to be followed in the case at hand,[58] does the Maharashdam move on to discuss the case of the husband who has been compelled by the court to grant a divorces, but imposes conditions for doing so. It is at this point that he makes the statement about conditional divorce, quoted above, which Israeli rabbinical courts have increasingly invoked.

Even if we assume, as rabbinical courts that rely on the Maharashdam's view do, that his remarks constitute a halakhic ruling intended for implementation, it is still not clear that they can be read as permitting imposition of monetary conditions that have bearing on the wife's rights. First, the Maharashdam himself insists that the

58 I.e., we must distinguish between what the Maharashdam stated as law intended to be put into practice (*halakha lemaase*) regarding an actual case, and remarks that are purely theoretical. In the responsum in question (EH #41), only the remarks on the case of the levir constitute law intended to be put into practice, not those made in the addendum. On the law/law to be put into practice distinction, the roots of which are very early, see M. Elon, *Jewish Law: History, Sources, Principles*, trans. B. Auerbach and M.J. Sykes (Philadelphia: 1994), 1456–60.

husband cannot impose a condition that is "almost impossible to fulfill," but only a condition that is "easy to fulfill." Is the demand that the wife pay back money or agree to reduced maintenance necessarily easy to fulfill? Rabbinical courts assume that this is the case, but devising tests for ease of fulfillment is very difficult, and there have been cases where the rabbinical court judges disagreed about whether a given condition was easy to fulfill.[59]

But even if the court reaches the conclusion that the condition is easy to fulfill,[60] an additional question arises: did the Maharashdam believe that every readily-fulfilled condition a husband imposes averts his being compelled to grant the divorce, or only conditions related to the divorce itself? This is an important question, because clearly, issues pertaining to child support and custody, for example, have nothing to do with the reasons for or consequences of the divorce. The rabbinical court panels that invoke the Maharashdam's view assume that every readily-fulfilled condition is legitimate. As we saw above, R. Izirer, for instance, stated that "the right to impose a condition does not exist only in monetary matters, but also in the realm of conduct, for instance, [stipulating] that she should not eat certain foods or wear certain clothes. . . . these demands . . . apply as part of the conditions for the divorce, and are binding, even in cases where the husband has been obligated to grant the divorce or compelled to grant the divorce."[61]

59 Bass, n. 30 above, 152, 155–57, 159–61. Clearly, whether a condition is easy to fulfill is subjective. As R. Dichovsky puts it: "Hence one must carefully weigh the condition's significance for the wife, taking the circumstances into account — not everything that is easy for one person is also easy for another" (n. 47 above, 157). And in fact, courts that uphold the Maharashdam's rule note at times that they have examined the wife's capacity to fulfill the condition. E.g., R. Izirer, in a supplement to his ruling (n. 41 above) speaks of the need for a "special determination by the court" on this point for every particular case.

60 In some rulings the court explicitly says that the condition is such, see, e.g., the ruling quoted in the text at n. 52 above.

61 See text above at n. 41. And similarly, the first ruling that invoked the Maharashdam's view asserted: "And from the Maharashdam it follows that he can impose any condition, and if they compel him, even ex post facto there is apprehensiveness about the validity of the divorce"; see Bibi et al., n. 23 above, 157.

Although R. Izirer qualifies this statement somewhat in his clarification,[62] he does not do so with respect to the substance of the condition, but rather, the ease of its fulfillment. It might seem plausible that the Maharashdam is referring to any type of condition, for he says in his responsum, "but if he wants to grant a divorce, but wants to impose some condition for granting the divorce, as to this they certainly did not say that they compel him to grant a divorce unconditionally." But there are difficulties with the assumption that he had in mind any type of condition. First, there is the contextual problem noted above: the concrete case addressed in the responsum has to do with imposing a condition on levirate release (*halitza*), so that the released widow would not marry a man who was already married to the levir's aunt. This condition is closely connected with the act of *halitza*, as it is the *halitza* that creates the possibility of a broken home that the levir seeks to prevent. But can we infer that it is the husband's right (or the levir's) to make the granting of a divorce (or levirate release) conditional on matters that are **not** related to the action he is being compelled to carry out? R. Dichovsky answers in the negative:

> Clearly, the husband cannot seek to impose any condition that he fancies, even if it is unrelated to the divorce, such as matters having to do with maintenance payments for the children. This is not merely a condition that is not related to the divorce, but also a condition that has no merit, for neither we nor the wife have the right to render others (the children) indebted to satisfy the desires of the recalcitrant husband.
>
> The whole matter of imposing conditions is an innovation, and there is nothing to it but this innovation, and why should we extend the innovation to areas unrelated to divorce?[63]

R. Ariel Yanai[64] and most likely also former Chief Rabbi Elijah Bakshi-Doron[65] concur with R. Dichovsky.

62 N. 42 above.

63 Dichovsky 2006, n. 47 above, 157. An additional distinction between the context of the Maharashdam's statements and the case of the husband who conditions the granting of a divorce on monetary concessions on the part of the wife is made by R. Zion Algrabli in Jerusalem District Rabbinical Court, case 3222-25-1 [3.1.2002], http://www.daat.ac.il/daat/psk/psk.asp?id=139.

64 In the ruling cited in n. 20 above, he argued that the Maharashdam's remarks do not entitle the husband to demand money from his wife.

65 5082-64-1, n. 28 above.

An additional consideration mentioned by R. Dichovsky is that of injury to a third party, in this case the children.[66] He argues that clearly, it was not the Maharashdam's intention to enable the husband to impose conditions that could injure a third party. This principle had already been elaborated on in a halakhic opinion by R. Samuel Landsman.[67] After he raises several questions about the plausibility of reliance on the Maharashdam's view, given that it manifestly does not follow from the views of the Early Authorities, as we will see, and that it suffers from a fundamental logical flaw, namely, that it renders compelled divorce virtually impossible,[68] he establishes that even according to the Maharashdam himself, the husband has no right to impose conditions that have bearing on the children:

> It appears that it was obvious to the Maharashdam that there needs to be some connection between the issues, that is, between the granting of the divorce and the matter on which he conditions granting the divorce. For without it, this is like the case of a husband who makes a condition affecting a third party, and not his wife, and then he certainly cannot delay execution of the ruling compelling him to grant the divorce, for what does the other party have to do with his condition? And this is the law if he imposes a condition on his wife that is not related to the divorce, for what does the granting of the divorce have to do with his condition? . . . And in our case too, his demand is not related to the divorce, for the divorce action and the child custody action are two separate suits without any connection. . . .
>
> Furthermore, in our case, where the husband stipulates a condition involving the children, they are considered a third party, for as far as the divorce itself is concerned, she is the litigant, and as far as child custody is concerned, even though she seeks to have them remain in her care, her status is only that of guardian and representative of the children. . . .[69]

2.3.2 *The Maharashdam's opinion and the classic decisors*

No less significant is the difficulty that follows from the innovative nature of the Maharashdam's opinion against the background of the views of the Early Authorities, which the Maharashdam himself

66 Dichovsky 2006, n. 47 above, 157.

67 Samuel Landsman, "Can a husband who is obligated to grant a divorce impose conditions?" (Hebrew), 2 *Divrei Mishpat* (1996), 146.

68 Ibid. R. Landsman tries to resolve this difficulty in various ways, none of which he finds satisfactory.

69 Ibid, 151.

acknowledges after presenting his view.[70] Two points in his statement merit examination. First, he admits that it was not easy to find a source for his opinion, which means that most of the Early Authorities who addressed this issue indeed thought otherwise. Needless to say, had there been an obvious source of this type, the rabbinical court panels who uphold the possibility of imposing conditions for divorce would not have had to resort to adducing the Maharashdam as their primary source, but would have relied on the earlier source.[71] Second, even after he found such a source, the Maharashdam was forced to analyze its language carefully in order to derive his conclusion from it.[72]

Examination of the views of the Early Authorities indeed shows that the Maharashdam's view is highly innovative, and even R. Joseph Caro, in whose *Beit Yosef* he found the source, apparently does not accept it:

(1) The source the Maharashdam relies on is *Responsa Haze Hatenufa* by R. Moses de Brussels, student of R. Asher b. Yehiel, the Rosh, which contains abridged versions of some of the Rosh's responsa.[73] The relevant responsum is the abridged version of the Rosh's responsum 43:12, which indeed discusses whether a husband can impose the condition, "with the intent (*al menat*) that you do not go to your father's home." His answer ends with the words: "But *ab initio*, if he is one of those who are compelled to grant a divorce, we compel him to grant it, and he cannot impose this condition in granting it." The Rosh, unlike his student, uses the word "this" only once, so the Maharashdam's

70 In the text at n. 27 above.

71 But see text below at n. 84 below.

72 His argument is based on the word "this," which appears twice in the sentence (also found in *SA*, EH 143:21): "If the husband granting the divorce is one of those who was compelled [by the court] to do so, and does not want to grant the divorce except on this condition, we do not listen to him, and he is compelled to grant the divorce without this condition." The Maharashdam concludes from this remark that only the condition 'so that you do not go to your father's home' or a condition that is difficult to fulfill, is invalid, but other conditions can be imposed even in cases of compelled divorce.

73 The responsa were published in R. Haim Joseph David Azoulay, *Responsa Haim Shaal* (Jerusalem: 1986), vol. 2, 249ff. The relevant responsum is in §4, p. 250. Next to each answer, R. Moses de Brussels indicated whether it is supported by evidence or is just speculation. Next to our responsum, he wrote "speculation."

linguistic argument is not derived from the Rosh. Moreover, it follows from another responsum by the Rosh[74] that a husband who has been obligated to grant a divorce cannot defer doing so because of monetary demands, "and therefore it is difficult to suppose that his student, whose statements are all based on his teacher's responsa, would write the opposite of what the Rosh said."[75]

(2) Contrary to the Maharashdam's singular view, the claim that, when it is being compelled by the court, the granting of a divorce cannot be conditional, appears in the writings of Early and Later Authorities alike.[76] Examples include the Rashba,[77] the Rashbash,[78] and the Rashbatz.[79] R. Zalman Nehemia Goldberg shows that the Maharashdam's view is also untenable on the basis of the *Tosafot*.[80]

(3) The responsum by the Rashba is cited by R. Joseph Caro in *Bedek Habayit*, a supplement to the *Beit Yosef*. *Haze Hatenufa*, on which the Maharashdam relies, is thus not the only source R. Joseph Caro adduces, and he also adduces the Rashba's opposed view. R. Caro did not comment on the disagreement between the two sources, which appears to indicate that he did not believe that it was possible to draw from *Haze Hatenufa* the broad inference that the Maharashdam draws from it.

Three additional points are in order. First, even if there is disagreement between the two sources, *Bedek Habayit* is undeniably later than *Beit Yosef*, and it is likely that it reflects R. Caro's final opinion. Second, there is no question about the fact that the Rashba's opinion takes precedence over that expressed in *Haze Hatenufa*, not only because of

74 *Responsa Rosh*, 43:3, discussed in Lavi, n. 54 above, 655–56.

75 Lavi, ibid., 648.

76 These sources are discussed in Lavi, 650–55. See also Bass, n. 30 above, 149–51. The ruling cited in n. 63 above also notes that various Early and Later Authorities, as well as Israeli rabbinical courts, have ruled that a husband who has been obligated to grant a divorce cannot make it conditional, and hence recommend that the Maharashdam's view be interpreted restrictively.

77 *Responsa Rashba*, 4:256. Although the Rashba speaks of a specific condition, it is precisely the condition that the Maharashdam addresses in the case he is ruling on, and allows. See also Lavi, n. 54 above, 650–51.

78 *Responsa Rashbash*, #383, §1.

79 *Responsa Tashbetz, Hut Hameshulash*, #6.

80 Case 5082, n. 28 above. The reference is to *Tosafot*, bKetubot 77a s.v. *kofim*. See also Bass, n. 30 above, 151.

his more authoritative status, but also because of the simple fact that he takes an explicit stand against a husband's imposing conditions, whereas the Maharashdam could derive the conclusion he wanted from the statements in *Haze Hatenufa* only from the specifics of their formulation, and "the Rashba's explicit assertions should not be set aside due to the Maharashdam's argument from specific wordings."[81] Third, it is significant that the Rashba's opinion and R. Caro's remarks in *Bedek Habayit* were not known to the Maharashdam. As R. Yanai puts it, "Apparently, the Maharashdam had not seen R. Caro's *Bedek Habayit*, which was published in 1605, fifteen years after the Maharashdam died, and volume four of *Responsa Rashba* was also published over a hundred years after his death."[82] And R. Lavi asserts:

> Given that the Maharashdam did not cite responsa by the Rashba, the Rosh, and the Rashbash, we can conclude that had he seen them, he would not have inferred the opposite from the responsum in *Haze Hatenufa*, but would have accepted the explicit opinion in the Rashbash's responsum, [namely,] that in cases where the rabbinical authorities issued a directive that [a husband] was to be compelled to grant the divorce, what good would their directive have done if he were able to impose conditions to prevent its execution?[83]

(4) It may be that the rabbinical court panel that pioneered use of the Maharashdam's approach was aware of these difficulties, and therefore cited the opinion of an Early Authority, R. Joseph b. Solomon Colon (Maharik), that might, on the surface, seem to suggest that a husband who is compelled by the court to grant a divorce can impose conditions for doing so.[84] The Maharik addressed the issue of whether a levir can

81 R. Jacob Castro (Maharikash), *Erekh Lehem*, EH 143.

82 Case 9707, n. 20 above.

83 N. 54 above, 652.

84 N. 23 above, 155; n. 21 above, 179. Note that in the first ruling (n. 23 above), there is only a reference to the Maharik's remarks, whereas the second ruling contains a quotation, and the panel concludes that a brother-in-law who is obligated to grant a levirate release (*halitza*) can defer the obligation by imposing monetary conditions. The panel also cites three Later Authorities (two of whom also address coercion to grant a levirate release), from which it is apparently possible to derive the conclusion the panel sought to derive. R. Lavi, n. 54 above, 653–54, and R. Yanai, n. 22 above, address the question of whether it can in fact be inferred from the sources in question that divorce can be made conditional on monetary demands or

make the granting of levirate release (*halitza*) conditional on receiving his deceased brother's monies, which the widow held — unlawfully, in his opinion. The Maharik's view is adduced by the Tel-Aviv District Rabbinical Court panel headed by R. Prover:

> In *Responsa Maharik*, #102, re coercing a levir to grant levirate divorce (*halitza*) [in communities where *halitza* takes precedence over levirate marriage, which they do not allow], he wrote as follows:
>
>> And the law allows that, since the precept of *halitza* takes precedence and he cannot keep the levirate precept ... he certainly must be compelled to grant levirate release so as to render [the widow] permitted [to remarry]. But if she is rich and the levir claims that the assets are in her possession by virtue of her having inherited them from his brother, we cannot exclude him from his brother's inheritance ... and thus it was customary to reach a compromise. And given that by law they can compel him to grant the levirate release so that he does not render her 'chained,' he puts forward a monetary claim, and thus only if the monetary claim is settled do they compel him to grant the levirate release ... for the only thing preventing compulsion is the monetary claim.
>
> We can see from the Maharik's remarks that even though the levir has an obligation to release his widowed sister-in-law so as not to 'chain' her [and there are no other mutual obligations], nevertheless, if he has a monetary claim, this claim defers [fulfillment of] the obligation.[85]

The rabbinical court's opinion does not cite the Maharik's responsum in full, but only the part conducive to its own argument. Examination of the entire responsum reveals that it does not appear to substantiate the claim that it precedes the Maharashdam in suggesting that a husband has the option of imposing conditions vis-à-vis divorce.[86] It is a lengthy responsum that addresses two situations, as the Maharik states at the outset: "It is proper to distinguish the case where the levir is married to another woman from that where he is not married to another woman; as to the latter case, the later decisors had a disagreement." If the levir is married, the 'ban of Rabbenu Gershom' prevents

demands to transfer the hearings on the matter to the rabbinical court. Even if these opinions are accepted, however, they are definitely minority views, even among the Later Authorities, as R. Lavi shows.

85 21 *PDR*, n. 21 above, 179.

86 My remarks here are based on R. Lavi's analysis, n. 54 above, 656–57.

him from contracting a levirate marriage and obligates him to grant a levirate release (*halitza*). In this case, his claims and conditions are not to be heeded: "And if so, it is proper for this levir to be banished and compelled by all types of coercive measures to grant the levirate release." In other words, it is clear that a purely monetary claim does not prevent compelled *halitza*. Yet the rabbinical court panel presents the Maharik's opinion very differently.

The quotation adduced by the panel is from the discussion of the second situation, viz., where the levir is not married. The Maharik states that in this case it is necessary to take into account the view that levirate marriage is possible, which will in any event give the levir possession of the assets he is demanding from the widow, and in any event preclude his being compelled to grant the levirate release. The Maharik bases this ruling on ordinances and customary practices of Ashkenaz (Franco-Germany) documented in the writings of Rabbenu Peretz, whom he quotes. They establish that in such a case, a compromise with the widow should be sought, and in the absence of compromise, the levir cannot be compelled to grant the levirate release. In other words, this is a specific ordinance, and it is doubtful whether it can be applied to other cases; it is not a general ruling, as is the Maharashdam's view (at least according to those rabbinical courts that invoke it), to the effect that monetary conditions for granting a divorce or levirate release can be imposed.

Furthermore, the Maharik begins his discussion of the case of the unmarried levir as follows:

> But if he is not married, if the widow (*yevama*) is in possession of her [deceased] husband's assets, I do not think we can compel him, except in the way indicated by R. Isaac of Corbeil in his *Sefer Mitzvot Katan*, [viz.,] to impose a ban and to isolate him until he grants the levirate release . . . because even according to those who say that we do not compel levirate release, as evidenced by the well-known fact that Rabbenu Tam often stated and forbade compelling the husband to grant a divorce on the grounds that she finds him loathsome (*meis alai*), and wrote that all who act on the basis of this claim are entirely in error and contribute to the proliferation of *mamzerim* among Israel — despite this, he wrote that various types of pressure can be exerted on him.

In other words, social isolation measures (*harhakot derabeinu tam*) can be levied against an unmarried levir who conditions the granting of levirate release on receiving money. If the Maharik believed that the Maharashdam's view was correct, why should the levir be liable to social sanctions for making *halitza* subject to a condition that the widow can easily fulfill, namely, paying him monies that she might even be legally obligated to return to him?

We can conclude that the Maharashdam's view certainly does not represent the predominant opinion of the decisors over the centuries, and it is highly doubtful whether there is even a single decisor from the period of the Early Authorities who upheld this approach. By contrast, there are many who disagreed with it. Moreover, examination of the view itself casts doubt on whether it is a satisfactory basis for the determination that a husband who can be compelled to grant a divorce can make it contingent on various monetary and procedural conditions.

It is no coincidence that in the past, rabbinical courts avoided this approach. We can assume that the growing recourse to it in recent years is due to the rabbinical courts' desire to establish a halakhic basis, however strained, for the notion that they can compel women to have the matters ancillary to divorce adjudicated in accordance with Torah law. Here again, the halakha serves as a tool for the rabbinical courts' efforts to expand their authority within the state's judicial system.

3 Recourse to civil court as grounds for divorce

The struggle over jurisdiction has intensified in recent years. One consequence of this escalation is that should a wife take the entirely legal step of approaching a civil rather a rabbinical court regarding a matter having to do with her rights in a dispute, this will result in her being deemed obligated to be divorced.

In three rulings issued in 2009 by a panel in Tel-Aviv that included R. Dov Domb, R. Aviran Halevi, and a third judge, it was determined that the very fact of a wife's having filed a maintenance- or property-related claim in family court rather than in rabbinical court is a self-standing ground for divorce, to wit, 'transgressing religious precepts' (*overet al dat*),[87] for which the wife is obliged to be divorced. Note,

87 In other words, causing her husband to transgress, see n. 95 below. See also B. Schereschewsky, *Family Law in Israel* (Hebrew), (Jerusalem: 1993), 314–17.

however, that in all these cases, the court held that additional grounds for divorce were present.[88]

The first case[89] involved a divorce suit by the husband, while the wife sought matrimonial reconciliation (*shlom bayit*). In parallel to her request for matrimonial reconciliation in rabbinical court, the wife turned to family court, seeking dissolution of partnership in the apartment, which, according to what is stated in the ruling, the husband also desired. It appears that the husband filed his suit for divorce in rabbinical court only after the wife approached the civil court. The rabbinical court mentions five grounds that support the husband's wish to have the court obligate his wife to be divorced, including:

> (b) The wife is definitely loathsome (*meusa*) to the husband, and there is confirmed cause, due to her conduct, and the divorce proceedings and dissolution of partnership that she initiated against him in civil court suffice. Add to this her complaints to the police and so on, as detailed in the file. According to him, the wife does not want to live with him as a spouse. And just as a husband must be obligated to grant a divorce on grounds of loathsomeness to her (*meis alai*) with confirmed cause, so must the wife be obligated, and the husband must certainly be exempted from the obligation to pay the wife maintenance . . . or be allowed to marry another woman, for Rabbenu Gershom did not issue his enactment to give her more power than him. Here it is edifying to cite the *Beit Yaakov*, EH #77: "Since she demands money that is not due her, and so on. He can divorce her against her will, for Rabbenu Gershom did not issue his ban with regard to such a case," and so on.
>
> (c) And not only that. Due to the very fact that she filed a claim elsewhere than in rabbinical court, she is to be regarded as transgressing religious precepts. Regarding the woman who refuses to have her matter adjudicated by Torah law, which is referred to as 'transgressing religious precepts,' see *Responsa Yabia Omer*, vol. 7, EH #3 and its many citations. And although some recent authorities disagree, the law is not in accordance with their view, and their opinion does not seem reasonable, and it is rejected. And although we refrain from discussing this, because we do not want to provide an opportunity for every husband and wife to cast aspersions on their spouse when their intention is insincere, in the case at hand

88 In another case, a rabbinical court ruled that the family court ruling regarding maintenance was liable to prevent settlement of the divorce, due to apprehensiveness that the husband's agreement to a divorce was obtained by obliging him to pay the maintenance imposed on him by the civil court. See Rehovot District Rabbinical Court, case 2693-21-1 [30.9.2009].

89 Tel-Aviv District Rabbinical Court, case 6548-21-1 [2.2.2009], 23 *HaDin Ve'haDayan* (2010), 7.

the situation is the very opposite. The wife holds on to Torah law just fractionally, having exhausted the possibilities offered by the civil courts. And this is not to be done.

Most of my analysis will focus on the second argument (c), which is repeated almost word for word in the other two rulings, but the first argument also merits consideration.

3.1 Is a wife who files suit in civil court deemed 'rebellious'?

According to the rabbinical court, turning to the civil court and to law-enforcement agencies renders the wife "definitely loathsome to the husband, and there is confirmed cause," and she can therefore be obligated to be divorced against her will. The claim that turning to the civil courts can be adduced as proof of a wife's loathsomeness to her husband has support in Jewish law, and there have been other rulings to that effect.[90] But the last part of that paragraph is highly problematic. To prove that the wife's turning to the civil courts generates the obligation to be divorced, the rabbinical court brings a truncated quotation from R. Jacob Lorberbaum of Lissa's *Beit Yaakov*. The problem is that examination of the full quotation in its proper context paints a more complex picture. R. Lorberbaum discusses the divorce of a 'classic' rebellious wife (*moredet*), that is, a wife who refuses to have sexual relations with her husband. He contends that, because of the ban of Rabbenu Gershom, which prohibits divorcing one's wife against her will, if the wife is willing to be divorced of her own volition provided she receives the sums specified in her marriage contract (*ketuba*) — and this is a case of divorce before twelve months have elapsed since the 'rebelliousness' (after which, according to the Talmud, the 'rebellious wife' loses her rights under the *ketuba*) — "he is forbidden to violate Rabbenu Gershom's ban and must pay the sums specified in the *ketuba* so that she can be willingly divorced."[91] By contrast, there is no need to pay the sums specified in the *ketuba* after twelve months, despite Rabbenu Gershom's ban:

90 See, e.g., Netanya District Rabbinical Court, case 3680-21-3 [4.5.2008], http://www.daat.ac.il/daat/psk/psk.asp?id=313, and the sources cited there.

91 *Beit Yaakov*, #77, §2 (Jerusalem: 2009, 16).

> Even if she is willing to be divorced if he pays the sums specified in the *ketuba*, he can in any case divorce her against her will, since she demands money that is not due her by law and denies him sexual intercourse. He can divorce her against her will, for Rabbenu Gershom did not issue his ban with regard to such a case, so that he would have to give her money that is not due her.

Let us set aside the fact that the wife turned to the civil courts seeking a dissolution of partnership on the basis of a divorce agreement to which the husband was also a party and in the execution of which he was interested, and that it is thus not at all clear that the money in question was not due her. The more difficult problem is the omission of an important phrase, and its replacement with the "and so on": "and denies him sexual intercourse." Clearly, in the original text, the wife's transgression is not that she makes unlawful monetary demands, but that she rebels in earnest, denying her husband sexual intercourse and also demanding that he pay her monies not due her if he wants to divorce her. It is difficult to say that this case is similar to the present case, in which the wife seeks matrimonial reconciliation, and it is the husband who does not want to remain married (the ruling even accepts her claim that the husband has relationships with other women). It appears that the court has omitted these words in an attempt to buttress its claim that the husband "can divorce her against her will" merely because she filed suit in civil court.

Furthermore, scrutiny of the context of the passage from the *Beit Yaakov* leads to the conclusion that it speaks of a wife who has already been deemed 'rebellious,' not a wife who became such by filing her claim in civil court. This point was made by Tel-Aviv Rabbinical Court judge, R. Zvi Ben-Yaakov:

> The Beit Yaakov [R. Lorberbaum] does not define as 'rebellious' a wife who does not wish to accept a divorce unless [her husband] gives her monies that are not due her. The Beit Yaakov speaks of a situation in which a wife has been declared 'rebellious' by the court in complete accordance with the law, and forfeited [the sums specified in] her *ketuba* for being rebellious, and after forfeiting her *ketuba*, she put forward a monetary claim that is not due her by law ([the sums specified in] her *ketuba*), and is willing to be divorced on condition this monetary claim [is paid]. And the question before the court is whether to allow the husband to marry another woman despite [Rabbenu Gershom's] ban, or, since there is a way of circumventing [i.e., avoiding breach of] the ban by having the wife be willingly divorced and paying her the [sums specified in her] *ketuba* to which she is not entitled by law, he should not be allowed to marry another

woman in addition to his wife. And to this, the Beit Yaakov answers, adducing R. Moses Isserles' opinion, that, in view of the fact that she demands monies that are not due her by law — with respect to such cases, Rabbenu Gershom did not issue his ban on marrying another woman in addition to one's wife, and there is no need to circumvent the ban, because the ban was not enacted with regard to a case such as this.[92]

Beit Yaakov is adduced by R. Aviran Halevi in the same way it is adduced in the ruling under discussion, namely, Tel-Aviv District Rabbinical Court, case 6548, in another ruling,[93] where it is quoted at the end of the paragraph entitled "The wife transgresses religious precepts," a definition to which we now turn.

3.2 Does a wife who files suit in civil court 'transgress religious precepts'?

Let us examine the rabbinical court's claim that by the very act of filing a property claim in civil court (which, in the opinion of the rabbinical court judges, violates the prohibition against recourse to Gentile courts),[94] a wife is deemed to 'transgress religious precepts,'[95] and as

92 R. Zvi Ben-Yaakov, *Mishpatekha Leyaakov*, 3:517–18. R. Ben-Yaakov speaks of Rabbenu Gershom's ban as a ban on taking a second wife, presumably because rabbinical courts in Israel prefer, in general, to grant permission to marry rather than to compel a wife to accept a divorce, but it is clear from the discussion in *Beit Yaakov* that the ban's intent is to prevent wives from being divorced against their will. Similar statements appear in a ruling by rabbis Eliezer Goldshmidt and Saul Israeli, see RHC, Appeal 1966/6, 6 *PDR* (1967), 325, 339–40, 352.

93 R. Aviran Halevi, "Obligating a wife to be divorced because of her conduct" (Hebrew), *Shaarei Tzedek* 10 (2010), 365–68. The ruling in question appears to have been issued by the Tel-Aviv District Rabbinical Court on 26.5.2009. The case involved a claim for maintenance and property that had been filed by the wife in civil court, following which the husband filed for divorce in rabbinical court (this is explicitly stated in the ruling on p. 365). R. Halevi concludes (368) by saying that if need be, they will use Rabbenu Tam's social sanctions, or alternatively, the sanctions listed in the *Rabbinical Courts Law (Enforcement of Divorce Judgments), 5755–1995*, "and additional means of enforcement."

94 See text at n. 50 above.

95 Post-talmudic halakha distinguishes between a transgressor of 'Jewish religious precepts' (*dat yehudit*), which refers to a woman who does not conduct herself in line with suitable norms of modesty, and a transgressor

such, she is obligated to be divorced (and to forfeit [the sums specified in] her *ketuba*). R. Halevi, with the approval of R. Domb, made very similar statements in other rulings as well.[96] One case[97] involved a long-lasting conflict between the spouses, in the course of which the wife filed suit for maintenance in civil court, and **two weeks later** "the husband filed a divorce suit in rabbinical court and attached to it all that was involved, that is, division of property, dissolution of partnership in the apartment, and maintenance." About a month later, the woman filed a claim in rabbinical court for "marital reconciliation," and sought "an injunction for the right to stay in the marital residence" (*mador spetzifi*).[98] Here too, R. Halevi notes five justifications for obligating the wife to be divorced, including:

> (c) The wife transgresses religious precepts
> By the very fact of her monetary claims filed in a non-rabbinical court, the wife is regarded as transgressing religious precepts. On a wife who refuses to accept Torah adjudication, who is therefore said to 'transgress religious

---

of 'the religion of Moses' (*dat moshe*), that is, a wife who causes her husband to violate a prohibition (see *SA*, EH 115:1, 4). Apparently, the reference here is to transgression of 'the religion of Moses' (although some regard women who refuse to submit to Torah law as transgressing 'Jewish religious precepts,' see R. Abraham Shapira, *Minhat Avraham*, 3:10–12). However, it is not clear that this is the original meaning of the term 'religion of Moses' in this context. See D. Frimer, "Grounds for Divorce due to Immoral Behavior (Other than Adultery) according to Jewish Law" (Hebrew), (PhD dissertation, Hebrew University of Jerusalem, 1980), 8–15.

96 Tel-Aviv District Rabbinical Court, case 8801-21-1 [24.6.2009], http://www.daat.ac.il/daat/psk/psk.asp?id=403; and the ruling mentioned in n. 93 above.

97 Case 8801.

98 "Right to stay in the marital residence" is a relief granted in rabbinical courts, in response to a request filed by the wife, generally at the same time as a marital reconciliation claim. Its essence is that the court declares the wife entitled to live in the couple's shared apartment to create an opportunity for reconciliation. Obviously, if the court grants this relief, it denies the husband's petition to dissolve the partnership in the apartment. In the case at hand, the court indeed maintained that the wife's request was submitted in bad faith, since she did not truly seek marital reconciliation, but only to increase her bargaining power in the divorce process.

> precepts,' see *Otzar Haposkim*, vol. 1, §10:10 (pp. 80–81)[99] and *Yabia Omer*, vol. 7, EH #3, and the sources cited there. We must be brief. And although we refrain from discussing this, because we do not want to provide an opportunity for every husband to cast aspersions on his spouse and ally, and every wife to cast aspersions on her husband, the hero of her youth, when his or her intention is insincere, in the case at hand the situation is the very opposite. The wife holds on to Torah law just fractionally. In the rabbinical court, she asks for "marital reconciliation" and "right to stay in the marital residence," but on the other hand, in actual fact, she concurrently sets forth her main claims, that is, for maintenance for herself and her daughter, in civil court. And this is not to be done. Therefore we must insist on the fundamental principles of the law, and render the determination that they must be divorced because she 'transgresses religious precepts.'

We can see that the above remarks are very similar to those made in the ruling handed down in the previous case discussed, 6548. R. Halevi notes that the letter of the law (*shurat hadin*) is clear (in case 6548[100] he adds: "and although some recent authorities disagree, the law is not in accordance with their view, and their opinion does not seem reasonable, and can be dismissed"): a monetary claim filed somewhere other than the rabbinical court renders the wife one who 'transgresses religious precepts.' The ruling goes on to say that rabbinical courts ordinarily do not rule in accordance with the letter of the law when it is clear that the husband's intentions are not honest. But in the cases at hand (6548 and 8801), precisely because the wife turned to the rabbinical court with a claim for marital reconciliation, though her claim for maintenance and division of property was filed in civil court, it was necessary to revert to the strict law and declare that there were grounds for determining that the wife had 'transgressed religious precepts,' obligating her to be divorced.

One can understand the judge's anger that the wife prefers to have some of her claims adjudicated in civil court, relegating to the rabbinical court only claims over which it has exclusive jurisdiction. There is no doubt that this anger, and the judge's belief that all of the wife's claims should have been adjudicated by the rabbinical court, had an impact on

99 This reference is unclear, because the references to §10:10 and to pp. 80–81 are both incorrect. The author apparently intended to refer to §15 of *Otzar Haposkim*, 1:82–3, which discusses the case of a wife who refuses to accept Torah law.

100 N. 89 above.

his ruling.[101] Indeed, examination of the three rulings in question reveals that in each case it was the court that took the initiative to declare the wife to have 'transgressed religious precepts' — the husband did not invoke this ground for divorce of his own initiative.[102] Moreover, all three rulings show that the husband filed for divorce in rabbinical court **only after** the wife filed suit in civil court, and it is very likely that this was in response to those suits.[103] But it is important to keep in mind that splitting claims is commonplace on the part of husbands and wives alike, and until the three cases in question, it never transpired that a husband or wife was deemed to 'transgress religious precepts' for doing so.[104]

Is there a halakhic basis for the determination that according to the letter of the law, suing in civil court indeed constitutes 'transgressing religious precepts'? The minority opinion in case 8801[105] thought otherwise. R. Isaac Zar argued:

> As to obligating the wife to be divorced because she went to the civil court system, and thus 'transgressed religious precepts' — this is certainly very serious, but it does not suffice to oblige her to be divorced because of it, and it does not constitute 'transgression of religious precepts.' For I dwell among my people, and [I know that] if it did, "you would leave no daughter to our forefather Abraham."[106] Women who do so, do it because they believe that the civil court will award them higher maintenance. And therefore she has not forfeited the right to file suit in rabbinical court as well, especially if she is not causing him to fail [to keep the precepts], and he too does not keep the Torah and its precepts.

101 See R. Halevi's fourth argument in case 8801, in which he explains why, from both the halakhic perspective and the legal, the rabbinical court must have authority, in the case of a petition for 'marital reconciliation,' to adjudicate all the wife's claims, even if the law allows her to split them.

102 As is the case in many rulings that retroactively annul divorces; see Radzyner 2009, n. 14 above, 163. As we will see, it is problematic for the husband to make this claim when he himself utilizes the civil courts.

103 N. 93 above and text at n. 97 above.

104 See, e.g., Tel-Aviv District Rabbinical Court, case 7270-21-1 [20.2.2005], http://www.daat.ac.il/daat/psk/psk.asp?id=137. R. Halevi was on the panel, and concurred with R. Moses Koller's ruling. The husband had split his claim between the rabbinical and civil courts, and the wife argued that the rabbinical court suit was brought in bad faith. The court rejected this claim, and justified the husband's conduct, arguing that it is not possible to prevent claim-splitting.

105 N. 96 above.

106 See text at n. 113 below.

First, it appears that R. Zar realizes that the court's position is highly innovative: deeming a wife who sues in civil court to be 'transgressing religious precepts' would make that designation applicable to most women in Israel who file claims against their husbands, an egregious outcome.[107] Indeed, to the best of my knowledge, it has not been applied by the rabbinical courts thus far to women who filed property or maintenance suits in civil court.

R. Zar makes two arguments to counter the claims of his colleagues on the panel regarding the rubric 'transgresses the religion of Moses,' and it appears that the letter of the law supports his view:

(1) "Women who do so, do it because they believe that the civil court will award them higher maintenance. . . . especially if she is not causing him to fail [to keep the precepts]:" R. Zar's point seems to be that the wife did not go to the civil system to suborn her husband to violate a prohibition (presumably, the prohibition against recourse to Gentile courts (*arkhaot shel goyim*), though it is by no means clear that the wife's having filed suit in civil court indeed suborns her husband[108]), but because she believed (and rightly so)[109] that the civil court would award her higher maintenance payments. Over forty years ago, R. Moses Feinstein, the leading American decisor, remarked in a similar vein:

> And what you wrote, that a woman who refuses to appear before the rabbinical court transgresses the law — though several recent authorities mention such a rule, this is not correct at all. This is not the case of transgressing the law that is mentioned in the Gemara, where she causes him to violate a prohibition. And especially since in the eyes of the public this is not considered to be a great sin in our day . . . and one should not be concerned about this at all.[110]

107 Many fewer suits for child custody, maintenance, and property matters, over which rabbinical and civil courts have parallel jurisdiction, are filed in the former than in the latter; see Halperin-Kaddari and Karo, n. 47 above, 81–93.

108 One who is sued in civil court, and thus forced to litigate there against his will, does not, so it seems, commit a transgression. See, e.g., the view of R. Ovadia Yosef, on which R. Halevi relies in his ruling, in *Responsa Yehave Daat*, 4:65, at the end s.v. *gam halom*.

109 Halperin-Kaddari and Karo, n. 47 above, 88.

110 *Responsa Igrot Moshe*, EH 3:29. The case discussed by R. Feinstein is much more serious than those we are discussing, because it deals with a wife who fled her home and for six years refused to litigate her husband's suit for divorce. In the cases we are discussing here, the wife does not reject the rabbinical court's authority to adjudicate the divorce, but merely seeks to have the monetary claims ancillary to the divorce adjudicated in civil court.

Indeed, the straightforward definition of 'transgresses the religion of Moses' is a wife who deliberately causes her husband to violate a prohibition, knowing that the thing is prohibited.[111] The woman's intentions and motive are important, and both Early Authorities and Later Authorities assigned them great weight with respect to declaring that a wife 'transgresses religious precepts.'[112] This is why R. Zar ascribes importance to the wife's reason for filing suit in civil court (her belief that the civil court will award higher sums than the rabbinical court), which is undoubtedly the reason for most of the civil court filings in matters ancillary to divorce.

Moreover, R. Feinstein's remarks indicate that we must take the prevailing mores into account, and today, filing suit in civil court is not perceived by the public as a great sin. Indeed, in bKetubot 72b, the Babylonian Talmud states that if we adopt R. Johanan's stance regarding the rubric 'transgresses Jewish religious precepts' (generally interpreted to mean 'behaves immodestly'), a wife would be categorized as such even for not covering her head in her own courtyard! The Talmud decrees that this is a problematic expansion of the concept, because most women do not cover their heads in their own courtyard, and were it adopted, "you would leave no daughter to our forefather Abraham."[113] In other words, customary practice is significant vis-à-vis establishing the existence of this ground for divorce. In many halakhic sources and court rulings, we find that a court must consider social norms when seeking to declare that a woman 'transgresses religious precepts,' even in cases where she transgresses important commandments.[114] As R. Dichovsky puts it:

> The husband cannot claim that it is his wife who transgresses religious precepts. For example, if she goes out with her head bare or with her arms uncovered where her habit, and that of the women in her area, is to go bareheaded and with uncovered arms. If we do not say so, every husband

111 See Schereschewsky, n. 87 above, 315; Frimer, n. 95 above, 36–7.

112 See, e.g., *Rema* and *Beit Shmuel*, EH 115:4.

113 See *Hidushei Haritba*, bKetubot 72b.

114 For sources, see Frimer, n. 95 above, 230–51. The concept was recently defined by the Haifa District Rabbinical Court, case 5922-21-1 [6.7.2008], http://www.daat.ac.il/daat/psk/psk.asp?id=292, which stated that the wife's permissive conduct must be assessed against the accepted norms of the secular society within which she lives, and thus she cannot be deemed to 'transgress religious precepts.'

> can become 'righteous' at an opportune moment, and make his wife, who conducts herself in accordance with the social norms that they both adhere to, into one who transgresses religious precepts.[115]

R. Feinstein was not the first to mention the impact of the norm of litigating in civil courts on the issues discussed here. Over a hundred years ago, the halakhic authority R. Eliezer Chaim Deutsch of Paksh, Hungary, pointed it out. He argued that it was wrong to say that a wife who refused adjudication by Torah law 'transgresses religious precepts,' among other reasons, because "it is known that nowadays there are many people who shirk Torah law and already construe that as normal, hence we cannot, at the present time, rule that one who shirks Torah law thereby falls under [the rubric] 'transgresses religious precepts.'"[116]

Later, R. Isser Judah Unterman, rabbi of Tel-Aviv and then Ashkenazic Chief Rabbi of Israel,[117] as well as other decisors,[118] reiterated this idea. Even R. Ovadia Yosef, whose opinion in *Yabia Omer* serves as the main source in R. Halevi's three rulings, recognizes the force of social mores with respect to the rubric 'transgresses the religion of Moses.'[119] Indeed, he states elsewhere that it is not a problem for a rabbinical court to undertake adjudication of a claim previously rejected in civil-court litigation, because "nowadays not everyone knows the law, and they think that the law prohibiting [Gentile] adjudication does not apply to the secular courts, because [the judges] are Jews, and 'the law of the land is the law,' and only a few outstanding individuals know the truth that adjudication in the civil courts is tantamount to recourse to Gentile courts."[120]

(2) "And he too does not keep the Torah and its precepts." R. Zar is arguing that because the husband is not precept-observant, he is precluded from claiming (and in the case under discussion, the court is precluded from making this claim for him) that by not observing the prohibition against recourse to Gentile courts, his wife is causing him to fail [to keep the precepts]. As in the ruling in case 6548,[121] it is also

115 Case 1390, n. 54 above.

116 *Responsa Pri Hasade*, 3:20. R. Deutch is quoted approvingly by R. Isaac Silberberg, *Atzei Zayit*, 2:69.

117 *Responsa Shevet Miyehuda* (Jerusalem: 1993), 2:240–41.

118 See R. Menahem Silber, *Responsa Moznei Tzedek*, vol. 3, EH #2, esp. 228–29.

119 R. Ovadia Yosef, *Responsa Yabia Omer*, vol. 3, EH #21.

120 *Responsa Yabia Omer*, vol. 7, HM #5, discussed below near n. 127.

121 N. 89 above.

apparent that the husband did not object to approaching the civil court to certify the divorce agreement. It is hard to believe that someone concerned about violating the prohibition against recourse to non-rabbinical courts would have his agreement certified in civil court when he could do so in rabbinical court.[122]

A basic principle, derived from dozens of sources, including Early Authorities, Later Authorities, and rabbinical court rulings,[123] is that a husband is precluded from claiming that his wife 'transgresses religious precepts' when he himself carries out similar acts, or when there is no reason to assume that he perceives the wife's actions as transgressions. Some of these decisors spoke harshly of this move on the husband's part, when, in their opinion, he made the claim only as a ploy to facilitate his divorce. For example, R. Ovadia Yosef, the source adduced by R. Halevi, made the following comments apropos a husband's demand that his wife wear modest clothing, a demand the court found insincere:

> If the husband's claim was not made sincerely and in good faith, and it is merely a pretext whereby he wishes indirectly to be rid of his wife, against her will and without [paying her the sums specified in] the *ketuba*, his words should not be heeded. . . . Otherwise every secular man, married to a secular woman, who wants to live with another woman, will make such claims and cast aspersions on his wife in order to divorce her against her will and without her *ketuba*, and she will not be able to meet his demands without being ridiculed by their friends. And he will thereby achieve his intent to divorce her without her *ketuba* and against her will. And we would be helping transgressors betray the wife of their youth and follow the capricious dictates of their hearts and their eyes.[124]

It is clear, in fact, that a husband who does not observe the Sabbath cannot seek to divorce his wife on the grounds that she desecrates the

122 On the halakhic problematics of having agreements certified in civil court, see Yigal Monisar, *The Law and Israel* (Hebrew), (Petach-Tikva: 2008), 255–72.

123 See, e.g. Schereschewsky, n. 87 above, 315; Frimer, n. 95 above, 233; Raphael Etzion, "Rabbinical Laws with Rationales no Longer Germane in the Rulings of Rabbis of Recent Generations" (Hebrew), (PhD dissertation, Bar-Ilan University, 2008), 284–85; *Mishpatekha Leyaakov*, n. 92 above, 3:44. See also R. Israel Grossman, "A ruling regarding a woman who transgresses religious precepts" (Hebrew), *Moriah* 8 (1979), 53; R. Isaac Shachor, "A woman who transgresses the religion of Moses" (Hebrew), in Dov Shahor (ed.), *Zekher Avot* (Hebrew), (Tel-Aviv: 1993), 198.

124 N. 119 above.

Sabbath. The same principle must apply also to turning to the secular courts in cases where it is reasonable to assume that the husband himself does not seek to have all his legal affairs adjudicated in accordance with Torah law. R. Dichovsky makes a salient comparison; note that the statements in the first paragraph represent the prevailing position in case law.

> Regarding [the rubric] 'transgresses religious precepts,' our predecessors have written in rabbinical rulings that a husband cannot claim, regarding his wife, that she transgresses religious precepts, unless he is precept-observant. But a husband who commits every type of abomination cannot wrap himself in righteousness and demand of his wife that she observe the precepts punctiliously, and not transgress religious precepts. We are speaking, of course, about things that do not render them forbidden to each other. Similarly, the husband cannot claim that it is his wife who transgresses religious precepts. For example, if she goes out with her head bare or with her arms uncovered where her habit, and that of the women in her area, is to go bareheaded and with uncovered arms. If we do not say so, every husband can become 'righteous' at an opportune moment, and make his wife, who conducts herself in accordance with the social norms that they both adhere to, into one who transgresses religious precepts.
>
> For the same reason, it seems to me that a husband cannot demand of his wife that their divorce be adjudicated in accordance with Torah law when he himself is not particular about doing so vis-à-vis his relations with others, and whenever it is beneficial to him, he turns to the civil courts. Nor can a husband who is not one of the righteous of his generation, and transgresses the law both out of irrepressible lust, and to flout the law, demand that his wife adhere to Torah law, because this is of financial benefit to him. And so too, a husband cannot demand adjudication in accordance with Torah law when he and those around him normally litigate in civil court, and rabbinical courts are beyond the pale for him. I have difficulty accepting [claims made by] someone who loudly broadcasts [lit., cries like a crane] his desire for adjudication by Torah law when he transgresses the Torah all the time.[125]

3.3 Halakhic sources of the rulings

R. Halevi, relying on R. Ovadia Yosef and *Otzar Haposkim*, states unqualifiedly, in his ruling in case 6548, that it follows from the halakhic sources that a wife who files suit in civil court for maintenance or property "should be regarded as transgressing religious precepts. . . . and although some recent authorities disagree, the law is not in accordance

125 Case 1390, n. 54 above.

with their view, and their opinion does not seem reasonable, and can be dismissed." But is it really so straightforward? The following points should be noted:

Reliance on R. Ovadia Yosef

The main source adduced by R. Halevi in the three rulings (and the sole source in two of them) is a responsum by R. Ovadia Yosef. We saw above that R. Yosef's position with respect to the 'transgresses religious precepts' rubric, as expressed in various response, does not, in fact, support the court's stance, but the responsum — *Responsa Yabia Omer*, vol. 7, EH #3 — merits careful examination. Perusal of the responsum reveals that the case it addresses is not at all similar to the three Tel-Aviv Rabbinical Court cases we are discussing. The case addressed by R. Yosef is as follows:

> About your question regarding the man . . . who is from the Sao Paulo Ashkenazic community, who separated from his wife in a civil divorce over a year ago, and paid her [the sums specified in] her *ketuba* and everything that was due her according to the laws of that country, and she promised him that afterwards she would accept a proper [Jewish] divorce from him, in full accordance with the laws of Moses and Israel. And now she refuses to appear before the rabbinate to be divorced, and has already been summoned to the court three times and has refused to go, despite the fact that they warned her that if she continues to stubbornly refuse to respond to the rabbinical court summons, to submit to adjudication by Torah law and receive the bill of divorce (*get*) from her husband, the court would issue her husband a dispensation to marry. Yet despite all this, she persists in her refusal to appear before the rabbinical court. And the husband, who has not yet fulfilled the precept of procreation, suffers a great deal because of this, because it is difficult for a man to be 'chained.' And he implores the court to allow him to marry another woman.

In other words, after a civil divorce, the wife refused to participate in the rabbinical court hearing to arrange the Jewish divorce, thereby preventing her husband from fulfilling the precept of procreation. R. Yosef emphasizes: "this is the law in the case at hand, where the wife refuses to submit to adjudication by Torah law, with her husband, and they have already divorced in civil court — it is clear that she transgresses religious precepts." This is not a woman whose only sin is **filing a monetary claim** in civil court, as in the three cases we are discussing, where the wives did not reject the rabbinical court's authority vis-à-vis their relationships with their husbands. On the contrary, in all three cases, the wives filed requests for marital reconciliation with the rabbinical courts.

Even if R. Halevi is convinced that in our cases the wives engaged in manipulative practices (although, as noted above, it appears that the move by a husband who files for divorce only in response to his wife's civil-court action is no less manipulative), his reliance on R. Yosef's ruling in the Sao Paulo case is unclear, since although R. Yosef's permits the husband to marry a second wife, he does so on the basis of her refusal to appear before the rabbinical court to arrange the divorce. Furthermore, the key factor in R. Yosef's dispensation is the fact that the husband had not yet fathered any children, and it was the wife who was preventing him from fulfilling this precept (some of the sources adduced by R. Yosef deem the wife to 'transgress religious precepts' specifically because she prevents her husband from observing the precept of procreation). This consideration is not germane in the cases we are discussing, where the couples had children.

Invoking numerous sources, R. Yosef deems the wife to 'transgress religious precepts,' but it is entirely clear that this determination, as well as the sources on which he relies (discussed below), apply to a wife who refuses to **have her divorce adjudicated** by a rabbinical court.[126]

Moreover, another responsum by R. Yosef appears to be far more relevant to our case.[127] This is a case that R. Yosef addressed as a judge on the Rabbinical High Court, also involving a wife who apparently made manipulative use of the rabbinical court, seeking its adjudication only regarding matters where she felt its rulings would be congenial, as in our cases:

> The wife filed a claim for matrimonial reconciliation in the Rehovot [District] Rabbinical Court, yet also filed a claim for spousal maintenance in civil court. The civil court indeed awarded her maintenance in the amount she requested. After a while, the husband and wife were summoned to the court, and the judge drafted a 'divorce agreement' between the two, which stated, among other things, that the spousal maintenance payments would cease the day the wife received her bill of divorce; the agreement focused mainly on the apartment that was registered under both their names. After a while the wife reneged on the

126 On the assumption R. Yosef's view can be relied on (as can the sources in *Otzar Haposkim*, discussed in the next section), why did R. Halevi not issue a dispensation for the husband to marry a second wife?

127 It is cited in n. 120 above. R. Yosef notes at the end: "and my colleagues, the eminent scholars R. Eliezer Waldenburg and R. Eliezer Shapira, of blessed memory, agreed with my ruling."

> agreement, after having signed it, and demanded that the entire apartment be transferred to her possession. The judge was offended by the wife's behavior and ruled that the order obligating the husband to pay spousal maintenance was to be cancelled immediately. When she heard this, the wife returned to the Rehovot [District] Rabbinical Court, requesting that her husband be obligated to pay her spousal maintenance. The rabbinical court considered her request on July 13, 1983, and after deliberating, ruled that it ought not accept her claim, since from the outset, she had had recourse to the civil court.

R. Yosef determined that the Rehovot District Rabbinical Court had erred, and that it ought to have adjudicated the wife's claim despite the fact that she had previously filed suit in civil court. It is clear from the facts of the case that here too, as in the other cases we are discussing, the husband was the one who filed for divorce, and the wife turned to the rabbinical court both for a matrimonial reconciliation order and to make demands that had been rejected by the civil court. Yet R. Yosef does not deem the wife's claim problematic, or suggest that the wife be declared a 'transgressor of religious precepts' for having turned to the civil court.

Reliance on *Otzar Haposkim*[128]

Granted, many decisors adduced in *Otzar Haposkim* (most of whom are also mentioned in R. Yosef's responsum) deem a wife who 'refuses to submit to adjudication by Torah law' to be one who 'transgresses religious precepts.' But we must reiterate a point made in the previous section: these decisors are speaking of a wife who refuses to have her divorce adjudicated by a rabbinical court, not one who files a monetary claim against her husband in civil court and refuses to have it adjudicated by a rabbinical court. Some of the sources explicitly address cases in which the husband has not yet fulfilled the precept of procreation, for example, the first source quoted, *Responsa Tirosh Veyitzhar*, #81, and the last, which is also mentioned in R. Yosef's responsum (*Responsa Yabia Omer*, vol. 7, HM #5).[129]

R. Halevi could also have adduced an additional source mentioned in *Otzar Haposkim*, which mentions many decisors who declare a wife who refuses adjudication by Torah law to be 'transgressing religious

128 See n. 99 above.

129 R. David Babad, *Responsa Havatzelet Hasharon*, vol. 2, EH #6.

precepts,'[130] but they too are speaking of a wife who refuses to submit to rabbinical court adjudication of her husband's suit for divorce, and addressing the question of whether he can be allowed to marry another woman. Thus it is by no means evident that there is a clear-cut halakhic source for the determination that filing a monetary claim in civil court renders the wife a 'transgressor of religious precepts.'[131]

What has been said up to this point should suffice to raise questions about the halakhic foundation of the rulings. But there are those who challenge even the correctness of deeming a wife who refuses to have the divorce claim itself (and not just the monetary claims) adjudicated in accordance with Torah law, that is, by a rabbinical court, to be 'transgressing religious precepts.' R. Halevi simply asserts, without elaboration, that "although some recent authorities disagree, the law is not in accordance with their view, and their opinion does not seem reasonable, and can be dismissed," but the basis for this statement is by no means clear.[132] In any event, it is difficult to say that these dissenting views are insignificant halakhic positions. We have already discussed R. Moses Feinstein's position,[133] and he is not alone. In the first volume of *Otzar Haposkim* (p. 83), which R. Halevi cites, there is only one opinion (*Responsa Mishne Sakhir*) that explicitly takes issue with the position of the other decisors quoted there and explains why a wife who refuses rabbinical court adjudication should not be regarded as 'transgressing religious

130 *Otzar Haposkim*, 77:54:3, vol. 21, 204–208.

131 There is indeed one contemporary decisor (known for the exceptional strictness of his rulings) who has asserted that filing a monetary claim in civil court causes a wife to be deemed 'rebellious' and a 'transgressor of religious precepts'; see R. Menashe Klein, *Responsa Mishne Halakhot*, 7:231; 12:355; 14:112.

132 It may be that R. Halevi is basing his statement on the responsum by R. Yosef that he cites in his ruling: "and although I saw some who disagree regarding a wife who refuses to submit to adjudication in accordance with Torah law. . . . In any event, in fact, most concur with the aforementioned decisors' view that a wife who refuses to submit to adjudication in accordance with Torah law is regarded as 'transgressing religious precepts,' and her husband is allowed to marry another woman" (*Yabia Omer*, vol. 7, EH #3). But note the difference between R. Yosef's characterization of this stance, and R. Halevi's.

133 N. 110 above.

precepts,'[134] but in vol. 21 of *Otzar Haposkim*, thirteen responsa that support this position are adduced.[135] Even if this is a minority view among the sources cited there, it does not seem that we can simply dismiss these opinions, as R. Haim Mordekhai Roller points out regarding the possibility of granting a dispensation to marry to a man whose wife refuses to submit to rabbinical court adjudication of his suit for divorce:

> As to the substance of the matter in cases where [the wife] truly refuses [to submit to rabbinical adjudication of the divorce]: permitting the husband to marry another wife by way of a 'dispensation by a hundred rabbis' exempting him from Rabbenu Gershom's ban, although this has been stated in several books, is not decided law (*halakha psuka*), for many dispute it, and among them, some of the greatest of the recent sages. . . . and they do not maintain, as do the majority of the sages, that we permit him [to marry another wife], even with a 'dispensation by a hundred rabbis.' And even though some sages did base their dispensation solely on the wife's refusal, most, if not all, of the later sages did not do so, but only where there were other grounds as well. And the stricter ones exclude themselves from being part of the 'dispensation by a hundred rabbis' when it is based only on the fact of the refusal.[136]

Let me conclude this section by adducing some distinctions made by R. Abraham Shapira when he served on the Rabbinical High Court.[137]

134 R. Issachar Teichtal, *Responsa Mishne Sakhir*, 1:74, §2. He distinguishes between various reasons for the wife's refusal, and therefore this source appears to be closer to the cases we are discussing than are the other sources adduced in *Otzar Haposkim*. Nor is it clear why his reasoned and well-argued statements are dismissed with the baffling claim that "their logic is implausible."

135 N. 130 above, 205–206.

136 *Responsa Beer Haim Mordekhai*, 3:57. It is true that in our cases R. Halevi did not use the 'transgresses religious precepts' rubric as the sole ground for his decision, and attached it to other grounds for obligating the wife to be divorced. Nevertheless, this source is important with respect to R. Halevi's statement that according to many decisors, "by the very fact of her monetary claims filed in a non-rabbinical court, the wife is regarded as transgressing religious precepts," and that the opinion of those who dispute this "can be dismissed."

137 R. Shapira's ruling was published in several places, including *Minhat Avraham*, n. 95 above; Itamar Warhaftig (ed.), *Edut Biyehosef: A Collection of Rulings by R. Joseph Kafih* (Jerusalem: 2004), 288. The latter work includes a ruling by R. Kafih in which he sharply criticizes a district rabbinical court that declared a wife 'rebellious' for failing to appear before the court.

After summarizing the opinions on which a wife who refuses to appear before the rabbinical court is deemed to 'transgress religious precepts,' R. Shapira raises two issues that are important for cases of the type we are discussing (although the case addressed by R. Shapira is more serious, because the wife refused to respond to the rabbinical court's summons to appear for adjudication of the husband's suit for divorce, and not just a secondary monetary claim):

> Therefore, in the case at hand, even if we assume that the wife's failure to appear in court was, at the time, deliberate and intentional, it does not seem that this is a case of 'transgressing religious precepts' as stated above, because it was asserted by the woman's representative, in her name, that from then on she would be willing to appear before the court, and in this case her two prior refusals [to appear for adjudication] certainly cannot be construed as rendering her refusal permanent. . . . Moreover, it seems clear that the rule of the wife who refuses [adjudication by Torah law] that is cited by the aforementioned decisors should not be invoked today by rabbinical courts in Israel as a basis for rendering judgment. For the rationale of this rule is that after the wife thwarts every attempt at adjudicating the conflict, and leaves the husband in limbo without the court's having reflected on and decided about the conflict, and it is impossible to rule for one side or the other, she is therefore deemed to be 'transgressing religious precepts.' And this was relevant abroad, where the rabbinical court had no authority to enforce the summons to the couple to appear before the court, as explicitly stated in *Responsa Sefer Yehoshua*, cited above. But in our day, the district rabbinical courts have the authority to compel the sides to appear and state their claims as to the disputed issue, be it matrimonial reconciliation or divorce, and the only possibility is for one of the sides, if it is interested in doing so, to seek to postpone the hearing from the date set by the court to a later, or much later, date, as is the case regarding any court proceeding between two people. But it is impossible to evade a hearing in rabbinical court entirely, and the parties know that it is impossible. And sooner or later, they will appear before the court even against their will. And this being so, a party that does not appear at the appointed time should definitely not be deemed to transgress Jewish religious precepts.[138]

In other words, in Israel's official rabbinical courts, there is no reason at all to regard a woman who refuses to submit to rabbinical court adjudication as 'transgressing religious precepts,' for the divorce will eventually be adjudicated by the rabbinical court, which is the only institution authorized to adjudicate divorce suits (even if the ancillary monetary claims are addressed in civil court).

138 *Minhat Avraham*, ibid., 12.

All the arguments adduced here indicate that R. Halevi's rulings are agenda-driven: they are, to a significant degree, innovative,[139] and their use of the halakhic sources they cite is quite problematic. In any event, it is problematic to assert that a wife who files spousal maintenance or property claims in civil court, especially in the case of a secular couple, 'transgresses religious precepts.' As I showed, we would have expected to find secular women declared as such in cases regarding other matters as well, but that was not the case. Why is it that only recourse to the civil courts prompts this designation? It appears, then, that this is an instance of halakhic 'creativity' that stems from the rabbinical courts' struggle to preserve their authority. Women who turn to the civil courts rather than the rabbinical courts are now at risk of finding themselves obligated to be divorced.

4 Dissolution of civil marriages

4.1 The Rabbinical High Court ruling in case 4276/63

If in the two previous contexts examined (the 'rebellious wife' and the wife who files suit in civil court), as well as the case of 'wrongful divorce,'[140] we witnessed the rabbinical courts' problematic invocation of halakhic sources, with a view to restoring authority that was taken from them, or to discourage adjudication in civil courts, the context we are about to explore is that in which problematic use of sources is intended to prevent the loss of authority the rabbinical courts presently possess. In other words, we will explore a case where rabbinical court judges made problematic use of halakhic sources and argumentation to

139 After all, for decades, various aspects of conflicts between couples were litigated in parallel in rabbinical and civil courts (see n. 107 above), yet it is only recently that a wife who files suit in civil court has been deemed to 'transgress religious precepts.' There was indeed one case where the court (in a ruling by R. Dichovsky) made such a declaration, see Ashdod District Rabbinical Court, case 2375/1980, 12 *PDR* (1980), 342, 347–48. But upon examination, the case can be seen to differ significantly from those we are discussing: the wife disappeared completely and did not obey numerous summonses to appear at hearings regarding her husband's suit for divorce. Here too, then, this was not a case of a wife who, alongside adjudication of her divorce in rabbinical court, also filed a monetary claim in civil court.

140 N. 14 above. On another difference between this situation and those discussed above, see n. 19 above.

protect the rabbinical courts' existing authority, specifically, to preserve their jurisdiction over divorce suits of civilly-married couples.[141]

At the end of 2003, the Rabbinical High Court (the panel comprised rabbis Solomon Dichovsky, R. Solomon Ben-Shimon, and R. Abraham Sherman), issued a revolutionary ruling: if a Jewish couple had voluntarily married in a civil marriage, dissolution of the marriage did not require a bill of divorce (*get*) (even a *get lehumra*[142]) at all, but could be effected through a judicial decision of the rabbinical court.[143]

141 There is no civil marriage in Israel, but Israeli law recognizes civil marriages entered into by Israelis abroad. However, regardless of the type of marriage, only the rabbinical courts have jurisdiction to adjudicate divorces where the spouses are Jewish; see Einhorn, n. 3 above, 216–17, 280–83.

142 I.e., a bill of divorce issued as a precautionary stringency, to preclude future doubts as to parties' personal status.

143 RHC, case 4276/63 [11.11.2003], www.daat.ac.il/daat/psk/psk.asp?id=93. In the ruling, the distinction between voluntary and non-voluntary civil marriage is presented as follows:

> Civil marriages, performed out of necessity, when there is no possibility of conducting a religious marriage, whether due to the lack of an ordained rabbi, or because the law of the state prohibits religious marriages, are viewed by the halakha as *nisuin lehumra*. This means that though the marriage ceremony was not conducted in accordance with Jewish law [lit., the religion of Moses and Israel], it is assumed that the parties regarded themselves as halakhically married, and thus, that the marital relations between them were tantamount to those of husband and wife, with the aim of conducting family life in accordance with the halakha. We assume that these couples wished to marry in accordance with Jewish law, but were prevented from doing so by the difficult times. Their underlying wish to be married in accordance with Jewish law must be 'translated' into their relationship, which must reflect the desire to establish a family in accordance with Jewish law, though they are prevented from doing so officially. . . . By contrast, civil marriages that are entered into by choice and with the wish not to marry in accordance with Jewish law, though the couple could have married in accordance with all the provisions of Jewish law, are considered marriages that are contrary to Jewish law. Couples who choose to marry in this way are declaring that they are not interested in the religious bonds of marriage. They do not want the sanctity of marriage. Their sole desire is to obtain the civil authorization. Since these couples are not interested in Jewish law, the marital relations between them take place on the basis of this attitude, and are intended to establish a family, but not in accordance

Examination of the halakhic sources adduced for the ruling raises serious questions, but before examining them, we must consider the circumstances of the case in question.

The ruling concerned a couple that had married in Cyprus because they did not want an Orthodox ceremony, the only marriage ceremony that the law allows Jews in Israel.[144] The marriage failed some time later, and the husband filed a suit in rabbinical court for "a declarative ruling that the parties are not married according to Jewish law [lit., in accordance with the religion of Moses and Israel], or alternatively, for divorce."[145] It is reasonable to assume that because the wife was not interested in divorcing or because she conditioned her consent to a divorce on various monetary conditions,[146] the district rabbinical court

---

> with Jewish law. . . . the operative conclusion is that in the second case there is no need for a bill of divorce handed by the husband to the wife. The marriage can be dissolved by issuing a divorce ruling. In the first case, a *get lehumra* is necessary. Very rarely, even in these cases, we allow the couple to separate without a bill of divorce.

The term "*get lehumra*" signifies a divorce that is granted to ensure that all opinions, even the most stringent, as to the validity of the marriage are taken into account, so that there will be no doubts or apprehensiveness that a marriage still exists between the parties, and therefore the wife remains married. The difference between this divorce and an ordinary one is that in cases where the rabbinical court encounters difficulties in arranging the divorce, it may consider waiving the need for a divorce in instances where it would be granted only as a precautionary stringency (*lehumra*), which is not possible in ordinary divorces. There have indeed been many instances where rabbinical courts have waived the need for a divorce in civil marriage cases where arranging a divorce was exceedingly difficult.

Case 4276/63 case is analyzed in Daniel B. Sinclair, "A definitive rabbinical court decision on the status of civil marriage," in idem, "Jewish Law in the State of Israel," 16 *Jewish Law Annual* (2006), 234–41. Sinclair's analysis differs from that presented here.

144 *RC Jurisdiction Law*, n. 3 above, §1–2. See Chigier, n. 3 above, 60–62. §1 of the Supreme Court ruling on the case, *Plonit v. Tel-Aviv-Jaffa District Rabbinical Court*, HCJ, case 2232/03 [21.11.2006], http://elyon1.court.gov.il/files/03/320/022/A16/03022320.a16.htm, notes that after the couple returned from Cyprus, "they had a private *kidushin* ceremony, conducted by a Reform rabbi, in Israel."

145 Case 4276/63, n. 143 above.

146 This seems clear from the husband's response to the wife's appeal to the HCJ, http://www.nevo.co.il/Psika_word/kitvey/03002232-a-kt.doc, §7, 8, 22.

found it sufficient to rule that "the parties are not married according to Jewish law."[147] The family court, which held a concurrent hearing about the couple's case, appeared to be perplexed by this ruling, and asked for clarifications regarding the personal (i.e., marital) status of the husband and wife, and their halakhic availability to wed other partners. The answer was as follows: "If the parties are not married to each other according to Jewish law, there is no need for clarification, and the woman is entitled to marry, as her status is that of one who is maritally-available (*pnuya*), as per the rabbinical court's ruling."[148] The wife, who suddenly and against her will found herself unmarried, and who understood that this ruling undermined her ability to negotiate the terms of the divorce, appealed the ruling to the Rabbinical High Court.[149]

In the appeal, she claimed that the Tel-Aviv-Jaffa District Rabbinical Court's ruling had only established that according to Jewish law [lit., the religion of Moses and Israel], the couple was not married. It did not, she claimed, have any ramifications for the legal validity of the civil marriage. Therefore, the rabbinical court was not entitled to make the determination that the couple were maritally-available, given that their civil marriage was valid. In her appeal, the petitioner claimed further that ending the civil marriage required a judicial decision, which would address the issue of the existence of grounds for divorce and the rights of the parties to the divorce. The determination that according to Jewish law the couple was not married did not suffice, she claimed, to dissolve the civil marriage.

The Rabbinical High Court accepted the wife's appeal, but its ruling was of no assistance to her: it asserted that it was, indeed, necessary for the court to issue a declaration that the couple was not married from the perspective of civil law either. The Tel-Aviv-Jaffa District Rabbinical Court then issued a ruling in which it asserted that "the parties are not married to each other according to Jewish law [lit., in accordance with the religion of Moses and Israel], and the court hereby

147 Ibid., §9; HCJ, n. 144 above, §2. Rabbinical courts in Israel do not have a consistent policy on civil marriage, but as we will see below, the prevailing view is that a *get lehumra* is needed, at least *ab initio*.

148 N. 146 above, §10–13; HCJ, n. 144 above, §3.

149 HCJ, n. 144 above, §4.

dissolves this marriage, and the parties are, according to Jewish law, maritally-available, and can marry."[150]

The wife then appealed to the High Court of Justice, claiming that it was inconceivable that the rabbinical courts could dissolve her marriage simply because it was not contracted in accordance with Jewish law. In her opinion, it is not possible that the court could dissolve the marriage without the agreement of both spouses and without examining the grounds necessitating their separation. The Supreme Court decided to request from the Rabbinical High Court the reasons for its ruling.[151] The Rabbinical High Court responded by issuing a ruling supplementing the ruling for which clarification had been requested.

It is this supplementary ruling that we will now examine. It opens with the statement: "The Supreme Court, sitting as a High Court of Justice, approached us — which it rarely does — with a request for clarification of the ruling." There seems to be no doubt that the Rabbinical High Court, and especially R. Dichovsky, who wrote the ruling,[152] understood that this was a pivotal moment and important touchstone in the complex relationship between the Rabbinical High Court and the High Court of Justice, which had, from the 1990s on, not hesitated to appropriate authority from the rabbinical courts or to impose on them the obligation to adjudicate various matters in a manner that was not in accordance with Torah law.[153] It understood that if the Supreme Court, and especially its President, Chief Justice Aharon Barak, who headed the panel adjudicating the case, was not satisfied with its explanation, that might well lead to loss of the rabbinical courts' exclusive authority to adjudicate the divorce suits of all Jewish couples in Israel, including those married in civil ceremonies, and to adjudicate them in accordance with Torah law.[154] Indeed, the issue of this authority is raised in Chief Justice Barak's ruling. Barak notes that the supplementary ruling he received from the Rabbinical High Court resolved that difficulty for him:

150 Ibid., §5–6.

151 The questions posed by the Supreme Court are presented at the beginning of the RHC ruling, n. 143 above, and also in the HCJ ruling, n. 144 above, §7–13.

152 The ruling was published as an article, see S. Dichovsky, "Recognition of civil marriage according to the halakha" (Hebrew), *Tehumin* 27 (2007), 239. And see text below at n. 171.

153 See n. 13 above.

154 See text below at n. 172, where this concern is stated explicitly.

> Does it not follow that where a Jewish couple does not require a *get lehumra* — as in the case before us — the rabbinical court has no authority to adjudicate their divorce? This question was difficult to answer in the past. Today, in light of the Rabbinical High Court's opinion that the Jewish couple, who were married abroad, are indeed married in its eyes (for purposes of 'external' relations[155]) according to Jewish law, it no longer raises any difficulty.[156]

Chief Justice Barak appears to be alluding to one of his own rulings, in which, as far back as 1985, he raised (but did not decide) a question that he takes to have been raised here by the wife: "another question is whether, within the scope of its jurisdiction, the rabbinical court is authorized to issue a divorce order for the sole reason that the marriage abroad was not contracted in accordance with Torah law."[157] As we will see, this question was of great concern to the rabbinical court, and its ruling was written with this question in mind.

The Rabbinical High Court now had to achieve two goals. First, it had to consolidate its legal and halakhic authority to rule on the status of civilly-contracted marriages, and decide how civilly-married couples were to divorce, not merely through the traditional means of a *get lehumra*, but by means of a "marriage-dissolution ruling,"[158] which was to a great extent an innovation, as we will see. Our main focus will be critique of this halakhic move. Second, it had to persuade the Supreme Court that in the case at hand, there were justifiable grounds for dissolving the marriage, and that the request of one party, as was the case here, sufficed for the grounds to be scrutinized to determine whether they indeed

155 The reference is to the marriage's ramifications for third parties. According to Barak, the ruling does not affect the marriage's 'internal aspect,' which pertains to the couple's mutual obligations to each other, HCJ, n. 144 above, §31.

156 Ibid., §29.

157 *Shmuel v. Tel-Aviv-Jaffa District Rabbinical Court*, HCJ 148/84, PD 39(4) 393, 398 (1985). See also P. Shifman, "Civil family law comes out of the closet: on Justice Barak's contribution to family law" (Hebrew), in C.W. Fassberg et al. (eds.), *The Judicial Legacy of Aharon Barak* (Hebrew), (Jerusalem: 2009), 575, 587.

158 As per n. 143 above, the ruling states that in general, when a civil marriage was involuntary, a *get lehumra* is issued, whereas when it was voluntary, a "marriage-dissolution ruling" is issued.

applied. For our purposes, however, the specifics of the justifications for the ground alleged to exist in the case at hand ("absence of any chance for marital reconciliation between the parties") are not relevant.

It is important to note that the ruling was highly gratifying to the Supreme Court, and Chief Justice Barak stated that he saw the Rabbinical High Court's ruling as "an important contribution to the development of marital law in Israel."[159] It is plain that by this he meant, among other things, that the ruling enabled him to make the sweeping determination — which it is unlikely the Rabbinical High Court had anticipated — that rabbinical courts have no authority to adjudicate any monetary issues related to the divorce of a civilly-married couple.[160] But the ruling was even more significant: the Rabbinical High Court ruling enabled Barak (on the basis of an assumption that, as we will see below, was mistaken, namely, the assumption that the Rabbinical High Court had set down a halakhic rule that would guide all the rabbinical courts) to claim that the obstacle to legislation that would allow for civil marriage in Israel had been removed:

> One of the difficult problems associated with recognizing civil marriage in Israel is that it entails recognition of civil divorce in Israel. And where civil divorce is not recognized by religious law, the woman is still considered married [to her original husband], and her offspring [from a subsequent relationship] will be considered *mamzerim* [born to a woman married to someone other than the father]. This is a difficult problem. But according to the rabbinical court's solution, whereby civil marriage is not marriage in accordance with Jewish law [lit., the religion of Moses and Israel], but is nothing at all, and does not require a *get lehumra*, the issue of *mamzerut* does not arise. This can open the door to civil marriage in Israel. But that is for the legislator to address.[161]

159 HCJ, n. 144 above, §28. The Attorney General supported and praised the RHC's position, see §20.

160 Ibid, §31. See also Shifman, n. 157 above, 590–91.

161 Quoted in "Barak: the road to civil marriages in Israel has opened" (Hebrew), 68 *Orekh Hadin* (2007), 40, 42. Barak makes similar statements in A.L. Bendor and Z. Segal, *The Hat Maker: Discussions with Justice Aharon Barak* (Hebrew), (Or-Yehuda: 2009), 169. Note that others who, for various reasons, support instituting civil marriage in Israel, also adduce this ruling as providing halakhic justification for such a move; see A. Picard, "According to the law of Moses and Israel" — the essence of marriage according to the halakhic decisors of the twentieth century: civil marriage as a test case" (Hebrew), *Democratic Culture* 12 (2009), 207, 243.

Clearly, the ruling now served a purpose that it is doubtful the Rabbinical High Court had envisaged, in removing one of the principal arguments against permitting civil marriage in Israel: apprehensiveness that when such marriages failed, they would, if not dissolved in accordance with Jewish law, lead to the birth of offspring deemed *mamzerim,* since though not in accordance with Jewish law, such marriages had some halakhic validity and required dissolution via Jewish divorce, or at least a *get lehumra.*[162] But if all that was needed was a "marriage-dissolution ruling," why did it have to be issued specifically by a **rabbinical** court?[163]

It is likely that the Rabbinical High Court was impelled by the need to protect its authority. It had to persuade the Supreme Court that there was a halakhic foundation for the mechanism called a "marriage-dissolution ruling," which would be issued in cases where it had been determined that there was no need for a divorce. For were there no such halakhic mechanism, and the court waived the need for a divorce, even a *get lehumra,* as the Tel-Aviv-Jaffa District Rabbinical Court indeed did in the case under discussion, it would follow that there was no need for any judicial act to dissolve the bond between the parties to a civil marriage. Such couples, who are recognized as married by Israeli law,[164] thus could, at least in theory, separate from each other without a decision by any judicial body. As we saw, the District Rabbinical Court saw no need to issue a clear judicial ruling (and made due with the factual determination that in its opinion the couple was not married), until the Rabbinical High Court obligated it to issue a ruling.

R. Dichovsky apparently understood that such an outcome would not be acceptable to Chief Justice Barak, and rightly so, as it would be

162 It is clear that this 'threat' is problematic, and it has been criticized in the past. Nevertheless, it is quite real, and has been voiced by important Israeli rabbinic authorities; see E. Shochetman, "On the question of instituting civil marriage in the State of Israel" (Hebrew), in Aharon Barak and Elinoar Mazuz (eds.), *Landau Book* (Hebrew), (Tel-Aviv: 1995), 3:1553, 1566ff.

163 It is possible that R. Dichovsky was somewhat aware that this claim might be put forward, and therefore ended his ruling with a statement that is hardly consistent with what was said in the body of the ruling: "The court will examine the possibility of executing a divorce, both from the halakhic perspective and the pragmatic. If it is not possible, from these perspectives, to arrange for a divorce, the marriage will be dissolved by means of a ruling."

164 N. 141 above.

inconceivable that a marriage recognized by Israeli law could be dissolved without some legal procedure; he understood that such an outcome would jeopardize the rabbinical courts' jurisdiction over civil marriage.[165] It thus stands to reason that R. Dichovsky was motivated by the desire to preserve the rabbinical courts' authority. As Pinhas Shifman put it:

> This is not the place to discuss the internal halakhic problems created by the rabbinical court's approach: does it not confer legitimacy on civil marriage, from which it has hitherto vigorously sought to distance itself? . . . And why is Noahide law not also deemed valid with regard to establishing mutual obligations between the spouses? It seems patently clear that the rabbinical court made a significant effort to adapt its rhetoric to the secular expectations — and all for the sake of not losing hold of its jurisdiction over this area.[166]

As might be expected of a ruling whose goal is to preserve the court's jurisdiction, the ruling raises significant difficulties.

4.2 Does the ruling reflect the judges' positions on civil marriage?

It appears that Chief Justice Barak's optimism was premature. The Rabbinical High Court's position on dissolution of a voluntary civil marriage without a divorce was almost never adduced in rabbinical court judgments. It had not been espoused before the court issued its ruling, nor was it adopted afterwards.[167] This appears to be due, primarily, to

165 When R. Dichovsky discussed his ruling (*Orekh Hadin*, n. 161 above, 42), he did not mention apprehensiveness about losing jurisdiction, but said that if neither a halakhic divorce nor a judicial decision was required, "we will reach absurd situations."

166 Shifman, n. 157 above, 590.

167 Although R. Dichovsky mentions "the rabbinical court custom of dissolving such marriages by issuing a ruling" three times in the ruling, it is hard to find evidence for the existence of such a "custom" (as opposed to an exceptional ruling). Even the District Rabbinical Court in the case under discussion, which exempted the husband from having to grant a divorce, did not do so by way of a ruling until the RHC required it to do so. Moreover, R. Dichovsky's remarks in the article cited in n. 161 above indicate that he was definitely aware of the innovativeness and creativity of his ruling: "And thus we reached the conclusion that a ruling was needed so as to recognize the [marital] separation between those who married as Noahides. And that is what I wrote in the ruling."

problems raised by the ruling's key argument, discussed below. Most rabbinical courts do not mention the ruling or invoke it to moderate their strict position, which mandates the issuing of a *get lehumra*, the position that most rabbinical court panels have taken in the past and continue to uphold.[168] Moreover, the ruling is also innovative relative to R. Dichovsky's own rulings. In a 1979 ruling, after a lengthy examination of the positions of past decisors, he concludes that "according to most of the later decisors, we should be lenient with regard to civil marriages, and release the wife without [requiring] a divorce. **But in practice they were not lenient, except in cases of 'chaining' (*igun*), where the husband did not appear before the court**."[169]

168 Although the rabbinical courts had previously issued rulings that waived the need for a divorce altogether, the prevailing position was undoubtedly to require a *get lehumra*, at least *ab initio*, and to consider waiving this requirement only if it turned out that this was not possible to arrange (see end of n. 143 above). See, e.g., Chigier, n. 3 above, 188; Einhorn, n. 3 above, 182, 216–17 (emphasizing the ruling's innovativeness); Shochetman, n. 162 above, 1571; R. Meir Mazuz, "The question of civil marriage and its validity" (Hebrew), *Oraita* 15 (1986), 219, 227; Haifa District Rabbinical Court, case 9579-21-2 [19.1.2006], http://www.daat.ac.il/daat/psk/psk.asp?id=295. Even a ruling that discusses the HCR ruling in case 4276/63, which is unusual, and mentions a similar case, that of a civilly-married wife who refused to be divorced though there was no chance of marital reconciliation, ruled in practice that "the couple must arrange a divorce in accordance with the custom of rabbinical courts in cases of civil marriage," see Haifa District Rabbinical Court, case 2177-21-1 [23.1.2008], http://www.daat.ac.il/daat/psk/psk.asp?id=360. And see too Tel-Aviv District Rabbinical Court, case 8711-68-1 [22.3.2009], published in 26 *HaDin Ve'haDayan* (2011), regarding a civilly-married couple, where the husband had long refused to grant a divorce. The wife's attorney sought to invoke the RHC ruling in case 4276/63 to have the marriage dissolved without a divorce. The court rejected the request, preferring to jail the husband to force him to grant the divorce.

169 Tel-Aviv-Jaffa District Rabbinical Court, case 4431/38, published in S. Dichovsky, "Civil marriage" (Hebrew), *Tehumin* 2 (1981), 252, 262 (emphasis in original). Although he states further down that the law as to a couple involuntarily married in a civil ceremony is more stringent than in the case of a couple that had a voluntary civil ceremony (see n. 143 above), his conclusion is sweeping: divorce is required in every case of civil marriage. R. Dichovsky refers to this article and to R. Mazuz's article (n. 168 above) in his HRC ruling in case 4276/63, as sources for his analysis of the "halakhic validity of civil marriage." As noted above, the position

An even more vexing problem arises from statements made by the rabbinical court judges who signed the innovative ruling. When R. Dichovsky published the ruling, he added a note that can have considerable impact on how the ruling should be read:

> In the wake of the supplementary ruling on which this article is based, the High Court of Justice ruled that the rabbinical courts have sole jurisdiction over dissolution of civil marriages, and civilly-married couples cannot 'divorce' in civil court. Note that were it not for this ruling, **there would have been a concern that jurisdiction over dissolution of civil marriages would be taken from the rabbinical courts and transferred to the family courts.**[170] (emphasis added)

Elsewhere, R. Dichovsky explicitly identified another key factor that impacts the manner in which the ruling should be understood. The ruling, he explained, reflected the fact that it was written at the request of the High Court of Justice, and was expected to be a foundational ruling on the halakhic approach to civil marriage (and indeed, this is how it was perceived by Barak, as we saw), and therefore its content did not reflect his personal opinion:

> Nor did I write the whole truth. In the framework of a ruling, I have to take into account not only what I think, but also what my colleagues think. It is not always possible to arrive at a consensus decision. This ruling was issued under unusual circumstances: the High Court of Justice approached us requesting that we issue a supplementary ruling clarifying the halakhic

---

voiced in these articles is incompatible with what R. Dichovsky presents, immediately after his reference to these articles, as "the rabbinical court custom" that to dissolve a voluntary civil marriage, "there is no need for a bill of divorce handed by the husband to the wife."

170 N. 152 above, n. 2. A similar concern seems to have been expressed in the body of the ruling as well. Before R. Dichovsky presents his argument, he states: "If the court is not authorized to issue a marriage-dissolution ruling, because this is a civil marriage, then not even a divorce arranged according to all the rules of the halakha can dissolve it; for if from a purely halakhic point of view the couple were not married in accordance with Jewish law [lit., the religion of Moses and Israel], there is no need for a divorce granted in accordance with Jewish law to dissolve the marriage, and if so, the court cannot purport to dissolve it, even from the perspective of state law." In my opinion, this sentence is asserting that the rabbinical courts' halakhic authority to dissolve civil marriages without a divorce must be consolidated, seeing that they have no jurisdiction to adjudicate dissolution of such marriages under state law.

> foundations of civil marriage. It is not possible to issue such a ruling by consensus. And my personal opinion does not match what I have written.[171]

In other words, the importance of the ruling required that it be issued unanimously, and that came at a price. R. Dichovsky does not even try to hide his opinion about the stance of his colleague on the panel, R. Abraham Sherman:

> In this ruling, my colleagues and I did not write what we thought. . . . Recently, a conference on this topic was held at the University of Haifa, and one of the colleagues who signed the ruling together with me was there, and told the audience that there is no such thing as Noahide marriage. Civil marriage [he said,] was null and void, like dust. I asked him, then why did you sign? He said, your conclusion was that the rabbinical court has jurisdiction. Set it up however you like, if the court has jurisdiction, I will agree to it.[172]

It is hard to exaggerate the severity of the criticism voiced here (although R. Dichovsky admits that he didn't write his real opinion either, and that preserving the rabbinical court's authority had been a weighty consideration in his eyes): a rabbinical judge signed a ruling expressing a halakhic approach that completely contradicts his real view, with the sole aim of preserving the rabbinical court's jurisdiction over dissolution of civil marriages! Yet the problem is even more serious than R. Dichovsky suggests. His statements imply that R. Sherman's position is that according to Jewish law, civil marriages

171 *Orekh Hadin*, n. 161 above, 42. Indeed, it appears that R. Dichovsky did not endorse the position he voiced in the ruling in case 4276/63, namely, that "over the course of time, all civilized countries instituted procedures for marriage and divorce in which the governmental authorities were involved. We can say that in principle, Jewish law also recognizes the binding validity of these procedures." In RHC, case 8958-21-1 [22.3.07], 15 *HaDin Ve'haDayan* (2007), 4, he states that civil marriage without sexual relations is not considered "Noahide marriage." This view is based on Maimonides' understanding of Noahide marriage, but it is very doubtful that it is consistent with the view expressed in *Tzofnat Paneiah*; see I. Shapira (1986), n. 184 below, 250–51 (which is cited in the RHC ruling in case 4276/63), and it is certainly inconsistent with R. Dichovsky's premise validating the marriages contracted in most countries today. Is there any country that makes the validity of civil marriages contracted according to its laws conditional on sexual relations?!

172 *Orekh Hadin*, ibid.

are invalid in any case, and therefore the intervention of the rabbinical court is not needed for their dissolution, but to satisfy the civil court, he agreed to the innovative "marriage-dissolution ruling." But R. Sherman's lecture at the conference, delivered on May 14, 2007, reveals something else entirely.

It is true that R. Sherman claims that he agreed to the ruling only because of his desire to preserve the rabbinical court's jurisdiction, and Torah law's monopoly, as it were, on the adjudication of marriage and divorce cases, but to this end he concealed his true opinion, which is rather stringent. Much of his talk was devoted to the stringent position of the Hazon Ish[173] and of R. Joseph Henkin.[174] On this view, there is no halakhic need for an intention to marry in accordance with Jewish law for a marriage to be contracted, hence civil marriages are halakhically valid, and *ab initio*, their dissolution requires a divorce, and not merely a *get lehumra* (which can be waived in various cases). In his talk, he mentions a ruling he had recently issued where he had misgivings about waiving the need for a divorce **even though the case involved a fictitious civil marriage** that was contracted in order to obtain a 'green card.'[175] And although the circumstances made it very difficult to arrange a divorce,[176] only a ruling by R. Shalom Joseph Elyashiv enabled him to waive the divorce requirement.

It is easy to see that if in this case he was apprehensive about dissolving the marriage without a divorce, he would be all the stricter in the case of a couple who had contracted a marriage fully intending to live as husband and wife, even if their civil marriage was voluntary. As noted above, when the surprised audience asked how this stringent position could be reconciled with the RHC ruling, R. Sherman answered that this was the way to ensure continued jurisdiction: the rabbinical

173 R. Abraham Karelitz, "On civil *kidushin*" (Hebrew), *Or Yisrael* 18 (1998), 12.

174 R. Joseph Henkin, *Peirushei Ibra* (NY: 1925), #4; *Lev Ibra* (NY: 1957), 12. On R. Henkin's approach, see E.G. Ellinson, *Non-Halachic Marriage: A Study of the Rabbinic Sources* (Hebrew), (Tel-Aviv: 1975), 152, 179.

175 There is doubt about the validity of fictitious marriages even if they are contracted in accordance with Jewish law. See, e.g., Ashkelon District Rabbinical Court, case 355/77, 10 *PDR* (1977), 317, but cf. another case in which the need for a divorce was waived in a fictitious civil marriage: Ashkelon District Rabbinical Court, case 2578-21-1 [4.12.2005], http://www.daat.ac.il/daat/psk/psk.asp?id=94.

176 See end of n. 143 above.

court would rule in accordance with its (real) interpretation of the halakha when its jurisdiction had been secured. R. Sherman's statements clearly indicate that he will continue to demand a divorce in the overwhelming majority of civil marriage cases.

In a well-known ruling in which R. Sherman called on rabbinical judges to follow the "preeminent sages of the generation" (*gdolei hador*) in matters of conversion,[177] he also elaborates on the need to accept their opinions in matters of marriage and divorce, and we can infer that he would be inclined to rule stringently regarding the need for a bill of divorce. To illustrate the need to act in accordance with the views of the generation's preeminent sages, he cites a responsum by R. Abraham Kahana Shapira, author of *Responsa Dvar Avraham*, which asserts: "The halakhic principle is that matters of law and legal rulings that apply to all Jewish communities, such as releasing a woman who married civilly, are usually [settled] by means of a *get lehumra*."[178] R. Shapira understood very well that the source on which the panel relied in handing down their ruling, a responsum by R. Joseph Rosin, the 'Rogachover,' takes a stringent view, requiring a divorce, and in his ruling R. Sherman even quotes R. Shapira in this regard: "without a divorce, it is altogether impossible to release her."[179]

It is clear that these statements, and R. Sherman's general conclusion in the ruling, namely, that "in matters of law and legal rulings that apply to all Jewish communities, such as releasing a married woman, one should never issue a ruling or enact ordinances without obtaining the consent and approval of the generation's preeminent Torah scholars and decisors,"[180] are incompatible with the ruling in case 4276/63,

177 RHC, case 6122-21-1 [10.5.2009]. The ruling was intended to consolidate the rabbinical courts' authority to annul conversions, in accordance with the stringent view that R. Sherman has endorsed in recent years. He maintains that his role is to carry out the instructions of the "preeminent sages of the generation," who have determined that conversions carried out without the convert's complete commitment to precept-observance are not valid.

178 Ibid., before the quotation from *Responsa Dvar Avraham*, 3:29.

179 R. Shapira's personal conclusion was that stringency was warranted, and each case had to be examined on the merits, and it was not possible to formulate a general rule applicable to every case, as the RHC ruling does (namely, the rule that the wife can be released without a divorce); see Ellinson, n. 174 above, 180–81.

180 N. 177 above.

which R. Sherman signed, and which appears to declare that in cases of voluntary civil marriage there is no need for a divorce. Moreover, it is evident that R. Rosin's opinion, the main halakhic source on which the ruling is based, altogether fails to serve the purpose of establishing that Jewish law recognizes the mechanism of a marriage-dissolution ruling.

4.3 Aptness of the principal source for the ruling: the Rogachover's responsa on civil marriage

The ruling in case 4276/63, I contend, should be regarded as a significant innovation born of fear and distress. Its innovativeness is also reflected in the main source on which the ruling relies. The ruling draws a distinction between halakhic marriage (and divorce), which is contracted by Jews, and marriage (and divorce) contracted by 'the nations of the world,' that is, non-Jews, as defined by Maimonides.[181] After identifying the latter with civil marriage, regarding which "the universal custom today is that the authorized judicial tribunal in each country is the body that declares the sides to be divorced, and the physical separation between the spouses is not sufficient," the ruling addresses the question of whether it is possible to apply the law of the nations to Jews, which would yield the desired conclusion, namely, that from the halakhic perspective it was also possible to dissolve a civil marriage between Jews by means of a 'marriage-dissolution ruling.'

To arrive at an affirmative answer, the court had to adduce a halakhic source, and the source it found was unconventional — a responsum by R. Joseph Rosin, the rabbi of Dvinsk (Daugavpils) in Latvia, known as "the Rogachover," after his birthplace (Rogachow). The manner in which it presented this source was also problematic. R. Rosin is considered an unconventional decisor, an original thinker in all areas of Jewish law.[182] In his *Responsa Tzofnat Paneiah*, there are six responsa that address the status of civil marriage.[183] They have been much discussed,

181 Maimonides, *Code*, Laws concerning Kings and Wars 9:8; the ruling also cites the Radbaz ad loc. and the Netziv.

182 See R. Solomon Zevin, *Leor Hahalakha* (Jerusalem: 2007), 73.

183 All six responsa — #1–4, 26 and 27 of the first volume of *Tzofnat Paneiah* — are mentioned in the RHC ruling, which also mentions R. Rosin's response to R. Shapira's view, discussed above at n. 179.

and the ruling cites some of the sources that address them.[184] The Rogachover's view has been summarized as follows:

> The basis of his method is that act of marriage forks off into two branches: marital possession [viz. sexual relations after matrimony] (*kinyan ishut*), and the prohibition against [the wife's having] sexual relations with others (*erva*). Marital 'possession' does not require intent that the marriage be in accordance with the Torah, because it is not unique to the people of Israel. Its source is in the Book of Genesis: "and he shall cleave unto his wife" (Gen. 2:24), from which we learn that even a Noahide is admonished against sexual relations with the wife of his fellow. Since this possession is common to Jews and the other nations . . . we can be satisfied, for Jews too, with ordinary intent without intent that the marriage be in accordance with the Torah. In such a case, the woman should not be released without a divorce, in order to terminate the 'possession,' but nevertheless, if someone else has relations with her, he does not violate the prohibition against sexual relations with a married woman in its full sense, and the children are not *mamzerim*, because the prohibition against sexual relations with others (*erva*) does not apply to the woman.[185]

There is no doubt that on this approach, a divorce is required even in cases of Noahide marriage, "even if the halakhic requirements of the divorce in question are weaker."[186] If so, this approach indeed supports

184 See, e.g., Menahem M. Tenenbaum, *Civil Marriage in the Teachings of the Rogachover* (Hebrew), (Kfar-Habad: 1988); Isaac Aaron Shapira, "The question of civil marriage in the Rogachover's responsa" (Hebrew), *Oraita* 15 (1986), 245; Shilo Raphael, "Civil marriage" (Hebrew), *Torah Shebeal Pe* 12 (1970), 108, 111–12; R. Israel Meir Lau, *Responsa Yahel Israel*, 3:51. The last three sources are mentioned in the RHC ruling as sources that provide an exposition of R. Rosin's position. Two additional sources, mentioned in the ruling in another context but also addressing R. Rosin's approach, are articles by rabbis Mazuz and Dichovsky, cited above in nn 168 and 169 respectively.

185 Ellinson, n. 174 above, 151–52.

186 RHC ruling, n. 143 above. On the differences between the two types of divorce, see I. Shapira (1986), n. 184 above, 255–56. R. Lau states, at the end of his responsum (n. 184 above), that the current rabbinical court practice of requiring a *get lehumra* is not based on the Rogachover's view, which R. Lau considers stricter than that which prevails in the rabbinical courts, since it does not permit any waiving of the divorce requirement in situations such as that of the *agunah*.

In the earliest of the six responsa (#3), the view expressed by R. Rosin, namely, that civil marriage may not require a Jewish divorce, and a separation "according to their [i.e., civil] laws" suffices, is rather dubious (see

the panel's claim that it is possible to apply the marriage laws of the nations to Jews as well, but at the same time poses a serious problem, because R. Rosin requires that civilly-married couples be halakhically divorced, whereas the panel is trying to claim that in the case at hand, there is no need for divorce.

To cope with this difficulty, R. Dichovsky 'splits' R. Rosin's position (*palginan dibura*): he accepts the applicability of "Noahide marriage" to Jews, but rejects the requirement that a divorce be issued. "The stringent approach taken by the author of *Tzofnat Paneiah*, which requires a bill of divorce handed by the husband to the wife . . . was not accepted by most of the decisors." But it is hard to understand this claim, as scrutiny of the remarks by halakhic authorities who discussed R. Rosin's view, including those adduced by the panel in its ruling, shows that indeed many rejected R. Rosin's approach, but rejected it in its entirety! That is, they maintain that the Noahide laws of marriage and divorce do not apply to Jews. In other words, the ruling in case 4276/63 presents a new approach, which accepts half of the Rogachover's innovative and very controversial approach, but ignores the fact that it mandates issuance of a divorce.

There is no doubt that R. Rosin's approach requires the issuance of a divorce. Indeed, prior to the ruling in question, his approach to the validity of civil marriage was considered, in light of this requirement, one of the most stringent. R. Dichovsky himself had so characterized it in the past, categorizing it as a view held by those who are "apprehensive as to [the ramifications of] the possible halakhic validity of civil marriages."[187] R. Meir Mazuz also characterized it as a stringent view in the article mentioned in the ruling:

> And indeed we found that one of those who were stringent, the eminent sage R. Joseph Rosin (Rogachover), mandated, in several of his responsa,

Shapira, ibid., 249). Indeed, Picard (n. 161 above, 236–37) adduces it to make the sweeping claim that according to R. Rosin, in the case of civilly-married couples, there is no need for a divorce. But aside from the fact that neither the halakhic authorities who discussed R. Rosin's stance, nor the RHC panel, shared this understanding of his view (which would have greatly facilitated the RHC's argument), from the five responsa on the subject that the Rogachover wrote subsequently (and which therefore have greater halakhic value), it is clear that it is not possible to waive the divorce requirement; see Tenenbaum, n. 184 above, 65.

187 N. 169 above, 257.

> the issuance of a divorce, which he termed "a liberating bill of divorce" (*get herut*) and not a "severing bill of divorce" (*get kritut*), for [it is stated] "he cleaved unto his wife — and not unto the wife of his fellow"; but he ruled that there need be no apprehensiveness about *mamzerut*, **even though without [receiving] a divorce, the woman is forbidden to be married to another.**[188] (emphasis added)

Moreover, this conclusion follows so directly from R. Rosin's remarks that his position was problematic for those who argued — just as Chief Justice Barak did on the basis of the Rabbinical High Court's ruling — that there need be no halakhic apprehensiveness about the 'married woman' problem [i.e., that of children born from a subsequent relationship] should Israel institute a system of civil family law.[189] One of the main voices calling for the institution of civil marriage made the following argument:

> It is clear that most, if not all, of the decisors who adopted a stringent approach on this point, did so only out of apprehensiveness about marriage (*kidushin*), or at most, doubtful marriage, but not out of any recognition that this is a full marital relationship from the religious point of view. One exception is R. Joseph Rosin of Dvinsk, known as the Rogachover, one of the most amazing thinkers of the previous generation, who adopted a position that differed in principle from that upheld by all his contemporaries. The Rogachover wrote several responsa on this subject, in most of which he adopted a stringent view for various reasons. But in his last responsum, he ruled in a comprehensive and unequivocal way that if a couple was civilly married, and in any event, if the couple regarded themselves as married, the woman was fully married according to the Torah. . . . The Rogachover's practice of not enslaving his rulings and decisions to those of earlier decisors — much like the practice of his main teacher, Maimonides — was not and is not accepted by the preponderance of Torah sages of our era, and therefore it is clear that despite his amazing erudition and incisiveness, and despite the great esteem in which he was held by the

188 N. 168 above, 228. The other articles cited in the ruling also refer to this stringency. And see a later ruling (which does not mention the ruling in case 4276/63), Ashkelon District Rabbinical Court, 2484-21-1 [17.11.05], http://www.daat.ac.il/daat/psk/psk.asp?id=53, which cites *Tzofnat Paneiah* as mandating issuance of a divorce (albeit a divorce that differs from an ordinary divorce) in cases of non-halakhic marriage.

189 See n. 161 above.

sages of his day, his opinion on this matter seems to have remained a minority view.[190]

Did any halakhic authorities accept R. Rosin's view as to the validity of Noahide marriage between Jews, but not with respect to the divorce requirement? R. Dichovsky appears to be the first to make this claim. A very few endorsed the view that Noahide marriages between Jews have halakhic status, but none accepted the notion presented in the Rabbinical High Court ruling in case 4276/63 that despite recognition of the marriage, issuance of a divorce is not required.

Let us examine two additional sources that consider the idea of Noahide marriage between Jews. In 1896, R. Isaiah Zilberstein, head of the Veitzen rabbinical court in Hungary, published a brief halakhic essay on the question of whether dissolution of civil marriages required issuance of a divorce.[191] Like R. Rosin after him, he was willing to assume that the giving of the Torah did not preclude the validity of the marriage laws that had applied earlier: if a Jew brought a woman into his home but did not do so in conformity with the laws of betrothal, he had still rendered her sexually prohibited to all others. The need for a bill of divorce did not change:

> And as clarified by Maimonides, in ch. 9 of *Melakhim*,[192] when he sends her away from his home, the marriage has ended, because among with the Gentiles, no rule was added requiring [that he issue her] a divorce, but among Jews, the Torah required issuance of a divorce in every case of betrothal (*kidushin*). Hence, even regarding this sort of [marital] possession, which remains from before the giving of the Torah, a divorce is necessary, as Scripture states, "he writes her a bill of divorcement . . . and sends her away from his house" (Deut. 24:1, 3) — even when he sends her away from his house, she needs a divorce.

190 Jacob Levinger, *Between Routine and Renewal* (Hebrew), (Jerusalem: 1973), 109–10. However, as Shochetman shows, n. 162 above, 1568–70, and as was manifest in R. Sherman's remarks, nn 174ff. above, the requirement that a divorce be issued is not a minority view voiced only by R. Rosin. Nor are his arguments for the requirement unique, though they are indeed special.

191 *Tel-Talpiot* 4 (1896), 5. In the same issue, the journal published various criticisms of R. Zilberstein's analysis. See also A.H. Freimann, *The Procedure of Betrothal and Marriage from the Canonization of the Talmud to Our Day* (Hebrew), (Jerusalem: 1964), 368.

192 Maimonides, *Code*, Laws concerning Kings and Wars 9:8, which is cited in the RHC ruling.

The second source is a responsum by R. Judah Leib Don-Yehia.[193] He also raised the possibility that "the Torah introduced the requirement that the Jews were commanded, by a positive commandment, to first acquire her in marriage in the presence of witnesses, but if he transgressed the positive commandment and conducted himself as before the giving of the Torah, she is nonetheless considered to be his wife." Further on, he has doubts as to whether it is necessary to divorce by means of a bill of divorce, but rules in practice that it is not possible to release wives without a divorce, "and the matter requires further investigation."

It appears that aside from these sources, no halakhic authorities accepted the premise that 'Noahide' marriage is applicable to Jews. Let me comment briefly on the sources R. Dichovsky adduces in the ruling:

> The stringent approach taken by the author of *Tzofnat Paneiah*, which requires a bill of divorce handed by the husband to the wife (even if the halakhic requirements of the divorce in question are weaker), was not accepted by most of the decisors (see *Dvar Avraham*, ibid.; *Sridei Esh*, 3:22; *Responsa Helkat Yaakov*, EH #74; *Responsa Yabia Omer*, vol. 8, EH #10 s.v. *hinei besifri*, and others).[194]

Perusal of these sources reveals that it is not correct to reduce their import to the claim that they rejected "the stringent approach taken by the author of *Tzofnat Paneiah*, which requires a bill of divorce" — they have difficulty with the entire concept of applying 'Noahide' marriage to Jews.

(a) *Dvar Avraham* (R. Avraham Kahana Shapira) R. Shapira does not distinguish between marriage and divorce, but raises a question about R. Rosin's approach in general: "Indeed, what the eminent sage [the Rogachover], of blessed memory, states about defining the relationship contracted with the woman, that it is divided into two elements — belonging to him and being prohibited to another, and so on — is a new trail he blazed for himself."[195]

(b) *Sridei Esh* 3:22 (R. Yehiel Jacob Weinberg) "But the very assumption that there are two elements, and so on, is something new that was not mentioned in the Talmud and the decisors, but rather, the

193 *Bikurei Yehuda*, vol. 1, Responsa, #3, 117ff., esp. 124.

194 Case 4276/63, n. 143 above.

195 N. 178 above.

Rogachover devised this novel view of his own accord, as was his way. And were it not for my being in awe of this great sage, I would say that one ought not heed this assumption at all."

(c) *Responsa Helkat Yaakov*, EH #74 (R. Jacob Mordekhai Breisch) After presenting R. Rosin's position, on which "if they separated, a divorce must be issued," he rejects R. Rosin's proofs from talmudic sources and the writings of early authorities, and concludes that it is not possible to accept his approach at all: "With respect to deciding the law, we must follow the *Shulhan Arukh* and the decisors, because we cannot fully comprehend the profundity of what he meant."

(d) *Responsa Yabia Omer*, vol. 8, EH #10 (R. Ovadia Yosef) Examination of R. Yosef's responsum reveals that he does not accept the view that 'Noahide' marriages in themselves have applicability among Jews. In his words, "And as to the Rogachover's stringent approach in *Responsa Tzofnat Paneiah* (#26–27) regarding civil marriages, requiring [that they be dissolved by issuance of] a divorce, which has been adopted by some of the more recent among the rabbis of our era — those who examine it carefully will see that his view is not mandatory."

Moreover, in an earlier ruling,[196] R. Dichovsky himself summarized the situation as follows:

> (9) The Rogachover's novel view that in civil marriage there is marital possession despite the fact that there is no prohibition against relations with others, was rejected by recent halakhic authorities: the author of *Dvar Avraham* (3:29), after quoting from the Rogachover's responsum, wrote: "Indeed, what the eminent sage [the Rogachover], of blessed memory, states about defining the relationship contracted with the woman, that it is divided into two . . . is a new trail he blazed . . . and those who scrutinize it will examine it, and embrace or reject it." And in *Responsa Sridei Esh* (3:22), [R. Weinberg] wrote: "But the very assumption that there are two elements . . . is something new that was not mentioned in the Talmud . . . I would say that one ought not heed this assumption at all." R. Herzog wrote: "And who would dare to introduce such an alarming innovation, of which there is not the slightest hint in the Talmuds!"[197] And see too the writings of R. Klems[198] in *Otzar Haposkim*, vol. 10, p. 362.

196 N. 169 above, 260.

197 *Responsa Heikhal Yitzhak*, EH 2:31.

198 R. Jacob Klems, a member of the Chief Rabbinate and the RHC, invokes a variety of arguments against R. Rosin's view that the notion of Noahide marriage between Jews is meaningful.

In other words, the sources adduced here, to which others can be added, show that R. Rosin's approach was rejected by the overwhelming majority of decisors, from its inception on, among other things because it is difficult to find a precedent for it in the writings of early authorities.[199]

In sum, as part of its effort to protect its jurisdiction over the dissolution of civil marriages, the rabbinical court, even when it reached the conclusion that it was unnecessary to issue a divorce, was forced to rely on a highly idiosyncratic opinion that was rejected by most decisors. But even this opinion does not allow the divorce to be waived, and therefore R. Dichovsky was forced to bisect it: to recognize its relevance with regard to marriage procedures, but not divorce procedures. This approach represents an innovation on the part of the rabbinical court, and has no precedent. In other words, to protect its jurisdiction, the rabbinical court was forced to invent a halakhic method *ex nihilo*. It is not surprising, therefore, that this approach (which succeeded in persuading the Supreme Court to let the rabbinical courts retain their jurisdiction over the dissolution of civil marriages) has not influenced rabbinical court rulings, and it is highly doubtful whether even the judges who signed the ruling in case 4276/63 actually apply it in practice.[200]

5 Conclusion

At the time the Chief Rabbinate, which included the system of official rabbinical courts, was established, its founders — the British Mandatory authorities and Rabbi Kook — made it clear that they expected the new institution to bring about needed changes in Jewish law, by both interpretation and enactments, and with respect to both procedural and substantive law.[201] And indeed, in the first decades of their operation,

199 See Freimann, n. 191 above, 355ff.

200 See n. 171, regarding a case in which it appears that R. Dichovsky tries to develop his innovative approach in a manner that fits the facts of the case at hand, but departs from his approach in case 4276/63.

201 Speeches of Herbert Samuel, Norman Bentwich, and R. Kook at the founding ceremony of the Chief Rabbinate, "Conference for the organization of the Chief Rabbinate in the land of Israel (Jerusalem, Mar. 22–24, 1921): Report," *Hator* [weekly], 4.3.1921, pp. 2, 4, 10.

the rabbinical courts generated major innovations.[202] As the legal scholar Samuel Eisenstadt noted in 1935:

> In the period that the Chief Rabbinate in Jerusalem and the Chief Rabbinate of the Yaffo-Tel-Aviv district have been in existence, there have emerged from the courts several fundamental rulings by which the rabbinical court judges directed the law, to a greater or lesser extent, along the channels of developing life in the land of Israel, consistent with the circumstances and needs of the times. In these rulings there are sometimes new interpretations of long-standing laws, and at times even halakhic innovations. These rulings are an important starting point for judicial renewal in the land of Israel.[203]

Clearly, the various enactments and innovations did not emerge in a void, and the rabbinical courts and their judges were influenced by modern approaches to law and by the needs of the time; some were even the result of external pressure.[204] It seems that this sort of innovativeness has disappeared from the rabbinical courts, and today there is no chance of revolutionary developments such as those introduced by rabbis Kook, Herzog, and Uziel.[205]

In this article, I have tried to show that it is possible to find in rabbinical court rulings innovativeness of a very different type. Even if triggered by external necessity, this innovativeness is not expressed in new enactments and attempts to adjust the law to the needs of the time and the litigants, but in novel rulings (both strict and lenient),[206] the

202 On procedural innovations, see Radzyner, nn 6–7 above. Substantive innovativeness was less extensive, see B. Eliash, "The limited influence of Israel rabbinical enactments on the Israeli rabbinical courts" (Hebrew), 10–11 *Dine Israel* (1981/83), 187; E. Westreich, "The legal activities of the Chief Rabbis during the period of the British Mandate" (Hebrew), in A. Sagi and D. Schwartz (eds.), *A Hundred Years of Religious Zionism* (Hebrew), (Ramat-Gan: 2003), 2:83.

203 Samuel Eisenstadt, "Comments on the *Rabbinical Courts Enactment* in the land of Israel" (Hebrew), 5 *Hamishpat* (1935), 8–9.

204 See Radzyner, nn 6–7 above.

205 See Eliash, n. 202 above. On halakhic creativity in the first decades of the official rabbinical courts, and its later demise, see Elon, n. 58 above, 824–35; 878–79; 1596–1600; 1807–809.

206 However, the strict rulings are generally law intended for implementation, whereas the lenient ones (e.g., waiving the divorce requirement in cases of civil marriage) have almost no practical import.

objective of which is to preserve the rabbinical courts' authority, to intimidate litigants who might consider exercising their legal right to turn to the civil courts, and even to bring litigants who have already done so back to the rabbinical courts.

As is generally the case with halakhic creativity inspired by necessity, the moves I have described raise significant concerns, both with regard to the sources adduced and the manner in which they are used. In some cases, the court's conduct raises other difficulties, as for example, that which is manifest in a comment by R. Dichovsky about one of the rulings that relied on the Maharashdam's approach:

> Similarly, we also had to repudiate another district rabbinical court ruling, dealing with a newly-penitent husband who endangered his child, and abused him, yet despite this demanded custody of him as a condition for granting a divorce; and the rabbinical court agreed. In my opinion, it is forbidden to hand down such rulings.[207]

Much has been written about the tribulations that the 'struggle for jurisdiction' in the State of Israel is causing for both litigants and the state rabbinical courts, the most significant halakhic institution in existence today. This article has discussed the impact of halakhic innovations that have been generated by these courts in response to this struggle.[208]

207 Dichovsky 2008, n. 25 above, 27.

208 I would like to thank Avishalom Westreich for his helpful comments.

The Jewish Law Annual, Vol. XX

Privacy in Jewish Law: A Historical and Conceptual Analysis

Arye Schreiber*

1. Introduction

Influential scholars of Jewish law, and the courts in Israel, have claimed that Jewish law recognizes and protects privacy, and indeed, this claim influenced both Israel's 1981 *Protection of Privacy Law*, and case law. Some have gone so far as to claim that Jewish privacy law has influenced the development of modern privacy law in general. In this article, I dispute these claims, demonstrating that while, in antiquity, Jewish law offered some protection of privacy, it did so only as far as was necessary for the protection of other interests, such as enjoyment of property or, later, the utility of the postal system. In contrast to personal dignity, which was valued and protected, privacy per se was neither valued nor protected, as is attested by, on the one hand, the close parallels between the concept of *boshet* (disgrace, shame,

* Advocate (Israel), Solicitor (England and Wales)

humiliation) in Jewish law and that of *inuria* in Roman law, and on the other, the lack of recognition of sexual privacy in the Jewish law of late antiquity.

The role of Jewish law in the Jewish homeland was a matter of controversy even before the establishment of the State of Israel; whether and how Jewish law could function as an independent legal system was much debated. In the decades preceding independence, several publications and institutions dedicated to preparing Jewish law for application in the Jewish state were founded.[1] Chief Rabbi of Palestine, and later, first Ashkenazic Chief Rabbi of Israel, R. Isaac Halevi Herzog was of the opinion that since the non-religious majority would not accept the authority of Jewish law, Jewish monetary law would be applied mainly in the context of arbitration. Others sought ways to adjust Jewish law to modernity and to Jewish independence, whether by imparting the spirit of the law into modern Israeli legislation, or through implementation of traditional Jewish law as the operative law of the State.[2] The debate over the role of Jewish law continued after the founding of the State.[3] With some notable exceptions, in recent decades the influence of Jewish law has been principally confined to 'animating' Israeli legislation with the spirit of Jewish law, and occasionally, its language and some minor provisions.

Privacy is one of the few areas in which Jewish law has had a readily-discernible and robust influence on Israeli law — both legislation and case law — principally due to the efforts of Nahum Rakover, deputy Attorney General in the 1980s and 1990s, and a member of the Kahan Commission, the committee that drafted Israel's *Protection of Privacy Law, 5741–1981* (henceforth *Privacy Law*). In the latter capacity, he directly influenced its content, including in it, for example, a provision that afforded correspondence some privacy protection. This provision, which ultimately became §2(5) of the *Privacy Law*, was inspired by the 'ban of Rabbenu Gershom' (*herem derabeinu gershom*), a c.1000 CE decree protecting the confidentiality of

1 M. Elon, *Jewish Law — History, Sources and Principles*, trans. B. Auerbach and M.J. Sykes (Jerusalem: 1994), 1:85–87.

2 For a summary of these efforts, see Z. Falk, "Book Review: J. Bazak, *Jewish Law in the State of Israel*," 1 *Dine Israel* (1969), 112, 114.

3 See D. Sinclair, "Jewish law," in A. Berlin and M. Grossman (eds.), *Oxford Dictionary of the Jewish Religion* (Oxford: 2011), 398–401.

correspondence.[4] Israeli courts, including the Supreme Court, have also cited Rakover's writings repeatedly in support of the general right to privacy and its roots in Jewish law.

Another scholar who has studied privacy in Jewish law, and who shares Rakover's general interest in applying Jewish law to contemporary legislation, is Itamar Warhaftig. Warhaftig concludes his study of Jewish privacy law thus: "If we want a Torah state — and we are duty-bound to act for its realization — we are obligated to address the legal questions that emerge, and to clarify the Torah's stance on these issues."[5] Rakover articulates the putative connection between Jewish law and the broader contemporary attitude to privacy as follows: "It seems that [the Torah], which on the one hand teaches about the value and uniqueness of the individual, and on the other, about the individual's connection to the public, has much to teach us about the right to privacy and its scope."[6]

The influence of Jewish law scholarship on Israeli privacy law warrants that we take a closer look at the halakhic sources, so as to gain a clear picture of the extent to which Jewish law indeed provides a basis, guidance or inspiration for contemporary privacy-related legislation. But before getting to the specifics of the issues in question, let me say a few words about methodology.

Menahem Elon, Deputy President of the Supreme Court of Israel, fought a long hard battle to have Jewish law recognized as first among equals of the legal systems that could assist in the development of Israeli law, by filling lacunae, and providing interpretive tools and legislative and judicial resources.[7] After observing that "despite growing recognition of the need to study Jewish law with a view to preparing it for practical application, most of the scholars did not

4 As will be described below, the recommendations made by Rakover and the Kahan Commission were watered down; they had recommended that reading other parties' correspondence be prohibited; §2(5) prohibits copying or using such correspondence, but not reading it. See N. Rakover, *Protection of Privacy in Jewish Law* (Hebrew), (Jerusalem: 2006) 100, 110. And see text at n. 192 below.

5 I. Warhaftig, *The Right to Privacy in Jewish Law* (Hebrew), (Ofra: 2009), 340.

6 Rakover, n. 4 above, 28.

7 Cf. A. Barak, *Interpretation in Law* (Hebrew). Vol. 2: *Statutory Interpretation* (Hebrew), (Jerusalem: 1993), 440–43.

sufficiently understand that such study required research into every period from the very beginning of Jewish law up to the present," he declared:

> The legal scholar who wishes to present the essence and character of a particular principle, especially when he wishes to draw conclusions with regard to adapting that principle for practical application, must know: (a) what were the various stages of this principle throughout all the periods of Jewish law, (b) what were the economic and social factors that brought about these various stages, (c) how Jewish law absorbed the changes during various stages and incorporated them as an integral part of its legal system, and (d) what were the legal methods Jewish law employed to integrate the new developments into existing law.[8]

Rakover and Warhaftig focus almost exclusively on Elon's first category above — the various stages of a given element of Jewish law — but ironically, despite the overall focus on periodization, their expositions lack sufficient chronological structure. As a rule, the Mishnah, in their writings, is hardly considered separately from its talmudic interpretation, and the two Talmuds are not often differentiated. These scholars frequently interpret earlier sources, such as the Talmud, in light of later sources, such as the *Shulhan Arukh*, and in this regard fail to discern the trajectory of the evolution of the laws that have bearing on privacy issues. Although their research sees privacy as a value motivating several distinct areas of the law, I will argue that the purported connections are tenuous at best.

This article attempts to revert to the methodology for the study of Jewish law championed by Elon. The traditionalist approach to Jewish law takes the academic study of Jewish law to be much like traditional study of the Talmud. Important though that may be, it fails to generate an understanding of Jewish law that would allow it to serve as an inspiration, with respect to ethos, form and substance, for Israeli law, which many, myself among them, see as its primary role today. The traditionalist approach to academic study of Jewish law also fails to generate either a rigorous intellectual history, or a consistent chronology, for the main concepts and principles of Jewish law. If the academic study of Jewish law is to remain relevant to the Israeli legal system, it must be rigorous and comprehensive. This mandates relinquishing exclusive reliance on the traditionalist approach, and adopting the new tools now

8 Elon, n. 1 above, 1: 87.

available for inquiry into the history and evolution of Jewish law, as per Elon's manifesto some twenty years ago. These include the tools of history generally, and archeology specifically; comparative law studies, such as comparative ancient law (Roman, Sasanian, Islamic); literary analysis of Tannaitic and Amoraic sources; and so on.[9]

In this article, I will adopt a hybrid approach,[10] analyzing the internal development of halakhic sources, but also identifying possible external sources of inspiration and influence in social, political, economic, and other realities — as Elon recommended. I will not explore privacy-related laws beyond the talmudic literature, with the exception of a brief discussion of Rabbenu Gershom's ban, nor does my exploration purport to be comprehensive. It is limited to two main areas — visual trespass and sexual privacy, and presents an analysis of the concept of *boshet* and its role in privacy protection. Beyond any substantive contribution, I hope this article contributes to the growing momentum of the hybrid traditionalist–eclectic methodology for studying Jewish law.

2. Privacy in Jewish law

The clear trend among the few researchers who have studied privacy in Jewish law is to find a unified overarching value and legal principle of privacy that underlies several areas of Jewish law. The three most prominent advocates of this stance are Nahum Rakover, Itamar Warhaftig, and Emanuel Rackman. As I noted, I will seek to show that there is, in fact, no such general value or principle, and certainly, no right to privacy in Jewish law in the talmudic literature, and that the several instances where Jewish law does mandate protection of privacy are unconnected, issue-specific laws that are not premised on the value of privacy per se.

9 Examples of the recent burgeoning of investigation into external influences on the Talmud include S. Secunda, "Talmudic text and Iranian context: on the development of two talmudic narratives," *Association of Jewish Studies Review* 33 (2009), 45–69; R. Hidary, "The agonistic Bavli: Greco-Roman rhetoric in Sasanian Persia," in S. Secunda and S. Fine (eds.), *Shoshanat Yaakov–Jewish and Iranian Studies in Honor of Yaakov Elman* (Leiden: 2012), 137–164.

10 On the hybrid approach, see C. Hezser "Introduction," in C. Hezser (ed.), *Rabbinic Law in its Roman and Near Eastern Tradition* (Tübingen: 2003), 1–11.

The significance of this claim goes beyond intellectual history, given that Rakover and Warhaftig have been adduced by Israel's Supreme Court in support of the claim that Jewish law endorses extensive protection of privacy, more so even than Israeli law,[11] and Rakover is cited by the Supreme Court in support of the notion that the constitutional right to privacy enshrined in the *Basic Law: Human Dignity and Liberty, 5752–1992* is based on Jewish law.[12] Likewise, lower courts have cited Rakover on visual trespass (*hezek reiya*) and determined that Israeli law is compatible with Jewish law as he presents it.[13] An alternate understanding of Jewish privacy law is therefore not merely of scholarly interest. I will survey these scholars' opinions briefly.

Rackman's 1996 article on Jewish privacy law is short and quasi-academic, but his opinion must be given due weight nonetheless[14]; indeed Rakover cites the article in his own book.[15] Entitled "The right to privacy in Jewish law," it claims that the right to privacy is a hallmark of modern democracy, and that "its source is unequivocally the Jewish religious tradition."[16] Rakover first published a paper on the protection of privacy in Jewish law in 1970, and, as noted above, was a member of the Kahan Commission that drafted Israel's *Privacy Law*; he wrote the chapter on Jewish law in the Commission's findings. Rakover's 2006 book on privacy has also been influential. Like Rackman, Rakover conceives of privacy as a general value[17] with which a variety of legal

11 *Benjamin Zweig v. Minister of Health et al.*, HCJ 9843/07, Tak-El 2010(2) 1583. In his ruling, Justice Rubenstein wrote that the Jewish law of privacy is premised on the biblical dictum "love your neighbor as yourself" (Lev. 19:18); cf. the ruling cited in the text at nn 173–74 below, which also invokes Leviticus 19.

12 *Eitan Parhi v. State of Israel*, CA 4988/08, Tak-El 2011(3) 2264, para. 12.

13 Specifically, with the notion that where it is clear that buildings will be built in close proximity to each other, buyers have waived their claims to visual trespass. See *Hollander v. Raanana Local Planning and Building Committee*, CA 3639/07 Tak-El 2010(4) 53638, paras. 71–76.

14 Emanuel Rackman, "The right to privacy in Jewish law," 8 *Justice* (1996), 44–47.

15 Rakover, n. 4 above, 16.

16 Rackman, n. 14 above, 44.

17 Jewish law is generally premised on obligations rather than rights. Presumably, Rakover would concede that to speak of 'rights' in Jewish law is a misnomer, and in this article 'value of privacy worthy of protection at law by imposition of obligations on third parties' and 'right to privacy' are effectively interchangeable.

provisions are imbued; in his view there is a general 'right to privacy' in Jewish law.[18] As he puts it: "We have sketched the general outlines of the legal nature of the right to privacy . . . we also showed how Jewish law endeavors to protect society against wrongful exploitation of this right. It is apparent that a number of basic elements of the right to privacy are as ancient as Jewish law itself."[19] Here Rakover not only asserts a general right to privacy, but goes further and suggests a theological anchor for the putative right: "[the] Jewish outlook that a person is not merely 'flesh and blood,' but rather a creation suffused with the image of God,[20] explains the fact that a matter novel to other legal systems [viz., privacy] has existed in Jewish law from its inception."[21]

Rakover's view of Jewish privacy law has been accepted by Israeli courts. Particularly emphatic was Justice Drori of the Jerusalem District Court, a Jewish law enthusiast, who wrote of Rakover's book that "whoever reads the books gets a comprehensive general picture, and it may be said that there is indeed, in Jewish Law, a general right to personal privacy."[22] Warhaftig's book is similarly premised on the existence of a general value of privacy in Jewish law.[23]

Both Warhaftig[24] and Rakover[25] attempt to define privacy, I leave for an other occasion analysis of their definitions. For now, let me note that what Prosser did for privacy law in 1960, Solove[26] and others are attempting to do now, namely, devise a taxonomy for the massive,

18 N. Rakover, "The protection of personal privacy in Jewish law" (Hebrew), 26 *Hapraklit* (1970), 563, 572–73.

19 Rakover, n. 4 above, English summary, xxvii.

20 There is no doubt that Jewish law gives tremendous weight to creation "in the image of God"; see Y. Lorberbaum, *Image of God: Halakha and Aggada* (Hebrew), (Tel Aviv: 2004). However, Rakover does not substantiate the claim that this is the basis for the alleged right to privacy.

21 Rakover, n. 4 above, xxix.

22 *Leora Berko v. State of Israel*, Various Petitions 4301/08 (Jm) (unpublished), para. 314.

23 Warhaftig, n. 5 above, 19, 47.

24 Ibid., 27.

25 Rakover, n. 4 above, 15, where he repeats the definition from his 1970 article (n. 18 above), which is also adduced, without credit, by MK Moshe Shahal during the first reading of the *Draft Law: Protection of Privacy, Reshumot* (Draft Laws) 1453 (1980), 3487, 3494.

26 D.J. Solove, *Understanding Privacy* (Cambridge MA: 2008).

unruly field of privacy law.[27] This is a crucial component missing from the work of Warhaftig and Rakover. Even in the days of Warren and Brandeis, the different elements of privacy were recognized: these founders of modern privacy law differentiate, for instance, between vertically and horizontally applicable privacy. Prosser approached his taxonomical work in terms of the harm being avoided by various actions for privacy, and the present generation of privacy scholars has sought to define and categorize privacy and its violations on the basis of space, behavior, choices, and information.[28]

This differentiation is missing from the aforementioned discussions of privacy in Jewish law, though it is clear that no plausible definition of privacy can be arrived at without reference to such analysis. Both Rakover and Warhaftig glide more or less seamlessly between privacy in the sense of protection of personal information and the right to be 'left alone,' to vertically-applicable constitutional privacy as per the US Constitution's Fourth Amendment, privacy in the sense of self-determination, and privacy in international human rights declarations.[29] Prosser's 1960 article is cited by Rakover in passing,[30] but the significance of Prosser's deliberate analysis of privacy case law into a multiplicity of different actions is missed. This is unfortunate, as had their conclusions been more nuanced, they would have been far more fruitful as a source of inspiration for jurists. Moreover, working within the frameworks of legal research on general privacy law would have been conducive to recognizing that the same multiplicity exists in Jewish law, and that many of the examples they adduce under the 'privacy' rubric are not really privacy issues at all.

There is one scholar who preempted me in making this claim. Aaron Kirschenbaum plainly disagrees with the aforementioned views of Rackman, Rakover, and Warhaftig. He states: "It cannot be said that the *halakha* here [allowing witnesses to be planted so that an offense will meet the requirements for severe punishment] intends to defend the privacy of an individual. Though there may be found isolated *halakhot* that do so, there is no general right to personal privacy in

27 On Solove's taxonomy, see D.K. Citron and L.M. Henry, "Visionary pragmatism and the value of privacy in the twenty-first century," 108 *Michigan Law Review* (2010), 1107.

28 See C.J. Bennett, *The Privacy Advocates* (Cambridge MA: 2008), 2–6.

29 Rakover, n. 4 above, 15–24; Warhaftig, n. 5 above, 26.

30 Ibid., 17.

Jewish law."[31] I fully agree. Kirschenbaum made this remark incidentally, but it is my central thesis in the present article, which will show that privacy is not a core value in Jewish law, and there is no general right to privacy in Jewish law. It will do so by examining three central areas related to privacy concerns — visual trespass, sexual privacy, and privacy of correspondence. I will show that insofar as privacy received some form of broad protection, it was human dignity that was being protected, and privacy was protected when its violation was also a violation of someone's dignity.

3. Visual trespass (*hezek reiya*)

Hezek reiya, literally 'damage through seeing,' will be referred to in English mainly as 'visual trespass'; it connotes such sight-related behaviors as gazing, gawking, leering, and so on. Visual trespass features prominently in bBaba Batra. Rakover and Warhaftig have written extensively on visual trespass, and I will repeat only as much of their discussion as is necessary to make my central argument, namely, that the laws of visual trespass protect privacy, but only to the extent required for peaceful coexistence between neighbors, and as part of a system of laws enabling civilized urban living. They do not protect some abstract legal principle of privacy.

"*Hezek reiya*" is the term used by the Babylonian Talmud to denote a set of laws that govern building practices, practices that secure various aspects of privacy, in particular: a wall or fence separating two halves of a formerly common courtyard now divided between the parties; and rules governing windows and doorways facing neighbors' houses or common courtyards, to preclude using these openings to look into the neighbor's house or the shared courtyard. The Mishnah states that one may not place a window overlooking common property directly opposite another window. The Talmud inquires as to the source of this mishnaic rule, and, in the name of R. Johanan, invokes a biblical verse:

31 A. Kirschenbaum, "Entrapment in Jewish law" (Hebrew), 15 *Dine Israel* (1989–90), 39–137, 58; see Drori's opinion in the ruling cited in n. 22 above, which quotes and dismisses Kirschenbaum's view. See also D. Frimer, "Medical examinations pursuant to court order and the right to personal privacy" (Hebrew), in Uriel Cohen (ed.), *Nediv Lev–A Collection of Articles by Rabbi Professor Dov I. Frimer* (Hebrew), (Jerusalem: 2010), 75–82.

Mishnah In a courtyard which he shares with others, one should not make a door facing someone else's door nor a window facing someone else's window. If it is small, he should not enlarge it, and he should not turn one into two. If it faces the public domain [i.e., the street], however, he may make a door facing someone else's door and a window facing someone else's window, and if it is small he may enlarge it or he may make two out of one.

Gemara Whence are these rules derived? R. Johanan said: From the scriptural verse, "And Balaam lifted up his eyes and he saw Israel dwelling according to their tribes"[32] (Num. 24:2). What did he see? He saw that the doors of their tents were not aligned one with the other, whereupon he exclaimed: These are worthy that the divine presence should rest upon them![33]

R. Johanan invokes the biblical verse in question in support of specific laws of visual trespass, but as I will argue, taken in its biblical context, the verse cited by R. Johanan is inconsistent with a privacy-based characterization of visual trespass. To determine the biblical source of the visual trespass laws, two other passages should be considered, one from Genesis and the other from 2 Samuel.

In Genesis 26:6–8, we read that during the sojourn of Isaac and Rebekah in Gerar, Isaac initially presented Rebekah as his sister. The narrative then states: "And it came to pass, when he had been there a long time, that Abimelech king of the Philistines looked out at a window, and saw, and, behold, Isaac was sporting (*metzahek*) with Rebekah his wife." The word "*metzahek*" here has a sexual connotation,[34] as is clear from the context: what Abimelech saw made it obvious

32 The new JPS translation reads: "encamped tribe by tribe."

33 bBaba Batra 60a. For textual variants, see M. Kasher, *Torah Shleima* (Jerusalem: 1992), 43:109.

34 See *Rashi*, Genesis 26:8. The new JPS translation reads 'fondling,' which makes the verb's sexual connotation evident. The verb is used in the same sexual sense in Genesis 39:14, where again, the old JPS translation ("to mock") is prudish, but the new JPS translation ("to dally") captures the sexual connotation. tSota 6:3 offers several interpretations of the lexical root *tz"h"k* that make this explicit.

to him that they were married, and not — as Isaac had claimed — siblings. In the Hebrew, it is ambiguous whether Abimelech was looking out of his own window or into Isaac and Rebekah's.[35] However, there is not even a hint that Abimelech's conduct, in looking out of his own window, or into Isaac's, and observing some intimate encounter between Isaac and Rebekah, was reprehensible. This episode is not too instructive, since we cannot ascertain whether or not Abimelech was watching in a prurient manner, and also because even if he was, his having been deceived by Isaac might neutralize any wrongdoing on his part in discovering the deception.

On the other hand, the story of King David and Bathsheba is unambiguously an archetypical instance of seeing private activity that is taking place on someone else's property: David, standing on his own royal rooftop, sees a woman bathing.

> Late one afternoon, David rose from his couch and strolled on the roof of the royal palace, and from the roof (*meial hagag*) saw a woman bathing. The woman was very beautiful. (2 Sam. 11:2)

The words "above the roof" may refer to Bathsheba's bathing on the rooftop, but a more plausible reading, reflected in the translation quoted above, was proposed by R. David Kimhe, the Radak (Narbonne, 1160–1235).[36] According to the Radak, the words "from [lit., above] the roof" (*meial hagag*) refer not to Bathsheba's bathing, but to David's leering. This reading is also supported by archeological evidence from the City of David, which places the palace at the top of the steep hill, above the site's Area G, meaning that it would have afforded a good vantage-point from which to see into houses below it.[37]

This adds an interesting dimension to the story: David specifically went to the roof in the "late afternoon," the time of day at which those who end a period of ritual impurity undergo ritual purification by immersing themselves in water, which the biblical text notes that Bathsheba had indeed done (2 Sam. 11:4). As the sun set, David would have been almost invisible to anyone immersing in a ritual bath in their home, as they would surely have lit a lamp, whereas he was standing outdoors in the twilight. We cannot be sure of David's *mens rea*, but at

35 See the *Daat Mikra* commentary ad loc.

36 Radak ad loc., and see too his comments on Psalms 68:24. See Jacob Medan, *David and Bathsheba* (Hebrew), (Alon Shvut: 1996), 27 n. 25, 33 n. 47.

37 As noted by Amnon Bazak.

the very least he was negligent; if he did not actually know, then he ought to have known that standing on his rooftop in the late afternoon or early evening was, literally, looking for trouble. Moreover, the verse adds that he was not just standing there taking in the afternoon air; he was "strolling," which may suggest that he was looking for an angle from which to catch a glimpse.[38]

The continuation of the story is well known: the episode led to much bloodshed and tragedy, all ensuing from David's visual trespass. Recognizing this, the Talmud states: "Do not become accustomed to engaging in contemptible conduct (*gnut*), on account of the incident that occurred."[39] The Soncino edition suggests alternative renderings for the antecedent clause: 'Do not frequent places where immodest sights are to be seen'; 'do not frequent roofs' — this latter version presumably based on emending the Hebrew word for "contemptible conduct" — *gnut* — so that it reads "roofs" — *gagot*. *Rashi* ad loc. elucidates the dictum as follows: " 'Do not become accustomed to engaging in contemptible conduct' — do not become accustomed to making your home in a public place, in a visible place; 'on account of the incident which occurred' — with David and Bathsheba." This is not framed as blaming the victim for bathing in a visible place, but rather, as advising prudent conduct in a hilly town such as Jerusalem. Indeed, the Talmud does not say that Bathsheba or Uriyah were in any way to blame.

The talmudic dictum in tractate Pesahim, as understood by Rashi, summarizes my interpretation of the talmudic approach to visual trespass in general. The talmudic directive is not 'do not walk on the roof,' 'do not look into the homes' of others, but rather, 'do not locate your home in too public a place, in too readily-visible a place, since that is asking for trouble.' This directive that one is to act in a manner conducive to peaceful coexistence in an urban environment is the idea underlying the concept of visual trespass. It is not motivated by the desideratum of protecting privacy as an abstract value, though the laws of visual trespass do indeed protect privacy. Let us now take a closer look at the halakhic sources on visual trespass.

38 bSanhedrin 107a, and *Maharsha* ad loc., suggest that at first David only saw her head, but then tried to glimpse her naked body, eventually succeeding.

39 bPesahim 113a.

i. Sources of the notion of visual trespass

R. Johanan states that the source for the rule against windows and doors that face each other is the verse: "And Balaam lifted up his eyes and he saw Israel dwelling according to their tribes" (Num. 24:2). But what was R. Johanan's basis for concluding that what so impressed and inspired Balaam was that the Israelites' tent openings did not face each other? And what is so extraordinary about tent openings that do not face each other? If every tent simply faced the same way (for example, due to sun or wind), or even faced different directions, they could easily be arranged so that openings did not face each other. Moreover, if X has a doorway facing Y's doorway, then the converse is also true. Assuming that no one wants their own doorway to be visually accessible to others, self-interest will ensure that everyone sees to it that their doorways are not in the sightline of neighboring dwellings.

Some have claimed that R. Johanan's statement is premised on the continuation of the biblical passage, namely, the verse "How fair are your tents, O Jacob" (Num. 24:5).[40] This interpretation seems attractive given the word "tents," which appears both in this verse and in R. Johanan's exegesis ("he saw that the doors of their tents were not aligned"), but this does not solve the problem: is there a plausible analysis of the verses that allows for R. Johanan's conclusion? Let me suggest an interpretive solution. It seems that what impressed Balaam, according to R. Johanan, was not the tent openings' not facing each other, but rather that different tribes faced their own members, not members of other tribes. This is in line with the plain meaning of the biblical verse that it was seeing Israel "dwelling according to their tribes" (*shokhen lishvatav*) (Num. 24:2) that inspired Balaam.

On this interpretation, R. Johanan is not suggesting that none of the Israelites' tent openings faced other Israelite tent openings, but rather, that the tent openings of one tribe were not facing those of another tribe. He is speaking of the conduct of the tribes, not of individuals. Each tribe was inward-facing, and did not pry into the affairs of other tribes. Several biblical episodes attest that the tribes considered

40 Interestingly, elsewhere R. Johanan related to the verse in a different manner, interpreting "your tents" as places of prayer and study (bSanhedrin 105b).

their wealth, specifically their land, to be communal (within the tribe).[41] This is also hinted at by the word *"shokhen,"* which the new JPS translates as 'encamped' and the old JPS as 'dwelling'. The lexical root of 'dwelling' or 'encamped,' *sh"kh"n*, is the same as that of the word 'neighbor.'[42] This explains the Talmud's 'joint courtyard' — 'tribe by tribe encampment' analogy in the *sugya* in bBaba Batra — the encampment was 'neighborly.' Each tribe was comparable to one family, and the public a-tribal space between the tribes was analogous to the common courtyard. Balaam saw that each tribe camped within itself, so to speak, and did not look out onto other tribes' space.

This suggests that insofar as there was privacy, a whole tribe was considered family, and there was no particular privacy within a tribe. Furthermore, the reason the tribes did not set up their encampments facing each other was not to avoid visual trespass, which presumably would apply equally within a tribe, but rather, so as not to provoke jealousy. This is supported by the narrative that describes what ensued after Israel conquered the land of Sihon (Num. 21:35). This conquest of rich pastures provoked the first major challenge to the unity of the Israelite tribes, when the tribes of Reuven, Gad and half of Menashe wanted to settle with their immense flocks in the conquered land, and not in the land of Israel proper (Num. 32:33). What Balaam saw was that the tribes were not jealous of each other. R. Johanan's analogy is telling: the Mishnah states that, within the common courtyard, one family may not make a window or doorway opposite that of another family. If this interpretation is correct, R. Johanan is stating that the law seeks, not to protect privacy and prevent voyeurism, but to create living conditions that discourage jealousy.

How authoritative is R. Johanan's invocation of the verse about Balaam? Rakover judiciously takes it to be alluding to visual trespass,[43]

41 The laws of inheritance were meant to ensure that land is not lost to a tribe, see Numbers 36:3–6.

42 As, e.g., in Exodus 12:4. In Numbers 23:9, just before the verse we are discussing, Balaam referred to Israel as "a nation that dwells (*yishkon*) alone," again using the lexical root *sh-kh-n*.

43 Rakover, n. 4 above, 270. Rakover was likewise cautious in the "Report of the Commission for Protection of Personal Privacy" (Hebrew), (Jerusalem 1976), c. 3.5, 8.

but Warhaftig[44] and Birnhack[45] have cited this talmudic *sugya* as the actual halakhic source for visual trespass. From a traditionalist-structuralist approach, this claim is not completely unreasonable,[46] but it is problematic. R. Johanan's statement was that, according to Balaam, the tribes' minding their own business, so to speak, made them "worthy of the divine presence." This is not a statement of a legal obligation, but commendation of an admirable, perhaps pious, mode of conduct. Furthermore, notwithstanding the interpretation suggested above, the connection between the verse about the tribes' encampment and the Mishnah's 'no facing windows' law is tenuous, and the exegesis deriving the law from Numbers 24:2 is not mentioned in Tannaitic sources. This suggests that R. Johanan was looking for, and found, some sort of textual support for his position. In the Babylonian Talmud, the question, "whence are these rules derived?" generally denotes a search for post facto support, including biblical support, for a Rabbinic law, rather than a search for a pre-existing source.[47] If the laws of visual trespass were an ancient law or tradition, they would surely have had a more plausible source. I contend, therefore, that the laws of visual trespass are one outcome of several processes that reached their zenith during the era of R. Johanan's leadership.

ii. The emergence and significance of the visual trespass laws

Both the Tosefta and the Mishnah are replete with building regulations that appear to be designed to prevent visual trespass. In particular, this includes rules such as: a wall X builds must be a prescribed distance from Y's window, so that it cannot be used by X to peep into Y's home (tBaba Batra 1:5, mBaba Batra 2:4); X may not make a window or

44 Warhaftig, n. 5 above, 86, 113.

45 M. Birnhack "Control and consent: the theoretical basis of the right to privacy" (Hebrew), 11 *Mishpat Umimshal — Law and Government in Israel* (2007), 17 n. 19.

46 Minister of Justice Tamir opened the first reading of the draft *Privacy Law* in the Knesset on June 23, 1980 with a reference to this claim, see *Reshumot*, n. 25 above. Tamir was apparently quoting from the Kahan Commission's findings, including Rakover's chapter on Jewish law.

47 This is not only recognized by academic scholars, but was also noted by R. Malakhi b. Jacob Hakohen, *Yad Malakhi*, 1:430.

doorway opposite Y's window or doorway (tBaba Batra 2:5[48]); and similar rules concerning a shared courtyard — windows may not be opened onto it, especially opposite another window (mBaba Batra 3:10). Also, upon dissolution of co-ownership of a courtyard, a fence must be erected between the parties' sections (mBaba Batra 1:1); bBaba Batra 2a-b suggests that this in order to prevent visual trespass, that is, to prevent the parties from seeing into each other's section.

Rakover writes: "The laws of visual trespass (*hezek reiya*) are manifold, and lawyers dealing with questions of town planning will surely find great interest in them. But our point here is chiefly to highlight the **principle** [of privacy — A.S.] underlying these matters, and to emphasize the legal aspect of this right."[49] In my view, however, the laws of visual trespass must be viewed in context, that is, among laws that address the distancing of noxious smells, insects, pigeons, and other nuisances; building codes and regulations pertaining to shared courtyards and walls; abutters' rights, easements and so on, all of which are discussed in tractate Baba Batra. Warhaftig[50] and Rakover[51] describe the debates as to the proper categorization of visual trespass among other torts, but their discussions are premised on the assumption that visual trespass is a good, or even the paradigmatic, example of the workings of the privacy principle in Jewish law. I am arguing that attending to the context of the visual trespass laws in tractate Baba Batra shows that they are but one of many instances of laws governing urban life, and the facilitation of urban life is the value being protected — not privacy.

Beyond the contextual evidence from mBaba Batra, a question presents itself: why is there no general prohibition against gawking?

48 It is difficult to construe this particular Tosefta as addressing visual trespass, see *Responsa Maharitatz*, #253; also *Nahmanides*, bBaba Batra 59a; cf. *Mordekhai*, bBaba Batra 1:471. See also S. Lieberman, *Tosefta Kifshuta* ad loc. The Tosefta appears to be discussing creation of a window above, i.e., on top of, not opposite, another window. It seems evident that this Tosefta addresses sharing responsibility for the structural soundness of a shared wall. It is interesting to note that the same rules were set down by Julian of Ascalon, see Besim S. Hakim, "Julian of Ascalon's treatise of construction and design rules from sixth-century Palestine," *Journal of the Society of Architectural Historians* 60 (2001), 4–25, 16.

49 Rakover 1970, n. 18 above, 571 (emphasis in original).

50 Warhaftig, n. 5 above, 87–8.

51 Rakover, n. 4 above, 269–80.

Later authorities do identify a general prohibition, the source for which is the talmudic discussion of an easement that generates visual trespass. The Talmud stipulates that one cannot claim an easement over someone else's property, even if the owner has expressly granted it, where that easement is for an activity that causes damage (bBaba Batra 23a). Thus, even if a landowner expressly waived her right to force a neighbor to share in building a fence between their adjacent courtyards, she can still force him to do so at any time.[52] Two explanations of the rule that one cannot claim an easement that causes damage are of particular relevance to the issue of visual trespass. Maimonides states that the rationale for the 'no waiver' rule is that the damage is intolerable and ongoing, hence it can be presumed that no one waives protection from such damage.[53] The Rashba (Barcelona, 1235–1310) takes a different approach, and explains that the rationale for the rule lies in the ethical element in protection from visual trespass: other damages can be waived, because they are merely a matter of debt, but not so those of visual trespass, since privacy has ethical value. Indeed, its violation distances the divine presence (*shekhina*).[54] According to the Rashba, then, the ethical dimension of protection from visual trespass trumps the right to waive compensation for such damage.[55] We see that Maimonides and the Rashba, each invoking the *sugya* in bBaba Batra 23a, both perceive visual trespass as something other than an ordinary tort or prohibited act. And indeed, visual trespass is neither an ordinary tort that can be waived, nor a prohibited act in the traditional sense. It is, perhaps, closest to tortious liability for breach of a statutory duty,[56] in this case the statutory duty being urban building codes.

Several prominent traditional authorities consider visual trespass an actual biblical prohibition, notably R. Jacob Lorderbaum[57] and

52 It appears that Maimonides limited the law to the case of division of co-owned property. The Rashba, cited below, extends this to opening windows overlooking adjacent homes.

53 Maimonides, *Code*, Laws concerning Neighbors 11:4. Cf. Maimonides, *Commentary on the Mishnah*, mBaba Batra 3:8.

54 *Responsa Rashba*, 2:268. This is a reference to R. Johanan's statement, discussed above, linking avoidance of visual trespass with the divine presence.

55 See Elon, n. 1 above, 2:943.

56 Governed in Israel by §63 of the *Torts Ordinance*.

57 *Netivot Hamishpat*, HM 154.

R. Yehiel Michel Epstein.[58] R. Meir b. Todros Halevi Abulafia (Rama),[59] and Nahmanides[60] both assert that there is a prohibition against gazing, and the *Shulhan Arukh*[61] sets down a prohibition against gazing that causes damage. Among academic scholars, Elon refers to a prohibition against visual trespass in Jewish law,[62] as does Rakover,[63] but I would argue that there is nothing in the Talmud to suggest such a prohibition. Rakover expressly situates visual trespass within the general framework of privacy protection.[64] He further notes that visual trespass is largely covered by Israeli law following the passage of the *Privacy Law*, §1(2) of which prohibits 'spying on or trailing a person, in a manner likely to harass him . . .', and §7 of the *Basic Law: Human Dignity and Liberty, 5752–1992*. In this regard I agree with Norman Lamm's assertion that "the Halachah insists upon the responsibility of each individual not to put himself into a position where he can pry into his neighbor's personal domain, and this responsibility can be enforced by the courts . . . visual or aural invasion of privacy is thus primarily a moral offence."[65] There is no Jewish civil law requirement that damages be paid for visual trespass; the only remedy is enforcement of the relevant provision.[66]

58 *Arukh Hashulhan*, HM 154. Others have also hinted at this. R. Joshua Falk, in *Sefer Meirat Einayim*, HM 154, does not state that there is a biblical prohibition against visual trespass; only that an easement cannot be allowed, as it enables a prohibited activity, as stipulated by the verse in Numbers regarding Balaam.

59 *Yad Rama*, Baba Batra 3:280; see Rakover, n. 4 above, 284.

60 Commentary on bBaba Batra 59a s.v. *ha detnan*. See Warhaftig, n. 5 above, 92 n. 35.

61 HM 378:5, though it is not clear that this is a reference to *hezek reiya*; see Warhaftig, ibid., 87–88 n. 13.

62 *Military Court of Appeals v. Vaknin*, PD 42(3) 837, 860 (1988).

63 N. Rakover, "The protection of privacy in Jewish law," in *Israel Yearbook of Human Rights* (Tel Aviv: 1975), 178; Kahan Commission Report, n.43 above, 8, citing *SA*.

64 Rakover, n. 4 above, 269; idem, n. 18 above, 570.

65 N. Lamm, "The Fourth Amendment and its equivalent in the halachah," *Judaism* 16 (1967), 300, 303–304. However, I am not aware of evidence for Lamm's conclusion that "the civil law and its requirements of monetary compensation" are derived from the moral offence of invasion of privacy (304).

66 In western law other tools exist to protect the enjoyment of property, including trespass and nuisance. Property rights are also subject to various constraints determined by the enjoyment of property. E.g., *Bernstein v. Skyviews and General* [1977] 2 All ER 902, 909 determined that property rights extend to the sky only insofar as is necessary for the enjoyment of the property.

This view of visual trespass is further reflected in Maimonides' classification of these laws in the Laws concerning Neighbors, in the Book of Property (*kinyan*) rather than in the Book of Torts (*nezikin*), notwithstanding the fact that Maimonides, in line with the apparent meaning of bBaba Batra 2b, rules that visual trespass is indeed a tort. In his subtitle to the Laws concerning Neighbors, Maimonides characterizes its subject as "the rules of dividing property between partners, and removing damage caused by any of them to their neighbor. . . ."

The Talmud's main discussion of visual trespass arises incidentally. bBaba Batra begins with a discussion about the meaning of the Mishnah's opening words: "Partners who want to make a *mehitza* (lit., split) in their [co-owned] courtyard."[67] Does *mehitza* signify a means of boundary demarcation such as a fence, or does it mean division, that is, dissolution of the co-ownership? Either meaning is plausible, since the notions are semantically connected. If it means 'demarcation,' the Mishnah is discussing norms regarding the demarcation and its construction — materials, height, ownership, etc. However, if it means 'division,' the Mishnah is discussing the dissolution of the partnership in this courtyard, and appears to stipulate what must be done — how the partners are to effect the dissolution. The Talmud appears to prefer the latter option, taking the Mishnah to say that upon dissolution of the co-ownership of a courtyard, the owners must put up a fence between their respective sections, suggesting that visual trespass is a real tort.[68]

According to Eidels, the dispute over the question of whether visual trespass (*hezek reiya*) is or is not an actionable tort (*hezek*) is limited to the issue of coercion: whether, upon dissolution of the co-ownership, the parties can force their former partners to build a fence.[69] In my view this is much too narrow a construction of the talmudic *sugya*, and even traditionalists have construed the dispute more broadly.[70] This further supports the claim that visual trespass cannot be viewed as an ordinary tort or prohibition.

Moreover, there is much in the Talmud that indicates that visual trespass is about enjoyment of property. For example, the Talmud contrasts the situation where co-ownership of a courtyard is dissolved

67 mBaba Batra 1:1.

68 *Tosafot*, bBaba Batra 2b s.v. *ta shma*

69 See Z. Eidels and E. Afarsemon, *Quality of the Environment; Visual Trespass* (Hebrew), (Hebron: 2009), 107ff.

70 Notably R. Zalman N. Goldberg.

with the situation where one person's roof looks out onto another person's courtyard. In the former case, the partners must build a wall at their shared expense, in the latter case, the roof owner must build a wall at her own expense. The Talmud explains that this is because the courtyard owner may claim: "I use my courtyard regularly, but you do not use your roof regularly, so I cannot know when you will go up to your roof, and I cannot conceal myself from you" (bBaba Batra 2b–3a). In other words, the roof owner is undermining the courtyard owner's enjoyment of his courtyard, so the roof owner must build a 4 cubit (2m) high wall to prevent her seeing into the courtyard. By contrast, in the case where co-ownership of a courtyard is dissolved, both parties use the courtyard regularly, so from the outset each party knows he cannot do personal, private things in his half.[71] This suggests that if there is a visual trespass tort, it protects residents' ability to enjoy their property.

It is not surprising that Roman law treated identical questions. In Roman law of this period, the action for dissolution of co-owned property was known as *action communi dividundo*.[72] The constitution of 294 CE provided that *in communionem vel societatem nemo compellitur invitus deteneri*, meaning that no person could be compelled to continue a co-ownership against his will,[73] and Paul, a "late classical jurist," stated that indefinite agreements between co-owners to prohibit a dissolution of the co-ownership had no force.[74] This is not to suggest Roman influence on the talmudic discussion. Roman law distinguished between the concepts of partnership (*societas*) and co-ownership (*communi*),[75] whereas in Jewish law they both fall under the rubric of partnership (*shutafut*). It is nonetheless the case that the relevant laws in tractate Baba Batra of the Mishnah, as understood by the Talmud, closely paralleled contemporary Roman law. In the discussion in mBaba Batra 1:1 regarding means of constructing a demarcating fence, the methods cited, though all based on local custom, also have parallels in Roman

71 See *Rashi*, bBaba Batra 3a s.v. *deitztena*.

72 See G. MacCormack, "The action *communi dividundo* in Roman and Scots law," in A.D. Lewis and D.J. Ibbetson (eds.), *The Roman Law Tradition* (Cambridge: 1994), 159ff.

73 Ibid., 160, citing C 3.37.5.

74 Ibid., citing D 10.3.14.2.

75 A.L. Udovitch, *Partnership and Profit in Medieval Islam* (Princeton: 1970), 35–6.

custom: "ancient Romans had various kinds of fences (*septa, sepes, vel sepimenta*), a wall (*maceria*), hedge, wooden fence, and ditch . . . for enclosing their gardens and orchards."[76]

Again, that is not to say that there was influence one way or the other,[77] but rather, these questions were common to all legal systems that addressed co-ownership of land and how to end it, and rules for proper fences between neighbors. The influence of Roman law in Babylonia in the Amoraic period is controversial,[78] but the principal route for Roman influence on the Babylonian Talmud was via the Tannaitic literature, including the Mishnah and Tosefta. We must, however, keep in mind that

> it is easy to draw parallels and contrasts between mishnaic law and the law of the Hellenistic and Roman empires, but it is not easy to determine influence or borrowing in either direction. Although the question remains open, surely it is a reasonable possibility that in some areas of the law, notably civil law . . . the Mishnah may have been influenced by the legal traditions of the Mediterranean.[79]

Whereas the Mishnah has laws relating to opening windows that face each other, the Tosefta (tBaba Batra 1:5) expressly addresses gazing, and is quoted in bBaba Batra 22b. The Jerusalem and Babylonian Talmuds differ markedly in their treatment of visual trespass. Though they do diverge on substantive law — for example, with regard to visual trespass in a garden[80] — the main divergence appears to be in the definition and conceptualization of visual trespass. Whereas the Babylonian Talmud engages in a lively discussion as to whether visual trespass is a recognized type of damage (bBaba Batra 2b), in the

76 A. Adam, *Roman Antiquities — An Account of the Manners and Customs of the Romans* (Philadelphia: 1807), 541.

77 See B. Cohen, *Jewish and Roman Law: A Comparative Study* (NY: 1966), 1–30; K. Kahana Kagan, *Three Great Systems of Jurisprudence* (London: 1955), 6–7. These works are now somewhat dated, and do not fully appreciate Saul Lieberman's contributions to the comparative study of ancient law.

78 See P. Crone, *Roman, Provincial and Islamic law* (Cambridge: 1987), 12ff.

79 S.JD. Cohen, "Judaean legal tradition and the halakhah of the Mishnah," in C. Fonrobert and M.S. Jaffee (eds.), *Cambridge Companion to the Talmud and Rabbinic Literature* (Cambridge: 2007), 121–143, 127.

80 Eidels and Afarsemon, n. 69 above, 157–58, citing *Ran*, bBaba Batra 3a s.v. *uleinyan*, and the Rosh, quoted in *Shita Mekubetzet*, bBaba Batra 2b s.v. *veharosh*.

Jerusalem Talmud, there appears to be no awareness at all of the concept of visual trespass. Does this imply that the concept of visual trespass entered the Babylonian Talmud via local Babylonian influence?

Herzog noted that the Jerusalem Talmud makes no mention of an abutter's rights (*bar metzra*), discussed at length in bBaba Batra, but dismissed the suggestion that this rule was derived by Jewish judges in Babylon from local Persian law.[81] This is also true, I would argue, in the case of visual trespass: its absence from the Jerusalem Talmud despite its inclusion in the Babylonian Talmud does not imply derivation from Persian law, though that is possible. The contrary is more likely in this case: the debate in the Babylonian Talmud suggests that the concept of visual trespass was less familiar, less well understood, to the Babylonian Sages than to the Sages of the Jerusalem Talmud. The Babylonian Talmud has trouble determining whether this concept even exists, and thus offers two radically divergent interpretations of mBaba Batra 1:1, one premised on its existence, the other making no such assumption. The Jerusalem Talmud finds no ambiguity in mBaba Batra 1:1. This suggests that the source for the laws of visual trespass should be sought, not in the Babylonian context, but in the Palestinian context, where they are taken to be straightforward and unproblematic.[82] Roman law is the obvious source for contextualizing the Jerusalem Talmud's straightforward understanding of laws that were so controversial to the Babylonian Talmud. Indeed, jNezikin appears to reflect considerable Roman influence,[83] and specifically, to have been influenced by the Roman laws against visual trespass. But regardless of whether this influence can be demonstrated, it is clear that there was a Roman background to the second- and third-century Rabbinic debates in the land of Israel. Roman law thus enhances our understanding of the Tannaitic, and therefore

81 R. I. Herzog, *Main Institutions of Jewish Law* (London: 1980), 1:386. Cf. D. Sperber, *Roman Palestine — 200–400; The Land* (Ramat-Gan: 1978), 200.

82 On the Palestinian Roman influence on the Babylonian Talmud, see R.L. Kalmin, *Jewish Babylonia between Persia and Roman Palestine* (Oxford: 2006).

83 C. Hezser, *Form, Function and the Historical Significance of the Rabbinic Story in Yerushalmi Nezikin* (Tübingen: 1993). In general, there are many parallels between the processes and methodologies of the Jerusalem Talmud and those of Justinian codification; see idem, "The codification of legal knowledge in late antiquity — the Talmud Yerushalmi and Roman law codes," in Peter Schäfer (ed.), *The Talmud Yerushalmi and Graeco-Roman Culture* (Tübingen: 1998–2002), 1:581–641.

the Amoraic, urban zoning laws, and can further our project of determining whether or not privacy per se was a core value protected by the halakha.

To be sure, seclusion was valued by the Romans, but inside the home, there was little that was considered private. "The Roman house, particularly that of an elite citizen, was anything but a private retreat from the public world of business. Because the owner had to conduct daily business in the house, it probably had no rooms that we would today consider 'private.' "[84] Yet obviously, the Roman citizen controlled access to his home. By the time of the High Empire (50–250 CE), the "dwelling of the ordinary individual was no longer, even for public display, the matrix of the formal patterns of family life. Great or small, it was a retreat from the collective life, a haven of informal and anonymous privacy, empty of any significance but that of personal fancy or indulgence."[85] The homes of middle-class Romans in the High Empire period in Italy were buildings five or six stories high,[86] in contrast to the two-story norm in Israel of that period. With such tall buildings, and considerable population density, building codes became tools to ensure sustained peaceful coexistence. Judging by the legal provisions, the Romans were much more interested in light than in privacy,[87] though there was sometimes a correlation between the two. One common solution was to place the windows of lower levels of homes relatively high up, both for security and for privacy,[88] allowing light, but not providing a view. The courtyard surrounded by living quarters — co-ownership of which is discussed in Baba Batra — is also familiar from the Roman *domus*.[89] The internal gardens, together with other areas, notably dining rooms and baths, were "an oasis of seclusion and the focal point of the private life of the family" for the Roman citizens affluent enough to enjoy them.[90]

84 J.R. Clarke, *Looking at Lovemaking — Constructions of Sexuality in Roman Art 100 B.C.–A.D. 250* (Berkeley: 2001), 93.
85 Ibid.
86 F.E. Brown, *Roman Architecture* (NY: 1968), 39.
87 O.F. Robinson, *Ancient Rome: City Planning and Administration* (London: 1992), 32.
88 J.P. Adam, *Roman Building — Materials and Techniques*, trans. A. Mathews (London: 1994), 305.
89 H.F. Jolowicz and B. Nicholas, *Historical Introduction to the Study of Roman Law* (Cambridge: 1972), 158.
90 F. Sear, *Roman Architecture* (London: 1989), 33.

Seclusion and privacy in Roman law seem to have been mainly tied to enjoyment of property. Going back to the earliest sources of Roman law, provisions of the Roman XII Tables "demonstrate an admirable feature of Roman law — that an owner of property has to show respect (in the use of his property) for the interests of his neighbour."[91] This civility was a requirement of private law, and Roman building law set out private remedies by way of servitudes to prevent obstructions of light and *prospectus* (view).[92] Third-century CE Roman law is characterized by increased interventionism — public legislation became more pronounced in governing use of private property, and private law less influential.[93] The Mishnah and Tosefta do not reflect such a transition, and seem to attest only to public law protection of seclusion on one's property. In stipulating the rules governing building, mBaba Batra uses the language of proscription ("may not make a door," "may not put up"; "must be kept distant"), in contrast with mBaba Kama, which governs torts and uses language of actionable rights ("if someone places a pitcher . . . he is liable for the injury"; "an ox that does damage . . .must pay"; "and if it did damage, the one that did the damage must pay"; "one who injures his fellow is liable to him"). Today we would say that Baba Batra is public law, and Baba Kama is private law. As I argue below, certain aspects of privacy were indeed protected by the laws of shaming (*boshet*) detailed in Baba Kama. Baba Batra is not about private interests, but rather public interests. In the case of visual trespass, the interest protected is urban coexistence, an emerging interest in the second and third centuries.

In seeking to ascertain the extent to which the laws of visual trespass protected privacy per se, two instructive sources, Julian of Ascalon (Ashkelon) and Justinian, provide context and historical–legal background.

Julian of Ascalon left a building code generally dated to c.530 CE, i.e., contemporaneous with Justinian and the *Corpus Iuris Civilis*.[94] Saul Lieberman claimed that Julian's code does not reflect Jewish law, but that

91 J.A. Borkowski, *Textbook on Roman Law* (Oxford: 1994), 160–61; A. Rodger, *Owners and Neighbours in Roman Law* (NY: 1972).

92 *Digest* 8.2.15ff.

93 Robinson, n. 87 above, 40–41.

94 Hakim, n. 48 above, 6; S. Lieberman, "A few words on the book by Julian the architect of Ascalon — The laws of Palestine and its customs," *Tarbiz* 40 (1970/71), 409–10.

parallels between it and Jewish law both reflect earlier Hellenistic, Roman, and local law.[95] Julian describes at length the rules of building windows and doors opposite those of a neighbor, just as the Mishnah does. Julian draws a distinction between new construction, on the one hand, and creating windows and openings in existing walls, on the other. Regarding the latter, Julian stipulates that if the window being added is intended for the purpose of providing light and air, it can be placed opposite a neighbor's window only if the new window is 3.5 cubits (about 1.75m) from the floor — i.e., too high to look out of unaided. If the window is intended for looking out of, the window can be built only if it is 20 feet from windows it faces.[96] This provision closely reflects the law in mBaba Batra 3:7 on co-owned courtyards, and tBaba Batra 2:14.

By contrast, regarding new buildings that would offer a sightline into others' property, Julian "maintains that only envious or spiteful owners of existing houses might obstruct the rights of others to build" and "suggests that if the owner of an existing house does not want to be overlooked, he should create his own defensive measures in the form of curtains or shutters on his windows."[97] This suggests that Julian's provisions may be premised on an implied 'easement' or a 'reasonable expectation.' If an existing adjacent home has a wall without windows, a neighbor is entitled to expect that this situation will continue, and can invest in and use her own property on that assumption. We might say that the owner of the house with the windowless wall is estopped from claiming the right to add a window, since the householder acts in reliance on the existing reality of a windowless wall. By contrast, new buildings make for new expectations, and in an urban environment it is unreasonable to expect a new building to be built without a sightline to any other property. Julian's stipulation that one may not stop construction of a new building despite the potential for visual trespass is, to my knowledge, without parallel in Tannaitic law.[98] The Mishnah only discusses creating a new window or door in an existing wall. If protection from visual trespass was, as Rakover and Warhaftig claim, an instance of the right to privacy, then a prohibition against visual trespass would apply a fortiori to new building — and perhaps they would

95 Lieberman, ibid.; Hakim ibid., 7.
96 Hakim, ibid.
97 Ibid., 15.
98 The distinction is made in the Gemara vis-à-vis erecting walls in recently built-up areas vs. those with longstanding buildings, see bBaba Batra 22b.

argue that it does. I would suggest that in light of Julian's stipulations, it is reasonable to take the Mishnah's silence on this matter as suggesting that there is no general prohibition against visual trespass. Where visual trespass does not violate some kind of reasaonable expectation, or more formally, an estoppel, then it is not actionable, and indeed, the language of chapter 3 of mBaba Batra is that of easements.

The second source that provides historical–legal background is Justinian. Justinian law distinguishes windows for light from windows for view.[99] But vis-à-vis visual trespass, the most telling law is in his 113th Constitution, an amendment to earlier decrees, which applies the 'ten feet' rule to balconies:

> We decree that between such structures, as between all others, a space of ten feet shall be left, for if this distance has been prescribed between buildings in order to prevent the violation of privacy, the same reason exists for establishing it between constructions of this kind. . . . Hence we order that no one shall place such balconies nearer than ten feet from the adjoining buildings; and we add that anyone who desires to change the facade of his house, and cover it with marble, cannot do so unless the space of ten feet still remains between his building and that of his neighbor, unless some right authorizing him to do so exists; or the time established by law for acquiring title by prescription has elapsed after the work has been completed; or a house has been erected by virtue of an agreement.[100]

The reference here to acquiring a right by prescription or agreement suggests this is a praedial rustic servitude,[101] that is, a building right that attaches to land, not its owner.[102] Thus, insofar as the Jewish laws of visual trespass were influenced by Roman law (or a source that influenced Roman law), it may be best construed as a right inhering in property, and as protecting property, not persons.

Beyond the relationship with Roman law, Jewish law must also be understood in light of the reality within which it operated. There is considerable archeological evidence that can help understand the Babylonian Talmud's visual trespass provisions. Julian lived in Ashkelon — a town of mixed Jewish and non-Jewish population,[103] and

99 G. Hermansen, *Ostia: Aspects of Roman City Life* (Edmonton AB: 1981), 94–5.

100 S.P. Scott translation.

101 Cf. D.8.2.2.

102 D.8.4.1.1., D.8.4.12.

103 See jPeia 3:17, regarding Gentile neighbors who planned to rob a Jewish-owned house while the owners were away.

as we saw, his laws are uncannily close to various mishnaic and later Rabbinic laws. Both Julian and Jewish law must be read in light of their local historical context. Hirschfeld identified three main types of house in Israel in the Roman-Byzantine period: simple houses; complex houses; and courtyard houses, as well as some minor categories, such as peristyle houses and shop-houses.[104] Simple houses were typical of rural settings, and complex and courtyard houses more common in urban settings. Simple houses that have been excavated range from 20–220 m^2. Courtyard houses are characteristic of private building in urban settings, with areas of at least 200–300 m^2. These were big houses, generally housing one wealthy family, and built around an internal courtyard. Finally, the complex house was a series of houses, each housing a separate family, built around one or more common courtyards. It is this complex house that appears to be the subject of mBaba Batra 1:1 and 3:7 on the division of a common (viz., co-owned) courtyard, and creating windows and doors that open onto the courtyard.

Beyond the structure of the courtyard, obviously the shape, size, and height of the windows, depth of the walls, and other such details pertaining to structure and materials, impacted a courtyard's privacy. Tannaitic sources provide some information on prevailing building norms, and archeology can fill in gaps. Walls were typically 50–85 cm thick,[105] and to best utilize sunlight would generally widen as they went inwards, such that there was just a narrow slit at the external wall.[106] Likewise, mBaba Batra 3:6 speaks of Egyptian windows so narrow that a person's head could not fit through them, and of Tyrian windows wide enough to fit a head through. tOhalot 14:3 states that windows in urban areas were a handbreadth (*tefah*) wide,

104 Y. Hirschfeld, *The Palestinian Dwelling in the Roman-Byzantine Period* (Jerusalem: 1995), 100ff. It has been argued that Hirschfeld's data was skewed by large houses, since, in the archaeological context, most distinguishable houses had belonged to the wealthy. In the Tannaitic literature, the word for 'house' (*bayit*) often means a room, as noted by Hirschfeld himself, and so in at least some Tannaitic contexts, a house was perhaps very small indeed. See A. Kosman, "The house, the small vegetable garden and the courtyard in the talmudic literature" (Hebrew), *Asufot–Yearbook of Jewish Studies* 11 (1998), 151–66.

105 Hirschfeld, 233.

106 Ibid., 258; Hirschfeld cites Leviticus Rabbah 31:7 as well as archaeological examples to corroborate this.

approximately 15 cm × 15 cm.[107] Courtyards were typically 3 × 4 m or 5 × 6 m.[108] With walls over half a meter thick, and windows 15–30 cm high, the sightline from 3–6 meters away was limited. Moreover, windows often had grills, making it difficult to see through, unless one was standing very close indeed, and even then, the view was limited.[109] Some of these features were not mandated by law, and presumably reflected local custom, which was determined as much by engineering requirements and availability of affordable materials as by concerns about privacy, light, and view.[110] From this evidence, too, it thus seems that privacy was at most just one of many considerations that informed local custom and laws governing buildings in the Tosefta, Mishnah, and Talmuds.

In conclusion, there are many indications that the rules of visual trespass (*hezek reiya*) cannot rightly be considered laws set down to protect privacy. These include: the biblical source put forward by R. Johanan; the public-law nature of the provisions, and their categorization in the Talmud under the rubric of nuisances and zoning regulations; the lack of a general prohibition against visual trespass in the Talmuds; the parallels with Roman law, where the relevant rights pertain to enjoyment of property and inhere in property, not persons. It appears to follow that the visual trespass rules are but one instance of a group of directives that govern peaceful urban co-existence. Visual trespass thus cannot be taken to attest to a general right to privacy in Jewish law or espousal of privacy as a core value in Jewish culture.

4. Sexual privacy

When we speak of sexual privacy today, this may refer to three distinct sorts of sexual privacy: (1) privacy during the coital act itself (i.e., no one watching); (2) privacy before and after the act (i.e., not having the fact and details of the intercourse publicized); and (3) vertically-applicable privacy (i.e., deregulation of sexual activity). As to the first kind of sexual privacy, I will argue that talmudic law protected the

107 Ibid.
108 Y. Hirschfeld, "Dwelling houses and private building," in Z. Baras et al. (eds.), *Eretz Israel from the Destruction of the Second Temple to the Muslim Conquest* (Hebrew), (Jerusalem: 1984), 2:134.
109 Ibid., 141.
110 See *Tosefta Kifshuta*, tBaba Batra 2:5, cited in n. 48 above.

privacy of intercourse, with an emphasis on the visual aspect. Other people's sexual intercourse, and even one's own to some extent, was not to be watched. As to the second, though the Talmud uses euphemisms, the extensive discussion of sexual acts, even beyond the purely legal context, demonstrates that the subject was not considered off-limits. Even great Tannaim and early Amoraim such as R. Eliezer and Rav discussed their personal sexual habits with their students. And as to the third sort of sexual privacy, let us consider Rackman's account of the general halakhic attitude to regulation of sexual activity.

Citing bBaba Batra 60a's invocation of Balaam, discussed above, Rackman asserts: "Privacy in the bedroom was one of the earliest of Jewish rights and Jews were proud of it."[111] He quotes from the US Supreme Court decision in *Griswold v. Connecticut*: "Would we allow the police to search the sacred precincts of marital bedrooms for telltale signs of the use of contraceptives? The very idea is repulsive to the notions of privacy surrounding the marriage relationship."[112] Rackman brings several examples to support his thesis that Jewish law protects the ideal of privacy in the bedroom, and in matters of religious ritual. One such example is the counting of days following genital discharges prior to purification via immersion in a ritual bath. Rackman makes much of the fact that people counted for themselves: "They are on their honour. Thus the Talmud interprets the verses. And in this way it expanded the right to privacy some two thousand years ago."[113] But in my view, this hardly suffices to establish respect for privacy, and was merely pragmatic: how else could this religious requirement be administered — only by some form of intrusive physical examination! That adults are responsible for the state of their own genitalia hardly demonstrates a "right to privacy." On the contrary, the specifics of talmudic law make it very hard to assert that adults are solely responsible for their genitalia: even in a victimless context, Jewish law regulates sexual conduct. bNida 13b, for instance, specifically mandates that a man who arouses himself (outside the context of lawful sex) be placed under a ban.[114] In support of his thesis, Rackman cites the fact that the offspring of incest and adultery are stigmatized as bastards (*mamzerim*), whereas those born of sex when the woman is menstrually impure are

111 Rackman, n. 14 above, 44.

112 *Griswold v. Connecticut*, 381 U.S. 479 (1965) 485.

113 Rackman, n. 14 above, 45.

114 See *Tosafot* and *Nahmanides*, bNida 13b s.v. *hamakshe*.

not.[115] However, stigmatization, considered unfair by a Tannaitic midrash that notes that this is visiting the sins of parents on their innocent children,[116] may be the result of social taboos, not only biological and religious ones. Clearly, incest and adultery have severe social ramifications that menstrually 'impure' sex does not,[117] and this may be reflected in the different levels of stigmatization.

As to Rackman's suggestion that Jewish law upholds privacy in the bedroom, and his reference to *Griswold* in support of that notion,[118] I disagree for two reasons. First, the comparison to *Griswold* certainly does not support Rackman's thesis, and indeed undermines it. *Griswold* involved the executive director (Griswold) and medical director (Buxton) of the Planned Parenthood League of Connecticut, who the lower court had convicted as accessories to the crime of preventing conception. The Supreme Court ultimately found that several constitutional freedoms, such as Fourth and Fifth Amendment rights, extended to marital sexual activity, and that the relevant Connecticut statutes were too broad, and invaded those freedoms.[119] Rackman's comparison between Jewish law and *Griswold* is misguided. If anything, the stance of Jewish law on sexual activity renders its approach analogous, not to the Supreme Court's decision, but to the freedom-curtailing Connecticut State law. Whereas *Griswold* determined that sexual relations (at least between a married couple) are beyond the state's purview, Jewish law has never made such a determination. Granted, it did not institute checks on whether women observe the menstrual laws properly, but neither did Connecticut law check whether people were using contraceptives. *Griswold* involved distributors, not end-users, of contraceptives. Setting aside enforcement of the law and focusing on its scope, we find that Jewish law is much more intrusive than the laws of any US state, and to this day adherents of Jewish law submit to its regulation of

115 Rackman, n. 14 above, 45.

116 Leviticus Rabbah, Torah portion 'Emor,' 32.

117 This is further supported by the fact that the prohibitions against incest and adultery are among the seven Noahide laws, whereas sex during menstruation is not. See Maimonides, *Code*, Laws concerning Kings and Wars 9:5.

118 Rakover, n. 4 above, 18 n.11, cites Rackman's declaration that Douglas J's ruling in *Griswold* is similar to views expressed in various Jewish legal sources. As I show, there is no such similarity.

119 *Griswold*, n. 112 above, 484.

a wide range of activities, from menstrual cleansing to dietary restrictions to restrictions on fabrics.

In adducing R. Johanan's statement that Balaam saw that the Israelites' tent openings did not face each other as reflecting a sentiment similar to that of the *Griswold* court, Rackman is conflating two different sorts of sexual privacy, as characterized above. R. Johanan's dictum would be relevant to type (1) of sexual privacy, namely, privacy of sexual activity between individuals,[120] but *Griswold* addressed the right of the state to interfere in marital sexual relations, that is, privacy (3), freedom from regulation of sexual activity.

Second, even with respect to the first and second categories of privacy delineated above — privacy of sexual activity between individuals and privacy in the sense of protection from having details of one's sexual activity publicized — there is little sexual privacy in talmudic law. I will now survey Amoraic sources, and demonstrate that even the most private of acts were not very private. More generally, I will argue that if there was any notion of sexual privacy in Rabbinic law, it was far removed from our current conceptions of sexual privacy.

The following story is related in tractate Berakhot:

> R. Kahana once went in and hid under Rav's bed. He heard him chatting [i.e. flirting] [with his wife] and joking [i.e., engaged in foreplay] and doing what he required [i.e., having intercourse]. He said to him: One would think that Aba's mouth had never sipped the dish before![121] He said to him: Kahana, are you here? Go out, because it is rude. He replied: It is a matter of Torah, and I must learn it.[122]

The same is related in bHagiga 5b, though without R. Kahana's final retort ("It is a matter of Torah . . ."). Rav showed his annoyance at R. Kahana by telling him to leave, because staying was impolite. From Rav's question, "Kahana, are you here?" and his reported response, it seems that R. Kahana may actually have stayed in the room throughout the sexual activity, and perhaps even after Rav's admonishment. In

120 I have suggested above that it is more plausible to interpret R. Johanan's comment as relating to inter-tribal relations. That would make Rackman's claim less incongruous, but neither Rackman nor anyone else I am aware of has put forward this reading.

121 Eating as a euphemism or allegory for sex is common in the Bible, see, e.g., Proverbs 30:20, and perhaps Genesis 39:6; and see *Rashi* ad loc.

122 bBerakhot 62a.

other words, Rav may have told R. Kahana to get out, only to learn that R. Kahana thought this was an important learning experience, at which point Rav continued despite knowing of R. Kahana's presence.[123]

There is room for confusion as to the exact identity of this R. Kahana. There were at least two Kahanas who were close to Rav. One appears to have been Rav's junior contemporary (*talmid haver*); another, sometimes called Kahana the Second, was Rav's student and protégé.[124] R. Kahana refers to Rav as "father" (*aba*), leading to speculation that R. Kahana was Rav's son from a second wife. This would add an interesting twist to the tale, as Kahana may thus have literally been in his own house, perhaps even in his own room. Perhaps he was a lad, and was presumed to be asleep. Moreover, it may mean that Rav was being intimate with R. Kahana's own mother, complicating things further. Hyman considers the word "father" here a term of endearment,[125] and sees this as indicating that the story involved the Kahana who was Rav's contemporary. Hyman takes Rav's sexual activity in bBerakhot 62b, as contrasted with Rav's apparent retirement from sexual life in bShabat 152a, as evidence that the two stories are about the two different Kahanas.[126] However, the fact that two people named Kahana felt free to involve themselves in or comment on Rav's sex life suggests strongly that they are one and the same. As to the fact that in one episode Rav is still sexually active, and in the other inactive, the passage of time explains this discrepancy easily — one predates the other by some years, and in the interim, Rav became sexually inactive.[127]

We cannot ascertain if the two *sugyot* recount episodes pertaining to the same R. Kahana, or his exact relationship — biological and academic — to Rav. But though R. Kahana's intrusive behavior apparently had a legitimate motive — learning proper sexual conduct[128] — at least until learning of this motive, Rav was annoyed. That R. Kahana's

123 I thus disagree with Boyarin's claim that the Talmud has "vigorously rejected" R. Kahana's behavior, see D. Boyarin, *Carnal Israel* (Berkeley: 1995), 123–25.

124 A. Hyman, *Toldot Tanaim Veamoraim* (Jerusalem: 1987), 3:843.

125 Ibid., 842.

126 Ibid., 843.

127 S. Friedman, "The further adventures of Rav Kahana," in Schäfer, n. 83 above, 3:251–2.

128 For a fascinating discussion of this incident as an extension of the study-hall into Rav's bedroom, see A. Kosman, *Women's Tractate: Wisdom, Love, Faithfulness, Passion . . .* (Hebrew), (Jerusalem: 2007), 127–46.

retort is in one version of the episode (bBerakhot), but not the other (bHagiga), suggests that the justification for his behavior is far from obvious, and appears to have been interpolated into bBerakhot, which discusses laws governing toilet habits, and briefly addresses how students can learn them. More generally, sexual privacy is obviously contextual, and the motives of one who invades sexual privacy are very important. In the talmudic context, learning Torah is about the best justification there can be, and indeed, Rav appears to be taken aback upon hearing R. Kahana adduce it.

In the Mississippi Supreme Court case *Plaxico v. Michael*,[129] a Mr Michael was involved in a bitter custody battle with his ex-wife, who lived in their (still co-owned) cabin, sharing it with one Rita Plaxico. Mr Michael photographed Ms Plaxico and the former Mrs Michael engaging in sexual activity; he then used the photos as evidence in the custody hearing. The majority ruled that "most reasonable people would feel Michael's actions were justified in order to protect the welfare of his minor child."[130] The *Plaxico* logic seems to be in line with R. Kahana's approach in bBerakhot: although his actions transgressed conventional behavioral norms, he invokes a fundamental value (learning Torah from his teacher) to render these actions not completely unreasonable in the given circumstances. We cannot be sure that R. Kahana's retort is part of the original version of this story, nor does the Talmud tell us whether and how Rav responded — did he resign himself to Kahana's presence, or show him out at once? Rav's words were, literally, "this is not the way of the land,"[131] that is, 'this is not

129 *Plaxico v. Michael* 735 So. 2d 1036, 1038 (Miss. 1999). See Jon L. Mills, *Privacy: The Lost Right* (Oxford: 2008), 257.

130 *Plaxico*, ibid., 1040. Cf. the story, told by Herodotus, of Candaules, king of Lydia in the 8th c. BCE, who boasted to his bodyguard Gyges of the Queen's beauty, and insisted that Gyges hide behind the bedroom door so he could see it for himself as she got ready for bed; see H. Licht, *Sexual Life in Ancient Greece* (London: 1969), 96–7. Note that Herodotus and Xerxes I, presumably the king in the Book of Esther, were roughly contemporary, and the story of Candaules is reminiscent of Esther 1:13.

131 A search for parallels for this phrase indicates that in general it reflects some indecent or otherwise inappropriate behavior, as, e.g., in bTamid 26b, which states that the older priests would sleep on the Temple grounds, but that to place beds there would be inappropriate. Other uses of this term concern behavior that might constitute infringement of the law, e.g. bSanhedrin 17a.

acceptable behavior.' From this we can infer that even Rav did not consider R. Kahana's conduct to be prohibited or immoral, but merely found it inappropriate.

Similarly, other intimate details of people's lives were far from secret or private. A woman's menstrual status was often public knowledge,[132] indicated by the special clothes she wore.[133] And as noted above, several leading figures of the Tannaitic and Amoraic periods were fairly open in discussing their sexual habits. It is plain that sex and sexuality in the Rabbinic era were not encumbered by the many taboos that arose in the medieval period.[134] Nahmanides (1194–1270), arguably the most prominent mainstream halakhic authority of his day, declared that "sex is disdained and deemed disgusting in the Torah, except for procreation, and when it will not lead to conception, it is prohibited."[135] And as late as the modern period, this attitude was prevalent even in Western societies, reaching new extremes during the Victorian period. Indeed, even in the United States in the 1970s, pregnant women were widely considered too openly associated with sex to be proper role-models for children. In 1974, the US Supreme Court considered the question of whether the Cleveland School Board was within its rights in insisting that, beginning with their fourth month of pregnancy, teachers had to take unpaid maternity leave.[136] The same question arose regarding married students. "As with a pregnant, married school-teacher, married students were simply too blatant an advertisement of sex. . . . Sex was a secret, undercover world. It was important for society to keep it that way."[137] Contemporary sensibilities still generally confine sex to the bedroom, but for much of the population and throughout history, there was no bedroom. Indeed, for many there was not even a bed of their own. Economic conditions dictated that

132 bKidushin 80a and bKetubot 72a speak of a woman who is known by her neighbors to be menstruating; *Rashi* ad loc. explains that she wears her menstrual clothes. Cf. Genesis 31:35, where Rachel matter-of-factly tells her father in public that she is menstruating.

133 See *SA*, YD 195:8.

134 Maimonides was quite liberal in *Code*, Laws concerning Forbidden Intercourse 21:10; but decidedly less so in *Guide for the Perplexed*, 2:36 and 3:8. And see Kosman, n. 128 above, 157ff.

135 *Nahmanides*, Leviticus 18:6.

136 *Cleveland Board of Education v. LaFleur*, 414 U.S. 632, 94 S. Ct. 791, 39 L.Ed.2d 52 (1974).

137 L.M. Friedman, *Guarding Life's Dark Secrets — Legal and Social Controls over Reputation, Propriety, and Privacy* (Stanford: 2007), 173.

> for the poor, sexual privacy was a luxury which they neither possessed nor could have desired. Living conditions were such that among the bulk of the population before the second half of the nineteenth century, whole families lived, worked, ate and slept in one or two rooms. Under such conditions sexual privacy for parents, or for married children living at home, was impossible, and children from an early age must have been familiar with the sight and sounds of the physical act of love. Only in summer — and then only on a dry day — was sexual privacy obtainable out of doors in the fields and woods.[138]

Many vestiges of the Victorian era are no longer found in liberal societies, though sexual reticence endures in traditional Jewish society. This reticence may also explain why two scholarly works on privacy in Jewish law, those of Rakover and Warhaftig, do not discuss sex. Many of the social taboos that developed around sex, menstruation, pregnancy, and birth in the medieval era, and remained in place, as I noted, until very recently, had not yet come into existence in the talmudic period, as reflected in the Rabbinic literature. As I will show, neighbors and family were practically expected to hear each other's sexual activities, to know when women were menstruating, and so on. Intercourse was not a secret or hidden act, and household members would be informed ahead of time that they were not to interrupt. Sex was not to be watched,[139] but it was known about, heard, and discussed.

The talmudic treatment of sexual activity seems to view it as private only in a visual sense. An example of how sexual activity was not considered secret is found in tractate Berakhot, where the Talmud, in the course of indicating how one can know when it is the second 'watch' of the night, states that at that time "a woman is talking with her husband," a euphemism for intercourse — presumably a reference to flirtatious banter.[140] Were people not expected to hear nearby love-making, it is hardly credible that the Talmud would give that as a sign. Other talmudic passages further support this hypothesis. The Talmud mentions a dictum of the ascetic Tanna R. Shimon b. Yohai that one should not have intercourse while any living creature is present.[141]

138 L. Stone, *The Family, Sex and Marriage in England, 1500–1800* (London: 1979), 384–85.

139 This may arise from the biblical treatment of sex. The Bible is sometimes quite visual in its references to intercourse, describing it as "seeing the nakedness," as in Leviticus 20:17 and, less obviously, Genesis 9:22.

140 bBerakhot 3a.

141 bNida 16b–17a.

Boyarin writes of this dictum that it mandates "extreme privacy for the sexual act,"[142] but it is hard to see this as "extreme" privacy unless the norm is no privacy at all. What R. Shimon proscribes is intercourse that other people can see, but he does not object to other people hearing the act, knowing of it, perhaps even being in the room and seeing that the couple is having intercourse under the covers. As Boyarin notes, the Talmud goes on to describe the act of ringing a bell to ensure that servants do not approach the bedroom while the masters of the house are having intercourse. Here too we see that the limits of sexual privacy dictated only that no one — not even slaves, in contrast with the Roman practice of having relations in the presence of slaves,[143] a custom that, from this talmudic source, seems to have spread among certain Jews of the time — was allowed to watch. Others were not necessarily kept away from the room, or prevented from knowing the act was going on, and there was nothing to stop them from hearing it and hearing about it.

Tractate Nedarim reports a discussion between R. Johanan b. Dabai and others about various sexual practices.[144] R. Johanan b. Dabai suggests a restrictive approach to sexual activity, prohibiting "turning the table,"[145] looking at and kissing a woman's genitalia, and talking during intercourse. Other Sages, such as R. Eliezer, Rabbi (Judah the Prince), and R. Johanan, are cited as opposing that position. Of particular note is R. Johanan — the second generation Amora in the land of Israel — who states: "anything that a man wishes to do with his wife he may do." This is the same R. Johanan who adduced the verse about Balaam as biblical support for the notion of visual trespass. Other stories are told of R. Johanan that further support the thesis that in R. Johanan's time, there was little sexual privacy in the second sense defined above. The Talmud relates that R. Johanan, who is reported by the Talmud to have been extremely handsome, would sit outside the ritual bath (*mikve*) where women would immerse themselves after menstruating, so that they would see his good looks and have beautiful babies.[146] The same R. Johanan once advised a woman to have

142 Boyarin, n. 123 above, 125.
143 Ibid., citing Veyne.
144 bNedarim 20a–b. See Boyarin, ibid., 110.
145 Generally interpreted as referring to different sexual positions and activities.
146 bBaba Metzia 84a.

intercourse with her husband on the river bank.[147] R. Johanan was thus consistent in espousing relative sexual freedom (within the limits of marital and ritual law), and rejecting sexual taboos.[148]

5. Three processes that impacted Jewish law on privacy

Three processes that were underway by the time of R. Johanan's leadership in the third century CE had significant ramifications for the Jewish world in the land of Israel and beyond. These processes go some way toward explaining the various phenomena connected with privacy that have been adduced above, including R. Johanan's reported relatively-easygoing stance on all things sexual,[149] the emergence of building codes with provisions offering some, albeit limited and perhaps incidental, privacy protection, and R. Johanan's effort to ground the latter in a biblical source. These three processes are: (i) urbanization of the population in the land of Israel; (ii) Romanization of the same population; and (iii) increasing polemical disputation with Christians. I now survey these processes briefly to explore how they may have impacted Jewish law on privacy.

i. Urbanization

One major process underway in the land of Israel in the second and third centuries CE was intense urbanization.[150] This urbanization had

147 bNida 66a; according to some versions of the incident, it was Rav who made the suggestion. But on the interpretation in *Bayit Hadash*, R. Johanan advised the woman to have sex with her husband in a secluded place, away from the jealous eyes of others.

148 For our purposes, it does not matter whether the dicta were actually R. Johanan's or merely attributed to R. Johanan. What we see is a consistent attitude associated with the most prominent Amora, the leader and symbol of the 3rd-century CE community in the land of Israel. We can assume that they reflect what R. Johanan might reasonably have said and thought.

149 The Babylonian Talmud also alludes to R. Johanan's effeminate appearance, and reports that Resh Lakish — soon to become his brother-in-law and protégé — jumped into the river in sexual pursuit of him, thinking he was a woman; see bBaba Metzia 84a. And see D. Boyarin, *Unheroic Conduct: The Rise of Heterosexuality and the Invention of the Jewish Man* (Berkeley: 1997), 129–34.

150 J. Liebeschuetz, *Decline and Fall of the Roman City* (Oxford: 2001), 57, 299. The process was reversed somewhat in the late Roman period, i.e., the 5th and 6th centuries.

far-reaching effects on the structure of society, the influence of the Rabbis and the law, and the law's evolution.

> During the second century the Palestinian Rabbis lacked institutionalized power. . . . Some argue that [this] changed at the end of the second or beginning of the third century. Previously the Rabbis had been located primarily in the villages and smaller towns, in rural areas. By the third century they were concentrated in such urban centers as Tiberias, Sepphoris, Caesarea, and Lod. The new urban setting increased the contacts between the Rabbis and the broad spectrum of the Jewish population of the province. As a result, the Rabbis seem to have become more tolerant of the masses. . . . They may also have become more open to Graeco-Roman civilization. The Rabbis also began to participate more in public life . . . holding positions of authority, such as judges and administrators. . . . The urbanization of the Rabbis parallels the urbanization of Palestine in general in the third century.[151]

Urbanization likely spurred the growth of commercial civil law: the laws of commerce, financing, contract, bailees, torts, partnerships, and so on, that is, the laws in tractate Nezikin. It is in this period that laws of urban coexistence, specifically zoning and building laws, became crucial and matured.[152] This urbanization was not unique to the Jewish community in the land of Israel, for by 300 CE, very few towns were demographically homogenous.[153] Jews and Gentiles alike were urbanizing, together, and needed rules to govern that process. Jewish and Gentile law and custom, reflected in tractate Baba Batra of the Talmud, Roman law and the laws of the Roman provinces, and Julian

151 D. Goodblatt, "The political and social history of the Jewish community in the Land of Israel c.235–638," in S.T. Katz (ed.), *Cambridge History of Judaism: The Late Roman-Rabbinic Period* (Cambridge: 2006), 4:425.

152 See N. Belayche, *Iudaea-Palaestina: The Pagan Cults in Roman Palestine, Second to Fourth Century* (Tübingen: 2001), 72ff.; Z. Safrai, "Urbanization in Israel in the Greco-Roman Period" (Hebrew), in Z. Avineri et al. (eds.), *Studies in the History of the Jewish People and the Land of Israel, presented to Azriel Shohat . . .* (Hebrew), (Haifa: 1980), 5:105–29; Baras, n. 108 above; Z. Weiss, "Greco-Roman influences on the art and architecture of the Jewish city in Roman Palestine," in H. Lapin (ed.), *Religious and Ethnic Communities in Later Roman Palestine* (Potomac MD: 1998), 219–46, 240 n. 54; M.D. Herr (ed.), *The History of Eretz Israel: The Roman Byzantine Period . . .* (Hebrew), (Jerusalem: 1985), vol. 5.

153 B. Isaac, "Jews, Christians and others in Palestine: the evidence from Eusebius," in M. Goodman (ed.), *Jews in a Graeco-Roman World* (Oxford: 1998), 73; see Weiss, ibid., 242 n. 58 for additional sources.

of Ascalon, likely influenced each other and came under some pressure to become more uniform.

Construction in towns with a strong Jewish presence in the Tannaitic and Amoraic periods — such as Sepphoris and Tiberias — seems to have been fairly similar to that in towns that were mainly pagan and Christian.[154] The same goes for towns in Syria. Dura and Palmyra were both Syrian towns with mixed communities that had a considerable Jewish presence in late antiquity; in both, Roman and Sasanian influences were felt, and both have yielded evidence that privacy was given consideration in urban housing. In both these towns, houses were found with entrances and vestibules that were offset to protect the occupants' privacy, and this was in evidence in all residential sectors: poor and wealthy, urban and suburban.[155] Roman conceptions of proper urban living — including rights to view, light, and seclusion — appear to be closely paralleled not only in Jewish law and custom, as we saw above, but also in actual buildings, as evidenced by archeological findings throughout Israel, Syria, and elsewhere in the region.

Privacy in the urban context was necessitated by economic and demographic shifts: Jews were increasingly living in built-up environments, where peaceable co-existence with neighbors was imperative. And since Jews had neighbors who were not subject to Jewish law, Jewish laws pertaining to building had to coexist, as it were, with other applicable law.

ii. Romanization

A second process well underway by the third century was Romanization.[156] The 212 CE *Constitutio Antoniniana*, which made all freeborn men of the Empire citizens, had a dramatic effect on the jurisdiction of the Jewish courts in the land of Israel, and on the Rabbis' influence. During the Tannaitic period, the jurisdiction of Jewish courts was, by all appearances, largely supported by the Roman authorities, and existed in parallel with the Roman courts.[157] This jurisdiction

154 See Weiss, n. 152 above.

155 K. Butcher, *Roman Syria and the Near East* (Los Angeles: 2003), 303–304.

156 See Belayche, n. 152 above, 49ff.

157 A. Oppenheimer, "Jewish penal authority in Roman Judaea," in Goodman, n. 153 above, 191. Cf. Seth Schwartz, *Imperialism and Jewish Society: 200 BCE to 640 CE* (Princeton: 2004), 110ff. which contends that the courts essentially had no jurisdiction.

appears to have come to an end upon the Bar Kokhba revolt, though it was reinstated sometime later, and continued until the *Constitutio Antoniniana*. But in 212 CE the courts of the Jews of Palestine, who had become Roman citizens, came under the aegis of the Empire.[158] While this appears to have reduced the influence of these courts, it increased the influence of the Rabbis, the most influential of whom was R. Johanan. "Romanization completely changed the political economy of Palestine and precipitated, both through the suppression of two local revolts, and through longer term processes which Palestine shared with other regions of the Roman Near East, extensive demographic shifts. . . . rabbinic culture was not merely a response to Roman imperial culture, but was in fact enabled (not to say created) by it."[159]

R. Johanan's prominence in communal affairs began with the inception of his leadership of the Tiberias community shortly after 200 CE, and lasted until his death around 280 CE. The *pax Romana* has ended, and this period came to be known as the 'anarchy' or the 'crisis of the third century' — five decades rife with instability, civil and external war, and hyperinflation, from the murder of Alexander Severus in 235 CE to the ascent of Diocletian in 284 CE,[160] and the period in which the Western and Eastern Empires began their separation. Throughout this period, the central authority in Rome weakened, and provincial Roman authorities wielded more power and had greater independence than before.

Sperber and others have shown that R. Johanan both influenced, and was influenced by, Roman law.[161] As we have seen, there is much to suggest that Roman and Jewish building codes of the period evolved in parallel, and perhaps there was also some direct influence, at least via local Roman provincial law. This may also be the case regarding

158 A.M. Rabello, *The Jews in the Roman Empire: Legal Problems, from Herod to Justinian* (UK: 2000), esp. ch. 12, "Jewish and Roman jurisdiction"; A. Linder, *The Jews in Roman Imperial Legislation* (Detroit: 1987), 77; Seth Schwartz, "Rabbinization in the sixth century," in Schäfer, n. 83 above, 3:59; P. Schäfer, *History of the Jews in the Greco-Roman World* (London: 2003), 170, 187.

159 H. Lapin, "Rabbis and cities: some aspects of the Rabbinic movement in its Greco-Roman environment," in Schäfer, n. 83 above, 2:51–80, 80.

160 See M. Harpaz, "R. Johanan B. Napcha — the Man and his Life-Work" (Hebrew), (PhD dissertation, Tel Aviv University, 1975) on R. Johanan's reactions to the loss of control manifested by the Roman authorities.

161 See Sperber, n. 81 above, 157 n. 44.

sexual privacy. It has long been thought that Zoroastrian-Sasanian influences dominate the Babylonian Talmud's attitudes to sexuality,[162] and these are mentioned in the Talmud and are adduced as the source for some suggestions that were assimilated into the prevailing Jewish customs. But the dominant cultural influence on the Tannaim, the Palestinian Amoraim, and to a lesser extent the Babylonian Amoraim, was that of Rome. The Romans paid little attention to type (1) sexual privacy, as noted above. They had sexual relations freely in the presence of others, and a couple's first act of intercourse likely took place in the presence of witnesses.[163] That Jewish practices vis-à-vis sexual privacy were by no means as permissive as those of the Romans is not saying much, and it is clear that the pervasive Romanization had a significant influence in this realm.

iii. Christian polemics

R. Johanan, generally associated with Tiberias, was a contemporary of Origen (c.185–c.254) — the Church Father who lived in Caesarea. Origen made quite a name for himself by his reported self-castration. Eusebius attributes this drastic move to Origen's literal interpretation of Matthew 19:12.[164] Eusebius' statement is controversial, particularly since Origen himself rejects a literalist interpretation of that verse, leading some to doubt the veracity of the story of his castration.[165] Yet Origen's castration — factual or apocryphal — can be viewed as a manifestation of the general inclination, among Christian thinkers from the second century on, to repudiate sexuality.[166] It has been argued that "permanent sexual renunciation and lifelong virginity were profoundly

162 I. Rosen-Zvi, *Demonic Desires: Yetzer Hara and the Problem of Evil in Late Antiquity* (Philadelphia: 2011), 118. Rosen-Zvi cites bKetubot 48a, bBerakhot 8a, bMegila 13a.

163 O. Kiefer, *Sexual Life in Ancient Rome* (London: 1956), 31. This has a counterpart in Jewish law, viz., the presumption that when newlyweds are secluded (*yihud*) they will have intercourse, and witnesses to their seclusion can attest that intercourse has occurred (bKidushin 65b).

164 Eusebius, *Ecclesiastical History* 6.8.1–5. Eusebius was born a decade or so after Origen's death.

165 See B. Chilton, "Resurrection in the Gospels," in J. Neusner and A.J. Avery-Peck (eds.), *Judaism in Late Antiquity* (Leiden: 2000), 215–42, 231.

166 M.D. Smith, *Sex and Sexuality in Early America* (NY: 1998), 123. See also S. Heid, *Celibacy in the Early Church* (San Francisco: 2000), 91ff.

important values in the first centuries of Christianity."[167] Sexuality was central to the Jewish-Christian polemics of the time, and the most prominent of Origen's Jewish contemporaries was R. Johanan.

It is controversial whether Origen and R. Johanan or another Rabbi, perhaps R. Abbahu, were personally acquainted,[168] but there was an ongoing intellectual and religious disputation between Origen and the rabbis of his day, as reflected in both the Amoraic literature and the Patristic.[169] Kimelman has demonstrated that R. Johanan and Origen were aware of each other's teachings and even related to each other polemically.[170] R. Johanan's views on sex and sexuality were diametrically opposed to those of contemporary Church Fathers, of whose teachings he was aware. Though it cannot be proven, it is not unreasonable to speculate that the repressive Christian notions of sexuality emerging at that time may have galvanized the relatively permissive stances of R. Johanan and others.

We can confidently conclude that the concepts of sexual privacy characteristic of present-day halakha and practice were largely absent from Jewish society and law of late antiquity. Intercourse, the most intimate of acts, was not private in the second sense articulated above: others could and often were made aware of the fact and details of sexual relations. This constitutes strong evidence that privacy was not a fundamental value of Jewish law during the Rabbinic era.

6. Privacy of correspondence

Rakover's treatment of R. Gershom's ban (*herem derabeinu gershom*) is comprehensive. Yet as Rakover himself hints, R. Gershom's ban is not really about privacy at all. Rakover notes the opinion of historian Haim Ben-Sasson, who asserted that R. Gershom's ban was principally

167 G. Taylor, *Castration: An Abbreviated History of Western Manhood* (London: 2002), 190.

168 N. de Lange, *Origen and the Jews* (Cambridge: 1976), 26–28. de Lange seems to think R. Abbahu was the most likely candidate. Others think a personal acquaintance is unlikely, see C. Hezser, *The Social Structure of the Rabbinic Movement in Roman Palestine* (Tübingen: 1997), 141–2; Katz, n. 151 above, 4:905 n. 15.

169 See Herr, n. 152 above, 221–22.

170 R. Kimelman, "Rabbi Johanan and Origen on the Song of Songs: A third-century Jewish-Christian disputation," *Harvard Theological Review* 73 (1980), 567–95.

intended to protect commercial secrets.[171] This argument was also made by Grossman, who explained all R. Gershom's bans — including those on polygamy, cancelling betrothals, and long distance travel without depositing a bill of divorce — on the basis of their socioeconomic background. Regarding the ban on reading others' correspondence, Grossman contends that

> R. Gershom's ban was of great importance, in view of the economic circumstances of contemporary German Jewry. The merchants, while away from home, sent letters to their wives and their partners by the hands of companions returning to Germany. In these letters they gave details of their business affairs (export and import), of goods they were seeking to buy in the hope of marketing them, of decisions not to buy merchandise which was no longer urgently needed, or economic links they had succeeded in establishing, or were planning to establish with local Jews, and so on. Naturally this information was confidential in character, for there was constant competition between these Jewish merchants for potential markets. Only the sacramental force carried by the ban could have overcome, or at least restrained, the great temptation to read these personal letters.[172]

The ban was mentioned in a decision by Supreme Court justice Elyakim Rubenstein, an avid supporter of Jewish law, who characterized it as "a ban on opening up someone else's letters without his permission," and claimed that it was an expression of "the prohibition against revealing secrets" rooted in the biblical command, "Do not go about as a talebearer among your countrymen" (Lev. 19:16).[173] I would argue, however, that Rubenstein was insufficiently precise here. The point of R. Gershom's ban was not to protect secrets per se, an idea

171 Rakover, n. 4 above, 108 n. 3; see also xv. Curiously, Ben-Sasson omitted this point in "The Middle Ages" in H.H. Ben-Sasson (ed.), *A History of the Jewish People* (Cambridge: 1976), 437–38, though he alludes to economic motivations for some of Rabbenu Gershom's bans (438). See also *Afikei Mayim v. Rani Fisher*, LA [National Labour Law Court] 1158/06 (Nazareth), Tak-Av 2008(2) 586 para. 4, which cites Rakover, arguing that R. Gershom's ban was principally motivated by considerations of commercial secrecy, and explaining why the general rules against revealing secrets were insufficient.

172 A. Grossman, "The historical background to the ordinances on family affairs attributed to Rabbenu Gershom Me'or ha-Golah ('The Light of the Exile')," in A. Rapoport-Albert and S.J. Zipperstein, *Jewish History; Essays in Honour of Chimen Abramsky* (London: 1988), 3–23.

173 *Clalit Medical Services v. Ministry of Defense*, CA 8825/03 (SC), Tak-El 2007(2) 166 para 22.

alluded to elsewhere in Scripture.[174] Rather, it sought to ensure that correspondence could serve the purpose of facilitating commerce, as Grossman explained. For the post to be valuable, it had to be not simply timely and reliable, but also confidential. In asserting that correspondence was not to be interfered with, R. Gershom's ban offered innovative protection for merchants and traders.

Modern legal provisions protecting correspondence have done so largely with the intention of protecting correspondence from the prying eyes of government. Until the twentieth century, the US Post Office often intervened to prevent distribution of immoral, scandalous, and — especially during the Civil War — seditious materials.[175] By 1948, privacy of correspondence was considered a fundamental human right; Article 12 of the Universal Declaration of Human Rights (UDHR) asserts: "No one shall be subjected to arbitrary interference with his privacy, family, home or correspondence, nor to attacks upon his honour and reputation." Similarly, Article 8 of the European Convention on Human Rights (ECHR), which adduces the UDHR, asserts that "Everyone has the right to respect for his private and family life, his home and his correspondence." The UDHR is not legally enforceable in any ordinary sense of the term, and the horizontal effect of the ECHR is not yet settled.[176] Likewise, though Article 7 of Israel's *Basic Law: Human Dignity and Liberty, 5752–1992* protects privacy of conversation and writings, it too has no direct horizontal effect, as per Article 11.

In the US it is a crime to interfere with and open mail that is in the possession of the postal service, or to obstruct its delivery. Provisions of this kind predate the constitution, being based on the laws governing the English post.[177]

> Whoever takes any letter, postal card, or package out of any post office or any authorized depository for mail matter, or from any letter or mail carrier, or which has been in any post office or authorized depository, or in the custody of any letter or mail carrier, before it has been delivered to the

174 Proverbs 11:13. On injunctions against revealing secrets, see Rakover, n. 4 above, 49–56; Warhaftig, n. 5 above, 127.

175 F.S. Lane, *American Privacy: The 400-Year History of Our Most Contested Right* (Boston: 2009), 23–37.

176 See, e.g., *Max Mosley v. News Group Newspapers Ltd* [2008] EWHC 1777 (QB), paras. 9, 126.

177 W. Diffie and S.E. Landau, *Privacy on The Line: The Politics of Wiretapping and Encryption* (Boston: 2007), 144.

> person to whom it was directed, with design to obstruct the correspondence, or to pry into the business or secrets of another, or opens, secretes, embezzles, or destroys the same, shall be fined under this title or imprisoned not more than five years, or both.[178]

Note that this US law, like R. Gershom's ban, seeks to protect users of the post from attempts to "pry into their business or secrets." In the US, England, Israel and elsewhere, the remedy for interfering with the post is criminal.[179] Note too that the crime involves opening mail that is in the possession of the postal service; it does not apply to mail not yet sent or already in the hands of the recipient, further demonstrating that personal privacy is not the rationale of this law. Indeed, these provisions existed in the US and England long before any meaningful recognition or horizontal application of the right to privacy, and in Israel they similarly predated both the *Basic Law: Human Dignity and Liberty* and the *Privacy Law*.

The 1765 English case *Entick v. Carrington and Three Other King's Messengers*[180] made it clear that "papers are the owner's goods and chattels; they are his dearest property; and are so far from enduring a seizure, that they will hardly bear an inspection; and though the eye cannot by the laws of England be guilty of a trespass, yet where private papers are removed and carried away, the secret nature of those goods will be an aggravation of the trespass." *Entick* directly influenced the US Constitution and even UDHR,[181] and predated Warren and Brandeis by over a century. So at common law, it seems that, as was the case regarding R. Gershom's ban, laws protecting the confidentiality of correspondence did not arise as expressions of an overarching principle that privacy was to be protected, but were localized instances of privacy protection arising from the protection of other interests.

> It is worth emphasizing that this legal shaping of postal policy was completely independent of the Bill of Rights, including the First and Fourth Amendments. Certainly many of the same people were involved in both postal policy and the shaping of the Bill of Rights. Nonetheless, the principle of privacy of correspondence effectively preceded the Bill of Rights.

178 18 USC 1702 — Obstruction of Correspondence.

179 The UK *Postal Services Act 2000*, §83 has similar provisions; as does the Israeli *Postal Law, 5746–1986*, §93, 101.

180 *Entick v. Carrington and Three Other King's Messengers* (1765) 19 St. Tr. 1029.

181 A. Schreiber, "Privacy: proprietary or human right? An Israeli law perspective," 89 *Intellectual Property Quarterly* (2009), 126.

> While everyone at the time saw that principle as embedded in postal law, no one saw it as a matter of constitutional law.[182]

The same is true of R. Gershom's ban — it was a postal policy, not a statement of rights.

Warren and Brandeis's seminal 1890 article on privacy law[183] was also a statement of private, not constitutional, rights. Yet it had a significant effect not only on private law, but also constitutional law. Additional branches of the right to privacy emerged or were identified after its publication.[184] In 1928, Brandeis himself wrote a powerful dissent in *Olmstead*,[185] helping to disseminate the Warren–Brandeis doctrine, which became entrenched in several areas of law. One such area was tort law: William Prosser broke down Warren and Brandeis's right to privacy into several strands, and Prosser enshrined his taxonomy of privacy actions in the Restatement (Second) of Torts in 1976, a project in which he played a central role.[186] Another area was Fourth Amendment law, where the US Supreme Court, in *Katz v. United States*,[187] overturned *Olmstead* and adopted Brandeis's dissent. Thus though, in their seminal article, Warren and Brandeis had addressed private law, they also influenced the development of constitutional law.

It has been claimed that Warren and Brandeis derive their notion of privacy from the 'a man's home is his castle' rule, presumably meaning that privacy is first and foremost associated with the enjoyment of private property.[188] This thesis arises from a misreading of Warren and

182 A.C. Desai, "Wiretapping before the wires: the post office and the birth of communications privacy," 60 *Stanford Law Review* (2007), 553, 568. Desai demonstrates that in *Ex Parte Jackson*, 96 U.S. 727 (1877), the US Supreme Court incorporated these postal provisions into Fourth Amendment law, but that doctrinally and historically, they were not only separate from, but also predated, the Fourth Amendment.

183 S.D. Warren and L.D. Brandeis, "The right to privacy," 4 *Harvard Law Review* (1890), 193.

184 See Mills, n. 129 above, 6.

185 *Olmstead v. United States*, 277 U.S. 438 (1928).

186 William Prosser, "Privacy," 48 *California Law Review* (1960), 383; *Prosser and Keeton on the Law of Torts*, §117 (5th ed. 1984); Restatement (Second) of Torts §652B-652E (1976).

187 *Katz v. United States*, 389 U.S. 347 (1967).

188 D. Shuger, *Censorship and Cultural Sensibility: The Regulation of Language in Tudor-Stuart England* (Pennsylvania: 2006), 141ff. See Schreiber, n. 181 above, 119.

Brandeis, who declare, at the very end of their article, that "the common law has always recognized a man's house as his castle, impregnable, often even to its own officers engaged in the execution of its commands. Shall the courts thus close the front entrance to constituted authority, and open wide the back door to idle or prurient curiosity?[189] Despite this "rhetorical flourish,"[190] their intent was plainly to contrast the clarity with which the common law protected the individual's right to freedom from government intrusion — namely, through the Fourth Amendment — with the lack of protection afforded by private law; it was not to suggest that vertically-applicable privacy protection be extended horizontally, *mutatis mutandis*. On the contrary, the very core of their argument was that the common law was evolving to protect violations of the individual's personal space — from physical assault to intellectual property infringements — and that the same, in the form of privacy, should be extended to one's inviolate personality. Private law, in the wake of Warren – Brandeis, influenced Fourth Amendment law, and not the reverse.

To return to Jewish law, R. Gershom's ban may have been motivated by the need for an effective postal service, but its pervasiveness and influence has spurred privacy as a value in Israeli law. With regard to the *Privacy Law*, this is certainly the case. As noted above, Rakover's discussion of R. Gershom's ban in the Kahan Commission's report was referred to, in the explanatory notes to the *Privacy Law*, as the basis for §2(5), which prohibits copying or using correspondence.[191] R. Gershom's ban, we saw, is also reflected in Israel's *Postal Law*, and has been incorporated into privacy law and even the *Basic Law: Human Dignity and Liberty*, much as the postal laws of the colonial era were incorporated into Fourth Amendment law.

A similar process may have taken place with regard to visual trespass. We saw that historically, the concept of visual trespass is related to land ownership, or perhaps possession, and from this perspective, should have been addressed in the context of building regulations. §2(3) of the *Privacy Law* defines "photographing a person while he is in

189 Warren and Brandeis, n. 183 above, 220.

190 H. Nissenbaum, *Privacy in Context: Technology, Policy, and the Integrity of Social Life* (Stanford: 2010), 95.

191 As noted above, the recommendations made by Rakover and the Kahan Commission were diluted; they had recommended that reading the correspondence of others be proscribed; see Rakover, n. 4 above, 100, 110.

a private domain" as an invasion of privacy; though the explanatory notes to this clause offer nothing by way of explanation, it appears to have been influenced at least in part by Rakover's survey of visual trespass in the Kahan report.[192] If my understanding of visual trespass and R. Gershom's ban are correct, then these two issues, which in Jewish law are only tangentially connected with privacy, have actually spurred major provisions in contemporary Israeli privacy law.

7. *Boshet and iniuria*

Scholars of privacy in Jewish law have not yet, to my knowledge, seriously considered the suggestion that revealing private information may be actionable under the rubric of *boshet* (disgrace, shame, humiliation). *Boshet* and the Roman action *iniuria* have much in common, and many instances of what would today be considered invasion of privacy were actionable in the past under *iniuria* and *boshet* in Roman and Jewish law respectively.

In comparing Roman law's *iniuria* to *boshet* in talmudic law, two key issues require elaboration: the value protected by the law, and the role of intent. Revelation of private information (the second of Prosser's four privacy torts[193]) is often embarrassing and an affront to dignity, and this would generally be actionable under *iniuria*.[194] *Iniuria* was broad in scope, including "any contumelious disregard of another's rights or personality."[195] Some verbal assaults that were protected by *iniuria* would today be protected by defamation laws, others by the tort of 'false light.' In Roman law, though there were several defenses against charges of *iniuria*, 'truth' was not one of them. In contemporary law, when a true but degrading detail of another person's life is shared, this may be an actionable invasion of privacy. *Iniuria* was an action against affront or insult, premised on the notion that honor is

192 *Reshumot*, n. 25 above, 207.

193 Prosser, n. 186 above.

194 W.L. Burdick, *The Principles of Roman Law and their Relation to Modern Law* (Rochester: 1938), 501; E. Descheemaeker and H.J. Scott (eds.), *Iniuria and the Common Law* (Oxford: 2012). According to Gaius, *iniuria* applies when someone "is struck . . . a vocal attack is made . . . when someone writes a defamatory book . . . and finally in many other ways" (*Institutes of Gaius*, trans. W.M. Gordon and O.F. Robinson (London: 1988), 3:220, 397).

195 B. Nicholas, *An Introduction to Roman Law* (Oxford: 1962), 216.

defensible at law. As pointed out by Warren and Brandeis, the notion of honor as defensible at law is alien to the common law.[196] They knowingly departed from the continental model that bases privacy on honor, as *iniuria* does, and turned instead to artistic property rights.[197] This reflects a fascinating and well-documented difference between the common law and civil law traditions. The case of Israeli law is instructive in this respect. Israeli law is generally considered a mixed common law–civil law system, and Israeli privacy scholars have debated whether Israeli privacy law is modeled on the continental European 'human dignity' model or the American 'liberty' model. It has been claimed that Israeli privacy law was initially premised on the American model, but that the 1992 passage of the *Basic Law: Human Dignity and Liberty*, esp. §7, which invokes privacy under a quasi-constitutional taxonomy, has effected a switch to the European model.[198] However, Israeli privacy law was initially based on a human-rights justification, as conceived by the Kahan Commission,[199] and Israeli Supreme Court case law quickly connected the protection of 'dignity' with the protection of privacy, not least through the *Basic Law: Human Dignity and Liberty*. I would thus argue that the model for Israeli privacy law has not changed.

Returning to Jewish law, we must ascertain the value protected by the laws of *boshet*, and the role of intent. It can be demonstrated that in the Babylonian Talmud, the value protected by *boshet* is dignity. In bBaba Kama 86b, R. Abba b. Memel inquires as to the law where A shames B while the B is sleeping, and B dies before awakening. Two explanations of R. Abba's question are put forward. R. Zevid explains the question thus: B was never embarrassed, but he was shamed, and R. Abba was investigating which of these — embarrassment or shaming — lies at the heart of the action for *boshet*. R. Papa understood the question differently: is *boshet* personal embarrassment — and B was never personally embarrassed, or does *boshet* protect the dignity of the family, which applies even if B dies in his sleep? Most authorities consider this

196 Warren and Brandeis, n. 183 above, 198.

197 See J.Q. Whitman, "The two western cultures of privacy: dignity versus liberty" 113 *Yale L.J.*, 1151, 1208 (2004); H. Beverley-Smith et al., *Privacy, Property, and Personality* (Cambridge: 2006), 8ff.

198 O. Tenne, "The right to privacy following the *Basic Law: Human Dignity and Liberty*: a conceptual, constitutional and regulatory revolution" (Hebrew), 8 *Kiryat Mishpat* (2009), 39.

199 Kahan Commission, n. 43 above, c 6, 30, para. 13.

question to have been left open: neither the proper interpretation of R. Abba b. Memel's question, nor the answer to it, are agreed on.[200] Some, however, interpret the Talmud as determining that *boshet* is premised on personal embarrassment.[201] We can thus argue, on good authority, that the *sugya* in bBaba Kama supports the claim that *boshet*, like *iniuria*, protects the victim's dignity, by making shaming or embarrassing someone an actionable tort.[202]

Israeli law attaches criminal liability to the malicious invasion of privacy.[203] §2(4) of the *Privacy Law* asserts that "publishing a person's photograph under circumstances in which the publication is likely to humiliate him or to bring him into contempt" is an invasion of privacy. The Supreme Court addressed an interpretive question about this: does the clause protect a person from having a photo that is not in itself embarrassing being published in circumstances that are embarrassing? For example, a harmless photo that is used in an ad for some immoral service. Chief Justice Barak said it does not, asserting that the *Privacy Law* protects privacy, not reputation; the *Defamation Law* protects reputation, not privacy. Barak noted that the court construes legislation on the basis of the legislator's intent — in this case, to protect privacy — and in a way that does not cause conflicts between laws — in this case, between the *Privacy Law* and the *Defamation Law*.[204] Invoking the *Privacy Law*'s explanatory notes to explain its legislative intent, Barak then stated that it was intended "to confront the technological and social changes on account of which 'the individual finds herself exposed to public view on matters that need privacy, and feels that her intimate

200 See Maimonides, *Code*, Laws concerning Wounding and Damaging 3:3; *Rashba*, bBaba Kama 86b; *SA*, HM 420:35.

201 *Tosafot*, bBaba Kama 86b s.v. *baisho; Rashba*, bBaba Kama 86b s.v. *veha; Rosh*, bBaba Kama 8:7; *Lehem Mishne*, Maimonides, *Code*, Laws concerning Wounding and Damaging 3:3; *Rema, SA*, HM 420:35, citing *Tur*. And see M. Weinstein, "Towards understanding *boshet*," *Alei Etzion* 9 (Alon Shvut: 2000), 55–65.

202 J.K. Crane, "Shameful ambivalences: dimensions of Rabbinic shame," *Association of Jewish Studies Review* 35 (NY: 2011), 61, 66, reaches this conclusion, but without reference to the *sugya* in bBaba Kama 86b. He may have been influenced by Weinstein, ibid., whom he cites.

203 *Protection of Privacy Law 5741–1981*, §5, §16. The latter is in the Database section of the law, but addresses revelation of personal information. §31(b) relates to minor database violations, but also requires "criminal intent or negligence."

204 *Biton v. Sultan*, Cr. FH 9818/01, PD 59(6) 554, 585 [40].

personal business will — without justification — enter the public domain.' "[205] In many US states, the tort of 'false light' fills the gap between privacy and reputation, protecting the victim's subjective feelings, whereas that of defamation protects their reputation. R. Abba's query, discussed above, is akin to the question of whether *boshet* is closer to false light or to defamation. As noted above, most authorities consider the issue of how *boshet* is best characterized to be unresolved, and we find a similar quandary in US law. The Supreme Court of Florida, echoing R. Zevid's interpretation of R. Abba's question, asserted:

> The use of a different standard, which is the main distinction between the elements of false light and defamation, is the theoretical mechanism for protecting the two different interests at issue. A false light plaintiff must prove that the publicity would be "highly offensive to a reasonable person," whereas a defamation plaintiff must prove injury to his or her reputation in the community. As explained by the Ohio Supreme Court in recognizing false light, "in defamation cases the interest sought to be protected is the objective one of reputation, either economic, political, or personal, in the outside world. In privacy cases the interest affected is the subjective one of injury to [the] inner person."[206]

Other courts, notably the Supreme Court of New Jersey, have emphasized how close these two actions are, to the point of being barely distinguishable.[207] Thus the highest courts in the US have perpetuated the talmudic discussion around *boshet* and what, exactly, it protects, with different courts reaching different conclusions. In summary, *boshet* appears to defend the individual's dignity — leaving open whether that is subjectively or objectively determined — and in this it reflects the Roman *iniuria* and the civil law tradition.[208]

We now come to the question of intent. As mentioned above, *iniuria* was actionable only when the offending party had intent to perform the act in question. In tractate Baba Kama, the Mishnah plainly states that *boshet* is only actionable where there was intent.[209] Liability under the *actio iniuriam* also required intent; by all appearances the intent required

205 Ibid., quoting *Reshumot*, n. 25 above, 206. Prior to his appointment as Attorney General, Barak was a member of the Kahan Commission.

206 *Jews for Jesus, Inc. v. Rapp*, 997 So. 2d 1098, 1109 (Fla. 2008).

207 *Rumbauskas v. Cantor*, 138 N.J. 173, 180–181, 649 A.2d 853 (1994).

208 Cf. *Mosley*, n. 176 above, paras. 212–14.

209 mBaba Kama 8:1. See also Sifre Deuteronomy, Torah portion 'Ki Teitze,' 293 s.v. *ish veahiv*.

was intent to perform the offending act, not intent to cause an affront.[210] The Talmud in bBaba Kama 86a appears to require intent to affront,[211] but elsewhere (27a) suggests that intent to carry out the offending act, generally assault, is required, similar to the requirement for *iniuria*.[212] Deuteronomy 25 reads:

> (11) If two men get into a fight with each other, and the wife of one comes up to save her husband from his antagonist, and puts out her hand and seizes him by his genitals, (12) you shall cut off her hand; show no pity.

mBaba Kama 8:1 derived the need for intent from these verses: "and puts out her hand and seizes him by his genitals" — one is not liable for causing embarrassment unless one intended to do so. Prima facie, the conclusion could follow from either "and puts out her hand" or "and seizes him by the genitals," each of which is an intentional act; it is thus unclear which conjunct suffices.[213] bBaba Kama 27a notes that the first, apparently superfluous conjunct ("and puts out her hand") teaches that intent to injure is sufficient. By contrast, Sifre ad loc. argues:

> Rabbi [Judah the Prince] says: since we find that there are cases of injury [specified] in the Torah where the unintentional is deemed intentional, could it be the same here? Therefore Scripture teaches, "and seizes him by the genitals" — to tell us that one is not liable for causing embarrassment (*boshet*) unless one did so intentionally.

According to the Sifre, the intention requirement is based on "and seizes him by the genitals," which suggests intent to shame. The same verse can therefore lead to two possible determinations of *mens rea* — intent to physically assault or perhaps to injure (bBaba Kama 27a) as in *iniuria*, or intent to shame (bBaba Kama 86a, Sifre).

The physical element of the two actions also merits comparison. According to R. Jose, *boshet* was only actionable if accompanied by

210 See Kenneth McK. Norrie, "The *actio iniuriarum* in Scots law: Romantic romanism or tool for today?" in Descheemaeker and Scott, n. 194 above.

211 *SA*, HM 421:1; and see *Sema* ad loc., which ties it directly to these verses. See also H. Ben-Menahem et al., *Windows onto Jewish Legal Culture: Fourteen Exploratory Essays* (London: 2011), ch. 7, "Law of the pursuer," 278ff., 287.

212 Maimonides, *Code*, Laws concerning Wounding and Damaging 1:12, but see Weinstein, n. 201 above, 55–66 for other interpretations.

213 Maimonides, ibid. 1:10, cites "and puts out her hand" as the source for the intention requirement; see *Mishne Torah* (Frankel edition) ad loc.

physical assault.[214] It is odd that this law does not appear in any Babylonian sources, and even in bBaba Kama 91a it is expressly quoted as "they say in the West [Israel] in the name of R. Jose b. Avin" (in the Jerusalem Talmud, "b. Bon"), a fifth-generation Amora in the land of Israel, meaning that the law reached Babylonia from Israel. jBaba Kama 3:8 asserts: "If he spat at him and the spittle did not touch him, what then? Said R. Jose, that is what was said: one who shames his fellow with words is not liable."

This illustrates R. Jose's rule that any *boshet* without physical violence is not actionable.[215] The Talmuds consider a case in which someone shames his fellow without touching him, by spitting in his direction (R. Jose) or by trumpeting in his ear (mBaba Kama 8:6). The mishnaic source is ambiguous — does it mean boxing someone's ear, or trumpeting into it? The latter is not obviously physical assault, and could suggest a position different from R. Jose's. Post-talmudic Jewish law accepted R. Jose's position,[216] though a different conclusion could be drawn from the Babylonian Talmud and Sifre. In support of this position, R. Menahem Hameiri (Perpignan 1249–1315), asserts of the case of one who screams in another's ear that while the perpetrator may have avoided liability for the four main types of actionable damage, he is still liable for *boshet*.[217] Since the Meiri is clear that words alone are not actionable, he seems to allow a very broad interpretation of R. Jose's 'assault' requirement, so as to include almost any physical intervention.

Despite the adage 'sticks and stones will break my bones, but words will never harm me,' shame is extremely powerful, and shame punishments have made a resurgence in modern penology. An affront to the body is also — if not primarily — an affront to our person and dignity. It is precisely this dignity that the Roman *iniuria* protected. Why, then, were words alone not actionable in Jewish law according to R. Jose and subsequent Jewish law? Daube's answer is that "mere

214 R. Jose, in jBaba Kama 8:6; cited in bBaba Kama 91a; Maimonides, *Code*, Laws concerning Wounding and Damaging 3:7.

215 Maimonides, ibid., 1:9; *SA*, HM 420:32. It is curious that R. Jose drew this conclusion, given the statement attributed to him that R. Zechariah b. Abkulas' words destroyed the Temple (tShabat 17:4). This statement is attributed elsewhere to R. Johanan; see Kalmin, n. 82 above, 43ff.

216 See *Tur*, HM 1; *Tur* and *SA*, HM 420:38.

217 *Beit Habehira*, bBaba Kama 90a, 91a, and *Rashi* and *R. Hananel* ad loc.

insulting words were not enough to justify proceedings . . . dangerous words such as hostile spells belong to a different class of delict altogether."[218]

As Daube noted, the laws of *boshet* and *iniuria* have followed a similar evolutionary course. In Roman law, a slap in the face — which generally results in hurt feelings, not physical injury — was the archetypical insult. Indeed, a slap or some similar assault without injury is the example of *iniuria* offered in the XII Tables (Table 7:7), where *iniuria* was distinct from *membrum ruptum, os fractum* (damaged limb, broken bone). However, *iniuria* later came to include injury. Daube makes a fascinating argument for a similar evolution in Jewish law. In response to a slap, Jesus invokes "eye for eye"' (Exod. 21:22), recommending instead, "turn the other cheek" (Matt. 5:38–39),[219] suggesting that "eye for eye" at that time was the basis for a legal action for shaming, namely, *boshet*. Daube puts forward the thesis that Matthew reflects a period when there was then no separate scriptural basis for an action for shaming, as it was included under the "eye for eye" rubric of Exodus 21, but that it later became separated. In the Tannaitic literature, he asserts, the verse in Deuteronomy 25:11 is invoked to support bringing suit for shaming. It is thus not surprising that Tannaitic and later sources do not agree on the correct interpretation of that verse, as we saw. Daube asserts that there is "no reason to assume any influence of Roman on Jewish law" and concludes that probably there was no such influence.[220] However, the emergence of *boshet* as an action at law over the course of the second century CE in ways rather similar to *iniuria*, and in a Roman province, suggests that similar forces guided the evolution of Roman and Jewish law at that time.

Returning to the role of *boshet* in protecting privacy, we can summarize that privacy as such was little valued in Roman culture, and barely meaningful in Jewish culture in late antiquity. There were, of course, institutions, such as the home and family, that provided sanctuary, seclusion, and privacy. But the notion of violating someone's privacy, particularly in the sense of revealing personal information, was of little significance. *Boshet* and *iniuria* protected the dignity of the individual. If one's dignity was violated, the violation was actionable. The mere

218 D. Daube, *The New Testament and Rabbinic Judaism* (Peabody MA: 1956), 259–65, 260.

219 Cf. Luke 6:29–30.

220 Daube, n. 218 above, 260–61.

fact of privacy violation was not in itself meaningful, and Shuger is basically correct in asserting that "the *Corpus iuris civilis* makes no mention of invaded privacy"; as shown above, there is some consideration of privacy in the urban setting.[221] Not only was privacy not a value to be protected, it was even an obstacle to the effective functioning of shame as a critical means of curbing misbehavior in Roman society.[222] *Dignitas*, by contrast, was a vigorously-protected value, and any revelation of private information that also violated dignity was actionable under the rubric of *iniuria*. Jewish law from the Tannaitic and Amoraic periods similarly seems to have accorded privacy little value, but to have deeply valued personal dignity, and much of what would today be a breach of privacy was then actionable under *boshet*.

8. Conclusion

The rubric 'Jewish law on privacy' is misleading. Several laws from the Tannaitic and later periods offered incidental protection of privacy, but all such laws had a different primary focus, and afforded protection to privacy only incidentally. Visual trespass is a concept that emerged to enable urban coexistence, protecting the enjoyment of private property. Rabbenu Gershom's ban on reading someone else's correspondence was similarly not intended to protect privacy as such, but rather, to facilitate reliable postal service. Even in what must surely be one of the most sensitive areas with respect to privacy, namely, the realm of sexual relations, there was, we saw, very little protection of privacy. Lastly, much of what might conceivably be considered invasion of privacy today would have been protected by the laws against shaming (*boshet*), which — like the Roman *iniuria* — offered protection against affronts to one's dignity. Jewish law protected property, correspondence, and human dignity, but did not view privacy as a fundamental value, or uphold a general right to privacy.[223]

221 Shuger, n. 188 above, 142.

222 C.A. Barton, *Roman Honor: The Fire in the Bones* (Berkeley: 2001), 21.

223 I thank Daniel Schreiber, Amram Tropper, Chanan Benayahu, Judah Galinsky, and Eric Descheemaeker for helpful comments and references.

The Jewish Law Annual, Vol. XX

HIV Vaccine Triage: Halakhic Considerations

Shalom C. Spira and Mark A. Wainberg*

1. Introduction

The halakhic questions arising from medical triage have received considerable attention over the past three decades.[1] This article will

* Rabbi Spira is a research assistant at the McGill AIDS Centre at the Lady Davis Institute for Medical Research at the Jewish General Hospital, Montreal. Dr. Wainberg is Director of the McGill University AIDS Centre, and a professor of medicine at McGill University.

1 In English: M.D. Tendler, "Rabbinic comment: triage of resources," *Mount Sinai Journal of Medicine* 51 (1984), 106–109, 116–20; M. Sokol, "The allocation of scarce medical resources: a philosophical analysis of the halakhic sources," *AJS Review* 15 (1990), 63–93; N. Amsel, *Jewish Encyclopedia of Moral and Ethical Issues* (Northvale NJ: 1994), 286–90; F. Rosner, *Biomedical Ethics and Jewish Law* (Hoboken NJ: 2001), 435–50; A. Steinberg, *Encyclopedia of Jewish Medical Ethics* (Jerusalem/Nanuet NY: 2003), 1:40–50; 3:848–60; D. Etengoff, "Triage in halacha: the threat of an avian flu pandemic," *Journal of Halacha and Contemporary Society* 55 (2008), 74–90; J. Goldschmiedt, "The division of scarce resources and triage in halacha," in J. Wiesen (ed.), *And You Shall Surely Heal: The Albert Einstein College of Medicine Synagogue Compendium of Torah and Medicine* (Jersey City NJ: 2009), 187–99; A. Lichtenstein, "Jewish philanthropy — whither?" *Tradition* 42 (2009), 7–32; J.D. Bleich, "Sacrificing the few to save the many," *Tradition* 43 (2010), 78–86.

build on this literature to offer preliminary, hypothetical suggestions on how Jewish bioethics might be applied to the distribution of a vaccine against HIV, should one become available in the future.

During a time of pandemic — and the rate of HIV morbidity and mortality in today's world represents a true pandemic — inoculating the public against HIV would have as much lifesaving potential as medications for the symptoms of patients already infected with HIV. Moreover, since none of the medications in question are presently capable of curing HIV, but can only suppress HIV plasma levels so they remain below a symptom-free threshold, the ubiquitous danger of infected patients developing drug-resistant viruses means that even patients currently being treated with medication could eventually experience a surge in plasma levels and die from AIDS. Thus, vaccination may be even more effective than medication in saving lives. It is therefore important to explore, through the prism of halakhic approaches to the allocation of scarce resources, the questions raised by the hypothetical possibility of dispensing an anti-HIV vaccine.

In Hebrew: S. Dichovsky, "Priority and preference in saving lives," *Assia* 3 (1982), 343–44; M. Hershler, "To what extent is there an obligation to spend money to rescue an endangered companion?," *Halakha Urefua* 3 (1982), 45–50; idem, "Priority and preferential treatment in the medical sphere," *Halakha Urefua* 4 (1984), 79–84; M. Weinberger, "Priority in healing the sick when there aren't enough physicians or medications," *Emek Halakha Assia* 1 (1985), 109–17; S. Dichovsky, "Priorities in communal life-saving," *Torah Shebeal Pe* 31 (1989), 40–51; I. Zilberstein, "Jumping the surgery queue," *Emek Halakha Assia* 2 (1989), 108–18; *Sefer Assia* 7 (1993): Shabtai Rappaport, "Priorities in allocation of public resources for medicine," 94–116; Y. Shafran, "Queue-jumping that makes others wait longer," 117–18; I. Zilberstein, "Special status and queue-jumping," 119–22; A. Steinberg, *Encyclopedia of Jewish Medical Ethics*, (Jerusalem: 1988-), 4:246–71; 5:498–544; J.D. Bleich, *Bintivot Hahalakha* (Hoboken NJ: 1996–2010), 1:118–26; R. S.E. Stern, *Shvivei Esh* (Bnei Brak: 2001), #66–67; *Sefer Assia* 9 (2004): I. Zilberstein, "Financial considerations in saving human life," 39–46; A. Nebentzal, "Forgoing one life for the sake of other lives," 47; *Assia* 81/82 (2008): A. Steinberg, "On the home front: halakhic considerations regarding triage, self-endangerment, and saving life," 5–39; U. Sedan, "Mass-casualty events," 40–48.

2. Selection for life vs. selection for death

R. J. David Bleich[2] and R. Shabtai Rappaport[3] have framed their respective analyses of medical triage in terms of the problem of selecting others for death. The issue is addressed by R. Shabtai Hakohen, the Shakh.[4] The Shakh discusses a scenario where the king has capriciously earmarked a specific number of innocent Jews for punishment (capital or financial). An outside Jew with imperial connections has the capacity to persuade the monarch to release one of those specified for punishment from the evil decree, but with the certain consequence that a different innocent Jew will be captured and punished instead, in order to meet the royal quota. May the Jew with imperial influence intervene in good conscience, to save an innocent co-religionist? The Shakh argues that this depends on whether the innocent Jew has already been captured by the king's servants. If he has, it is forbidden to persuade the sovereign to free him when this will inevitably result in the same punishment befalling a different Jew. But if he has not been captured yet, then it is permitted to persuade the sovereign to exempt a fellow Jew from the punishment, even though this guarantees that a different Jew will be punished instead. The argument is based on bJebamot 79a, which relates the events recounted in 2 Samuel 21, and describes King David approvingly as having prayed that Mephibosheth would be spared from delivery into the hands of the Gibeonites.

R. Bleich and R. Rappaport both explain that although it is strictly forbidden to earmark an innocent person for death, even for the sake of saving many others,[5] a principle underscored by the "we do not set aside one life for another" principle,[6] the law is in accordance with the ruling in the *Shakh*, because persuading the king to exempt the Jew is fundamentally a beneficial act of saving life (*hatzala*), namely, selecting the individual in question for life, whereas what the Jerusalem Talmud prohibits is the callous act of handing someone over to be put to death (*mesira*), that is, selection for death. Indeed, even if the earmarked Jew has already been captured by the king's servants, the principle of saving life should still authorize the Jew with imperial connections to

2 *Bintivot Hahalakha*, n. 1 above.
3 N. 1 above.
4 *Shakh, SA*, HM 163:18, which endorses the view in *Responsa Mahari b. Lev*, 2:40.
5 See jTerumot 8:4 (47a).
6 mOhalot 7:6.

intervene. However, the Talmud imposes a limit on the extent to which rescue is permitted when saving one life ipso facto endangers another. This limit in essence proscribes emotionally-inspired favoritism (*maso fanim*).[7] Based on the ruling in the *Shakh*, R. Bleich and R. Rappaport construct a legal-philosophical system of medical triage whose operative rubric is that of saving life rather than that of handing someone over to be put to death.

The Shakh's ruling is challenged by R. Jacob Ettlinger.[8] R. Ettlinger observes that David merely prayed to God that Mephibosheth be spared. God is the Master of all life, and a human being can request something of God, without fear of rendering an erroneous 'lifeboat ethics' decision. There is no indication that David took any physical action to actually save Mephibosheth at someone else's expense. R. Ettlinger thus denies that the *sugya* in bJebamot 79a can be adduced in support of the Shakh's view.[9]

7 bJebamot 79a. In effect, the proscription of favoritism in bJebamot 79a corresponds to that implicit in bBaba Metzia 62a, where two travelers have but a single canteen of water. The law is in accordance with the view of R. Akiva, who requires the legal possessor of the canteen to drink his own water and save his own life, even though this spells death for his companion. The Talmud implies that the unfortunate companion is forbidden to steal the canteen, which would constitute an act tantamount to homicide. Indeed, R. Chaim Ozer Grodzinski, in *Responsa Ahiezer* 2, YD 16:6, cites an earlier authority to the effect that if the companion were to steal the canteen in order to save his own life, he would be liable to death at the hands of heaven. Likewise, *Hazon Ish*, bBaba Metzia 62a, Likutim, 20, states that for the companion to steal the canteen would be tantamount to his stealing the life of the canteen owner. Similarly, R. Moses Feinstein rules in *Igrot Moshe*, YD 1:145 that the companion must forfeit his life rather than steal the canteen. So too, the captured Jew who could theoretically be saved by his compatriot's imperial connections must not be saved in this manner. In other words, the favoritism proscribed in bJebamot 79a is tantamount to the theft of life-sustaining water proscribed in bBaba Metzia 62a.

8 *Arukh Laner*, bJebamot 79a s.v. *veakati*.

9 The Shakh's view that the outside Jew may — before the impending decree has actually been issued — ask the king to exempt a potential victim from the decree, is also criticized in R. Moses Leib Tziltz, *Responsa Milei Deavot* 1, HM #4. However, though he disagrees with its theoretical basis, R. Tziltz proceeds to find a technical way to defend the Shakh's conclusion: R. Tziltz distinguishes between speaking directly to the king (which, he claims, retroactively removes the potential victim from the ambit of the imperial danger altogether) and all other means of rescuing the potential victim, which he prohibits for the reason noted by R. Ettlinger. We do not find

In our opinion, a methodological parallel can be drawn between the dispute between the Shakh and R. Ettlinger, on the one hand, and contradictory rulings that are found in different versions of a responsum by R. Moses Feinstein regarding medical intervention when someone is moribund (*goses*).[10] In the immediately preceding responsum (2:73:1), R. Feinstein invoked the view of R. Nissim Gerodi (Ran), that, under limited circumstances, it is permitted to pray for an incurably moribund patient (*goses*) to die.[11] R. Feinstein then proceeds, in the next responsum, to extrapolate from that dispensation to the conclusion that it is permissible, and even appropriate, to refrain from using medications to prolong the life of the same patient. After all, if we can pray for the death of the moribund patient (*goses*), why must we intervene medically to keep her alive? Thus, R. Feinstein seeks to derive a law regarding medical ethics from a law pertaining to prayer. This is the conclusion of the version of the responsum that appears in the Yeshivat Ohel Yosef edition of *Igrot Moshe* published in Bnei Brak and the Noble Book Press edition published in Brooklyn.

However, in the Moriah Offset Company edition, also published in Brooklyn, several further lines are added to R. Feinstein's responsum. R. Feinstein reports that his grandson R. Mordechai Tendler objected that perhaps there was a difference between praying for the death of one who is in the throes of dying, which is proper, and intervening medically to prolong the patient's life. Praying has no physiological effect on the patient, whereas medical treatment does, at least momentarily, physiologically help the patient, and perhaps is thus even obligatory in light of the pivotal obligation to save life (*pikuah nefesh*).[12] That is,

R. Tziltz's distinction convincing, but in any event, in essence R. Tziltz accepts R. Ettlinger's position.

10 HM 2:74:1.

11 *Ran*, bNedarim 40a.

12 The practice of medicine is considered a mode of saving life (*pikuah nefesh*), as per *SA*, YD 336:1. According to *Biur Halakha, SA*, OH 329:4, the Sabbath is to be desecrated even to save the life of one who is dying (*goses*). It follows, we contend, that there is a halakhic obligation to medically intervene to extend the life of one who is dying by every additional moment that is technologically possible. R. Feinstein himself states, in the last paragraph of *Igrot Moshe*, YD 2:174:1, that one who is dying should receive lifesaving intervention. See also *Bintivot Hahalakha* 3, n. 1 above, 161–78, on the question of the obligation to provide medical treatment to, or undertake heroic measures to resuscitate, someone who is dying.

R. Tendler argued against R. Feinstein's analogy, and maintained that the patient's life should be prolonged. R. Feinstein responds to R. Tendler's observation with the words, "this claim merits further examination," meaning he acknowledged that it might have some validity. Evidently, then, according to this version of the responsum, there is uncertainty as to whether Rabbenu Nissim's remarks on praying for the death of someone who is suffering a painful demise constitute a precedent for permitting someone dying (*goses*) to die without medical intervention. Presumably, in light of the rule that a doubt regarding danger to life is to be decided in favor of saving life,[13] one must set aside the Ran's view and opt to medically extend the life of one who is dying.

Thus, the first edition of the responsum is in line with the Shakh's premise that one extrapolates from prayer to deciding questions of life and death, whereas the second edition is in line with R. Ettlinger's doubts about that premise. Since R. Feinstein was apparently unable to decide between these positions, we would argue that one must follow R. Ettlinger's cautious approach, since the question at hand concerns an unresolved doubt regarding saving a life.

Moreover, as R. Bleich himself concedes, a ruling by R. Moses Isserles, the Rema, appears to be inconsistent with the Shakh's view. The Rema rules that if one sees that she is in imminent danger of harm, she may rescue herself, even though this will automatically cause the

---

In a letter published by R. Bleich in *Bioethical Dilemmas: a Jewish Perspective*, vol. 1 (Hoboken NJ: 1998), vol. 2 (Southfield MI: 2006), 1:71, R. Aaron Soloveitchik opposes extrapolation from prayer to medical treatment, consistent with the view in *Arukh Laner* and the second version of R. Feinstein's responsum. R. Soloveitchik does not, however, argue that one who is dying need be given medical treatment (apparently on the strength of the view expressed in *Rema, SA*, YD 339:1); rather, he circumvents the problem of medical treatment of the *goses* by simply positing that there are "very few, if any" patients today who meet the halakhic criteria for deeming someone to fall into that category. By contrast, both R. Feinstein, in *Igrot Moshe* YD 2:174:1 and version 2 of HM 2:74:1, and R. Bleich, do mandate treating even a patient who satisfies the criteria for deeming someone to be dying, and suggest alternative interpretations of *Rema, SA*, YD 339:1. Medically, however, there seems to be at least one — and perhaps it is the only one — pathological condition that can truly be said to render a patient a *goses*, namely, cardiac arrest. It should, however, be noted that R. Moses David Tendler, in *Responsa of Rav Moshe Feinstein* (Hoboken NJ: 1996), 75–82, 135–48, maintains that the view in the first edition of *Igrot Moshe*, HM 2:74:1 represents the normative determination of the law.

13 bYoma 83a.

harm in question to befall someone else.[14] R. Joshua Falk infers from the Rema's stance that this applies only before the harm ensues, but once the harmful event is taking place, the victim may not save himself when doing so will cause the harm to be inflicted on someone else.[15] On the other hand, it has been argued that the Shakh's position is to always permit one to rescue himself, even after he himself is captured, and that it is only when rescuing a third party that the Shakh distinguishes between the pre-capture and post-capture situations.[16] If so, there seems to be a clear difference of opinion between the Rema and the Shakh.[17]

14 *Rema, SA*, HM 388:2.

15 *Sefer Meirat Einayim* (Sema) ad loc., §10. The *Sema*'s exposition is affirmed in R. Yair Bacharach, *Responsa Havot Yair*, #213 and R. Abraham Tzvi Perlmutter, *Damesek Eliezer*, gloss on p. 4. Cf. R. Meir Auerbach, *Imrei Bina*, OH 13:5, who contends that the *Sema* distinguishes between deflecting the source of danger from oneself onto others by taking action against the source of danger — which is prohibited — versus taking action vis-à-vis oneself, i.e., fleeing the danger, which is permissible. R. Perlmutter argues against R. Meir Auerbach's view by considering the following scenario: suppose a dangerous deluge has begun flooding someone's field. R. Falk's view in the *Sema* would proscribe erection of a barrier in the middle of the field to deflect the deluge onto neighboring fields, even though the land-owner is merely taking an action vis-à-vis his own property. R. Perlmutter contends that the correct distinction to make is that between pre-capture actions and post-capture actions. However, we would argue that there is no substantive halakhic difference between the views of R. Perlmutter and R. Meir Auerbach. R. Auerbach would presumably concede to R. Perlmutter that once the torrent of water has entered a landowner's field, it becomes 'his' water, and so for him to construct a barrier in the middle of his field to deflect the onslaught would be to act against the source of the danger, which is categorically forbidden. Thus, R. Auerbach and R. Perlmutter, like R. Bacharach, appear to uphold the view endorsed in the *Sema*.

16 *Gilyon Yad Avraham, SA*, YD 157:1. The reasoning here is that favoritism is tantamount to causing homicide (see n. 7 above), but the concept of causing homicide is inapplicable when one of the two travelers has legal ownership of the flask of water, in which case he may drink the water even though this consigns his fellow to death. So too, one who has the diplomatic know-how to rescue herself may do so, even though this condemns her fellow to death.

17 This difference of opinion is identified in R. Nathan Gestetner, *Responsa Lehorot Natan*, 11:103, §15, which cites *Gilyon Yad Avraham*. In addition, it is identified in a responsum by R. Samuel Landau published in his father's *Responsa Noda Biyehuda*, 2nd edition, YD #74 s.v. *veefshar leya-shev*. Yet inexplicably, R. Landau proceeds to ignore the objections to the Shakh's view voiced by R. Isserles and R. Falk, and rule in accordance with

We contend that the wording of the Rema's ruling implies that one may save himself and only himself from danger before the danger arrives, but not save someone else (even before the danger arrives) when this will cause the harm to automatically be displaced onto others. This position reflects the concern raised by R. Ettlinger in *Arukh Laner* about adducing the *sugya* about praying for the death of a moribund sufferer to draw conclusions about medical intervention.

Why does R. Ettlinger allow one to save himself before the danger arrives, as the Rema rules, even though the danger is thereby shifted to someone else? The explanation seems to lie in the distinction between saving (*hatzala*) and handing someone over to be put to death (*mesira*).[18] To save oneself before the danger is actually present is not a reprehensible act of selecting someone else to be put to death, but rather, it is the salutary act of selecting oneself for life, even though the inevitable consequence of this selection is that someone else will die. The proof-text for this principle, which is articulated in the talmudic *sugya* of the two travelers with just one canteen of water, is "that your brother may live with you" (Lev. 25:36), for which R. Akiva offers the exegesis "your life takes precedence over your fellow's."[19] That is, even R. Ettlinger accepts the conceptual distinction between saving someone and handing someone over to be put to death that is invoked by both R. Bleich and R. Rappaport in constructing their respective analyses of halakhic triage, though he takes its practical application to be more limited.[20]

---

it. We do not find his argument for doing so to be compelling. Indeed, R. Landau himself candidly admits at both the beginning and the end of his responsum that it was difficult for him to arrive at a ruling on the matter.

18 Earlier, R. Chaim Sofer provided an unambiguous characterization of the saving — handing-over dichotomy in *Responsa Mahane Haim* 2, EH #19 s.v. *venahafokh hu*.

19 bBaba Metzia 62a.

20 The distinction is also adduced in a thought experiment in *Hazon Ish*, HM, Sanhedrin #25 s.v. *veyesh leayen*. It reflects on the predicament of an outside observer who beholds a lethal projectile launched at a large group of people. The observer faces a conundrum: she possesses the capacity to deflect the projectile from its original trajectory, thereby saving the large group of people, but the deflected projectile will instead kill a smaller number of people in the new location where it will land. R. Karelitz, the Hazon Ish, tentatively suggests that it might be permitted to deflect the projectile, because the deflection is fundamentally a noble act of saving many people — with the unfortunate and unintended side-effect of killing

3. Saving oneself vs. saving others

In line with R. Akiva's dictum "your life takes precedence over your fellow's," we see that Jewish law permits — indeed, commands — the individual to utilize whatever resources he possesses to save his own life before rescuing the lives of others.

In the event that the prospect of danger is unequal, with some facing a greater risk of death than others, in the absence of sufficient vaccine for all, and where the owner of the available vaccine is at a lower risk of dying, the following question arises: should/can the owner of the vaccine forfeit his vaccine in order to save others? This

---

a smaller number of people — rather than a vicious act of handing someone over to be put to death (*mesira*). But he proceeds to raise a counterargument that perhaps the deflection should be proscribed because — absent the observer's intervention — the smaller number of people would have lived, and thus the observer can be said to have, with his own hands, actively sacrificed the smaller number of people, which is unconscionable. Ultimately, the Hazon Ish leaves the conundrum unanswered.

However, as suggested in Dichovsky 1989, n. 1 above, careful reflection on the Hazon Ish's language reveals that he implicitly endorses the Shakh's position, though without mentioning any of the decisors who debated the issue. R. Dichovsky bases this conclusion on the fact that the sole consideration raised by the Hazon Ish against deflection of the lethal projectile is that the observer would thereby be "killing with his own hands" (*horeg beyadayim*) by physically manipulating the controls so that the projectile is propelled to a new target. But if the observer could rescue the larger group at the expense of the smaller group without having any tactile contact with the source of the danger, then the Hazon Ish might well have argued that the intervention should be carried out. This position would be consistent with the views of Mahari b. Lev, the Shakh, and R. Samuel Landau, but unacceptable to rabbis Isserles, Falk, Bacharach, Ettlinger, Meir Auerbach, Perlmutter, and Tziltz (in most cases). We thus contend that the ruling implicit in the *Hazon Ish* should not necessarily be taken as dispositive, seeing as R. Karelitz did not address the countervailing position of so many authorities.

It should be noted that R Karelitz is apparently assuming that when one has been targeted by an airborne projectile that is already en route, he is not regarded as already have been 'captured.' Were he already regarded as captured, then even the Shakh would forbid a third party to rescue him at the cost of someone else's life. This point is itself independently questioned by R. Perlmutter, and hinges on the dispute among the decisors as to whether a vessel that has been targeted by a horizontally-fired arrow is already regarded as virtually destroyed; see *Bintivot Hahalakha*, n. 1 above, 2:180–84 for an exploration of this dispute.

question is in turn reducible to the halakhic dispute over whether one is obligated or even permitted to risk his life in order to rescue someone else from certain death. R. Naftali Zvi Berlin takes the *sugya* of the two travelers with one canteen (bBaba Metzia 62a) to address precisely such a conundrum; and concludes that one is forbidden to risk one's life to save someone else's life.[21] Although, on the basis of the Jerusalem Talmud, which permits and indeed obligates an individual to risk his life in order to rescue his fellow from certain death, R. Joseph Caro reaches the opposite conclusion,[22] the majority of decisors concur with R. Berlin's ruling.[23] Accordingly, the owner of a dose of the vaccine should always inoculate himself rather than forego his dose to save someone else's life.

Should the risk to the owner of a scarce resource be medically remote, but still sufficiently significant to frighten the general population, while others face certain death (or — more accurately — a greater risk of death), the problem of whether the owner should forfeit the resource appears analogous to the dilemma of living renal donation. R. Ovadia Yosef rules that such donations are permissible and praiseworthy, though not mandatory.[24] However, in our opinion, the danger of contracting HIV in today's society can never be regarded as remote, and thus one who owns an HIV vaccine should always use it for herself rather than forego it to save someone else.[25]

When the question of HIV vaccine allocation is a matter of oneself vs. others, then, one inoculates oneself first.[26] A more difficult question

21 *Haamek Sheeila*, #147.

22 *Beit Yosef*, HM 426.

23 See R. J.D. Bleich, *Contemporary Halakhic Problems* (NY: 1977-), 4:275–79; R. Jonathan Goldberger, *Responsa Avnei Hefetz* 3:79; R. Ovadia Yosef, *Responsa Yabia Omer* 9, HM #12; 10, HM #6.

24 *Responsa Yabia Omer* 9, HM #12.

25 This assessment is evidently shared by R. Bleich, who asserts that the entire populace must be halakhically envisaged as endangered by the HIV global pandemic, see *Bintivot Hahalakha*, n. 1 above, 3:64.

26 R. Michael Broyde has argued that since one's immediate obligation to act charitably mandates caring for one's closest relatives, as stated in *SA*, YD 251:3, this generates an automatic triage priority in the context of the obligation to save life. An individual in (lawful) private possession of several doses of lifesaving vaccine must inoculate himself and his immediate relatives first, notwithstanding the needs of the broader society. R. Zvi Spitz supports this view, arguing that an individual is obligated to

arises when the owner of a vaccine is already inoculated and must choose between other parties to whom he is not related.

4. Lives of the many vs. lives of the few

Contemporary decisors take it to be axiomatic that, when rendering a triage choice between two groups, one always saves the group with the greater number of members.[27]

---

be charitable to outsiders only after having taken care of his relatives' needs, see *Mishpetei Hatora* (Jerusalem: 1997), 3:126–27. Dichovsky 1982, n. 1 above, and Goldschmiedt, n. 1 above, similarly direct a rescuer to save the lives of immediate relatives before saving the lives of non-relatives. R. Spitz lists the order of priority among relatives, for lifesaving purposes, as follows: (1) parents, (2) children, (3) parents-in-law, (4) siblings, (5) siblings-in-law. This ordering seems surprising, since that given in *Rema, SA*, YD 251:3 places siblings immediately after children. Another question that requires clarification is the rank assigned to one's spouse. Is saving a spouse the first priority, even over a parent?

R. Dichovsky and R. Spitz caution that prioritization of a rescuer's relatives is only pertinent to allocation of resources that are privately owned by the rescuer. If the rescuer is distributing resources belonging to the public or to a corporate entity, he obviously has no right to favor his own relatives.

27 See R. Bleich, *Bioethical Dilemmas*, n. 12 above, 1:153–59; *Shvivei Esh*, n. 1 above, #66, §3–5. R. Steinberg (*Assia* 2008, n. 1 above), ascribes this position to R. Joseph Shalom Eliashiv, *Kovetz Teshuvot*, 3:159. Examination of that responsum appears to leave unresolved the question of whether saving one Torah scholar outweighs saving many ignoramuses, but the clear implication of R. Eliashiv's remarks is that, other things being equal, the rescuer must indeed select the larger group.

This rule is also implicit in the discussion in *Hazon Ish* cited in n. 20 above. R. Karelitz expressed doubt regarding saving the larger group of people at the expense of the smaller group only because on the envisaged scenario, the observer could be accused of actively killing the smaller group. However, where no killing is involved, and one is simply coming to the aid of victims by providing them with the scarce medical resources one possesses, R. Karelitz would, we can assume, also take it as axiomatic that the larger group should be saved.

As Goldschmiedt, n. 1 above, suggests, this rule is apparently based on bNazir 47b, which compares the sanctity of a deputy High Priest to that of a priest who leads the army. The former has higher standing, and in a situation where one of the two must be defiled by tending to an abandoned

In a previously unpublished responsum, R. Solomon Zalman Auerbach extends this principle to a novel frontier.[28] He describes the following triage problem: two deathly-ill patients, one wealthy, the other impoverished, are in the hospital waiting for a hemodialysis machine. The wealthy patient has the wherewithal to offer a substantial donation to the hospital in exchange for the right to use the machine, while the poor patient obviously cannot do so. "If the wealthy man's donation can expand the hospital unit, and he will [thereby] save himself as well as others, why should he not possess the right of precedence? Behold, he takes what is his and he also gives to others!" In other words, although the pauper will die if the magnate gets the machine, just as the magnate will die if the pauper gets the machine, more lives will saved by the rich man's getting the machine. His donation will subsidize the hospital's hemodialysis unit, allowing the hospital to pay for more equipment, medications, and staff that will save the lives of other patients as well. On the envisaged scenario, even with the magnate's generosity, another hemodialysis machine cannot be acquired in time (otherwise, there would be no ethical problem and the question need not have been posed to R. Auerbach), hence the death of the poor patient is inevitable. Nevertheless, inasmuch as a greater number of lives will be saved, the triage choice is correct.

Two caveats are in order. Firstly, the group with the greater number of patients is to be preferred only when both groups face an equal medical danger and have the same medical prognosis. However, when one group is anticipated to improve more thanks to the medical intervention (because it is in greater initial danger and/or because it is anticipated to respond better to the intervention), then R. Auerbach himself

---

corpse, it is the latter who should suffer defilement. Nevertheless, continues the Gemara, if a rescuer can only save the life of one of the two priests, he must select the military priest, because "the many depend on him." *Rashi* ad loc. explains: for he leads the public in war. In other words, rescuing the military priest will save the lives of the many, whose survival depends on him, and this consideration outweighs saving the individual life of the deputy High Priest.

28 It was published in R. Simha Bunim Lazerson, *Shulhan Shlomo, Erkhei Refua* (Jerusalem: 2006), 2:47 (henceforth *Shulhan Shlomo*).

is quoted elsewhere in the same volume (p. 14) as ruling that the group that will fare better takes priority with respect to triage.[29]

29 His ruling is based on R. Joseph Teomim's *Pri Megadim, SA*, OH 328 and *Mishbetzot Zahav*, §1. Without directly referring to R. Teomim's rulings, the same point is made in *Igrot Moshe*, HM 2:73:2. R. Feinstein rules that if two very ill patients arrive at a hospital simultaneously — one who can survive only for a very brief interval (*hayei shaa*), and one who can be cured, extending her life significantly (*hayei olam*) — and resources only exist to save one of them, then the hospital should save the patient who can be cured. R. Samuel Wosner, *Responsa Shevet Halevi*, 6:242, who also seems to uphold the view in *Pri Megadim*, though without citing it explicitly, similarly directs a healthcare worker to rescue one whose life can be extended significantly (*hayei olam*) before one whose remaining life will be very brief (*hayei shaa*). R. Wosner subsequently (10:167) demands that a rescuer confronted with two very-ill patients rescue the more dangerously-ill patient first.

R. Feinstein further argues that a patient who can be saved and whose life can be significantly extended takes triage priority over a patient who can only be saved for a very brief interval, even if the one whose life can be significantly extended is only possibly in mortal danger, whereas the patient who can only be saved for a very brief interval is definitely in mortal danger. This claim is innovative, and cannot be inferred from *Pri Megadim*. According to R. Steinberg (*Assia* 2008, n. 1 above), R. Feinstein reached this novel conclusion on the basis of his understanding of R. Akiva's dictum in bBaba Metzia 62a, which he takes to imply that the significantly-extended life (*hayei olam*) of one patient is worth more than the very brief remaining life (*hayei shaa*) of two.

In a subsequent responsum (HM 2:75:2), R. Feinstein clarifies that for triage purposes, a patient deemed to have 'life for very brief interval' refers to a patient whose medical prognosis is such that — even with medical intervention — he is anticipated to have less than a year left to live, whereas a patient deemed to have the potential for 'significantly-extended life' refers to a patient who is anticipated to live a year or longer if treated. The distinction, it is argued, originates from the principles governing one who is mortally-ill (*treifa*). But cf. *Bioethical Dilemmas*, n. 12 above, 2:239–75, which challenges the extrapolation from the principles of the mortally-ill patient (*treifa*) to the *hayei shaa* vs. *hayei olam* dichotomy with regard to hazardous medical procedures. R. Bleich defines 'significantly-extended life' as any statistically-predicted length of survival in a given patient, if treated, that exceeds the prognosis of the same patient if left untreated. If R. Bleich similarly contests R. Feinstein's definition of 'significantly-extended life' vis-à-vis triage, this would render triage determinations extremely complicated, since in every set of competing patients there would have to be an assessment of who was anticipated to live longer. Arguably, an echo of this putative approach is discernible in the

This caveat is illustrated by a talmudic *sugya* in tractate Gitin.[30] It recounts an incident in which R. Johanan b. Zakai asked the emperor Vespasian to save at least a small number of Jews living in the land of Israel, rather than asking him to spare the entire Jewish community, as it was certain that the lesser request would be accepted, but uncertain whether the larger one would be accepted. Analogously, when there is a good medical reason for determining that the poor patient should get the hemodialysis machine, the poor patient must be accorded priority.[31]

---

controversial opinion of those decisors who advocate assigning priority to minors of at least bar or bat mitzva age (see sec. 5 below). Presumably, *ceteris paribus*, a younger patient has a longer life expectancy, if treated, than a more senior patient. On the other hand, R. Bleich might not necessarily dispute R. Feinstein's view as applied to triage, since the distinction between one who is mortally-ill (*treifa*) and one who is not may be so fundamental as to merit consideration in line with R. Teomim's view. As a third possibility, R. Bleich might both accept the distinction between one who is mortally ill and one who is not as relevant to R. Teomim's analysis, and also mandate that even among two patients who are either both mortally-ill or both non-mortally-ill, the patient whose life is anticipated to be longer is to be granted priority.

30 bGitin 56b, invoked by R. Chaim Sofer to illustrate the medical triage point in *Responsa Mahane Haim* 2, EH #19 s.v. *vekhen ala bedaati*.

31 Admittedly, prima facie, this conclusion appears inconsistent with that arising from the talmudic sugya in bNazir 47b about saving the priests, discussed in n. 27 above. The Talmud there rules that although the deputy High Priest has greater sanctity than the military priest, the military priest should be saved, and not the deputy High Priest, because saving the military priest is tantamount to saving the many. Thus, whereas bGitin 56b suggest a principle of taking into account factors other than sheer numbers, bNazir 47b puts forward the principle that numbers are determinative, and the largest group should be saved. To resolve this apparent conflict, a distinction must be made between different types of non-quantitative factors. Factors that are intrinsically related to saving life (*pikuah nefesh*) through physical causality, e.g., facing greater danger and/or having a greater chance of rescue, confer halakhic priority on smaller groups, and may outweigh the quantitative advantage of larger groups. But factors unrelated to saving life through physical causality, but rather based on considerations of spiritual superiority (e.g., greater priestly sanctity), are ignored, and the triage decision is based on saving the grater number of people.

Our suggestion for reconciling bGitin 56b with bNazir 47b is consistent with the accepted principle that the obligation to save life mandates only recourse to methods of rescue that can be anticipated to succeed on the strength of causality, i.e., established causal relations (*refua beduka*). Spiritual means of rescue are not recognized, see *Contemporary Halakhic Problems*, n. 23 above, 4:203–17. It is also in line with R. Feinstein's

Second, R. Solomon Auerbach's directive to — in essence — auction off the right of triage priority to the bidder who will donate the most — provided the competing patients all have the same medical need — might be operative only in a hospital where the competing patients are not actual stakeholders in the hospital themselves. For example, if the hospital was privately built, and the two competing patients are not those who paid for its construction; or alternatively, if the hospital was publicly funded, but the competing patients are visiting from abroad. On such scenarios, the non-stakeholder who can offer a larger donation to the hospital should be granted priority. However, if the competing patients are both stakeholders, it might not be possible to summarily dismiss the poorer patient's claim for treatment, as she is an actual part-owner, and, as explained above in sec. 3, the owner of a scarce resource deserves priority in benefitting from it. How such a scenario should be managed requires further consideration.[32]

principle that rescuers are only halakhically authorized to intervene medically to prolong or improve a patient's life in a physiological sense, but not a spiritual sense; an example of the latter would be intervening to allow the patient to fulfill the precept of fasting on Yom Kippur; see *Igrot Moshe*, OH 3:90. The same point is reflected in R. Bleich's concept of "maximization of life quanta" when rendering decisions regarding patient care; see *Bioethical Dilemmas*, n. 12 above, 2:239–75.

32 According to the Maharsha (R. Samuel Edels), bBaba Metzia 62a, when a scarce lifesaving resource is owned jointly by two partners, it must be shared by both of them. *Igrot Moshe*, YD 1:145 rules as does the Maharsha, emphasizing that this is the law even if the supply of jointly-owned water happens to be held by one of the co-owners. The same conclusion is reached by R. Efraim Oshry in *Responsa Mimaamakim*, 5:1. Obviously, unlike a supply of water, a hemodialysis machine is indivisible and would be useless if 'shared' by two patients. (More precisely, its only real use as a shared commodity would be to be sold with near-instantaneous swiftness, the proceeds then being divided between both patients, who would each proceed to beg for emergency donations to cover the rest of the cost of a hemodialysis machine so that each would have access to her own machine.) Nevertheless, appropriating the part-ownership of the machine from one patient to give full use of the machine to the other does not appear to be halakhically justifiable. Nor does there appear to be a justifiable halakhic basis for permitting one of the patients to altruistically waive her share in the resource so that the other will live. No one has halakhic license to waive his life, as is explained in R. Solomon Zevin, *Leor Hahalakha* (Tel Aviv: 1956), 318–35.

The case of a scarce resource owned jointly by partners must be distinguished from that of a totally ownerless scare resource. R. Chaim Sofer

With respect to an HIV vaccine, all members of any given society would appear to be roughly equal. The danger of exposure to HIV in that society, and the lifesaving efficacy of the vaccine, are identical for all citizens. Accordingly, if a hospital owns a circumscribed number of HIV vaccine doses, and there is competition between different non-stakeholder patients seeking to be inoculated, it would appear that a patient who is willing to make a donation to help expand the hospital's facilities, so that more patients can be treated, should be given priority, since by saving him one is saving the greater number of patients.

5. Unresolved triage disputes

There are a number of outstanding disputes among the decisors regarding triage, which we hereby survey in the hope that contemporary decisors will provide definitive guidance.

---

rules that if the two thirsty travelers were to chance upon an abandoned canteen of water, R. Akiva would obligate them to share it equally, even though one of them has the physical agility to pre-empt the other and drink all the water himself (*Responsa Mahane Haim* 2, EH #19 s.v. *akh nire li lehadesh*). This is also the ruling of R. Joseph Soloveitchik, as cited by R. Hershel Schachter at a conference on Dec. 28, 1988 (http://www.yutorah.org/lectures/lecture.cfm/711848/Rabbi_Moshe_D._Tendler/Definition_of_Death_II, 47:00 into the recording). Although the rulings by R. Sofer and R. Soloveitchik may seem similar to that of the Maharsha, we would argue that the former follow, not from the concept of partnership in a resource, but from analysis of the question, discussed above in sec. 2, of whether, once one has been captured, she may permissibly rescue herself when that will shift the danger onto others. The thirsty individual who theoretically has the physical agility to seize the ownerless canteen, is consigned to death should he choose to congenially share the canteen with his companion. He can extricate himself from death by drinking all the water instead of sharing it, but this will cause his companion to be 'captured,' i.e., consigned to an earlier death than otherwise. As we saw, the Shakh and those who accept his view permit this, whereas the Rema and those who accept his view forbid it. In essence, R. Sofer and R. Soloveitchik subscribe to the Rema's position (or at least recognize that it is sufficiently strong to warrant a stringent ruling). Accordingly, if a scarce lifesaving resource is ownerless, and gravely-ill patients are competing for it, the conclusion of sec. 2 above dictates that it be divided among them.

Age

Both R. Feinstein[33] and R. Solomon Z. Auerbach[34] emphatically deny that an age difference between two individuals competing for medical triage should be granted any significance in establishing priority. R. Jacob Emden[35] and R. Solomon Dichovsky,[36] however, maintain that a younger person does have priority, so long as she is sufficiently old to be obligated to observe the precepts.[37]

Lineage

The majority of decisors incorporate the lineage guidelines found in tractate Horayot[38] into medical triage algorithms.[39] Some, however, have questioned their relevance.[40] And some contemporary decisors,

33 *Igrot Moshe*, HM 2:75:7.
34 *Shulhan Shlomo*, 2:14.
35 *Sefer Birat Migdal Oz*, Even Bohen, pina alef, §92.
36 Dichovsky 1982, n. 1 above.
37 A bioethics team at the U.S. National Institutes of Health recently proposed an algorithm comparable to the guidelines suggested by R. Emden and R. Dichovsky, see G. Persad et al., "Principles for allocation of scarce medical interventions," *Lancet* 373 (2009), 423–31.
38 "A priest takes precedence over a Levite, a Levite over an Israelite . . . a proselyte over an emancipated slave" (bHorayot 13a).
39 *Igrot Moshe,* HM 2:74:1; 75:2; R. Solomon Auerbach, quoted in *Shulhan Shlomo*, 2:14, 17; *Bintivot Hahalakha*, n. 1 above, 1:123; Hershler, n. 1 above; *Responsa Shevet Halevi*, 10:167; *Mishpetei Hatora*, 2:140.
40 *Sefer Birat Migdal Oz*, Even Bohen, pina alef, §89, expresses uncertainty as to whether the priority assigned to priests (*kohanim*) and Levites (*leviim*) applies today, since present-day priests and Levites are deemed to be such only on the basis of a presumption (*hazaka*), given that it is not possible to authenticate this status by tracing their family histories back to ancient times. R. Eliezer Waldenberg, *Responsa Tzitz Eliezer*, 18:1, asserts that the lineage rules in tractate Horayot are only relevant vis-à-vis giving charity, but not saving life. We would argue that, since in bKidushin 80a the Talmud declares that presumptions are sufficient even for adjudicating matters of life and death, there is no reason to disregard lineage in matters of medical triage just because present-day priests and Levites are only presumptively deemed to be such. However, what R. Emden clearly intends to convey is that since, as noted in *Magen Avraham, SA*, OH 201:4, some authorities doubt that there is even a valid presumption today that putative priests are indeed of priestly lineage, there may be room to question the role of priestly and Levitical lineage vis-à-vis triage.

while concurring with the majority who incorporate the lineage rules, admit that such calculations would be difficult, and implausible, for healthcare workers to carry out.[41]

Dosage divisibility

Although the law is in accordance with the view of R. Akiva in bBaba Metzia 62a, namely, that the water canteen owner is to drink his own water so as to gain a significant extension to his life (*hayei olam*), rather than divide it between himself and his companion to enable both of them to live for a brief interval (*hayei shaa*), as Ben Patura advocates, the decisors disagree on how to interpret R. Akiva's algorithm when an outside rescuer who owns the water (and whose life is not endangered) encounters two very thirsty travelers. Some say that in the latter situation, R. Akiva would concede to Ben Patura, and the rescuer must divide the water equally[42]; others hold that R. Akiva's exegesis of the verse "that your brother may live with you" (Lev. 25:36) entails that rescue that leads to a significant extension of one patient's life is always preferable to rescue that extends two lives by a short interval only, and hence the rescuer should give all the water to one patient.[43] Remarkably,

41 R. Solomon Auerbach, cited in *Shulhan Shlomo*, 2:14. Cf. *Igrot Moshe*, HM 2:74:1, which, after emphatically insisting on the applicability of the bHorayot lineage rules, somewhat incongruously adds, "even though in these cases it is difficult to orchestrate an action without great analysis."

42 See, e.g., R. Waldenberg, *Responsa Tzitz Eliezer*, 9:28:3, based on R. Naftali Hertz Landau, *Heker Halakha*; R. Moses Sternbuch, *Teshuvot Vehanhagot*, 1:858.

43 R. Solomon Auerbach, cited in *Shulhan Shlomo*, 2:17; *Responsa Shevet Halevi*, 6:242. In *Responsa Mishne Halakhot*, 17:175 s.v. *od katav sham*, R. Menashe Klein expresses incredulity at R. Naftali Landau's comments in *Heker Halakha*, cited in n. 42 above, claiming that they direct the rescuer to deny the water to both patients, allowing both to die; R. Klein dismisses this course of action as ethically absurd, and instead rules that the water be allocated entirely to one patient, so that his life will be extended significantly (*hayei olam*). R. Klein seems to have misunderstood R. Landau's view, which is accurately captured by R. Waldenberg: the water should be divided between the two patients, allowing each to live for a brief interval (*hayei shaa*). Thus, although R. Klein concurs with the view of R. Solomon Auerbach and R. Wosner, unlike them, he does not acknowledge the possibility of an alternative interpretation of bBaba Metzia 62a.

the Hazon Ish contradicts himself on this question,[44] and R. Chaim Sofer ambiguously asserts that one may adopt the second approach,[45]

44 In *Hazon Ish*, bBaba Metzia 62a, Likutim, 20, R. Karelitz upholds the second approach. Yet according to the posthumously-published edition of his *Gilyonot Al Hidushei R. Haim Halevi Al Harambam, Code,* Laws concerning the Fundamental Principles of the Torah 5:1, he actually endorses the first approach (i.e., equal division).

R. Weinberger, n. 1 above, suggested two ways to account for this discrepancy. One possible explanation notes that there are two versions of the dispute between Ben Patura and R. Akiva: the talmudic version, and that presented in the Sifra. On a literal reading of the talmudic *sugya*, Ben Patura's position represents an a priori assumption, which is only challenged by R. Akiva because of the exegesis that yields the conclusion "your life takes precedence over your fellow's." Otherwise, R. Akiva would agree to the default position of equal division of the water, and hence a third-party rescuer should divide the water accordingly. But according to the Sifra (as well as the Ritba's interpretation of the Talmud), Ben Patura's opinion too is derived by scriptural exegesis; it is not an a priori assumption. Thus there is no default assumption as to what to do in the case of a third-party rescuer. In the *Gilyonot*, the Hazon Ish based his opinion on the Talmud's version, which, Weinberger claims, compelled him to affirm the putative default position — equal division. In the *Likutim*, however, R. Karelitz was relying on the version in the Sifra (and the Ritba's commentary on the talmudic *sugya*), which enabled him — but did not require him — to take the position that all the water should go to one traveler. R. Weinberger does not explain why the Hazon Ish felt that, on the basis of the Sifra, he had to conclude that all the water should go to one traveler.

A second possible solution advanced by R. Weinberger is that the Hazon Ish's two incompatible conclusions reflect the dispute between the *Tosafot* and Maimonides regarding the reason homicide is prohibited even under force majeure, as elucidated in R. Chaim Soloveitchik, *Hidushei R. Haim Halevi Al Harambam, Code,* Laws concerning the Fundamental Principles of the Torah 5:1. R. Weinberger argues that the *Tosafot* would require that the water be divided, whereas Maimonides would not. In his *Gilyonot*, where the Hazon Ish is arguing against R. Soloveitchik's interpretation of Maimonides (and is claiming that even Maimonides accepts the position that R. Soloveitchik ascribes to the *Tosafot*), this compelled him to rule that the water be divided. But this does not explain why he rules to the contrary in the *Likutim*. He rejects R. Chaim Soloveitchik's interpretation of Maimonides, so there is no 'Maimonides' to follow in the *Likutim*. And even according to R. Soloveitchik's interpretation of Maimonides, there is no specific mandate that the water go to just one of the travelers. See n. 61 below for further elaboration of this point.

45 *Responsa Mahane Haim* 2, EH #19 s.v. *veala bedaati lehavi reaya*.

which — taken literally — could be interpreted to mean that the rescuer has the discretion to choose either mode of distributing the water.

This dispute is not relevant to triage of a hypothetical HIV vaccine, which presumably would not be divisible and so could only be given to one of the patients, but is extremely germane to triage of the many types of antiretroviral drugs (including reverse transcriptase inhibitors and protease inhibitors) currently employed to save the lives of HIV seropositive patients. Is it better to give enough medicine to two patients to extend each of their lives for a very limited time, or to direct all of the medicine to one patient so as to extend her life significantly?

Statistically-guaranteed future dangers

R. Ezekiel Landau[46] and R. Moses Sofer[47] set down the landmark principle that, by definition, saving life (*pikuah nefesh*) is only obligatory when there is a patient in immediate danger, whether definite or vague.[48] Patients who may hypothetically become ill in the future are not taken into account for purposes of saving life. Therefore, the needs of presently-endangered patients automatically override the need to prepare for hypothetical future patients, who are simply not on the halakhic radar screen.

R. Karelitz, however, asserted that statistically-guaranteed future endangered patients are to be treated as presently-endangered with respect to saving life.[49] His novel thesis appears to have gained universal acceptance,[50] precipitating a triage dispute among the decisors as to whether the claims of statistically-guaranteed future patients can override the need to care for present-day patients. For instance, a hospital may have a scarce resource (say, a life-support machine) that can be used to save the life of a patient who is in immediate mortal distress. The hospital administrator calculates that it is actuarially guaranteed

46 *Responsa Noda Biyehuda*, 2nd edition, YD #210.

47 *Responsa Hatam Sofer*, YD #336.

48 In a tour de force discovery, R. Klein (*Responsa Mishne Halakhot*, 3:42) correctly assigns credit for the initial articulation of this principle to *Tosafot*, bPesahim 46b s.v. *raba*. Note too that *SA*, YD 251:11 implicitly codifies this principle.

49 *Hazon Ish*, YD 208:7, a ruling he derives from bEruvin 45a.

50 See sources adduced in Dichovsky 1989, n. 1 above; *Bioethical Dilemmas*, n. 12 above, 1:154–57; and nn 52–56 below. This is also the ruling in R. Israel Harfenes, *Responsa Nishmat Shabat*, 2:276.

that other patients of higher triage-priority will materialize at the hospital in the future, and will require this scarce resource. Is the administrator justified in passively denying[51] the resource to the presently-endangered patient on the grounds that it will be needed for the future higher triage-priority patients? According to rabbis Solomon Z. Auerbach,[52] Moses Sternbuch,[53] and Eliezer Waldenberg,[54] the answer is yes; according to rabbis Samuel Wosner[55] and Menashe Klein,[56] it is no.[57]

51 It is crucial to emphasize that only passive denial of the resource for the sake of triage is countenanced by Jewish law. Once a patient has already been granted access to a resource, it most certainly cannot be withdrawn for triage purposes. This follows as a direct consequence of the principle that medical triage can only make selections for the purpose of saving life (*hatzala*), and never for acts that consign a patient to death (*mesira*), as explained in sec. 2 above. And see n. 62 below.

52 Cited in *Shulhan Shlomo*, 2:16–17.

53 *Teshuvot Vehanhagot*, 1:858.

54 *Responsa Tzitz Eliezer*, 17:72:14–23.

55 *Responsa Shevet Halevi*, 6:242.

56 *Responsa Mishne Halakhot*, 17:175.

57 Cf. R. David b. Solomon ibn Zimra, *Responsa Radbaz*, 4:13, which addresses the bizarre predicament of an incarcerated Jew who is prevented by his captors from engaging in precept-observance, and whose captors have now granted him the option of a one-day reprieve, any day of the year he wishes. The Radbaz requires him to take the soonest possible day as his day of reprieve, and not wait for a 'mitzva-laden' day, such as Yom Kippur, even though it is statistically guaranteed that by taking his reprieve on the earlier day, he will be unable to observe Yom Kippur, with its greater 'load' of precepts. The Radbaz reasons that "we do not bypass the opportunity to observe precepts" (as per bYoma 33a), hence the prisoner must seize the first opportunity to observe precepts, even if they are of lesser stature than the statistically-guaranteed future observances that are thereby forfeited.

A diametrically opposed approach appears to be adopted in *Responsa R. Akiva Eger*, 1st edition, #9. R. Eger rules that even on the view that phylacteries (*tfilin*) are not donned on the intermediate days of a Festival (*hol hamoed*), if, during the intermediate days of the Sukkot Festival, a poor Jew has sufficient means to purchase either a set of the four species (i.e., *lulav* and *etrog*) or phylacteries, but not both, he must purchase the phylacteries, because it is statistically guaranteed that an occasion on which the precept of phylacteries — which is of greater stature than that of ritually 'taking' the *lulav* on the intermediate days — is observed will soon arrive. There is a parallel dispute among the decisors regarding a borderline seriously-ill patient who is told by his physician that by fasting on the third day of the

Theoretically, the dispute could be explained as hinging on the question of whether R. Karelitz maintains that statistically-guaranteed future patients are treated as definite cases where lifesaving action is called for, even if this necessitates violating precepts (*pikuah nefesh*) — in which case they will compete for resources with existing patients — or treated as doubtful cases of *pikuah nefesh* — in which case they assuredly justify violation of the Sabbath and other precepts, but do not compete with definitely-endangered existing patients, as per the view of R. Joseph Teomim in *Pri Megadim*, discussed in sec. 4 above. Indeed, a controversy along these lines arose over a *sugya* in tractate Gitin, between rabbis Moses Tendler and J.D. Bleich, on the one hand, and Ovadia Yosef and Joseph S. Eliashiv, on the other.[58]

---

month of Tishre (the Fast of Gedalia), he will be unable to fast on the tenth of Tishre (Yom Kippur). Some hold that the patient must still fast on the third of Tishre because that is the first opportunity to observe the precept of fasting; others hold that he should eat on the third of Tishre in order to be capable of observing the far more important fast of Yom Kippur. See R. Simcha Rabinowitz, *Piskei Teshuvot* (Jerusalem: 1996), 6:248.

As noted in *Responsa Yabia Omer* 10, OH #55 (gloss on *Rav Pealim,* OH 2:54), the Radbaz is addressing the case of an individual facing a triage-like decision regarding precept-observance. But when the community as a whole faces such a decision, the Radbaz concedes that the weightier precept is automatically granted priority. Since the obligation to save lives devolves on the community no less than on individuals, we consider it obvious that the triage dispute regarding statistically-guaranteed future decisions cannot hinge on the controversy between the Radbaz and R. Akiva Eger, both of whom would agree that the weightier lifesaving mission takes priority. Rather, the dispute between rabbis Solomon Auerbach, Sternbuch and Waldenberg on the one hand, and Wosner and Klein on the other, must be explained in terms of how the notion of a 'weightier' lifesaving mission is defined.

58 The Talmud, in bGitin 45a, prohibits redeeming a hostage for a sum greater than the going rate for the typical ransom. The Talmud asks whether this is intended to keep the community from impoverishment or to deter future piracy. R. Bleich, in *Contemporary Halakhic Problems*, n. 23 above, 5:xxviii–xxxi, presents an analysis on which *SA*, YD 252:4 rules in accordance with the latter view. Since, by definition, redemption of a hostage is an instance of saving life, R. Bleich argues that the fact that the *Shulhan Arukh* countenances refraining from redeeming a present hostage for the sake of deterring future piracy means that statistically-guaranteed future dangers are considered definite cases where lifesaving is mandated, which compete for resources with present endangerments.

R. Tendler, n. 1 above, not only endorses R. Bleich's argument, but deems it applicable even on the view that the law against paying high

Alternatively, even if statistically-guaranteed future patients are considered to be doubtful cases where lifesaving action is mandated, perhaps it could be argued that doubtful cases where lifesaving action is mandated in which the lives of the patients will be extended for significant periods (*hayei olam*) take precedence over definite cases

---

ransoms is intended to save the community from impoverishment. For poverty too is connected with statistically-guaranteed future dangers: present-day impoverishment jeopardizes the ability to maintain law and order, which will inevitably render the society endangered later on. R. Tendler's thesis is supported by *Responsa Hatam Sofer*, HM #177, which asserts that "if the community is financially oppressed, and especially at a time when the nations of the world have power [over it]," this is a situation that mandates lifesaving intervention. Similarly, R. Joseph Engel, *Responsa Ben Porat*, 2:10, states that "public funds are tantamount to lives."

But the passage in bGitin 45a is understood quite differently by R. Ovadia Yosef. In *Responsa Yabia Omer* 10, HM #6, §21, he contends that the law stated in Gitin is a limited enactment pertaining to the particular case of ransoming hostages, and exemplifies the Sages' seldom-invoked power to order that a precept not be observed, pursuant to bJebamot 90b. In any other situation, however, society is certainly obligated to spend all its available resources on saving life. R. Yosef would reject the contention that bGitin 45a is a basis for equating, in the triage context, statistically-guaranteed future dangers with definite cases where lifesaving intervention is mandated. This view is also upheld by R. Eliashiv in *Kovetz Teshuvot*, 1:124.

This debate can be reduced to the fundamental question of how to interpret *SA*, YD 251:11, which states that during a famine, available food must be provided to a starving ignoramus who materializes at a rescuer's doorstep, even if this results in the possibility that a Torah scholar will die of starvation in the not-too-distant future. The Talmud, in bHorayot 13a, states that Torah scholars have triage priority over the unlearned, yet the *Shulhan Arukh* seems equally clear that the statistically-guaranteed future mortal danger of scholars cannot compete with the present mortal danger facing an ignoramus. Arguably, R. Bleich and R. Tendler would explain that the *Shulhan Arukh* refers only to the possibility that scholars might die of starvation in the future; if the danger to scholars was certain, then the ignoramus must be allowed to die so that the food can be reserved for the scholars to have later. By contrast, R. Yosef and R. Eliashiv would apparently maintain that the *Shulhan Arukh* refers even to scenarios where the future danger of the scholars is certain, and would assert that under any circumstances, the ignoramus's life must be saved, as he is the one who is presently endangered.

This question also appears to drive the dispute between *Igrot Moshe*, YD 1:144 and R. Yom Tov Schwarz, *Maane Leigrot*, #138. R. Feinstein regards a statistically-guaranteed future need for charity as being immediately present, R. Schwarz disagrees.

where lifesaving action is mandated in which the lives of the patients will be extended only for very brief intervals (*hayei shaa*) — a situation not presented in these terms by R. Teomim. This might, in fact, constitute the focus of the controversy between rabbis Solomon Auerbach, Sternbuch, and Waldenberg, and rabbis Wosner and Klein.[59]

Intriguingly, the formulation of R. Karelitz's remarks on the third question discussed in this section, namely, that of dosage divisibility, suggests that it arises from the question we are now discussing, namely, that of statistically-guaranteed future dangers.[60] If one believes that statistically-guaranteed future dangers do not compete with present dangers for triage purposes, then a third-party rescuer who encounters two patients is obliged to divide the medicine between them in order to extend each of their lives by a brief interval (*hayei shaa*), since it is only this situation that is of immediate interest, given that whether or not a patient can survive for an extended period (*hayei olam*) is a statistically-guaranteed future concern. By contrast, if one believes that statistically-guaranteed future dangers do compete with present dangers, then it is possible (though not necessary) to rule that the medicine should all be given to one patient, whose life will be significantly extended.[61]

59 As described in n. 29 above, R. Feinstein (*Igrot Moshe*, HM 2:73:2) explicitly rules that a patient whose life can be significantly extended takes triage priority over a patient who can only be saved for a very brief interval, even if the former is only possibly in mortal danger, whereas the patient who can only be saved for a very brief interval is definitely in mortal danger.

60 *Gilyonot*, n. 44 above, s.v. *veein haveiro*. We thank R. M. Kornfeld for drawing our attention to this conceptual link.

61 The conceptual link between the issues of dosage divisibility and statistically-guaranteed future dangers creates a contradiction for the view of R. Wosner and R. Klein. They both rule that statistically-guaranteed future dangers cannot compete with present dangers, yet argue that the entire dosage should be given to one patient so that her life will be significantly extended. In any event, on the basis of this conceptual link, let us suggest a novel resolution to the contradiction between R. Karelitz's view in the *Gilyonot* and that in the *Likutim*, described in n. 44 above. The *Gilyonot* is explaining that, if one believes that statistically-guaranteed future dangers do not compete with present dangers, then a third-party rescuer must divide the medicine between the two patients. On the other hand, the *Likutim* can rule that the entire dose be directed to one patient, because it is speaking from the perspective that statistically-guaranteed future dangers do compete with present dangers. However, this does not explain why, on the view expressed in the *Likutim*, it is essential that the resource be directed to one patient only; presumably, dividing it is also plausible

6. First come, first served

A paramount halakhic triage principle is that once a patient's care has commenced, she cannot be abandoned for the sake of another patient, even if the other patient enjoys a higher triage priority.[62] This follows from

---

on the view endorsed in the *Likutim*. But the same rejoinder we made to R. Weinberger's two suggested resolutions (n. 44 above) will apply to this third suggested resolution. On all three proposed solutions, it is clear why division is mandated in the *Gilyonot*, but it is unclear why, on the account in the *Likutim*, the entire resource must be directed to one patient.

We contend that a better solution to the Hazon Ish's apparent inconsistency can be suggested on the basis of a comment in R. Zvi Hirsch Meisels, *Responsa Mekadshei Hashem* 1, Shaar mahmadim, note 2. R. Meisels quotes a point made in R. Isaac Meir Alter, *Hidushei Harim*: Ben Patura's concern in bBaba Metzia 62a is that the owner of the canteen not **see** the death of his fellow — the focus is the horror of watching someone die without being able to help. Although R. Akiva challenges Ben Patura when the owner himself requires the water, R. Akiva would concede that when the owner does not require the water (because he is a third-party rescuer), he is obliged to minimize the number of deaths that he observes, and so he must give all the water to one traveler (and thus only have to witness one death, not two) rather than divide it between the travelers and ultimately see both perish.

A similar approach is taken in R. Jacob Ettlinger, *Responsa Binyan Tzion*, #175. It considers a scenario where the traveler who does not own the water is very thirsty, but not as thirsty as the canteen owner, such that if the water is shared, the canteen owner will die, whereas if the canteen owner drinks it all, he will live and his companion will die. Under these circumstances, avers R. Ettlinger, even Ben Patura agrees that the owner should drink all the water, because, one way or another, one traveler will see the other die, and so the owner should save his own life. R. Ettlinger echoes R. Alter's insight that the goal is to minimize the number of deaths to which one is a helpless spectator. Hence R. Ettlinger would presumably agree with R. Alter that a third-party rescuer should give all the water to one traveler.

The Hazon Ish's *Likutim*, we contend, can be similarly understood as mandating that the entire dose be given to one patient. In his *Gilyonot*, the Hazon Ish is, in essence, qualifying the conclusion of the *Likutim* by noting that it is only true if statistically-guaranteed future dangers are taken to compete with present dangers. However, if statistically-guaranteed future dangers do not compete with present dangers, then the third-party rescuer must divide the resource between both patients and thereby save the lives of both patients in the short term.

62 *Igrot Moshe*, HM 2:73:2; *Shulhan Shlomo*, 2:14–16; *Responsa Shevet Halevi*,

the saving vs. handing-over dichotomy discussed in sec. 2 above: a rescuer can only select for life and never for death. To divert attention from a patient who is already being treated would constitute selection for death.

It follows that the dangerously-ill patient who presents himself first to the rescuer for care must be treated first. The rationale here is the legal fiction that if a patient has arrived earlier, his care is regarded as having commenced earlier. There are two talmudic sources for this legal fiction in tractate Sanhedrin. The first, bSanhedrin 8a, interprets "for the judgment is God's" (Deut. 1:17) as commanding a judge to hear cases according to the sequence in which prospective litigants assemble. The second, bSanhedrin 32b, interprets "Justice, justice shall you pursue" (Deut. 16:20) as offering guidance on determining the right-of-way between two vessels that must pass each other on a narrow river. It can be inferred from the talmudic discussion that if one vessel arrived at the narrows earlier, it must be granted the right-of-way, no matter how compelling the other vessel's need to reach its destination.[63]

10:167; *Halakha Urefua*, 4:84; *Bintivot Hahalakha*, n. 1 above, 1:123; *Shvivei Esh*, #66, §11–12.

Accordingly, a life-support machine can never be withdrawn from a machine-dependent patient for the sake of redirecting the machine to a higher-priority triage patient's life, even if the machine is automatically deactivated from the first patient via a 'Sabbath clock' (i.e., a timer). The Sabbath clock would preclude any charges that homicide has been committed by the attending staff, by satisfying even the stringent opinions (e.g., *Igrot Moshe*, YD 3:132; HM 2:73:1) that regard deactivation of a life-support machine that sustains a machine-dependent patient as homicide. But since the life-support machine — even while deactivated — is still physically attached to the first patient, who needs that machine (in its reactivated state) for his continued existence, the staff are forbidden, according to Jewish law, to detach the machine from the patient, just as a physician cannot abandon a patient once she has begun to treat him. There would be no choice but to reactivate a life-support machine that had been deactivated by a Sabbath clock. Thus, Sabbath clocks are technologically useless for resolving triage problems.

63 R. Spitz, *Mishpetei Hatora*, 1:306, rejects invocation of Deuteronomy 1:17 as support for halakhic recognition of queuing as determining treatment priority, on the grounds that such recognition may be limited to the context of judges hearing court cases. However, he recognizes queues as determining treatment priority on the basis of Deuteronomy 16:20. We would argue that, after having accepted the argument from Deuteronomy 16:20, the argument from Deuteronomy 1:17 should be accepted as well, in light of the exegetical rule that analogies may be drawn between non-equivalent contexts that have a common factor (*hatzad hashave shebeineihen*). On the strength of the two scriptural injunctions, therefore, we conclude that there

In essence, then, queuing order is the decisive determinant in prioritizing lifesaving activity; all other considerations enumerated above are pertinent only when competing sets of patients present themselves simultaneously. And as noted above, once a patient's care has commenced (or at least commenced as a matter of legal fiction), she cannot be abandoned for the sake of another patient with a higher triage priority.

The propriety of managing triage through a queue has been challenged in the bioethical literature:

> It favors people who are well-off, who become informed, and travel more quickly, and can queue for interventions without competing for employment or child-care concerns. Queues are also vulnerable to additional corruption. . . . those who could figuratively (and sometimes literally) push to the front of the line would be vaccinated and stand the best chance for survival.[64]

---

is a biblical obligation to assign treatment priority in accordance with the patients' queuing order.

Recognition of the biblical mandate to recognize queuing order as determining treatment priority must not be confused with the weaker Rabbinic prohibition against tortious interference, the classic example being the poor person rummaging through the ashes for a morsel of cinder-cake (*ani mehapekh baharara*), from whom it is forbidden to snatch the cake, even though it is ownerless (bKidushin 59a). In cases of tortious interference, a prospective buyer is pushed aside by another prospective buyer, who forces his way ahead of him. The transgression is merely Rabbinic, because the seller has the freedom to sell or decline to sell her wares to whomever she wishes. By contrast, a judge is obligated to hear rabbinical court cases, and a society is obligated to regulate right-of-way issues, and cannot refuse. In both these cases, the Talmud establishes a biblical obligation to respect queuing priority. It is only logical that the same should hold true for medical triage, since healthcare workers are obligated to save lives without the possibility of refusal.

Cf. R. Zilberstein, n. 1 above, who infers from *Beit Habehira*, bSanhedrin 32b that the validity of medical triage line-ups is a matter of custom and compromise rather than strict law. We do not concur, but maintain that the Meiri should be understood as stating that when two competing groups arrive simultaneously, the question of who is accorded the right-of-way is a matter of custom and compromise. But the Meiri does not deny the plain meaning of the Talmud that when one group arrives first, it must be granted the right-of-way as a matter of law. Hence, queues have biblical validity in assigning triage priority, as R. Moses Sternbuch indeed rules in *Teshuvot Vehanhagot*, 4:318.

64 Persad et al., n. 37 above.

We acknowledge the soundness of these observations, but still uphold queues as halakhically correct and altogether moral. The concern that those who cannot take time off work are hindered in their ability to compete for fastest access to a lifesaving queue is indeed valid, and is addressed by the Talmud,[65] which cites the biblical verse "You must pay him his wages on the same day . . . for he is needy and sets his soul upon it [i.e., urgently depends on it]" (Deut. 24:15). The Talmud explains that people risk their lives for the sake of their livelihood, and hence an employer is divinely mandated to pay her workers on time. Potentially-diminished access to a lifesaving medical queue as a consequence of one's employment represents a facet of the risk accepted by the worker, for which she is entitled to financial compensation from her employer.[66]

The concern about fairness toward patients who are burdened with child-care responsibilities can also be addressed on the basis of another

65 bBaba Metzia 112a.

66 It is ordinarily forbidden for an individual to voluntarily endanger himself, for one is not the owner of his life, as explained in Zevin, n. 32 above, but as bBaba Metzia 112a informs us, for the sake of one's livelihood, such endangerment is permitted. It is on the basis of this consideration that *Responsa Noda Biyehuda,* 2nd edition, YD #10, permits safari expeditions as a means of livelihood, but prohibits going on the identical expeditions for recreational purposes.

As noted in R. Hershel Schachter, *Beikvei Hatzon*, #34, the principle articulated in bBaba Metzia 112a mirrors another principle, presented in bAvoda Zara 27b, which authorizes an individual to risk his life in the short term (*hayei shaa*) for the sake of significantly extending his life (*hayei olam*) by undergoing a hazardous medical procedure. This is because earning one's living (at the subsistence level) is itself ultimately a matter of sustaining and thus saving life, as per bShabat 69b. Risking one's life for one's job constitutes jeopardizing life in the short term for the sake of the longer term, much like undergoing a hazardous operation, and is thus proper, according to R. Bleich's analysis in *Bioethical Dilemmas*, n. 12 above, 2:239–75.

Identification of bAvoda Zara 27b as an instance of the principle articulated in bBaba Metzia 112a solves a mystery that has puzzled many, including R. Schachter and R. Bleich. The principle that life in the short-term should be risked for long-term healing, stated in bAvoda Zara 27b, is grounded in the biblical episode of Gehazi and his sons (2 Kings 7:3–5). But why does the Talmud assume that Gehazi and his sons acted properly? Once it is appreciated that Gehazi and his sons were implementing the mandate grounded in the verse "for he is needy and sets his soul upon it" (Deut. 24:15), the acceptability of their actions is clear.

consideration. R. Jacob Emden tentatively speculates about whether an individual could be allowed to sacrifice his life in order to save his child.[67] Similarly, R. Zvi Hirsch Meisels considers the possibility that one's child be regarded as the equivalent of oneself with respect to the saving–handing-over dichotomy outlined in sec. 2 above.[68] R. Bleich justifies these opinions philosophically by invoking the notion that a child can be regarded as its parent's alter ego, as per the "in place of your fathers shall be your children" (Ps. 45:17) principle. This dictum is invoked by the Talmud in bBaba Batra 159a.[69] Although the doubts expressed by R. Emden and R. Meisels lead to the conclusion that, as a matter of the law to be put into practice, one dare not sacrifice his life even for his child, and a child dare not be regarded as the triage equivalent of oneself with regard to saving vs. handing-over, nevertheless, the theoretical possibility to the contrary is sufficient to justify using order in a queue to determine triage priority, despite the aforementioned argument that queuing is unfair to the disadvantaged. The reasoning here is that since it is theoretically plausible that a parent could rightfully sacrifice himself for the sake of his child, other patients who are not saddled by child-care concerns are

67 *Sefer Birat Migdal Oz*, Even Bohen, pina alef, §85. Somewhat similarly, in *Teshuvot Vehanhagot*, 4:323, R. Moses Sternbuch tentatively raises the possibility that a terminally-ill but pregnant cancer patient has the option of voluntarily refraining from undergoing life-prolonging chemotherapy so as to allow her fetus to survive until parturition, if she so chooses. The woman's wish to give birth to a living child may trump her own self-survival obligation.

68 *Responsa Mekadshei Hashem* 1, Shaar mahmadim, ch. 3. R. Meisels upholds the Shakh's position (sec. 2 above), viz. that Leviticus 25:36 authorizes an individual to rescue himself, in a manner that deflects the danger onto someone else, even after he has been captured, but one may not rescue anyone else in this manner. R. Meisels was deliberating whether rescuing one's child was tantamount to rescuing oneself.

Of course, as we showed in sec. 2 above, many decisors, led by the Rema, reject the Shakh's position. But this does not detract from the cogency of R. Meisels's suggestion, since — even on the Rema's view — Leviticus 25:36 gives rise to a saving vs. handing-over dilemma vis-à-vis saving oneself and saving others. For according to the Rema, before one is actually captured, one may rescue oneself in a manner that deflects the danger onto someone else, whereas one may not rescue anyone else in this manner.

69 See R. Solomon Kluger, *Imrei Shefer*, Torah portion 'Kedoshim,' §14; R. Elhanan Wasserman, *Kovetz Shiurim*, 2:12; *Bintivot Hahalakha*, n. 1 above, 1:125–26; R. J.D. Bleich, "The problem of identity in Rashi, Rambam and the Tosafists," *Tradition* 41:2 (2008), 28–30.

entitled to take advantage of this halakhic plausibility to outrun their competitors in the chase to the queue. R. Joseph Teomim clearly mandates that a patient with definite priority be given treatment priority over a patient with doubtful priority.[70]

Insofar as corruption is concerned, the problem can be remedied by appropriate supervisory monitoring, law enforcement, and public education. A patient dare not push to the front of the line, just as in the paradigmatic scenario presented in bBaba Metzia 62a, the thirsty traveler dare not steal the canteen from his thirsty companion, its rightful owner.[71]

Nevertheless, there is one possible complicated exception to the 'first come, first served' principle. Since, as described in the previous section, an unresolved dispute exists among the decisors as to whether statistically-guaranteed future dangers can compete for triage with present dangers, it emerges that — in the opinion of some authorities — the patient who will experience the statistically-guaranteed future danger is virtually present at the head of the line together with whichever current patient is physically present at the head of the line. This would — according to that opinion — justify pushing some later arrivals ahead of earlier arrivals.[72]

70 See text above at n. 29.

71 See rulings cited in n. 7 above, prohibiting the thirsty traveler from snatching the canteen from its rightful owner. Indeed, R. Chaim Hirschensohn, *Hidushei Haraha*, 1:382, directs the captain of a naval vessel to establish a system of rules for abandoning ship in an orderly fashion, to prevent passengers who have already reached the lifeboat from being displaced. (We are grateful to R. Daniel Z. Feldman for bringing this source to our attention.)

72 Cf. *Igrot Moshe*, HM 2:73:2, which stipulates that medical triage is to be administered on the basis of a queue, but that a later-arriving patient whose life can be significantly extended (*hayei olam*) should be pushed ahead of one whose life can be only briefly extended (*hayei shaa*) who arrived earlier, provided that the latter patient's treatment has not yet begun. We would argue that the second clause in this ruling is only justified if the arrival of the patient whose life can be significantly extended, was already statistically guaranteed at the time the first patient, whose life can be only briefly extended, arrived, and one assumes that either (a) statistically-guaranteed future dangers are deemed definite cases of imperilment where lifesaving intervention is mandated (*pikuah nefesh*), or (b) uncertain imperilment where life can be significantly extended overrides definite imperilment where life can be only briefly extended. As we saw (n. 29 above), (b) is indeed assumed by R. Feinstein, and as is suggested in the final paragraph of n. 58 above, (a) is as well.

Ultimately, however, as applied in practice to HIV vaccination, it seems to us that 'first come, first served' is largely moot altogether. This is because R. Feinstein defines a triage queue as the population of patients for whom a healthcare worker has been called to provide succor, and not merely the population of patients who have physically assembled before the healthcare worker.[73] Hence 'first come, first served' really means 'first called, first served.' Since it is well publicized among all healthcare workers that 100% of the population is presently at risk for contracting HIV, and therefore that 100% of the population has a need for inoculation, on the envisaged scenario where a vaccine against HIV has become available, all healthcare workers are being simultaneously summoned to vaccinate the entire citizenry.[74] Thus, no meaningful queue is possible for

73 *Igrot Moshe*, HM 2:74:1 (final paragraph). R. Stern, in *Shvivei Esh*, #66, §13, points out that, on R. Feinstein's view, it is not the patient's call summoning emergency medical services that places the patient in line, but rather the rescuer's professional assessment that the patient needs her lifesaving assistance.

However, R. Feinstein proceeds to rule that if there is a second call, from a patient who is in even greater danger or who stands a better chance at life prolongation than the first, then the physician should respond to the second call, "and the decision as to the matter depends on the physician's opinion." We would argue that R. Feinstein's directive can only be justified if the second patient's call was already statistically guaranteed at the time of the first patient's call, and one assumes that statistically-guaranteed future dangers are treated as definite cases where saving life is mandated. One cannot argue here, in contrast to the responsum discussed in n. 72 above, that R. Feinstein holds that uncertain imperilment where life can be significantly extended overrides definite imperilment where life can be extended only briefly, since there is no indication in the current responsum that the first caller is one whose life can be only briefly extended.

74 That healthcare workers' impressions should play a role in determining priority of treatment appears to follow from the idea that "to a significant extent, the halakhic concept of danger reflects a sociological perception rather than a raw statistical quantification" (*Bioethical Dilemmas*, n. 12 above, 2:295). Likewise, R. Solomon Auerbach is cited in *Shulhan Shlomo*, 1:231, as maintaining that

> The definition of *pikuah nefesh* is anything concerning which people are afraid or hysterical even on weekdays on account of concern about danger. . . . It seems to me that this definition is quite correct, and resembles that which the Sages said in several places in the Talmud [e.g., bJebamot 72a]: "in the present day . . . 'God preserves the simple-minded' (Ps. 116:6)"; i.e., that which people are accustomed to handle without fearfulness is a case where we are allowed to rely on the

HIV vaccination: every human being alive at the time the vaccine is developed will already be present at the head of the queue.

The only possible 'first called, first served' prioritization will involve babies born after the envisaged discovery of the HIV vaccine. Since these babies had not yet been born at the time the HIV vaccine was first synthesized, as cases of uncertain imperilment where lifesaving intervention is mandated (*safek pikuah nefesh*), their call for inoculation must wait to be answered until after all those already alive at the time the vaccine is introduced have been inoculated. Subsequently, as babies are born, they are added to the inoculation queue.

7. Capricious modes of rationing: whim vs. lottery

When all triage factors are equal among patients competing for a scarce lifesaving medical resource, it becomes necessary to resort to arbitrary means of decision-making. Under such circumstances, Jewish law directs rescuers to decide swiftly, relying on personal whim to arbitrarily choose which patient to save.[75]

> assumption that "God preserves the simple-minded" [meaning, fearfulness is unwarranted].

In other words, R. Auerbach holds that a risk that is not accepted with equanimity by society at large is deemed a case where life may be imperilled and thus lifesaving intervention is mandated (*safek pikuah nefesh*). This is reiterated on pp. 262–63, in discussing an ammunition carrier stationed near Jewish soldiers' barracks on the Sabbath. R. Auerbach rules that if experts perceive the carrier's proximity as a danger, such that even on a weekday they would be worried enough to make taking steps to move the carrier a priority, then the Sabbath may be desecrated in order to move the carrier.

These considerations are obviously germane in the context of avoiding HIV contagion, where, as R. Eliashiv writes in *Kovetz Teshuvot* 2:28: "all over the world, no one ever approaches [a patient] to treat him — neither physician nor nurse — without taking every sort of precaution, out of fear lest they be infected." It is thus not surprising that R. Auerbach (*Shulhan Shlomo* 1:245) countenances desecration of the Sabbath to quarantine someone so as to prevent him from possibly infecting others, or becoming infected himself, with a dangerous pathogen.

75 This is manifest in the language used by R. Karelitz (*Hazon Ish*, bBaba Metzia 62a, Likutim, 20), who states that the rescuer should "give it to the one he wants [to give it to]" (*yiten leehad sheyirtze*). Likewise, R. Dichovsky rules that the rescuer should "save whomever he wishes" (*matzil mi sheyirtze*), see Dichovsky 1982, n. 1 above.

A philosophical argument for capricious triage on the basis of the rescuer's whim can be modelled on R. Bleich's analysis of pregnancy reduction.[76] An obstetrician is entitled to randomly destroy the minimum number of fetuses necessary to allow the other fetuses a chance to survive in an overcrowded womb, because the omniscient Creator already knows in advance which fetuses will be eliminated, so those fetuses were never viable in the first place, and thus the prohibition against abortion never applied to those fetuses. By the same token, where it is impossible for a rescuer to save all patients, and the criteria for triage prioritization have already been applied, the Creator knows in advance which patient will be randomly selected for rescue, and so — by definition — whatever choice the rescuer makes is the correct choice.

In the halakhic literature, there are occasional references to arbitrary resolution of medical triage dilemmas by means of a lottery conducted by the rescuer, rather than relying on personal whim.[77] At first glance such a directive seems incomprehensible, since the Talmud explains the legal mechanism behind a lottery's effectiveness in adjudicating competing claims of individuals as a kind of joint acquisition where the partners waive their individual rights to make decisions.[78] Prospective partners would not agree to engage in the same commercial enterprise unless an authoritative means of resolving their disputes is created in advance. By way of a formal act of acquisition (*kinyan*), the partners transfer to one another the rights to be governed by the lottery's decisions, enabling them to jointly benefit from their willingness to work together co-operatively. This rationale cannot possibly apply to medical triage, when no one possesses the right to waive her life, or the resources necessary to save her life, in advance.[79] Accordingly, a lottery seems like a pointless and counterproductive expenditure of precious time in the triage context.

We would argue that a lottery is never mandated per se in administering arbitrary medical triage. However, a lottery may be needed to fulfill the obligation of "you shall be clear before the Lord and before Israel" (Num. 32:22), from which the Talmud derives the obligation to

76 *Bioethical Dilemmas*, n. 12 above, 1:269–81.

77 *Igrot Moshe*, HM 2:75:2; *Mishpetei Hatora*, 2:138–40.

78 bBaba Batra 106b.

79 See R. Zevin, *Leor Hahalakha*, n. 32 above.

avoid even the appearance of wrongdoing.[80] Without a lottery, onlookers might suspect that a healthcare worker who was in charge of distributing society's resources had falsely claimed that the triage criteria had been exhausted so as to prematurely appropriate authority to follow his personal whim. Perhaps the rescuer had some vested selfish interest in rescuing a specific patient (e.g., a relative or business associate) who was in fact a lower triage priority than the other patients. By forcing the rescuer to resort to a lottery, suspicions of misbehavior are preempted.

This analysis leads to the conclusion that it is only when a rescuer distributes publicly-owned resources arbitrarily that he must resort to a lottery. If the rescuer personally possesses surplus resources, there is no need for a lottery, and the rescuer should swiftly apportion the resources in accordance with her personal whim.

The foregoing also explains an episode, described by R. Tendler, in which R. Feinstein directed an Israeli hospital as to its distribution of a scarce supply of penicillin.[81] Israel's Chief Rabbinate was uncertain how to proceed, and telephoned R. Feinstein in New York for urgent guidance. R. Tendler reports that Rabbi Feinstein answered, without any hesitation, that the penicillin should be given to "the first bed you come to." In effect, R. Feinstein cleverly devised an instant lottery for the physician to conduct in distributing the penicillin, because the penicillin supply was owned by the hospital as a whole, and the physician was obligated to adhere to the biblical mandate of avoiding even the appearance of wrongdoing. On the other hand, had the doses of penicillin been privately owned by the physician, he would have been halakhically required to administer them on the basis of personal whim.

Accordingly, a rescuer who inoculates patients with societally-owned doses of an HIV vaccine must do so on the basis of a lottery, whereas a rescuer who possesses her own supply of surplus doses of HIV vaccine must inoculate others on the basis of personal whim.

80 He who distributed donations made to the Temple "did not enter the chamber wearing either a bordered cloak or shoes or . . . lest if he became poor, people might say that he became poor because of an iniquity committed in the chamber, or if he became rich, people might say that he became rich from the appropriation in the chamber. For it is one's duty to be free of blame before men as before God, as it is said: 'you shall be clear before the Lord and before Israel' (Num. 32:22)" (mShekalim 3:2).

81 Tendler 1984, n. 1 above.

8. Triage in the Noahide Code

The foregoing sections have analyzed allocation of an HIV vaccine insofar as a Jewish rescuer is concerned. Application of the relevant halakhic postulates to a Noahide rescuer requires independent arguments, as the above sections were premised on the sacrosanct obligation which devolves on Jews to save their own lives as well as those of others (*pikuah nefesh*). One may legitimately inquire whether this Torah obligation also devolves on Noahide healthcare providers.

Invoking tractate Sanhedrin of the Talmud, which interprets the biblical verse "whoever sheds the blood of man, by man shall his blood be shed" (Gen. 9:6) as an injunction to bystanders to prevent a homicidal pursuer (*rodef*) from achieving his nefarious goal,[82] R. Isaac Shmelkes argues that since the injunction that homicide is to be prevented is part of the Noahide Code, Noahides are obligated to save the lives of endangered fellow human beings.[83] R. Shmelkes concedes, however, that elsewhere in the tractate,[84] the same biblical verse is interpreted quite differently, and — as explained by R. Ezekiel Landau[85] — Maimonides rules in accordance with this second *sugya*, thereby undermining the supposed source for obligating Noahides to save imperiled lives (*pikuah nefesh*). Moreover, R. Shmelkes's argument that if Noahides are obligated to neutralize a pursuer (*rodef*), this means that they have been mandated to save lives, is itself disputed by R. Chaim Soloveitchik. R. Soloveitchik takes any putative Noahide obligation vis-à-vis a pursuer to follow from the Noahide obligation to maintain law and order.[86] On this reasoning, the injunction that homicide is to be prevented (Gen. 9:6) does not serve to establish that a Noahide bystander must intervene if someone is dying in a non-violent manner — say, succumbing to AIDS.

An alternative attempt to identify some sort of medical-assistance obligation devolving on Noahides might invoke a *sugya* in tractate Baba Kama that establishes that the biblical verse, "But for your own

82 bSanhedrin 72b.

83 *Responsa Beit Yitzhak*, YD 2:162.

84 bSanhedrin 57b.

85 *Responsa Noda Biyehuda*, 2nd edition, HM #59, at the end.

86 *Hidushei R. Haim Halevi Al Harambam,* Laws concerning Murder and the Preservation of Life 1:9.

life-blood I will require a reckoning"[87] (Gen. 9:5), which is part of the Noahide Code, prohibits suicide.[88] This prohibition is elaborated on by R. Nissim Gerondi to include a prohibition against passive suicide by refraining from eating or drinking long enough for death to result.[89] Seeing as Maimonides equates the imbibing of lifesaving medicine with the consumption of life-sustaining food and drink,[90] it should follow that Noahides are positively obligated to save their own lives with medicine that they personally possess. This would apparently require a Noahide to inoculate herself with an HIV vaccine that she personally owns.[91]

87 New JPS translation, which replaced the earlier rendering, "And surely your blood of your lives will I require."

88 bBaba Kama 91b.

89 *Ran, Alfasi*, bShevuot 25a.

90 In his commentary on mPesahim 4:9, discussed in *Bioethical Dilemmas*, n. 12 above, 1:72–74.

91 This assertion is complicated by the fact that failure to inoculate oneself with an HIV vaccine will by no means lead to certain death, but only to possible endangerment by death. Thus, it is necessary to investigate whether Noahides are held responsible for doubtful infractions of the Noahide Code. This issue is explored in R. Isaac Yosef, *Yalkut Yosef*, Isur Veheter (Jerusalem: 1998), 2:403–19, in discussing ramifications of the dispute among the Early Authorities as to whether the principle that a doubt regarding Torah law is decided stringently (*safek deoraita lehumra*) is a matter of Torah law (as the Rashba argues in his novellae on bKidushin 73a) or a matter of Rabbinic law (as Maimonides argues in *Code*, Laws concerning Corpse Uncleanness 9:12). If it is a matter of Torah law, then Noahides must avoid even doubtful transgressions of the Noahide Code. If it is a matter of Rabbinic law, then doubtful transgressions of the Noahide Code are permitted, since Noahides were never obligated to observe Rabbinic legislation. R. Yosef advances another reason for leniency vis-à-vis Noahides. Even if the law is in accordance with the Rashba's view, the Rashba's scriptural source may have been addressed only to Jews, but not Noahides, generating a compound doubt, and matters regarding which there are such doubts are decided leniently (*sfek sfeika lekula*).

However, a stringent ruling seems to follow from *Bintivot Hahalakha*, n. 1 above, 2:140–43, where R. Bleich shows that it can be argued that Rabbinic legislation applies even to Noahides, under the 'courts of justice' requirement as per Maimonides, *Code*, Laws concerning Kings and Wars 10:11. If so, then the first layer of the purported compound doubt is undermined, and Noahides must indeed avoid even doubtful transgressions of the Noahide Code. Hence a Noahide possessing HIV vaccine would be required to inoculate himself.

As noted in the text below at n. 102 in the name of R. Shimon Sofer, it can

However, the Hazon Ish challenges Maimonides' view, distinguishing food and drink from medicine.[92] He does so on the basis of a talmudic discussion that interprets the biblical dictum "and shall cause him to be thoroughly healed" (Exod. 21:19) as granting physicians license to heal.[93] The fact that the practice of medicine requires special biblical authorization, whereas eating and drinking does not, he claims, illustrates a fundamental difference between these two spheres of human action: eating and drinking is an activity through which the righteous serve God, whereas medicine — while unquestionably necessary in light of the overriding obligation to save life (*pikuah nefesh*) — is presented in the Bible as a post facto endeavor, a response to injury inflicted in the course of transgression.[94] It would be better had the need for healing never arisen, and physicians been superfluous. If indeed we reject the equation of medicine with food and drink, it would follow that there is no biblical source to obligate a Noahide to save her own life with medicine.[95]

---

also be argued that Noahides are potentially bound by the talmudic dictum "[keep My statutes and My judgments, which, if a man do] he shall live by them" (Lev. 18:5) — but not die by them" (bYoma 85b), which would render them obligated to rescue themselves even from possible mortal danger. On this argument, Noahides definitely have an obligation to inoculate themselves against HIV.

92 R. Abraham Karelitz, *Emuna Ubitahon*, 5:5.

93 bBaba Kama 85a.

94 The Hazon Ish is referring to the biblical context of the injunction to heal, namely, "And if men quarrel together, and one strikes another with a stone, or with his fist, and he dies not, but keeps to his bed; If he rises again, and walks out with his staff, then shall he who struck him be acquitted; only he shall pay for the loss of his time, and shall cause him to be thoroughly healed" (Exod. 21:18–19).

95 R. Karelitz's position seems to be shared by R. Moses Feinstein, as quoted by R. Tendler (recording cited in n. 32 above, at 57:30 into the recording). R. Tendler reports that R. Feinstein expressed concern that withholding water from an incapacitated patient in one's care, as distinct from the withholding of medicine, might be regarded as homicide. Although not explicitly specified by R. Tendler, it seems clear from his presentation that food and water are interchangeable for these purposes, particularly since — in an intensive care environment — all nutrition is delivered to the patient in liquid form. Accordingly, R. Feinstein seems to be extrapolating from the ruling of Rabbenu Nissim, cited in n. 89 above, that denying oneself food is suicide; R. Feinstein tentatively deduced from this that denying food to someone else may be homicide. Thus, for R. Feinstein, as for the Hazon Ish, food and medicine are not deemed to be equivalent.

Nevertheless, although he does not address R. Karelitz's objection, R. Bleich offers an effective defense of the Maimonidean position.[96] R. Bleich adduces *Midrash Temura* to argue that two verses in Genesis, 1:29 and 3:19,[97] indeed mandate the consumption of food, thereby validating the equivalence between medicine and food. And if the consumption of food is described by the Hazon Ish as an act of serving God, then surely the medical maintenance of one's life can similarly be envisaged as an act of praising the Creator.[98] If this line of reasoning is accepted, then a Noahide is indeed subject to the obligation to medically sustain his own life (including self-inoculation with an HIV vaccine). Moreover, R. Bleich emphasizes that even according to R. Karelitz, who does not equate food and medicine, it is certainly permissible for Noahides to practice medicine, since he deems the passage in tractate bBaba Kama authorizing physicians to heal a "conceptual delineation of human prerogatives."[99]

That being so, it seems to us that even R. Karelitz would agree that a Noahide is obligated to save his own life using medicine, on the strength of an argument put forward by R. Joseph Babad in *Minhat Hinukh.*[100] R. Babad asserts that although it is questionable whether a Jewish community may — if this is necessary to save the entire community — hand over to oppressors an innocent member of the community already designated for death by these oppressors, and hence the law to be implemented in practice is that this is impermissible,[101] for a Noahide the same

96 Fred Rosner and J. David Bleich (eds.), *Jewish Bioethics*, augmented edition (Hoboken NJ: 2000), 24–25.

97 We would also point to Genesis 2:16.

98 *Bioethical Dilemmas*, n. 12 above, 1:118–19.

99 Personal communication, Sept. 9, 2009.

100 *Minhat Hinukh*, precept 296 (§28 in Jerusalem Institute edition).

101 *Bioethical Dilemmas*, n. 12 above, 1:295; *Bintivot Hahalakha*, n. 1 above, 3:72. But cf. *Responsa Yabia Omer* 10, HM #6, §1–4, where R. Yosef appears inclined to authorize surrender of the designated victim on the basis of *Shakh, SA*, YD 242, which is also cited elliptically by R. Bleich in *Bioethical Dilemmas*, 2:298. However, scrutiny of R. Yosef's responsum indicates that he seems to have merely considered adducing the ruling in the *Shakh* as a mitigating consideration to be combined with a separate mitigating consideration. Namely, rather than permit actively surrendering a designated victim, R. Yosef is prepared to consider passively allowing hostages who have already been captured in a terrorist attack (whom he deems to be 'designated victims') to remain captured, for the sake of protecting the citizenry from further attacks. However, he ultimately rejects this argument, which leaves R. Bleich's conclusion unchallenged.

act of surrendering a designated victim would be permitted, since Noahides are not subject to the law forbidding the handing-over of such victims. And since Noahides are permitted to so act, R. Babad continues, Noahides are actually obligated to save their own lives by surrendering the designated victim, since the biblical dictum, "But for your own life-blood I will require a reckoning" (Gen. 9:5) obligates a Noahide to do everything he can permissibly do in order to save his life. *Mutatis mutandis*, the same should apply to taking medicine he owns.

In support of this line of reasoning, we can add an argument made by R. Shimon Sofer.[102] He contends that the talmudic dictum "he shall live by them" (Lev. 18:5) — but not die by them," which authorizes an individual to override the precepts in order to save (or possibly save) her own life, among other things, by medical interventions, applies to Noahides no less than to Jews.[103] R Shimon b. Tzemah Duran understands the dictum to constitute an obligation, arguing that where one is entitled to transgress a commandment in order to save his life, he is directed by the verse to do so.[104] And this is true all the more so where the rescue can be accomplished without transgression of any other commandment. Hence a Noahide must inoculate himself against HIV by employing a dose of vaccine that he possesses.

Is there a Noahide obligation to provide medical treatment to others? There is some evidence suggesting that Noahides are mandated to give charity[105]; if so, the obligation of charity would presumably

102 *Responsa Hitorerut Teshuva*, 1:222.

103 This thesis is also put forward by R. Eliashiv in *Kovetz Teshuvot* 3:69 and 3:122, without mentioning R. Sofer's responsum. R. Sofer and R. Eliashiv evidently both reject the argument in *Minhat Hinukh*, precept 296 (§3 in Jerusalem Institute edition) that bYoma 85b is irrelevant to Noahides. Cf. R. Akiva Eger's novellae on *SA*, YD 62, where *Teivat Gome* (by the author of *Pri Megadim*) on Exodus 4:24 is also cited as denying that the dictum in bYoma 85b applies to Noahides. We would argue that scrutiny of *Teivat Gome* reveals that its import is more accurately captured in *Pithei Teshuva*, YD 155:4, which states that *Teivat Gome* is undecided on this point. In any event, R. Eliashiv rejects the argument from Exodus 4:24.

104 *Responsa Tashbetz* 3:37 s.v. *veharamban*.

105 *Hidushei Haran*, bSanhedrin 56b maintains, on the strength of Genesis 18:19, that Noahides are obligated to give charity. This is also the position in R. Joseph Rosin, *Tzofnat Paneiah, Code*, Laws concerning Gifts to the Poor 7:7. Likewise, *Sefer Rokeiah*, §366, imposes the obligation of giving charity on Noahides on the basis of the culpability of the people of Sodom, as reflected

encompass providing lifesaving medical treatment to the best of one's ability, including HIV vaccination. After all, the act of saving a life is the greatest act of charity an individual can perform.[106] Moreover, one opinion regards prayer as mandatory for Noahides.[107] Prayer, in essence, consists of beseeching the Almighty to provide for one's own personal needs (including life, health, and welfare). In light of the axiom that the way one is treated by Heaven mirrors the way one treats others,[108] it tentatively follows that, on the view that Noahides have an obligation to pray, they likewise have an obligation to provide medical care for others' needs to the best of their ability. If we accept R. Shimon

---

in Ezekiel 16:49. This view is upheld in R. Isaac Arama, *Akeidat Yitzhak*, Genesis, gate 20, and in R. Naftali Zvi Berlin's approbation for R. Israel Meir Kagan's *Ahavat Hesed*. R. Berlin adds, citing Psalms 89:3, that giving charity is required as a matter of natural law, to which Noahides are subject.

On the other hand, *Talmudic Encyclopedia* (Hebrew) 3:357 notes that *Rashi* and *Beit Habehira*, bSanhedrin 56b, as well as Maimonides, *Code*, Laws concerning Kings and Wars 10:10, appear to deny any Noahide obligation to give charity. This is also the opinion of R. Elijah Rogoler, *Yad Eliyahu*, Ktavim, s.v. *bnei noah* and R. Meir Dan Plocki, *Kli Hemda*, Torah portion 'Vayera,' §1. See also the Oz Vehadar–Metivta edition of the Talmud, Biurim, bSanhedrin 56b, which observes that *Yad Rama* is inconsistent on this point.

106 But cf. R. Eliashiv's surprising thesis in *Kovetz Teshuvot* 3:122 that the obligation to give charity does not necessarily encompass an obligation to save the recipient's life. In context, R. Eliashiv is elucidating Maimonides' stance that a Jew must provide financial support for a poor 'residing stranger' (*ger toshav*), but cannot desecrate the Sabbath to save the latter's life. R. Eliashiv takes this to mean that the Jew has no duty to save the life of a 'residing stranger' who is dying of something other than poverty (e.g., drowning). But R. Eliashiv concedes that his novel thesis is untenable, as it conflicts with Maimonides' explicit ruling that a Jew is obligated both to charitably support and save the life of a 'residing stranger.' R. Eliashiv proceeds to explain that the dispensation to override the Sabbath is conceptually unrelated to the obligation to save life. We would therefore argue that his claim in *Kovetz Teshuvot* 3:122 should be rejected. Indeed, *Hitorerut Teshuva*, which *Kovetz Teshuvot* completely overlooked (see nn 102–103 above), argues that the obligation to give charity does encompass an obligation to save the recipient's life despite the prohibition against desecrating the Sabbath on behalf of a 'residing stranger'.

107 R. Samuel b. Hofni, Genesis 34:12.

108 bSota 8b-13a.

Sofer's thesis that the "he shall live by them" (Lev. 18:5) — but not die by them" dictum applies to Noahides, and R. Shimon b. Tzemah Duran's interpretation thereof, the argument can be made that a Noahide has an obligation to save, by medical intervention, not only his only life, but also the lives of others.[109]

A more rigorous source for a Noahide obligation to render medical care is bBaba Batra 7b, which authorizes citizens of a town to compel one another, by law, to erect fortifications for protection against possible attacks by marauders. Though there is no present danger to the town, even just one citizen may demand that this expensive protection be provided, and no one else may excuse himself from paying his share of the cost by pleading that he chooses to accept the danger of being ransacked.[110] The rationale is the implicit social contract within a community to promote the public's well-being by providing certain services, among them protection from invasion. Analogously, R. Bleich maintains that even a single citizen can insist that society establish programs and institutions to thwart the transmission of HIV.[111] This provision applies fully to a Noahide society, because the

109 This would be in line with R. Isaac Schorr, *Responsa Koah Shor*, #20, which states that a Noahide may violate the Noahide Code to save not only his own life but also the life of a fellow Noahide. That claim is disputed in *Minhat Hinukh*, precept 296 (§4 in Jerusalem Institute edition), which argues that a Noahide is forbidden to transgress the Noahide Code to rescue anyone other than himself. In *Contemporary Halakhic Problems*, n. 23 above, 4:195, R. Bleich suggests that the dispute between *Koah Shor* and *Minhat Hinukh* may reflect the unresolved doubt in *Tosafot*, bSanhedrin 59a s.v. *leika*, as to whether a Noahide obstetrician is permitted to abort a fetus so as to save its endangered mother.

110 *SA*, HM 163:1–2.

111 Personal communication, July 2002. Safety from infectious disease is no less important than safety from enemy invasion. Indeed, as noted above, *Hazon Ish*, YD 208:7 specifically compares control of infectious disease by public health departments to neutralization of hostile military forces, as described in bEruvin 45a. R. Karelitz extrapolates from the case of defensive warfare to that of public protection from imminent contagion, viewing both as instances where saving life is mandated (*pikuah nefesh*), whereas R. Bleich extrapolates from the case of pre-emptive warfare to that of public protection from future contagion, see *Bintivot Hahalakha*, n. 1 above, 1:80–82.

bBaba Batra 7b is similarly invoked by R. Bleich in support of an implicit social contract to ensure the provision of training for physicians (*Bintivot*

obligation to fulfill contractual commitments is subsumed under either the Noahide commandment prohibiting theft (according to Maimonides[112]) or the Noahide commandment mandating justice (according to Nahmanides[113]).

R. Shlomo Goren has argued that when one has accepted a societally-imposed duty to protect the lives of others, he is legally responsible for negligence in executing these duties, and any such negligence is tantamount to directly harming those dependent on his professional diligence.[114] Although R. Goren is speaking of a military commander, his remarks surely apply to civilian healthcare workers as well. This principle would then obligate those dispensing an HIV vaccine to do so to the best of their ability so as to save the lives of members of the society. What does "to the best of their ability" mean in the context of Noahide triage decisions? As we said, a Noahide personally possessing a dose of HIV vaccine must inoculate herself first, on account of the biblical mandate that Noahides sustain themselves with the food they possess. The obligation of Noahides to save the lives of others, where it exists, is obviously no weightier than the obligation

---

Hahalakha, 3:197–200), health insurance (*Bioethical Dilemmas*, n. 12 above, 1:16–20), and medical research (*Bioethical Dilemmas*, 2:200–205).

R. Solomon Auerbach is cited in *Shulhan Shlomo*, 2:204–05 as claiming that society's waging of 'war' on disease through research may call to mind the notion of an 'obligatory war' (*milhemet mitzva*). But as the editor of that volume notes, R. Auerbach's remark appears hyperbolic, since obligatory war would certainly override the Sabbath as a matter of the duty to save life, which is by no means true of scientific research in general. Rather, as follows from R. Bleich's various writings, biomedical research should be envisaged as a valuable mission akin to pre-emptive war, which serves as commendable preparation for observance of the precept of saving life, but does not intrinsically constitute an act of saving life. But cf. *Contemporary Halakhic Problems*, n. 23 above, 3:254–57, where R. Bleich notes that *Beit Habehira* and *Kneset Hagedola*, bSota 44b, adopt a non-conventional reading of the *sugya*, according to which the majority view of the Sages does regard medical research as an obligatory war. R. Auerbach could therefore be construed as adopting their maverick reading, although this attribution is not compelling, especially since, as R. Bleich notes, some argue that the passage in *Beit Habehira* should be emended.

112 *Code*, Laws concerning Kings and Wars 9:14, as elucidated in *Responsa Hatam Sofer* 6:14.

113 Commentary on Genesis 34:13, as elucidated in *Responsa Hatam Sofer*, ibid.

114 *Meshiv Milhama*, vol. 1 (Jerusalem: 1984), 30–39.

that binds Jews; a Jewish rescuer saves his own life first, and therefore the same must hold true for a Noahide rescuer. R. Joseph Babad's ruling that a Noahide community may save itself by surrendering a member already earmarked for death[115] implies that saving many patients whose lives can be significantly extended (*hayei olam*) takes triage priority over saving one patient whose life can be extended only briefly (*hayei shaa*). R. Babad proceeds to express doubt as to whether the community can similarly surrender a member who has not yet been earmarked for death, but rather, has been capriciously designated for this purpose by the community. The practical impact of this doubt would apparently be that such handing-over is prohibited.[116] Accordingly, a Noahide rescue worker, like his Jewish counterpart, could not withdraw medical care from one patient in order to save another, or even in order to save an entire group of other patients.[117] A major issue with which decisors adjudicating questions of Noahide triage will have to grapple is undoubtedly the question of whether the Noahide obligation to establish a judicial system entails that Noahides must follow the same civil procedures that govern Jews, or are halakhically entitled to institute their own civil norms.[118]

9. Conclusion

Allocation of scarce resources — whether doses of a hypothetical HIV vaccine or other types of lifesaving medical care — is a daunting task. We have endeavored to elucidate various halakhic principles governing medical triage. Medical triage must always be selection for life and never selection for death; for this reason, once a dangerously-ill patient is receiving a resource, the resource cannot be withdrawn even to save a higher-priority patient. The biblical imperative, "you shall choose life" (Deut. 30:19) articulates this mandate.

In light of the paramount importance of the obligation to save life (*pikuah nefesh*), the ideal pre-emptive solution is, of course, for human civilization to harness its creative energies and find ways to dedicate

115 See text above at nn 101–102.

116 See n. 91 above, from which it emerges that doubtful violations of the Noahide Code cannot be countenanced.

117 See n. 62 above.

118 For an analysis of conflicting sources on this issue, see *Bintivot Hahalakha*, 2:154.

more funding to healthcare in general, and HIV treatment/vaccination in particular. More realistically, the imperative that societal decisions "not be made from an amoral perspective that exempts society from ethical imperatives, but rather with a full appreciation of the infinite worth of human beings, that will enable us to do a lot more with the little that we have,"[119] will, we hope, resonate with many.[120]

119 Tendler 1984, n. 1 above.

120 We are grateful to R. Shalom Carmy, R. Alfred Cohen, R. Aaron Glatt, R. Edward Reichman, R. Michael Shmidman, R. Avraham Steinberg, and Dr. Joel Wolowelsky for reviewing an earlier version of this article.

Contractual Consequences of Cohabitation in American Law and Jewish Law

Ronnie Warburg*

1. Contractual consequences of cohabitation in American law

> They live near you — in a house, apartment, or trailer, in urban centers, small towns, or on farms. They may both be professionals or wage earners; they may work separately or together in various enterprises of their own; one of them may act as a homeowner while the other works outside the home for pay. They share your neighborhood activities, your civic concerns, your national and international problems. Their life-style may be avant-garde or traditional. . . . In one respect, however, they differ from most couples: they are not married.[1]

Cohabitation without undertaking the formalities of marriage has become a widespread phenomenon over the past four decades.[2] How

* Beth Din of America

1 H. Hill Kay and C. Amyx, "Marvin v. Marvin: preserving the options," 65 *California Law Review* (1977), 937.

2 U.S. Bureau of the Census: 1960 Census of Population, *Persons by Family Characteristics*, table 15, 4b; 1970 Census of Population, *Persons by Family Characteristics*, table 11, 4b; Current Population Reports, Population Characteristics, *Households, Families, Marital Status, and Living Arrangements*, March 1984 (Advance Report); G. Spanier, "Living together in the eighties," *American Demographics* 4 (1982), 17; L. Bumpass et al., "Trends in cohabitation and implications for children's family contexts in the US," *Population Studies* 54 (2000), 29–30; Eric Schmitt, "For first time, nuclear families drop below 25% of households," *NY Times*, May 15, 2001; G. Blumberg, "The regularization of non-marital cohabitation: rights and responsibilities in the American welfare state," 76 *Notre Dame Law Review* (2000/01), 1265, 1268–269. On the legal issues, see W. Weyrauch, "Informal and formal marriage — an appraisal of trends in family organization," 23 *University*

does cohabitation differ from common-law marriage? In a common-law marriage, in the absence of the ex ante imprimatur of the state or solemnization by a church, the parties live together and agree between themselves to be married, present themselves to the community as husband and wife, and live together for a significant period.[3] Many elements of cohabitation are identical to those associated with traditional and common-law marriage: sexual relations, living together, children together, common housing, joint domestic budget, common ownership of property.[4] However, whereas in conventional marriage or common-law marriage, marital or quasi-marital intent exists, in cohabitation, the parties either do not express long-term commitments, or express private commitments regarding permanent union outside the marital or quasi-marital frameworks.[5] Moreover, whereas termination of common-law marriage requires divorce, cohabitants can simply

of Chicago Law Review (1960), 88; M. Grossberg, *Governing the Hearth: Law and Family in Nineteenth Century America* (1985), 83–102; Homer Clark, *The Law of Domestic Relations in the United States* (St. Paul MN: 1987), §2.4; A. Dubler, "Note: Governing through contract: common law marriage in the nineteenth century," 107 *Yale L. J.* (1998), 1885; *Nestor v. Nestor*, 15 Ohio St. 3d 143, 145; 472 N.E. 2d 1091, 1094 (1984); *Etheridge v. Yeager*, 465 So. 2d 378, 379–80 (Ala. 1985).

3 See A. Dubler, "Wifely behavior: a legal history of acting married," 100 *Columbia Law Review* (2000), 957, 1011.

4 G. Blumberg, "Cohabitation without marriage: a different perspective," 28 *University of California–Los Angeles Law Review* (1980/81), 1125; Steven Nock, "A comparison of marriages and cohabiting relationships," *Journal of Family Issues* 16 (1995), 53.

5 See S.A. Coolidge, "Rights of the putative and meretricious spouse in California," 50 *California Law Review* (1962), 866, 873; M. Ploscowe et al., *Family Law: Case Law and Materials* (Boston: 1972), 81; William Reppy Jr., "Property and support rights of unmarried cohabitants: a proposal for creating a new legal status," 44 *Louisiana Law Review* (1983/84), 1677, 1706; J.T. Oldham, "Lessons from Jerry Hall v. Mick Jagger regarding U.S. regulation of heterosexual cohabitants, or, can't get no satisfaction," 76 *Notre Dame Law Review* (2001), 1409, 1410–411; M. Garrison, " Is consent necessary? An evaluation of the emerging law of cohabitant obligation," 52 *UCLA Law Review* (2005), 815, 840; cf. Milton Regan Jr., "Calibrated commitment: the legal treatment of marriage and cohabitation," 76 *Notre Dame Law Review* (2001), 1435, 1437; *Dennison v. Dennison*, 35 Md. 361, 381 (1872); *In re Brush*, 25 A.D. 610, 613, 49 N.Y.S. 803, 806 (1898); *Hewitt v. Hewitt*, 77 Ill. 2d 49, 394 N.E. 2d 1204, 1208–1209 (1979); *Knauer v. Knauer*, 323 Pa. Super. 206, 228, 470 A. 2d 553, 564 (1983).

separate.[6] Rights, including those to insurance proceeds and employment retirement benefits, which exist in common-law marriages, do not necessarily attach to cohabitation agreements. And jurisdictions that recognize common-law marriages do not automatically grant status rights to cohabiters.

Formerly, we lived in a binary legal world where a couple was either married or not married. In the nineteenth and early twentieth centuries, courts analyzed the legal rights and responsibilities of common-law spouses who 'acted married' within non-solemnized relationships. With the gradual decline of jurisdictions that recognize common-law marriages, domestic relations law has expanded. It divides family relations into different components, protecting some but not all aspects of a couple's relationship (alimony, inheritance rights, worker's compensation) in the grey area known as 'cohabitation' that has emerged between the normative categories of marriage and non-marriage. Assessment of the legal status of non-marital cohabitation involves not only the rights of two individuals, but also the very institution of marriage itself.[7] The issue is not simply that of determining when expectations of unmarried couples should be enforced, but also the impact of enforcing the rights of cohabitants on the definition of marriage.

The dilemma of how cohabitation fits into existing legal frameworks is reflected in the response to the three *Marvin* cases, perhaps one of the most significant series of domestic relations cases in the last several decades.[8] In 1976, the Supreme Court of California was called upon to establish guidelines for determining the financial rights and responsibilities of non-marital partners in the highly-publicized case of *Marvin v. Marvin*, which has been described as "one of the most misunderstood decisions of modern times."[9]

Plaintiff Michelle Triola and defendant Lee Marvin lived together, unmarried, for close to seven years, during which time all their real and

6 Samuel Green and John Long, *Marriage and Family Law Agreements* (NY: 1984), 162.
7 *Hewitt v. Hewitt*, n. 5 above, 77 Ill. 2d 63, 394 N.E. 2d 1210; *Knauer v. Knauer*, n. 5 above.
8 *Marvin v. Marvin*, 557 P.2d 106 (Cal. 1976); *Marvin v. Marvin*, 5 Family Law Rptr. (BNA) 3077 (1979); *Marvin v. Marvin*, 176 Cal. Rptr. 555 (Cal. Ct. App. 1981).
9 Kay and Amyx, n. 1 above, 954.

personal property was placed in the defendant's name. After the relationship ended, Triola sued him for breaching an oral agreement that entitled her to half the property acquired and to support payments in exchange for giving up her movie career and performing the domestic services of a housewife. As Triola had suffered no legally recognizable injury, the trial court granted judgment on the pleadings for the defendant, and dismissed the suit.[10] The court of appeal affirmed, stating that no rights are acquired in cases where a "meretricious" relationship, i.e., cohabitation, is "itself the consideration for the agreement."[11]

Finding that the agreement alleged by the plaintiff did not rest upon unlawful consideration, the California Supreme Court reversed and remanded the case for trial.[12] It concluded that the plaintiff's complaint did state a cause of action for breach of an express agreement, and that Triola could amend her complaint to reflect various legal and equitable remedies that might govern property distribution among unmarried couples.

Justice Tobriner, who authored the majority opinion, observed that in the absence of an express agreement, the courts may look to other theories of recovery, including

> an implied contract . . . of partnership or joint venture . . . or some other tacit understanding between the parties. The courts may, when appropriate, employ principles of constructive trust . . . or resulting trust. . . . Finally, a nonmarital partner may recover in quantum meruit for the reasonable value of household services rendered less the reasonable value of support received if he can show that he rendered services with the expectation of monetary reward.[13]

When the *Marvin* case was considered on remand by the Superior Court of Los Angeles in 1979, the trial court found that neither the words nor the conduct of the parties demonstrated the existence of an express or implied agreement to apportion property.[14] The trial court

10 18 Cal. 3d 665; 557 P.2d 110; 134 Cal. Rptr. 819.

11 18 Cal. 3d 667; 557 P.2d 111; 134 Cal. Rptr. 820.

12 *Marvin v. Marvin*, No. 44359, slip op., 22 (Cal. Ct. App. 2d Dist. July 23, 1975).

13 18 Cal. 3d 684; 557 P.2d 123; 134 Cal. Rptr. 832.

14 5 Family Law Rptr, 3085. Although the intent of the award was rehabilitation and reeducation, the media labeled the award 'palimony,' implying that a cohabiter was granted support similar to that received by a lawful spouse. See H. Foster and D. Jonas Freed, "*Marvin v. Marvin*: new wine in old bottles," 5 *Family Law Reporter* (1979), 4001, 4009; Kay and Amyx, n. 1 above, n. 104.

did not endorse the equitable remedies that had been suggested by the California Supreme Court.[15] Nevertheless, pursuant to the Supreme Court's guidelines, the trial court awarded an equitable remedy of $104,000 so that the plaintiff could upgrade her existing employment skills or acquire new ones.[16] In 1981, the $104,000 award was reversed on appeal, on the ground that it was not within the issues articulated in the pleadings.

The import of the *Marvin* cases lies in Tobriner's holding that to assert claims arising from cohabitation agreements, the parties must furnish adequate proof of the existence of the arrangement to satisfy contract doctrines of enforceability. The majority opinion's analysis thus opens with the enforceability of the oral agreement. The plaintiff asserted that she and the defendant had an oral contract which provided that they would live together and share equally any and all property they accumulated individually or jointly, and that she would be supported for the rest of her life. The plaintiff further alleged that she agreed to serve as a companion to the defendant and furnish her services as a homemaker.

The California Supreme Court concluded that there was a cause of action for breach of an express pooling agreement with respect to the disposition of the couple's jointly-acquired property.[17] How did it reach this conclusion? In a series of cases dating back to the nineteenth

15 Mary DeNevi, "Reasonable expectations in nonmarital cohabitation: a proposal for recovery," 21 *B.C.L. Rev.* (1980), 889, 890.

16 5 Family Law Rptr, 3085; 18 Cal. 3d 684; 557 P.2d 122–23; 134 Cal. Rptr. 831–32.

17 The court's conclusion was predicated on the plaintiff's evidence that there was indeed an express agreement and that the plaintiff's services were performed in consideration for the cohabiter's promise of property rights or remuneration. The agreement is enforceable, like a promise that induces reliance; see 1A A. Corbin, *Contracts*, §194 (1963); Stanley Henderson, "Promises grounded in the past: the idea of unjust enrichment and the law of contracts," 57 *Virginia Law Review* (1971), 1115, 1160–64. But cf. *Hill v. Estate of Westbrook*, 39 Cal. 2d 458, 461, 247 P.2d 19, 21 (1952), where recovery was denied because of insufficient evidence to prove either the existence of an oral agreement, or that the plaintiff's services were performed gratuitously, without expectation of remuneration; *Beckman v. Mayhew*, 49 Cal. App. 3d 529; 122 Cal. Rptr. 604 (1975); *Warren v. Warren*, 94 Nev. 309, 579 P.2d 772 (1978).

century,[18] courts have held that living outside the bonds of marriage implies that the parties are engaged in illicit sexual relations, and have refused to uphold contracts between cohabiters where the agreement rests on the illegal consideration of meretricious sexual services.

> A promise is not enforceable if part or all of the consideration for it is illicit sexual intercourse or the continuance of such an illicit relationship. This is true even though the relationship is not adulterous or otherwise criminal; the bargain is contra bonos mores in any case and the parties are regarded as in pari delicto.[19]

The illegal consideration doctrine has been characterized as "a means of upholding the morals of society and discouraging opprobrious sexual behavior. . . . the doctrine provides a convenient way to dispose of cases involving the division of property, since the courts do not have to divide the property that the cohabitors have accumulated and inextricably mixed."[20] Cohabitation agreements were deemed contrary to public policy interests or public morals, and even construed as contracts for prostitution.[21]

The *Marvin* court rejected Corbin's equation of cohabitation and prostitution. Tobriner held that the nature of the sexual relations involved in cohabitation arrangements was qualitatively different from those characteristic of prostitution:

> The nonenforceability of agreements expressly providing for meretricious conduct rested upon the fact that such conduct, as the word suggests,

18 *Vincent v. Moriarty*, 31 App. Div. 484, 52 N.Y.S. 519 (1898); *Trutalli v. Meraviglia*, 215 Cal. 698, 12 P.2d 430 (1932); *Hill v. Estate of Westbrook*, 95 Cal. App. 2d 599, 213 P.2d 727 (1950); *Lovinger v. Anglo Cal. Nat'l Bank*, 243 P.2d 561 (Cal. App. 1952); *Bridges v. Bridges*, 125 Cal. App. 2d 359, 370 P.2d 69 (1954); *Wellmaker v. Roberts*, 213 Ga. 740, 101 S.E. 2d 712 (1958); *Beckman v. Mayhew*, 49 Cal. App. 3d 529, 122 Cal. Rptr. 604 (1975). See Carol Bruch, "Property rights of de facto spouses including thoughts on the value of homemakers' services," 10 *Family Law Quarterly* (1976), 101, 108.

19 6A A. Corbin, *Contracts* §1476, 621–22 (1962).

20 G. Smith, "*Hewitt v. Hewitt*: non-marital cohabitation and the doctrine of immorality," 69 *Illinois Bar Journal* (1981), 368.

21 On the role of public policy in contract law, see P. Winfeld, "Public policy in the English common law," 42 *Harvard Law Review* (1928), 76; W. Gellhorn, "Contracts and public policy," 35 *Columbia Law Review* (1935), 679; J. Shand, "Unblinkering the unruly horse: public policy in the law of contract," 30 *Cambridge Law Journal* (1972), 44.

> pertained to and encompassed prostitution. To equate the non-marital relationship of today to such a subject matter is to do violence to an accepted and wholly different practice.[22]

In other words, labeling a cohabitant a "meretricious spouse" fails to reflect the nature of the cohabitation relationship.

Another court made a similar argument:

> Defendant has referred to plaintiff as a meretricious spouse living in a meretricious relationship. The adjective should be examined in its precise meaning, i.e. "of, pertaining to, befitting, or of a character of a harlot" (Shorter Oxford English Dictionary, 1934), or "of or relating to a prostitute" (Webster's New Collegiate Dictionary, 1973). . . . The well-pleaded facts contradict the terms in showing that the parties lived, and for a time, enjoyed a most conventional, respectable and ordinary family life. . . . nothing discloses a scandal, an affront to family living or society, or anything other than that the parties were known as husband and wife.[23]

The *Marvin* court upheld the validity of the oral agreement in question. Relying on prior California case law, it applied the doctrine of severability. As Corbin put it, "A bargain between two persons is not made illegal by the mere fact of an illicit relationship between them, so long as that relationship constitutes no part of the consideration bargained for and no promise in the bargain is conditional upon it."[24] That is, if an agreement consists of a provision that is contrary to public policy, but has other provisions that are severable from the tainted provision, the court will uphold the contract. In our scenario, an agreement between cohabiters to pool resources may be enforceable if the essence of the exchange and its consideration are severable from the sexual relationship. The *Marvin* court thus had to ascertain the existence of two separate agreements: an agreement to pool resources, and a second, independent agreement

22 18 Cal. 3d 683–84; 557 P.2d 122; 134 Cal. Rptr. 831. The distinction between cohabitation and prostitution was recognized in other cases; see, e.g., *In re Estate of Alexander*, 445 So. 2d 836, 842 (Miss. 1984) (Lee J., dissenting).

23 *Hewitt v. Hewitt*, 62 Ill. App. 3d 861, 863; 380 N.E. 2d 454, 456–67 (1978), *rev'd*, 77 Ill. 2d 49; 394 N.E. 2d 1204 (1979).

24 Corbin, n. 19 above. See also *Restatement (Second) of Contracts*, §184, 195 (1979).

to live together. Relying on the holdings in *Trutalli v. Meraviglia*[25] and *Vallera v. Vallera*,[26] *Marvin* states:

> Adults who voluntarily live together and engage in sexual relations are nonetheless as competent as any other persons to contract respecting their earnings and property rights. Of course, they cannot lawfully contract to pay for the performance of sexual services. . . . So long as the agreement does not rest upon meretricious consideration, the parties may order their economic affairs as they choose, and no policy precludes the courts from enforcing such agreements.[27]

Though the *Marvin* court held that sexual relations could not provide consideration in cohabitation agreements, and acknowledged that contracts between cohabitants are made in contemplation of a sexual relationship, it nevertheless found that there were other bases for consideration, namely, nonsexual services such as income and property.[28] In viewing the sexual relationship as severable from the economic agreement, the court was, arguably, invoking a legal fiction.

> The concept of severability in the cohabitation agreement case takes on a shape somewhat different from its normal use. For example, in a covenant not to compete agreement, the terms that are overly broad and offensive can be separated without affecting the essence of the agreement. . . . While it is entirely possible that sexual relations may be either a minor or collateral element in a contractual transaction, this is usually not the case in cohabitation agreements. The living arrangement and sexual relations probably provide the true impetus for the usual promise to . . . jointly acquire property. For this reason the use of the severability concept in cohabitation agreement cases may require a rather unrealistic application of the concept.[29]

25 N. 18 above.

26 21 Cal. 2d 681; 134 P.2d 761 (1943). On California courts, prior to *Marvin*, that upheld the concept of severable agreements, see Bruch, n. 18 above, n. 24. On the case law, see Kay and Amyx, n. 1 above, 942–45. At the same time as *Marvin*, the Oregon Supreme Court concluded that inability to sever an agreement from an illicit affair did not invalidate the agreement; see *Latham v. Latham*, 274 Or. 421, 547 P.2d 144 (1976).

27 18 Cal. 3d 674; 557 P.2d 116; 134 Cal. Rptr. 825. As the *Latham* court stated: "We are not validating an agreement in which the only or primary consideration is sexual intercourse. The agreement here contemplated all the burdens and amenities of married life" (*Latham v. Latham*, ibid., 147).

28 134 Cal. Rptr. 823.

29 Harry Prince, "Public policy limitations on cohabitation agreements: unruly horse or circus pony?" 70 *Minnesota Law Review* (1985/86), 163, 206.

Exposing the gullibility involved in asserting that the parties would have entered into an agreement for homemaker services in the absence of sexual consideration, the court in *Hewitt v. Hewitt* states:

> It would seem more candid to acknowledge the return of varying forms of common law marriages than to continue displaying the naiveté we believe involved in the assertion that there are involved in these relationships contracts separate and independent from the sexual activity, and the assumption that those contracts would have been entered into or would continue without that activity.[30]

Adoption of the doctrine of severability allowed the *Marvin* court to uphold the Marvins' agreement while avoiding the need to pass moral judgment on their relationship.[31]

The *Marvin* court, after framing the issue in terms of illegality and severability, concluded with a 'changing mores' argument: "In summary, we believe that the prevalence of non-marital relationships in modern society and the social acceptance of them, marks this as a time when our courts should by no means apply the doctrine of the unlawfulness of the so-called meretricious relationship to the instant case."[32]

Thus, in the final analysis, the court acknowledged cohabitation as a preparation for marriage that reflected "the mores of . . . society."[33] It thereby imparted recognition to a lifestyle practiced in our diverse and pluralistic society: cohabitation on the basis of the couple's mutual agreement.

Though the court's decision regarding the enforceability of the oral agreement mandated reversal of the trial court's judgment, due to the submission of briefs requesting recovery in the absence of an agreement,

---

Marvin's reasoning has been characterized as "an agile flight of fancy (fantasy?) to enforce cohabitants' agreements" in J.T. Oldham and D. Caudill, "A reconnaissance of public policy restrictions upon enforcement of contracts between cohabitants," 18 *Family Law Quarterly* (1984), 93, 126.

30 N. 5 above, 77 Ill. 2d 60; 394 N.E. 2d 1209. See also Howard Hunter, "Essay on contract and status: race, marriage and the meretricious spouse," 64 *Virginia Law Review* (1978), 1039, 1091.

31 Whereas the *Marvin* court exercised its judicial authority to recognize cohabitation arrangements on the basis of a strained use of the severability doctrine and contract theory, the court in *Hewitt*, ibid., 77 Ill. 2d 66; 394 N.E. 2d 1211, argued that the state legislature was the proper forum for addressing social changes such as increased cohabitation.

32 18 Cal. 3d 683; 557 P.2d 122; 134 Cal. Rptr. 831.

33 Ibid.

the court focused on other bases for recovery that would protect the lawful expectations of the unmarried but cohabiting partners.[34] Since most cohabiters do not think of their relationship in contract terms,[35] and consequently, do not make express agreements, oral or written, courts have no framework for dealing with the dissolution of their relationships. The court thus suggested that other theories of recovery be adduced. Eschewing a narrower compass for its holding, the court addressed the propriety of various legal and equitable remedies.

The *Marvin* court examined the expectation of compensation for homemaker services and acquisition of property rights by the non-income-generating party, through the prism of the doctrine of implied-in-fact contracts.[36] On this doctrine, an agreement is inferred, by the courts, from the conduct of the parties rather than from their oral or written statements.[37] Whereas in earlier decisions,[38] California courts

34 Ibid.

35 Homer Clark, "The new marriage," 12 *Willamette Law Journal* (1976), 441, 451; Bruch, n. 18 above, 102, 135; H. Folberg and William Buren, "Domestic partnership: a proposal for dividing the property of unmarried families," 12 *Willamette Law Journal* (1976), 453, 465; Comment, "Property rights upon termination of unmarried cohabitation," 90 *Harvard Law Review* (1977), 1708, 1718. Despite the steady increase in nonmarital unions over the last twenty-five years, there seems to be a tacit understanding between the parties that their property remains separate. "The main defect with contract as the conceptual underpinning for claims between intimate partners is that couples do not in fact think of their relationship in contract terms" (Ira Ellman, "Contract thinking was *Marvin*'s main flaw," 76 *Notre Dame Law Review* [2000/01], 1365, 1367). On the paucity of express agreements for intimate relationships, see Bruch, 135. Cf. Lenore Weitzman, "Legal regulation of marriage: tradition and change," 62 *California Law Review* (1974), 1169, 1249–55; Kay and Amyx, n. 1 above, 969.

36 On other theories of recovery utilizing implied-in-fact contracts in the context of partnership agreements and constructive and resulting trusts, see Bruch, n. 18 above, 118–26.

37 D. Dobbs, *Handbook on the Law of Remedies* (St. Paul MN: 1973), §4.2, 234; *Restatement (Second) of Contracts*, §4, comment b (1979). If it is the case that cohabiters do not think of their relationship in contract terms, as argued above, then a theory that directs courts to infer agreements from the parties' actions is misguided. Yet many courts have utilized this technique to grant relief in cohabitation cases.

38 *Vallera v. Vallera*, n. 26 above; *Lovinger v. Anglo Cal. Nat'l Bank*, n. 18 above, 569; *Keene v. Keene*, 57 Cal. 657, 371 P.2d 329, 21 Cal. Rptr. 593 (1962).

held that in the absence of an express agreement there can be no recovery at all, the *Marvin* court was the first California court to acknowledge the potential enforceability of a putative implied-in-fact cohabitation agreement between meretricious spouses.

The efficacy of an implied-in-fact contract requires that the parties intend a contractual relationship. The household or business services allegedly performed under this contract must have been rendered with the expectation of receiving remuneration, and the recipient must have indeed expected to pay for them. Prior to *Marvin*, California courts were reluctant to utilize the implied-in-contract theory as a technique for awarding property rights in a non-marital union on the basis of services provided by the non-income-generating spouse, whether as a homemaker or by working in a family business.[39] Courts predicated their denial of recovery on the unreasonableness of inferring an agreement to pay for the services rendered when the relationship (even a meretricious one) between the parties makes it natural that the services were offered gratuitously.[40]

The unfairness resulting from those holdings, which denied relief for the value of homemaker services, was articulated by Justice Curtis in his dissenting opinion in *Vallera v. Vallera*:

> Unless it can be argued that a woman's services as cook, housekeeper, and homemaker are valueless, it would seem logical that if, when she contributes money to the purchase of property, her interest will be protected, then when she contributes her services in the home, her interest in property accumulated should be protected. . . . To permit the defendant to retain the entire fruits of their joint efforts is contrary to the dictates of simple justice.[41]

The irony emerging from these decisions did not go unnoticed:

> The courts were willing to recognize that the feelings of affection in family-like circumstances made it reasonable to assume homemaker services were offered without thought of future payment. But courts denied the corollary that a well-established quasi-family relation also could raise

39 Comment, "Property rights of unmarried cohabitants — a proposal," 14 *California Western Law Review* (1979), 485, 497.

40 *Keene v. Keene*, n. 38 above; *Vallera v. Vallera*, n. 26 above.

41 Ibid., 686–87.

> other expectations based upon the structure of the relationship, such as equal rights to property accumulated throughout the relationship.[42]

Overcoming this historical unwillingness to ascribe value to household services, and affirming the scholarly criticism of this inequity,[43] *Marvin* recognized that implied-in-fact contracts should serve as a basis for recovery in cases of cohabitation. It held that both implied and express cohabitation arrangements were not contrary to public policy and were thus enforceable. Where other courts preferred to assume that services rendered were rendered gratuitously, rather than examine the expectations of cohabiters in non-marital relationships, the *Marvin* court adopted a functional approach and legitimized relationships that share the basic features of a traditional family unit. On this approach, if the non-marital union resembles a family unit, then there is a presumption that "the parties intend to deal fairly with each other." In the absence of legislative standards, the judge, with a view to remedying potential injustices, will approach each cohabitation case with a technique such as that of implied contract, and attempt to divine what the parties had in mind.

Nevertheless, various courts in the 1980s remained concerned that these relationships were against public policy, and consequently affirmed only express agreements, denying relief where the contracts were implied.[44]

> The problem with judicial lawmaking [of this type] . . . is uncertainty. If the availability of the remedy is to depend simply on the idiosyncrasy of the judge acting in accordance with his or her perception of a need to ameliorate a situation involving an injustice, and who does so without the certainty of enacted prescription, then unless judges come to act in such a way as a matter of predictable habit, thereby charting new law, the injustice cannot be said to have been removed.[45]

42 C. Fernandez, "Note, Beyond *Marvin*: A proposal for quasi-spousal support," 30 *Stanford Law Review* (1978), 359, 383.

43 See Harold Havighurst, "Services in the home," 41 *Yale L. J.* (1932), 386; Herma Kay, *Text, Cases, and Materials on Sex-Based Discrimination* (St. Paul MN: 1974), 142; Bruch, n. 18 above, 113.

44 *Morone v. Morone*, 50 N.Y. 2d 481, 407 N.E. 2d 438, 429 N.Y.S. 2d 592 (1980); *Trimmer v. Van Bomel*, 107 Misc. 2d 201, 434 N.Y. S. 2d 82 (1980); *Carnes v. Sheldon*, 109 Mich. App 204, 311 NW 2d 747 (1981); *Tapley v. Tapley*, 122 N.H. 727, 449 A. 2d 1218 (1982).

45 H. Finlay, "The informal marriage in Anglo-Australian law," in J. Eekelaar and Sanford Katz (eds.), *Marriage and Cohabitation In Contemporary Societies* (Toronto: 1980), 156, quoted in Reppy, n. 5 above, 1690 n. 54.

"Approaching each case on an ad hoc basis," as Reppy puts it, without prescribed guidelines, allows the judge to impose his own notions of fairness, colored by his personal beliefs regarding the propriety of this type of relationship, in the guise of inferring the existence of an agreement.[46] Persuaded of the unreliability of this doctrine, Justice Clark, in his dissenting opinion in *Marvin*, concludes that "under the majority opinion a party may recover half the property acquired during the relationship on the basis of general equitable principles."[47]

In the absence of an express or implied agreement, the *Marvin* court viewed the relationship between the parties as based on mutual affection rather the mutual consent to contract domestic affairs. However, in the absence of contrary evidence, a court may treat the relationship as legally equivalent to traditional marriage and apportion the assets pursuant to community property principles.[48]

What are the jurisprudential implications of this legal analysis of the *Marvin* and post-*Marvin* cases? We must bear in mind that "it is hard to produce a systematic view of an unsystematic subject, and perhaps family law must always be ad hoc, responsive to local

46 Reppy, ibid. And see Robert Casad, "Unmarried couples and unjust enrichment: from status to contract and back again," 77 *Michigan Law Review* (1978/79), 47, 49; Ruth Deech, "The case against recognition of cohabitation," in Eekelar and Katz, ibid., 273; Blumberg, n. 4 above, 1166; I. Ellman, "The theory of alimony," 77 *California Law Review* (1989), 1, 21–23; Ann Estin, "Love and obligation: family law and the romance of economics," 36 *William and Mary Law Review* (1994/95), 989, 1043–44. On proposals for statutory regulation as opposed to ad hoc judicial solutions, see, e.g., *Connell v. Francisco*, 898 P.2d 831, 837 (Wash. 1995); *Koher v. Morgan*, 968 P.2d 920 (Wash. Ct. App. 1998); Folberg and Buren, n. 35 above; Judith Younger, "Marital regimes: a story of compromise and demoralization, together with criticism and suggestions for reform," 67 *Cornell Law Review* (1981), 45, 99–102; Martha Fineman, "Law and changing patterns of behavior: sanctions on non-marital cohabitation," 1981 *Wisconsin Law. Review* (1981), 275; Ellman, n. 35 above, 1377–79.

47 18 Cal. 3d 660; 557 P.2d 106; 134 Cal. Rptr. 815, 832.

48 Comment, "Property rights," n. 35 above, 1716. Others, however, argue that marriage involves equal sharing, whereas in cohabitation, entitlement is proportionate to one's investment, mandating contribution-based recovery; see Ann Estin, "Ordinary cohabitation," 76 *Notre Dame Law Review* (2001), 1381, 1399–1403; Carolyn Frantz and H. Dagan, "Properties of marriage," 104 *Columbia Law Review* (2004), 75, 81–84.

conditions, sensitive to the day's sensibilities, and willing to compromise irreconcilable differences."[49]

Marvin v. Marvin presents a window through which to view the relationship between legal rules and social beliefs. Social norms (which include moral norms) may figure in judicial reasoning at various levels. On one level, the *Marvin* court transformed a matrix of social beliefs about marital behavior into an ex post facto legal standard for cohabitation. The court invoked the language of contract, but whether cohabitation arrangements were to be recognized depended on the degree to which they conformed to a set of social norms pertaining to relationships and their significance, rather than to principles of contract. For *Marvin*, the implicit assumption was that there exists a clear set of norms 'out there' that enables a relationship to be deemed 'cohabitative,' norms that the court accepted uncritically, without due legal reflection.

On another level, the *Marvin* holding implicitly addresses the long-standing academic debate over the relationship between legal change and social norms. Do legal rules simply reflect social phenomena, do shared public values cause legal change, or is law 'fundamentally constitutive' of social life, and thereby able to influence social morality? Do law and legal change reflect social morality, or does law have autonomous content? Does *Marvin* simply suggest a means of providing legal and equitable relief on the basis of the parties' lawful expectations, or does it give its judicial imprimatur to the cohabitation relationship and thereby undermine traditional marriage?

In *Hewitt v. Hewitt*,[50] the Illinois Supreme Court examined the implications of *Marvin* for the institution of marriage. The case involved

49 Carl Schneider, "The next step: definition, generalization, and theory in American family law," 18 *University of Michigan Journal of Legal Reform* (1985), 1039, 1048. See too Martha Minow, "Forming underneath everything that grows: toward a history of family law," 1985 *Wisconsin Law Review* (1985), 819–27. Clearly, the difficulty in articulating conceptual categories and developing a 'meta-narrative' is not limited to family law, and despite the difficulties, scholars continue their efforts to make sense of the reality of family relationships. See, e.g., Mary Ann Glendon, *The Transformation of Family Law: State, Law, and the Family in the United States and Western Europe* (Chicago: 1989); John Witte, *From Sacrament to Contract — Marriage, Religion and Law in Western Tradition* (Louisville KY: 1997).

50 *Hewitt v. Hewitt*, n. 5 above.

a couple who separated after living together for fifteen years; the woman filed for divorce. The trial court dismissed the claim, because the woman admitted that no formal marriage had occurred and that the couple had never procured a marriage license. However, the court allowed her to amend the complaint, whereupon the plaintiff alleged economic dependence on her former partner, and requested an equal share of the property accumulated during the couple's relationship, whether held in joint tenancy or not.[51]

The Illinois Supreme Court noted that other courts had enforced oral contracts between unmarried cohabiters. Some of the jurisdictions recognized two separate agreements: one grounded on illicit sexual consideration, another based on the pooling of efforts and assets. Rejecting the appellate court's decision to recognize these express agreements between cohabiters, the Illinois Supreme Court argued that the underlying issue was "whether it is appropriate for this court to grant a legal status to a private arrangement substituting for the institution of marriage sanctioned by the State,"[52] and concluded that this should be a legislative rather than a judicial determination.

> It is said that because there are so many unmarried cohabitants today the court must confer a legal status on such relationships. . . . If this is to be the result, however, it would seem more candid to acknowledge the return of varying forms of common law marriage. . . . We cannot confidently say that judicial recognition of property rights between unmarried cohabitants will not make that alternative to marriage more attractive by allowing the parties to engage in such relationships with greater security. . . . we believe the appellate court decision in this case contravenes the [Illinois statute's] policy of strengthening and preserving the integrity of marriage.[53]

In effect, the *Hewitt* case expresses the need to develop a conception of society that encompasses but goes beyond our social mores. Roberto Unger observes:

> [The classic social theorists] wanted to create a body of objective knowledge of society that would not be at the mercy of metaphysical speculation . . . and, up to a point, they succeeded. But now we see that to resolve its own dilemmas, social theory must once again become, in a sense, both metaphysical and political. . . . The doctrines theory embraces are ideals as

51 Ibid., 1208–09.
52 Ibid.
53 Ibid.

> well as descriptions: the choices theory must make are choices among conceptions of what society ought to be as [well as] among views of what it is. These choices are neither arbitrary nor capable of logical or empirical proof. They build upon speculative conceptions of the requirements of social order and of the demands of human nature.[54]

Faced with dramatic changes in the structure of living arrangements and intimate relationships, the *Hewitt* court engaged in the "channeling function of law,"[55] which seeks to support desirable social institutions.[56] It promoted the integrity of the institution of marriage by penalizing sexual relations outside the legally and socially controlled institution of marriage, which has been described as "monogamous, heterosexual and permanent."[57] The existence of an alternate lifestyle, it contended, does not in itself warrant legal ratification of that conduct.

Implicitly adopting a conceptualization of society that seeks to preserve the institution of the family, *Hewitt* harnesses the channeling function of law to that end. *Hewitt*'s progeny, rendered in many jurisdictions, deny cohabiters statutory benefits — such as wrongful death, worker's compensation, inheritance tax status, spousal support, and recovery for negligent infliction of emotional stress — traditionally reserved for married couples, as well as the common-law right of a married person to recovery for loss of a spouse's consortium.[58] Rather

54 Roberto Unger, *Law in Modern Society* (NY: 1976), 267.

55 See Carl Schneider, "The channeling function in family law," 20 *Hofstra Law Review* (1992), 495; idem, "State-interest analysis and the channeling function in family law," 55 *Albany Law Review* (1992), 669; J.T. Oldham, *Divorce, Separation and the Distribution of Property* (NY: 2001), §1.02.

56 Schneider, "State-interest," 671. The channeling function can also work by impeding less-desirable institutions: "Sometimes competing institutions are merely disadvantaged. For instance, the rule making contracts for meretricious considerations unenforceable traditionally denied unmarried couples the law's help in resolving some disputes" ("The channeling function," 503). See too Lynn Wardle, "Deconstructing family: a critique of the American Law Institute's 'Domestic Partners' proposal," 2001 *Brigham Young Law Review* 1189, 1224–27.

57 Schneider, "The channeling function," n. 55 above, 500–501.

58 *Chiesa v. Rowe*, 486 F. Supp. 236 (W.D. Michigan 1980), 413 A. 2d 165 (1980); *Tremblay v. Carter*, 390 So. 2d 816 (Fl. App. 1980); *Sostock v. Reiss*, 92 Ill. App. 3d 322, 415 E 2d 1094 (1980); *Sawyer v. Bailey*, 413 A. 2d 165 (Me. 1980); *Haas v. Lewis*, 8 Ohio App. 3d 136, 456 N.E. 2d 512 (1982); *Tapley v. Tapley* 122 N.H. 727, 449 A. 2d 1218 (1982); *Nieto v. City of Los Angeles*, 138 Cal. App. 3d 464, 188 Cal. Rptr. 31 (1982); *Schwegmann v. Schwegmann*, 441

than paying lip service to the *Marvin* doctrine, but holding that the contract is neither proven nor implicit, these courts, following *Hewitt*, affirm the integrity of marriage and refuse to grant relief to meretricious spouses for claims to benefits associated with the status of marriage, as opposed to contractual remedies.

Though *Hewitt* and other courts claim that *Marvin* sought to resurrect the doctrine of common-law marriage and derogate from the institution of marriage, the *Marvin* court, aware that its holding could be misconstrued, emphasized the following:

> Lest we be misunderstood, however, we take this occasion to point out that the structure of society itself largely depends upon the institution of marriage, and nothing we have said in this opinion should be taken to derogate from that institution. The joining of the man and woman in marriage is at once the most socially productive and individually fulfilling relationship that one can enjoy in the course of a lifetime.[59]

In effect, the court is affirming a view of marriage as a means of personal fulfillment at both the individual and the social levels.[60]

How does the *Marvin* court legally define the status of a man and woman who are living together as spouses? Are all long-term, stable

---

So. 2d 316 (La. Ct. App. 1983), cert. denied, 443 So. 2d 1122 (La.), cert. denied, 104 S. Ct. 2389 (1984); *Felch v. Air Florida*, 562 F. Supp. 383 (D.D.C. 1983); *Laws v. Griep*, 332 N.W. 2d 339 (Iowa 1983); *Hendrix v. General Motors Corp.*, 146 Cal. App. 3d 296, 193 Cal. Rptr. 922 (1983); *Slocum v. Hammond*, 346 N.W. 2d 485, 491 (Iowa 1984); *In re Estate of Alexander*, 445 So. 2d 836 (Miss. 1984); *Elden v. Sheldon*, 164 Cal. App. 3d 745, 210 Cal. Rptr. 755 (1985); *Ledger v. Tippitt*, 164 Cal. App. 3d 625, 210 Cal. Rptr. 814 (1985); *Feliciano v. Rosemary Silver Co.*, 401 Mass. 141, 514 N.E. 2d 1095 (1987); *Elden v. Sheldon*, 46 Cal. 3d 267, 758 P.2d 582, 250 Cal. Rptr. 254 (1988). See Sonja Soehnel, "Annotation, Action for loss of consortium based on nonmarital cohabitation," 40 A.L.R. 4th 553 (1988).

59 *Marvin*, n. 28 above, 831.

60 On the educational and social functions of marriage, see, e.g., Weitzman, n. 35 above, 1241–45; Kelly Martin, "Note, Loss of consortium: should California protect cohabitants' relational interest?" 58 *Southern California Law Review* (1985), 1467, 1475–77; Lynn Wardle, "The use and abuse of rights rhetoric: the constitutional rights of children," 27 *Loyola University Chicago Law Journal* (1996), 321, 327–28. On its role in personal fulfillment, see Glendon, n. 49 above, 115, 173–74. For a communitarian perspective emphasizing traditional family relationships, see, e.g., Milton Regan Jr., *Family Law and the Pursuit of Intimacy* (NY: 1993), 118–25.

relationships to be subsumed under the category of marriage? Traditionally, married spouses are those considered to be married pursuant to state law. The legal regulation of marriage focuses on the terms of the marriage, enforcing them through the sanctions of the legal system.

A second type of spousal relationship is that involving the putative spouse. A putative spouse is an individual who erroneously, but in good faith, believes the relationship to be a legal marriage. Some states have statutorily accorded various rights, including property rights, to putative spouses, and others have created rights for putative spouses judicially. Are individuals who have an ostensibly-marital relationship deemed to be putative spouses? In 1973, a California appeals court, in *In re Marriage of Cary*,[61] concluded that living arrangements that resembled those of a normal family would shift the spouses "from the category of meretricious spouse to the category of putative spouse." Thus, without regard to the existence of a private agreement, express or implied, upon dissolution of the ties, there would be a division of property, traditionally reserved for legally-married couples only. Rejecting this judicially-created right for cohabitants, *Marvin* argued that property benefits could be expected only in situations where there was a legal marriage or a putative spousal relationship. It refused to accord status to a meretricious relationship and grant cohabiters rights analogous to those of married or putative spouses under California law. In effect, *Marvin*'s rationale reflects the desire to preserve the integrity of the status of marriage.

However, the *Marvin* court rejected the judicial approach taken by *Hewitt*,[62] which totally bars recovery of property rights for cohabiters. Whereas *Hewitt* rejected *Marvin*'s "changing mores" argument and claimed that recognition of cohabiters' property rights amounts to de facto recognition of common-law marriage, *Marvin* insisted that the granting of legal and equitable remedies neither reinstates

61 *In re Marriage of Cary*, 109 Cal. Rptr. 862, 866–867 (Ct. App. 1973). For critique of the decision, see "Note, *In re Cary*: a judicial recognition of illicit cohabitation," 25 *Hastings Law Journal* (1974), 1226, 1227–29; Kay and Amyx, n. 1 above, 951–54. A decision issued in the same year as *Marvin*, adopting the same approach as *Cary*, granted de facto status to a meretricious relationship, see *Latham v. Hennessey*, 87 Wash. 2d 550, 554, P.2d 1057 (1976).

62 *Hewitt*, n. 7 above, 1208–209.

common-law marriage nor undermines the institution of marriage.[63] Michelle Marvin's claims differed significantly from those that would have been made in a case involving common-law marriage. To substantiate the existence of a common-law marriage, it must be demonstrated that the parties live together, agree to be husband and wife, and hold themselves out to the community as married. Michelle Marvin's claim for relief was based on contract theories, not marital-status theories.

Marvin's granting of relief to cohabiters was predicated on the recognition that a court can take the lead by identifying a norm of conventional morality and establishing a new legal rule on the basis of this social norm. On the one hand, the court was mindful of Holmes's admonition:

> As law embodies beliefs that have triumphed in the battle of ideas and then have translated themselves into action, while there still is doubt, while opposite convictions still keep a battle front against each other, the time for law has not come; the notion destined to prevail is not yet entitled to the field.[64]

Recognition that the norm exists is not sufficient. One norm may be perceived by the community as more prevalent than another; one norm may be more resilient than another, or may better reflect the community's moral standards. In the final analysis, courts are obliged to discern the prevailing social morality, ascertain the requisite social support, and bring legal rules into congruence with the norms in question.[65] "In his application of precedent, as in the interpretation of statutes, the judge must take note of major shifts in public opinion and social policy, of developments sufficiently fundamental to be accepted by the consensus of public opinion."[66]

Granting that social mores are 'out there' and can be 'discovered,' they represent only the first step in establishing a new rule. An apparent norm of social morality may reflect only the mores of a single group. The prerequisite for the establishment of a new rule is the existence of

63 Cf. M. Willemsen, "Justice Tobriner and the tolerance of evolving lifestyles: adapting the law to social change," 29 *Hastings Law Journal* (1977/78), 73, which contends that *Marvin's* "changing mores" arguments reflect the judge's personal ideology.

64 Oliver W. Holmes, *Collected Legal Papers* (NY: 1920) 291, 294–95.

65 Melvin Eisenberg, *The Nature of the Common Law* (Boston: 1988), 18–19.

66 Wolfgang Friedmann, *Law in a Changing Society* (NY: 1972), 54.

a broad social consensus that renders it conventional morality.[67] It is thus social consensus regarding cohabitation which mandates that the *Marvin* court fashion remedies to protect those in cohabitation relationships.

Does *Marvin* invoke a moralistic stance regarding informal unions? Clearly, it does not, holding that the law should be neutral as to the morality of alternative living arrangements. Rejecting the court of appeal's moralistic approach, *Marvin* states: "the mores of society have indeed changed so radically in regard to cohabitation that we cannot impose a standard based on alleged moral considerations that have apparently been so widely abandoned by so many."[68]

Rather than validate contracts that contemplate a non-marital relationship, Justice Tobriner in *Marvin* asserted that "so long as the agreement does not rest upon illicit meretricious consideration, the parties may order their economic affairs as they choose, and no policy precludes the courts from enforcing such agreements."[69] In effect, by employing the doctrine of severability, *Marvin* removes from judicial consideration the moral question of whether the state can validate a contract based on what some deem a morally-offensive relationship. By asserting that the sexual relationship was a minor part of the agreement and by excising the agreement's putatively 'immoral' element, the court sidestepped the need to pass judgment on the relationship's moral propriety.[70]

Marvin argued that the vocabulary of morality manifest in prior case law should be replaced by a different language, drawn from contract theory. Rather than raise moral questions, it held that we must address "the reasonable expectations of the parties." In the absence of an express agreement, the *Marvin* directive is to grant relief on the basis of other contractual and equitable theories, such as an implied agreement, constructive or resulting trust, or the quantum meruit doctrine. Furthermore, *Marvin* recognized the need to apply market-like

67 Ibid. Cf. John Ely, *Democracy and Distrust* (Boston: 2006), 63–69.

68 *Marvin*, n. 28 above, 831. A similar disavowal of the appropriateness of moral condemnation of informal unions is expressed in *In re Estate of Thornton*, 81 Wash. 2d 72, 76 499 P.2d 864, 867 (1972).

69 See text at n. 27 above.

70 Hunter, n. 30 above, 1077, and see text above at n. 31. *Marvin's* labeling the relationship "meretricious" is inconsistent with its advocacy of moral neutrality regarding the propriety of informal unions.

concepts, viz., contractual constructs, to domestic situations.[71] Whereas prior to *Marvin*, its proximity to marriage was the measure of a relationship's legal significance, "the legal system of a society which now accepts non-marital cohabitation must protect the reasonable expectations of those persons choosing the alternative lifestyle."[72] In effect, marital status had become merely one of the tests for ascertaining a relationship's significance. Rather than defining family relationships in accordance with the nuclear family model, which recognizes only relationships that arise from marriage, the *Marvin* court adopts a functional approach, inquiring whether the relationship functions in a manner similar to that of a legally-married couple, and therefore should be accorded the same recognition and protection.

Marvin deems it theoretically feasible to legally regulate domestic relationships on the basis of a contractual construct combined with de jure marriage. Aptly characterized as a "hybrid model," it has been described thus:

> Without accepting the socially-defined status of marriage, parties can enter any type of contractual relationship they wish without fear that the relationship will be deemed a de facto marriage. Contract remedies, and possibly tort and equitable remedies will be available if the relationship breaks down, on the theory that unmarried couples are entitled to the same range of remedies as partners in a business arrangement. The arrangement is not considered meretricious, and therefore illegal, unless sex is explicitly made consideration for an agreement. . . . The couple is also free to decide on marriage if both so agree.[73]

Without delineating the practical differences between a married couple and cohabitants, *Marvin* held, in effect, that a married couple is governed by a status-oriented approach, and cohabiters by a contractual approach.[74] Contract theory allows cohabiters to opt for an informal union that allows for a degree of flexibility in ordering their financial affairs, rather than marriage, where the terms of the relationship — such as federal income tax liabilities, and social security and pension repercussions — are dictated by the state. Whereas *Hewitt* and its

71 Havighurst, n. 43 above.

72 W. Glucksman and M. Mitchelson, "Equal protection for unmarried cohabitors: an insider's look at *Marvin v. Marvin*," 5 *Pepperdine Law Review* (1978), 283–85.

73 Ellen Kandoian, "Cohabitation, common law marriage, and the possibility of a shared moral life," 75 *Georgia Law Journal* (1986/87), 1829, 1856.

74 On the ramifications of this distinction, see Hunter, n. 30 above, 1084–96.

progeny promote the publicly-imposed value of traditional marriage, *Marvin* and its progeny defer to the value of individual freedom, whereby the state, through its lawmakers, allows individuals to choose between competing lifestyles.

Though many courts reject the *Marvin* holding[75] and argue for the preservation of a firm distinction between the legal treatment of married and unmarried unions, numerous jurisdictions[76] invoke the *Marvin* contract rubric, imposing obligations on cohabiters on the basis of explicit agreements or implied agreements emerging from the parties' behavior or grounded in a quasi-contractual quantum meruit theory.[77]

75 See n. 58 above.

76 See, inter alia: *Dombrowski v. Somers*, 41 N.Y. 2d 858, 393 N.Y.S. 2d 706, 362 N.E. 2d 257 (1977); *Humiston v. Bushnell*, 394 A. 2d 844 (N.H. 1978); *Jiminez v. Jimenez*, 68 Ill. App. 3d 651, 25 Ill. Dec. 376, 386 N.E. 2d 647 (1979); *Gilbert v. Cliché*, 398 A. 2d 387 (Me. 1979); *Kozlowski v. Kozlowski*, 403 A. 2d 902 (N.J. 1979); *Morone v. Morone*, 413 N.E. 2d 1154, 1157 (N.Y. 1980); *In re Estate of Steffes*, 95 Wis. 2d 490, 290 N.W. 2d 697 (1980); *Hill v. Ames*, 606 P.2d 388 (Alaska 1980); *Glasgo v. Glasgo*, 410 N.E. 2d 1325 (Ind. Ct. App. 1980); *Joan S. v. John S.*, 121 N.H. 96, 427 A. 2d 498 (1981); *Artiss v. Artiss*, 8 Fam. L. Rep. (BNA) 2313 (Hawaii Cir. Ct. 1982); *Poe v. Estate of Levy*, 411 So. 2d 253 (Fla. Dist. Ct. App. 1982); *Merill v. Davis*, 100 N.M. 552, 673 P.2d 1285 (1983); *Alexander v. Alexander*, 445 S. 2d 836 (Miss. 1984); *Hay v. Hay*, 100 Nev. 196, 678 P.2d 672 (1984); *Mason v. Rostad*, 476 A. 2d 662 (D.C. Ct. App. 1984); *Nelson v. Nevel*, 154 Cal. App. 132, 201 Cal. Rptr. 93 (1984); *Eaton v. Johnston*, 672 P.2d 106 (Kan. Ct. App. 1984); *Carroll v. Lee*, 148 Ariz. 10, 712 P.2d 923 (1986); *Watts v. Watts*, 405 N.W. 2d 303 (Wis. 1987); *Goode v. Goode*, 396 S.E. 2d 430 (W. Va. 1990); *Shuraleff v. Donnelly*, 817 P.2d 764 (Or. Ct. App. 1991); *Wilbur v. DeLapp*, 850 P.2d 1151 (Or. Ct. App. 1993); *Connell v. Francisco*, n. 46 above; *Bright v. Kuehl*, 650 N.E. 2d 311, 315 (Ind. Ct. App. 1995); *Byrne v. Laura*, 60 Cal. Rptr. 3d 908 (Ct. App. 1997).

77 *Beal v. Beal* 282 Or. 115, 577 P.2d 507 (1978); *Rogelis v. Pettis*, 49 Or. App. 537, 619 P.2d 1339 (1980); *Holloway v. Holloway*, 63 Or. App. 343, 663 P.2d 798 (1983); *In re Marriage of Lindsey*, 678 P.2d 328 (Wash. 1984); *Warden v. Warden*, 36 Wash. App. 693, 676 P.2d 1037 (1984); *In re Marriage of Burton*, 758 P.2d 394 (Or. Ct. App. 1988); *Foster v. Thilges*, 812 P.2d 523 (Wash. Ct. App. 1991); *In re Marriage of Lindemann*, 960 P.2d 966 (Wash. Ct. App. 1998); *Koher v. Morgan*, n. 46 above; *Mitchell v. Moore*, 729 A. 2d. 1200 (Pa. Super Ct. 1999); *Salzman v. Bachrach*, 996 P.2d 1263 (Colo. 2000); *Pederson v. Anibas*, 2001 WI. 969176 (Wis. Ct. App. 2001).

Some states have invoked matrimonial property principles as a basis for property distribution on the termination of cohabitation, see *Connell v. Francisco*, n. 46 above; *Marriage of Lindsey; Wilbur v. DeLapp*, n. 76 above; *Pickens v. Pickens*, 490 So. 2d 872 (Miss. 1986).

Other states, such as Oregon and Washington, have, in the footsteps of *In re Marriage of Cary*, eschewed contract theory as a basis for relief. Instead, they have assimilated informal unions into the legal framework of marriage by awarding property rights and benefits such as health insurance, pensions, and insurance rights on the basis of cohabitation that is long-term, stable, and pseudo-marital. In effect, these jurisdictions have adopted a 'domestic partnership' model and invoked a status approach to long-term cohabitation, a perspective endorsed by many American jurists.[78] Nevertheless, this legal status falls short of marriage by failing to link rights to responsibilities. "To date, partnerships have conferred benefits only; the most logical progression is for partnerships to include responsibilities of support, commitment and obligation within the economic partnership construct of emerging family law."[79]

Though 'domestic partnership' is not treated like legal marriage in all respects, the line between informal unions and traditional marriage has been blurred nonetheless.[80] Indeed, even the jurisdictions that

78 American Law Institute, Principles of the Law of Family Dissolution: Analysis and Recommendations (Tentative Draft 4, 2000), §6.02, 10–14; Blumberg, n. 4 above; Folberg and Buren, n. 35 above; Ellman, "Theory of alimony," n. 46 above; Deech, n. 46 above; "Note, "Living together: the need for a uniform nonmarital cohabitation act," 2 *Adelphia Law Journal* (1983), 79; Craig Bowman and Blake Cornish, "Note, A more perfect union: a legal and social analysis of domestic partnership ordinances," 92 *Columbia Law Review* (1992), 1164; Amy Lim, "Comment, In defense of Washington's equitable treatment of pseudomarital property," 29 *Idaho Law Review* (1992), 975; Cynthia Bowman, "A feminist proposal to bring back common law marriage," 75 *Oregon Law Review* (1996), 709; Rebecca Bailey-Harris, "Law and the unmarried couple — oppression or liberation?" 8 *Child and Family Law Quarterly* (1996), 137.

A few states have imposed the obligations applicable to married couples on cohabiting couples. See *In re Marriage of Cary*, n. 61 above, 866–67; *Estate of Atherley*, 119 Cal. Rptr. 41, 46–48 (Ct. App. 1975); *Evans v. Wall*, 542 So. 2d 1055, 1056–1057 (Fla. Dist. Ct. App. 1989); *Sullivan v. Rooney*, 533 N.E. 2d 1372, 1374 (Mass. 1989); *Pickens v. Pickens*, n. 77 above, 875–876; *Latham v. Hennessey*, n. 61 above; *Foster v. Thilges*, n. 77 above; *Connell v. Francisco*, n. 46 above.

79 Raymond O'Brien, "Domestic partnership: recognition and responsibility," 32 *San Diego Law Review* (1995), 163. And see Reppy, n. 5 above, 1716–23.

80 On the one hand, some states have enacted legislation recognizing the partnership model, see Sanford N. Katz, "New directions for family law in

adopted the *Marvin* contract rubric have contributed to this outcome, by allowing the consequences of cohabitation to resemble those of marriage. Though *Marvin* seeks to uphold a hybrid of traditional marriage and cohabitation, and not to blur the distinction between them, empirical reality reveals that cohabiters are fulfilling exactly the same functions as, and assuming roles analogous to those of, their married counterparts. Responding to this social change, the law has created legal constructs that regard cohabitation as de facto marriage, providing for third-party benefits traditionally available only to family members. Cohabiting partners, who presumably espouse an ethos of individualism and freedom of self-definition, are increasingly being granted legal protection for this autonomy.

That judicial decisions are a function of social forces was remarked on by Felix Cohen nearly eighty years ago:

> A truly realistic theory of judicial decisions must conceive every decision as something more than an expression of individual personality, as concomitantly and even more importantly a function of social forces, that is to say, as a product of social determinants and an index of social consequences. . . . Behind the decision are social forces that play upon it to give it a resultant momentum and direction. . . . Only by probing behind the decision to the forces which it reflects, or projecting beyond the decision the lines of its force upon the future, do we come to an understanding of the meaning of the decision itself.[81]

Undoubtedly, social forces impacting the prevalence of marriage and alternative modes of cohabitation/partnership shaped *Marvin* and its progeny, and these decisions cannot be said to simply reflect personal ideologies of the judges who made them. They illustrate that law and legal change are not autonomous, self-contained entities, but context-driven products of social morality.

---

the United States" (2007). *Boston College Law School Faculty Papers*. Paper 202, p. 13 n. 24. On the other hand, numerous jurisdictions have resisted extending marital benefits and privileges to the unmarried; see text at n. 58 above. On the varying approaches to awarding legal benefits to cohabitants, see, e.g., Martin, n. 60 above; Carol Bruch, "Cohabitation in the common law countries a decade after *Marvin*: settled in or moving ahead?" 22 *University of California Davis Law Review* (1989), 699, 729–33.

81 Felix Cohen, "Transcendental nonsense and the functional approach," 35 *Columbia Law Review* (1935), 809, 843. See also idem, "Field theory and judicial logic," 59 *Yale L. J.* (1950), 238.

2. Contractual consequences of cohabitation in Jewish law

Contract is a legal mechanism for ordering certain areas of conduct and for the creation of financial obligations between parties; it is a means of governance. As we have seen, American law does not evince a uniform attitude to contractual governance of financial relationships between unmarried partners. Does the Jewish legal system, as reflected in contemporary sources,[82] recognize, enforce, and adjudicate disputes over, financial duties emerging from informal unions? To develop an analytical framework for investigating this question, let us first examine Jewish law's view of the financial responsibilities of individuals within the wider context of marital and non-marital relations, beginning with the marital relationship itself.[83] Basically, in Jewish law, the marital relationship can be said to be an agreement, albeit a special one, that establishes the personal status of *ishut* on the basis of the parties' willing consent.

What are the components of this consensual agreement to establish a marital relationship? Marriage consists of two separate acts, *kidushin* (betrothal) and *nisuin* (the marriage ceremony). These have been characterized as follows:

> In practical terms, *kidushin* as the primary state of Jewish marriage can be . . . normatively constituted through the presence of five halakhic elements. . . . At the helm stands *kavanah*: intention. But intention for what? Two divergent directions emerge. . . . According to one authority, the intent of the couple must be for at least the most minimal and natural characteristics of the marital experience. . . . That decision, however, must also include the stipulation that the wife shall be exclusively related to her husband and prohibited to all others. From this intent of *leshem ishut* will then flow all other authority which will bestow legitimacy and direction

82 Jewish law is recorded in various authoritative literary sources, including the Talmud, the classic commentaries, novellae, codifications, and responsa (juridical authorities' decisions on legal queries from judges and communal leaders). On these sources, and on the adjudicative tools of Jewish law, see M. Elon, *Jewish Law: History, Sources, Principles*, translated by B. Auerbach and M.J. Sykes (Philadelphia: 1994).

83 See B.Z. Shereschewsky, "Marriage" and "Husband and wife," in M. Elon (ed.) *The Principles of Jewish Law* (Jerusalem: 1975) 356, 379–387; J. David Bleich, "Jewish divorce: judicial misconceptions and possible means of civil enforcement," 16 *Connecticut Law Review* (1984), 201, 227–30, 256–57; Michael Broyde, *Marriage, Divorce and the Abandoned Wife in Jewish Law* (NY: 2001) 119–23, 184.

> upon the formal ceremony and simultaneously form the foundation of the *kidushin*. The other view finds the natural standard utterly inadequate. . . . What, then, shall be the normative canon for *kavanah*? It must be *lekidushei Torah* or *leshem kidushin* . . . a conscious awareness that the ceremony must be *kedin*, in faithful fulfillment of the hallowed imperatives of Jewish law. . . .
>
> The intention to marry must be visibly objectified, in order both to articulate as well as to inculcate the core ideas of that *kavanah*. Jewish tradition, therefore, devised two more patterns of action to achieve tangibility. One of them was the *amirah*, an official verbal declaration of marital *kavanah* to be made directly by the groom to his bride in a formal and public style. . . . The other act . . . was the *netinah*, giving, initiated again by the groom and complemented by the parallel *kabbalah*, receipt, by the bride. These sequential acts of "give and take" involve an object . . . traditionally a ring. . . .
>
> But not only must these facets of *kavanah* be shared between bride and groom. Normally, the halakhah also demands . . . *ratson* — a fourth element, involving the couple's voluntary assent to all parts of the *erusin* [i.e., *kidushin* (RW)]. . . .
>
> Finally, a Jewish marriage must be witnessed by at least two qualified *edim*, whose responsibility is two-fold. When necessary, they . . . can help establish the facts and certify the . . . degree of compliance with the prerequisites of Jewish marriage law. Yet, even more critical is their role as . . . witnesses who by their very presence and participation at the ceremony constitute the validity of the *ma'aseh kidushin* [act of betrothal (RW)].[84]

In short, the subjective marital intentions of the man and woman are translated into reality via verbal articulation and other modes of concretization, under the scrutiny of witnesses and in the presence of an officiating rabbi and public assemblage, for the express purpose of establishing a consensual marital union.

The betrothal (*kidushin*) relationship too may be said to be a consensual agreement,[85] again, a very special agreement that establishes a personal status, namely, that of a *mekudeshet*, a woman designated for a particular man and prohibited to all others.[86] The establishment of this status (*ishut*) renders both spouses subject to various prohibitions, e.g.,

84 Norman Frimer and Dov Frimer, "Reform marriages in contemporary halakhic responsa," *Tradition* 21 (1984), 9–11.

85 On elements that establish voluntary assent, see *SA*, EH 26, 37–39, 43–44.

86 "The woman becomes prohibited to all others in the same way as that which is consecrated to the Temple (*hekdesh*) [becomes prohibited for other uses]" (bKidushin 2b).

sexual relations with various relatives become prohibited.[87] The act of betrothal also creates financial obligations that will be transformed into spousal duties on completion of the marriage ceremony (*nisuin*).[88]

Given the multi-dimensional nature of the marital bond, are financial relations between spouses grounded in the norms of Jewish civil

87 See Eli Lifshitz, "The ordering of marital relations" (Hebrew), in E. Lifshitz et al. (eds.), *The Obligations of Husband and Wife* (Hebrew), (Har Etzion: 1984), 7–35.

88 Whether these financial obligations arise from the essence of betrothal or are derivative, and the ramifications of this distinction, are beyond the scope of this article; see R. Asher Weiss, *Minhat Asher*, Baba Batra, #36 and Berachyahu Lifshitz, "The substance and framework of the doctrine of community property" (Hebrew), 3 *Hamishpat* (1996), 239, 247–48. Though generally, these obligations come into being after the marriage ceremony (*SA*, EH 55:4–6, 56:3, 61:1) and any marriage is pursuant to this presumption (see 6 *PDR* [Israeli Rabbinical Court Rulings] 353, 366–67), Jewish law recognizes that betrothal can create monetary duties that are dormant unless activated by a contractual agreement between the betrothed couple. E.g., prior to betrothal, when there is no personal–legal tie between the couple, a prenuptial property arrangement is null and void. Hence, an agreement whereby the prospective husband renounces his future rights in his prospective wife's property (*siluk*) [e.g., "I have no rights in this woman's property . . . and its fruits and the fruits of its fruits in perpetuity"] is null and void. See 1 *PDR* 289, 300–302. Though this type of agreement destroys the presumption established by the default rule, viz., the prescribed matrimonial property regime (discussed in Schereschewsky, "Dowry," in Elon, n. 83 above, 390–92), after the betrothal, the parties can negotiate such an agreement. See *Sema, SA*, HM 209:21; R. David b. Samuel, *Turei Zahav, SA*, HM 209:3; *Ketzot Hahoshen*, HM 209:13. According to some contemporary decisors, pursuant to specific rules governing obligations, such agreements can be finalized prior to betrothal; see 7 *PDR* 353, 366; R. Tzvi Ben-Yaakov, *Mishpatekha Leyaakov*, 2:47; Simcha Meron, *Proposals for Agreements on Property Arrangements between Spouses* (Hebrew), (Jerusalem: nd), 4; R. Yoezer Ariel, *Torat Hamishpat*, 389–92 (in the name of R. Z.N. Goldberg); Basil Herring and Kenneth Auman, *The Prenuptial Agreement: Halakhic and Pastoral Considerations* (NY: 1997), R. Solomon Dichovsky, "Prenuptial agreements" (Hebrew), *Tehumin* 21 (2001), 279. On prenuptial agreements, see also *Responsa Havot Yair*, #47; *Responsa Avodat Hagershuni*, #50–51; R. Arye Leib Heller, *Avnei Miluim*, EH 92:5; R. Abraham Eisenstadt, *Pithei Teshuva*, EH 92:1. Note that though the spouses must generally begin to fulfill their respective obligations at the onset of marriage, there is precedent for awarding spousal support to a betrothed woman whose marriage is not consummated. On the rationales for awarding such support, see 3 *PDR* 44, 51.

law, or in the marital relationship (*ishut*) that exists between the spouses?[89] Without addressing the entire gamut of spousal financial relations, let us focus on how various Israeli rabbinical courts understand spousal maintenance (*mezonot*).

On the one hand, spousal maintenance is similar to a conventional debt. Though it is an obligation *ex lege*, an obligation imposed by the system by dint of the marriage rather than a contractual duty, it is similar to a debt in that the wife may, if she so chooses, opt out of receiving spousal maintenance from her husband. Furthermore, if spousal maintenance funds for a prescribed period of time are either stolen or lost while in the wife's possession, since the husband's duty (*hiyuv*) has been discharged, he is exempt from reimbursing his wife for the lost funds.[90] Further, payment of spousal maintenance does not take precedence over any liens placed on the husband's property by his creditors.[91]

On the other hand, there are many provisions indicating that the spousal maintenance obligation is qualitatively different from a conventional debt. Unlike other legal systems which preclude tort actions between spouses for personal injury on the basis of the interspousal immunity doctrine, Jewish law allows spouses to sue each other for injuries incurred during marriage. What happens if a husband claims to have been injured by his wife, and she is unable to compensate him for the inflicted injury? Is the husband entitled to offset his tort claim against her from the maintenance due her? One Israeli rabbinical court concluded that the wife is entitled to her maintenance, and should the couple later divorce, the offset vis-à-vis the tort claim is to be resolved

89 1 *PDR* 289, 313. On private ordering in domestic relations, see Z. Warhaftig, *Studies in Jewish Law* (Hebrew), (Ramat-Gan: 1985), 136–47; Maidi Katz, "The married woman and her expense account: a study of the married woman's ownership and use of marital property in Jewish law," 13 *Jewish Law Annual* (2000), 101–41; R. Warburg, "A comparative analysis of a wife's capacity to pledge her husband's credit for domestic necessities in Anglo-American law and Jewish law,"13 *Jewish Law Annual* (2000), 213–38; idem, "The varying approaches in arrangement of spousal monetary relations" (Hebrew), *Hadarom* 71–72 (2001), 129.

90 1 *PDR* 333, 339; 11:193, 208; 16:44, 52. Cf. R. Jacob Blau, *Pithei Hoshen*, Inheritance and Marriage, 360 n. 10.

91 3 *PDR* 109, 112, 114, 299, 309. On the various rationales for this rule, see 17 *PDR* 311, 315. See *SA*, EH 70:8 and *Rema* ad loc. regarding an additional similarity between spousal maintenance and conventional debts.

at that time.[92] Indeed, there can be no reduction of spousal maintenance payments due to any monetary claim a husband may have against his wife.[93] Invoking the rule regarding assessment of what a creditor is entitled to collect from his debtor (*mesadrim lebaal hov*), a rabbinical court will exempt certain items from being levied, for example, foodstuffs for thirty days.[94] Nevertheless, a husband who has ample food for only thirty days must share his food with his wife in compliance with his spousal maintenance obligation.[95] Similarly, when food and bedding is insufficient for both spouses, the wife is accorded priority.[96] And whereas an oral loan agreement may be levied only against the debtor's movable assets, and a written loan agreement creates a lien on the debtor's realty,[97] an impoverished husband is obligated to find employment in order to maintain his spouse.[98]

The rationale for the aforementioned provisions is the notion that marriage, by its very essence, generates a personal servitude (*shiabud ishi*) of the husband to the wife.[99] In effect, spousal maintenance is a unique monetary obligation that arises from the status of being in a marital relationship. Spousal maintenance (*mezonot*), by definition, constitutes a "support obligation"[100] rather than a debt to be repaid. Hence, an impoverished husband is obligated to find gainful employment, a husband's actionable tort claims against his wife are deferred, and priority is accorded to the wife's physical necessities. R. Moses Sofer (Hungary, 1762–1839), the *Hatam Sofer*, declares: "if spousal maintenance is absent, there is no marital relationship

92 1 *PDR* 333, 338–39.

93 2 *PDR* 97, 99; 7:136, 154; 11:193, 208; 16:156, 158.

94 *SA*, HM 97: 6–11, 23.

95 *Rema*, *SA*, EH 70:3; 2 *PDR* 65, 87; 3:299, 309; 7:290, 296–98.

96 7 *PDR* 290, 303. However, a destitute husband is exempt from the duty of spousal maintenance, see B. Schereschewsky, *Family Law in Israel* (Hebrew), (Jerusalem: 1993), 110, 112.

97 *SA*, HM 111.

98 2 *PDR* 68, 88; 3:109, 114; 7:290, 303; 10:165–66. For earlier sources, see M. Elon, *Freedom of the Individual in Debt Collection in Jewish Law* (Hebrew), (Jerusalem: 1964), 71–110.

99 Whether this personal servitude is created by the act of marrying or by the ongoing existence of the couple's marital union is a matter of debate, see 2 *PDR* 65, 79; 5:292, 302.

100 2 *PDR* 65, 86–7; 3:110, 114; 17: 313–14.

(*ishut*)!"[101] These words resonate throughout the rabbinical court holdings I have adduced. Conversely, if there is no marital relationship (*ishut*), there is no obligation to pay maintenance. Hence a husband has no obligation to maintain a wife who refuses to engage in sexual relations (*moredet*) or is found to be adulterous.[102]

Many of the rules governing spousal maintenance are thus anchored in the institution of marriage, the personal status it confers (*ishut*), and its multidimensional nature.[103] In addition, they also reflect standard principles of monetary obligations that are actuated at the time of betrothal.[104]

101 *Responsa Hatam Sofer*, EH #131.

102 On the 'rebellious wife' (*moredet*), viz., the wife who refuses to engage in sexual relations, see 1 *PDR* 345; 2:233; 4:321; 6:5; 6:338; 8:261; 9:171; 11:89, 193, 275. Though most authorities concur regarding this characterization of the 'rebellious wife' (see 1 *PDR* 340, 344–45; 6:33, 46), a minority view contends that a wife who fails to engage in her marital duty of housework or contributing earnings from outside work to the family finances, is also a 'rebellious wife' and need not be maintained; see 10 *PDR* 225, 231. On the exemption from the spousal maintenance obligation in the case of an adulterous wife, see 3 *PDR* 257, 267; 4:157, 162. Although there is controversy as to whether an adulterous wife is entitled to maintenance in a case where she will accept a divorce but the husband refuses to grant one, i.e., where she is deemed to be prevented by her husband from remarrying (*meukevet*) (see 3 *PDR* 53; 4 *PDR* 162), the basis for maintenance in this situation differs from that of a maintenance order based on marriage; see 1 *PDR* 74, 77–80; 3:44, 52, 208; 7:290, 294; 10:294.

103 The thesis that these norms reflect the personal status conferred by marriage as well as the standard rules of the law of obligations was put forward by Schereschewsky, n. 96 above, 111 n. 20, 112 n. 21, 127–28. As Berachyahu Lifshitz has argued, the norms governing a widow's maintenance and the distinction between present and past maintenance obligations may serve other purposes.

104 The role of the element of personal status created by marriage in generating the rules of maintenance is borne out in the decisions by Israeli rabbinical court judge R. Eliezer Goldschmidt. In one of his earliest decisions (2 *PDR* 65, reprinted in E. Goldschmidt, *Ezer Mishpat*, 130–49), R. Goldschmidt addresses the propriety of attaching the property (*ikul*) of the obligor husband to satisfy his maintenance obligations to his obligee wife. If a wife is concerned about the future availability of her husband's assets because she fears he is dissipating them, and thus wishes to attach them prior to the date a maintenance payment is due, it might seem that she ought to receive these assets, as she would in the case of a conventional debt, as collateral security. R. Goldschmidt demurs, arguing that

The preceding discussion establishes the analytical framework for defining the nature of the maintenance obligation within the context of permitted marital relations. Let us now move on to the context of prohibited marital relationships.

The classic examples of prohibited marriages are marriage between a *kohen* (descendant of the priestly class) and a divorcee, and marriage between a woman who committed adultery and was divorced by her husband, and the lover with whom she had the adulterous relations.[105] In such cases, the marriage is permitted after the fact (*bediavad*), and prohibited *ab initio* (*lekhathila*).[106] In other words, though the marriage is recognized as valid after the fact, the halakhic system does not allow a

---

there is controversy as to whether the obligation to pay maintenance is created at the time of marriage and the debt is paid off daily, or it is created daily. Those who take the latter approach contend that since the debt does not exist, one can never attach property to satisfy future spousal maintenance payments. Hence, a wife's request for attachment ought to be rejected.

However, realizing the reasonableness of the wife's concerns that the husband might dissipate his assets and flee the rabbinical court's jurisdiction to avoid paying maintenance, R. Goldschmidt invokes civil court procedures (rather than the norms of debt repayment), and mandates the property attachment so as to prevent the husband from dissipating or absconding with his wife's maintenance.

Upon further reflection, R. Goldschmidt concludes that even in the absence of reasonable grounds for ordering an attachment, all decisors (even those who claim that the debt is created daily) concur that the personal servitude (*shiabud ishi*) element of marriage in itself is a sufficient ground for attaching the husband's assets; he thus allows the court to coerce a husband to pay his future spousal obligations in the present.

105 *SA*, EH 6:1; 5 *PDR* 219, 221; *SA*, EH 11:1. For other examples of prohibited but valid marriages, see Schereschewsky, "Marriage, prohibited," in Elon, n. 83 above, 361–62; E. Shochetman, *Legal Validity of Actions involving Transgressions* (Hebrew), (Jerusalem: 1981), 83.

106 For a jurisprudential perspective on the relationship between '*ab initio*' and '*ex post facto*' in Jewish law, see Shai Wozner, "Consistency and effectiveness in the halakhah, as reflected in the *lekhathila-bediavad* distinction" (Hebrew), 20–21 *Dine Israel* (2001), 43, 49. On the ex post facto validity of prohibited marriages, see bJebamot 23a; R. Ezekiel Landau, *Responsa Noda Biyehuda*, 2nd edition, EH #50; *Responsa R. Akiva Eger*, #129; *Hidushei Harashba*, bKidushin 67b. Though valid, the court generally compels the dissolution of such marriages, see *SA*, EH 6:1; *Rema, SA*, EH 154:21.

rabbi to officiate at such a wedding, as that would constitute approval of a prohibited marriage.[107]

The danger of validating these marriages does not lie simply in rewarding sinners for their misdeeds. In the words of the Rabbinical High Court of Appeal,

> It is clear that one may not demand of the Court that it violate the *halakhah* and certify and support a ruling that they are husband and wife. . . . this would mean that the Court itself would set a precedent that would validate the marriages of every such couple that succeeds somehow . . . in placing the Court in a position after the fact, as if it were facing an "existing fact"; that is, the Court would aid with its own hands in tearing hole after hole in the fabric of family life in Israel.[108]

In other words, issuing declaratory judgments validating these marital unions would invite additional requests to recognize such marriages and thereby contribute to weakening of the family.

Moreover, once the system serves as the arbiter of which intimate relationships are to be recognized under the rubric of marriage, the institution of marriage itself provides the normative model for the legal regulation of prohibited marriages. The legal consequence of contracting a prohibited marriage, is, as in the case of a permissible marriage, a change in legal status. The wife acquires the status of a presumptive married woman (*hezkat eishet ish*), who is entitled to maintenance. However, since here, unlike the case of a permissible marriage, Jewish

107 On the ramifications of the legitimation of prohibited marriages a priori, see, e.g., R. Abraham Kook, *Responsa Ezrat Kohen*, #20; 6 *PDR* 288, 289; J. David Bleich, *Bintivot Hahalakha*, 1:56–6; Getsel Ellinson, *Non-Halakhic Marriage* (Hebrew), (Jerusalem: 1980), 88–90. Cf. 4 *PDR* 306; Shimshon Ettinger, "The High Court of Justice — a retreat for captives of marriage?" (Hebrew), 4 *Mishpatim* (1972), 428; I. Englard, *Religious Law in the Israeli Legal System* (Jerusalem: 1975), 159–77; P. Shifman, *Doubtful Marriage in Israeli Law* (Hebrew), (Jerusalem: 1975), 133–43; Ariel Rosen-Zvi, "A Jewish and democratic state: spiritual paternity, alienation, and symbiosis — can one square the circle?" in idem (ed.), *A Jewish* and *Democratic State* (Hebrew), (Tel Aviv: 1996), 11, 36–37. And see n. 109 below.

108 App. 80/1956, cited in E. Shochetman, *Seder Hadin* (Hebrew), (Jerusalem: 1988), 177 n. 80, translated in Shochetman's "Civil marriage in the State of Israel," in M. Freeman (ed.), 13 *Jewish Law Association Studies* (2002), 131, 163.

law seeks dissolution of the marital union, the wife is not entitled to maintenance.[109]

Despite its disapproval of imposing the duty of maintenance when a marriage is prohibited, Jewish law does recognize the validity

109 bJebamot 85a; *SA*, EH 116:1; 6 *PDR* 281, 289. Cf. R. Johanan's position (according to one tradition) in jJebamot 9:5; Maimonides, *Code*, Laws concerning Marriage 24:4; R. Vidal of Tolosa, *Magid Mishne* ad loc. If the husband knows that the marriage is prohibited, his wife will be entitled to payment of the sums specified in the marriage contract (*ketuba*). Upon the husband's demise, the widow is entitled to maintenance from his estate, see 4 *PDR* 157; Schereschewsky, n. 83 above, 213–15, 326–29; M. Chigier, *Husband and Wife in Israeli Law* (Jerusalem: 1985), 146–47. The reasoning here is that whereas entitlement to maintenance in a prohibited marriage may aid the sinners and undermine the family, a widow's claiming maintenance from her husband's estate will not encourage these marriages, see 5 *PDR* 219, 223. To facilitate dissolution of such marriages, a recalcitrant husband who refuses to divorce his wife and thereby prevents her from remarrying is obligated to pay her maintenance. See R. Isaac Herzog, *Responsa Heikhal Yitzhak*, EH 1:1, R. Ben-Zion Uziel and R. Moses Toledano, *Otzar Haposkim* 2, note on p. 8; 1 *PDR* 51, 54, 55, 235, 238; 2:9–14; 3:44–57; 11:300–308. The idea that "a sinner ought not be rewarded" (bJebamot 92b) motivates the Talmud (bJebamot 85a) and others (6 *PDR* 281, 288) to impose the duty of maintenance on the husband. Hence during the marriage, the wife is not offered financial support, as an incentive for her to voluntarily dissolve the marriage. If, upon expressing willingness to do so, she is confronted with a recalcitrant husband, the system deems her to be prevented from remarrying (*meukevet*), and mandates support. See Chigier, 112.

There is a controversy among the decisors as to whether the obligation to pay maintenance to a wife who is prevented from remarrying is a continuation of the preexisting marital duty or a new obligation, see 1 *PDR* 65; 3:44; 8:174; 10:110. Clearly, in the context of a prohibited marriage, obligating the husband to maintain his wife when the court deems her to be prevented from remarrying implicitly reflects the latter approach.

Whether imposition of a monetary penalty in the form of the duty to pay maintenance risks rendering a subsequent divorce coerced (*get meuse*) is much debated, see Z. Warhaftig, "Coercion to grant a divorce in theory and practice" (Hebrew), 3–4 *Shenaton Hamishpat Haivri* (1976/77), 153, 166–67; J. David Bleich, *Contemporary Halakhic Problems* 3 (NY: 1989), 337–40; Solomon Shanon, "Modes of coerced divorce" (Hebrew), *Tehumin* 11 (1990), 203.

of supplementing the basic amount specified in the *ketuba*[110] with an additional amount (*tosefet ketuba*), which is entered into the document during the wedding ceremony,[111] generating a financial obligation that is binding on the husband. Even in cases where the marriage is incestuous (*gilui arayot*), and thus void *ab initio*,[112] Shochetman observes, this obligation, once undertaken, is enforceable.[113]

To summarize, the common denominator between permitted and prohibited marital relationships is that both give rise to the personal status of marriage (*ishut*), which, in principle, mandates payment of spousal maintenance. However, as the parties to a prohibited marriage are forbidden to cohabit and under a duty to divorce, the system precludes the wife from submitting a claim for maintenance, so that those who break the law do not benefit from their misdeed. Despite the exemption from maintenance, certain self-imposed obligations in these marriages, such as supplemental *ketuba* amounts, and maintenance based on explicit agreements between the parties, are enforceable. Upon dissolution of both permitted and prohibited marital unions, a bill of divorce (*get*) is delivered by the husband to his wife, but "the *get* is nothing more than the recession of the contractual obligations of marriage and of the restrictions that flow therefrom."[114]

Execution and delivery of the bill of divorce means that the woman is no longer someone's wife (*eishet ish*), enabling the parties to remarry.

110 On contemporary valuations of the *ketuba* amounts, see M. Broyde and J. Reiss, "The value and significance of the *ketuba*," *Journal of Halacha and Contemporary Society* 47 (2004), 101.

111 Maimonides, *Code*, Laws concerning Marriage 24:3; *Turei Zahav*, *SA*, EH 116:3. Whereas *Rashi*, bKetubot 101a s.v. *aval tosefet*, construes the additional amount as a gift, Maimonides contends that it is an obligation undertaken in exchange for the bride's consent to reserve herself for her husband during their marriage.

112 By contrast, a marriage consummated with a menstruant (*nida*), when intercourse is prohibited, is valid, see *SA*, EH 61:1; *Rema* ad loc. Cf. Maimonides, *Code*, Laws concerning Marriage 10:2.

113 Shochetman 1981, n. 105 above, 220–21. This point will be elaborated on below at n. 209.

114 Bleich, n. 83 above, 256, see also 201, 219. In Jewish law, a divorce is not a judicial decree, but executed by the couple themselves, though as Berachyahu Lifshitz has pointed out (in an oral communication, RW) in some instances this is imprecise. E.g., after twelve months, a rebellious wife (*moredet*) loses her rights, but the law requires that she receive a bill of divorce nonetheless.

The concepts that demarcate the boundaries of marriage, whether permitted or prohibited, are thus betrothal (*kidushin*), the marriage ceremony (*nisuin*), and delivery of the bill of divorce.

What are the defining concepts of civil marriage? Ought such a relationship between Jews forge a religious matrimonial bond that can only be dissolved by the execution and delivery of a bill of divorce?[115] If the answer is yes, ought we conclude that this act of matrimony pursuant to civil law rather than Jewish law ('the religion of Moses and Israel') effects a change in the parties' personal status and generates obligations such as spousal maintenance? In a 1946 exchange of correspondence between rabbis Ben-Zion Uziel, Sefardic Chief Rabbi of Mandatory Palestine; Avraham Rodner, a rabbi in Kiryat Eliyahu, Haifa; and Zvi Pesach Frank of Jerusalem, R. Uziel states:

> According to those who contend that civil marriages are dissolved solely through a divorce, it is clear that the husband is obligated to pay her maintenance, since the reason and rationale for maintenance is [the principle that] 'a man does not engage in promiscuous intercourse' (*ein adam ose beilato beilat znut*).[116]

Let us examine this presumption, and how it was understood by the Talmud[117] and early decisors. R. Abraham di Boton, a sixteenth-century commentator on Maimonides' *Code*, asserts that the presumption was invoked in the Talmud in situations "where there was an aspect of betrothal (*kidushin*), or the man had previously been betrothed

115 On the halakhic status of civil marriages, see the sources cited in Nahum Rakover, *Otzar Hamishpat* (Hebrew), 1 (Jerusalem: 1975), 363–65; 2 (Jerusalem: 1990), 368–70; idem, *Multi-Language Bibliography of Jewish Law* (Jerusalem: 1990), 641–42.

116 Quoted in R. Abraham Rodner, *Mishpetei Ishut* (Hebrew), (Jerusalem: 1949), 140, reprinted in *Responsa Mishpetei Uziel*, EH #77. See also *Mishpetei Uziel*, 2nd edition, YD #60; EH #4. Invoking this presumption presupposes that it is operative in contemporary times, but given the moral decay of modern society, numerous decisors would argue that it is not. See R. Israel Isserlein, *Responsa Trumat Hadeshen*, #209; R. Joseph di Trani, *Responsa Maharit*, EH #1; R. David b. Zimra, *Responsa Radbaz*, 1:351; R. Efraim Margolis, *Responsa Beit Efraim*, EH #42; R. Yehiel Weinberg, *Responsa Sridei Esh*, 3:22; R. Ovadia Yosef, *Responsa Yabia Omer*, vol. 6, EH #1; R. Abraham Freimann, *Seder Kidushin Venisuin* (Jerusalem: 1964), 346–84.

117 bJebamot 107a; bKetubot 72a–73b, bGitin 81a–b.

to the woman."[118] R. di Boton's reference to an "aspect" of betrothal is an allusion to the possibility of effecting betrothal through intercourse (*bia*), betrothal that is deemed to be of doubtful validity.[119] As explained above, the normative practice is to consummate betrothal by verbal articulation and concretization of the couple's intent under the scrutiny of witnesses and in the presence of an officiant and public assemblage. Nevertheless, numerous sources, beginning with the Mishnah, recognize the possibility of betrothal by intercourse (*kidushei bia*).[120] Such betrothal is predicated on intent to consummate an exclusive conjugal relationship (*kavana leshem kidushin* or *kavana leshem ishut*).[121] The presumption that 'a man does not engage in promiscuous intercourse' is a corollary of this rule. Since, unless the parties had the proper intention, their acts have no legal efficacy, the presumption is rebutted if there are grounds for assuming that the parties are engaging in licentious behavior.[122] Hence, the question arises whether this presumption applies where the parties in question are not generally committed to observing Jewish law.

If the parties are apostates, all agree that it does not.[123] However, if the involved parties do not observe the laws of family purity or are promiscuous, but refrain from adultery, there is much debate regarding the presumption's aptness.[124] Some decisors maintain that

118 *Lehem Mishne, Code,* Laws concerning Marriage 1:4.
119 See Ellinson, n. 107 above, 115, nn 2–3.
120 mKidushin 1:1; bKidushin 2a, jKidushin 1:1. Cf. R. Shimon Duran, *Responsa Yakhin Uboaz*, 2:10; *Responsa Beit Efraim*, EH #42, #59; *Responsa Hatam Sofer*, EH #58; *Responsa Beit Yitzhak*, EH #29; *Responsa Helkat Yaakov*, 1:1, which reject the post-talmudic applicability of betrothal by intercourse, a position also upheld in R. Shaar Yashuv Cohen, "A couple that cohabits without *hupa* and *kidushin*" (Hebrew), *Tehumin* 13 (1992/93), 186–87.
121 Ellinson, n. 107 above, 129–47, 154–69; 7 *PDR* 35.
122 R. Isaac b. Sheshet, *Responsa Ribash*, #6. Whether one can invoke this presumption with regard to couples living together without marriage is subject to debate, see Maimonides, *Code*, Laws concerning Marriage 1:4; *Rabad* ad loc.; *Rema*, *SA*, EH 33:1.
123 *Terumat Hadeshen*, #209; R. Moses Lima, *Helkat Mehokek*, *SA*, EH 26:3.
124 See 7 *PDR* 35, 43, 52–64; Frimer and Frimer, n. 84 above, n. 78. In addition to the debate over the presumption's applicability, there is also much debate over its interpretation. The differing understandings of the presumption are articulated by R. Isser Judah Unterman, a former Ashkenazic Chief Rabbi of Israel, in *Shevet Miyehuda*, 4:13; and see *Responsa Sridei Esh*, 3:41; R. Meir Simha Hakohen of Dvinsk, *Or Sameiah*;

non-commitment to the halakhic system, non-observance of the laws of family purity, and sexual licentiousness, indicate that the party in question is not engaging in sexual union with the proper intent; these decisors do not consider civil marriage valid.[125]

Other decisors perceive the issues connected with civil marriage differently. R. Moses Feinstein, a twentieth-century decisor, concludes a lengthy responsum on civil marriage by saying that those who opt for a civil marriage are indeed establishing conjugal ties, but without intent to engage in religious matrimony[126]; other decisors argue that civil marriage does not ipso facto entail the absence of religious intent. R. Joseph Henkin, another twentieth-century decisor, writes that a Jew "who takes into his house" a Jewess intends to establish a permanent and exclusive conjugal relationship rather than engage in wanton intercourse. That is, R. Henkin maintains that the intent of the relationship is matrimony, and thus should it be dissolved, a Jewish divorce is required.[127] In light of the wide range of opinions, an Israeli rabbinical court decision reflects the prevailing attitude among contemporary decisors: "Usually the status of civil marriages is to be decided on the basis of each individual case and the situation of each couple, [as well as] the time and the place."[128] In short, whether proper intent — intent

---

Maimonides, *Code*, Laws concerning Divorce 10:19; *Responsa Hatam Sofer*, EH #68; *Responsa Dvar Avraham*, 3:29.

125 *Responsa Maharam Schick*, EH #21; *Responsa Heikhal Yitzhak*, EH 2:31; *Mishpetei Uziel*, vol. 1, EH #59. R. Jacob Moses Harlap argues that those who opt for a civil marriage are products of a morally-decadent society; he thus rejects the 'a man does not engage . . .' presumption, see *Responsa Beit Zevul*, 1:27. See too *Responsa Beit Efraim*, EH #42; *Responsa Yabia Omer*, vol. 6, EH #1; R. Haim Epstein, *Sefer Teshuva Shleima*, vol. 2, EH #17.

126 *Igrot Moshe*, EH 1:74–75; 2:19. And see R. Shimon b. Tzemah Duran, *Responsa Tashbetz*, 3:47; R. Abraham Shapiro, *Responsa Dvar Avraham*, 3:29; *Responsa Sridei Esh*, 3:22; *Responsa Helkat Yaakov*, 1:1; *Responsa Mishpetei Uziel*, vol. 2, EH #59.

127 *Teshuvot Ibra*, #3; *Lev Ibra*, 12–20. See R. Zilberstein, *Otzar Haposkim*, EH 26:1 (6b). R. Zvi Hirsch Ferber argues that the presumption applies even in situations where the civilly-married parties are licentious; see *Birur Halakha*, 5, 8, 10, 16.

128 9 *PDR* 352, translated in Shochetman 2002, n. 108 above, 154. Though most authorities concur with R. Harlap's view (see n. 125 above) that a civil marriage does not constitute a halakhic marriage, for various reasons, many decisors mandate that should they terminate their relationship,

to engage in religious matrimony — is a sine qua non for establishing a marital bond, is debatable.

Let us now return to R. Uziel's view[129]:

> According to those who contend that civil marriages are dissolved solely through divorce, it is clear that the husband is obligated to pay her maintenance, since the reason and rationale for maintenance is [the principle that] 'a man does not engage in promiscuous intercourse.'[130]

R. Uziel is asserting that according to certain decisors, invoking the presumption that 'a man does not engage in promiscuous intercourse' lays the groundwork for recognition of the spousal maintenance obligation. The presumption itself, however, is compatible with various religious criteria for determining whether a sexual relationship constitutes promiscuous intercourse or a permissible conjugal relationship.

In response to R. Uziel's presentation, R. Rodner counters: "The decisors who argued cautiously with regard to civil marriage, acted stringently, in that they mandated that the husband deliver a bill of divorce [to his wife]; but if he indeed wishes to divorce her, he is exempt from [the duty of] spousal maintenance."[131] R. Rodner's position, which exempts the husband from having to pay spousal maintenance, is affirmed by R. Frank. Subsequently, both R. Yehiel J. Weinberg[132] and

---

such couples, given that on some views their relationship was tantamount to marriage, require a divorce as a precautionary stringency (*get lehumra*), so that there will be no doubts as to their personal status. See Schereschewsky, n. 96 above, 81. Cf. *Responsa Even Yekara*, EH #12; *Responsa Mishpetei Uziel*, vol. 2, EH #59; *Responsa Pri Hasade*, 3:9; *Bikurei Yehuda*, vol. 1, *Responsa*, #3; *Responsa Helkat Yaakov*, EH #74; *Responsa Yabia Omer*, vol. 8, EH #10. In recent years, Israel's rabbinical courts have increasingly had to address questions pertaining to the dissolution of civil marriages, see, e.g., RHC, case 4276/63 [11.11.2003] (rabbis Dichovsky, Ben Shimon, Sherman), www.daat.ac.il/daat/psk/psk.asp?id=93 ; Haifa District Rabbinical Court, case 2177–21-1 [23.1.2008] (rabbis Nahari, Shani, Yagoda), www.daat.ac.il/daat/psk/psk.asp?id=360

129 See text at n. 116 above.

130 Rodner, n. 116 above, 138.

131 Ibid., 142. Berachyahu Lifshitz notes (oral communication, RW) that if the spousal maintenance duty is based on an implied agreement, it might conceivably continue to exist even after the divorce.

132 *Responsa Sridei Esh*, 3:41.

the Rabbinical High Court of Appeal in Jerusalem reaffirmed this position.[133]

Both the Rabbinical High Court of Appeal and R. Weinberg contend that there is a recognized procedural rule, the rightful possession presumption — "the burden of proof is on the one who has a claim against his fellow" (*hamotzi mihavero alav hareaya*) — which preempts the possibility of a rightful claim to maintenance. For this approach mandates that a bill of divorce be delivered to terminate the marriage,[134] because it is uncertain, but possible, that, from the halakhic perspective, a betrothal took place (*safek kidushin*).[135] Hence this is a situation where doubt (*safek*) exists, and in cases of doubt, one is precluded from appropriating someone else's assets.[136] But there is a more fundamental reason for the exemption from spousal maintenance. Most of the decisors who have been cited conclude that civil marriage does not involve an act of betrothal (*kidushin*), and hence there is no spousal maintenance obligation.[137] And even some of those who argue that a civil marriage does involve an act of betrothal reject the notion that it generates a maintenance obligation.[138] Their argument is that, given that the relationship does not confer the personal status of being married (*ishut*), there are no spousal monetary obligations, and the rules of spousal maintenance (*mezonot*), as outlined above, are not applicable. There exists an exclusive conjugal relationship, like that of a cohabiting couple as discussed above vis-à-vis American law, but it is not deemed to fall under the category of marriage.

133 3 PD 369, 378–79.

134 R. Judah Tsirelson, *Responsa Maarkhei Lev*, #32, #87, #149.

135 See Schereschewsky, n. 96 above, 81.

136 bBaba Kama 46a.

137 See Schereschewsky, n. 96 above, 78–81. For arguments against recognizing civil marriage, see R. Elijah Aaron Milikovski, *Responsa Ohalei Aharon*, 2:50; Meir Issachar Mazuz, "Civil marriage and its consequences" (Hebrew), 3–4 *Shenaton Hamishpat Haivri* (1976/77), 233, 253.

138 R. Henkin, n. 127 above; R. Abraham Price, *Mishnat Avraham*, #10; R. Judah Leib Don-Yihye, *Bikurei Yehuda*, 1:3. The Hazon Ish argues that should the parties execute an agreement, concerns about betrothal via written declaration (*kidushei shtar*) would arise; see R. Abraham Karelitz, "On civil marriage" (Hebrew), *Or Yisrael* 18 (1998), 12. However, in the absence of a document, where the parties have no intent to be married religiously, he concedes that there is no betrothal; see *Hazon Ish*, EH 43:10.

Among the few decisors who believe that a civil marriage creates a halakhic marriage is R. Joseph Rosin, 'the Rogachover,' who asserts that the very fact that a woman "binds herself to a particular man" creates a marital bond ("this . . . is the definition of marriage") with the ensuing obligations, including spousal maintenance.[139]

In sum, those decisors who contend that civil marriage is neither an act of marriage nor an act of betrothal or even doubtful betrothal maintain that it does not generate a spousal maintenance obligation, and, apart from the Rogachover, even those who contend that it is a proper marriage deny that there is such an obligation.

On my reading of the majority view, both an exclusive conjugal relationship that is solemnized by the state, that is, civil marriage, and the relationship of a cohabiting couple, are to be viewed as examples of concubinage (*pilagshut*).[140] Though in civil marriage there is indeed marital intent, and termination of the relationship requires a civil divorce, whereas in cohabitation there is no expression of long-term commitment and the couple can merely separate, nevertheless, the decisors view both relationships as forms of concubinage.[141] The contemporary rabbinic consensus is that cohabitation, like civil marriage, does not effect a valid halakhic marriage.[142] Hence in both cases, there is no spousal maintenance obligation.

139 R. Joseph Rosin, *Responsa Tzofnat Paneiah*, 1:4.

140 *Responsa Ezrat Kohen*, #38; R. Eliezer Waldenberg, *Responsa Tzitz Eliezer*, 2:19; *Responsa Rivash*, #6; R. Joseph Caro, *Responsa Avkat Rokhel*, #80. Others define a concubine (*pilegesh*) as either a woman who is betrothed halakhically without a *ketuba*, or a woman who lives with a man but consorts with other men; see E. Shochetman, "Need there be apprehensiveness about uncertain betrothal in the relationships of those 'known to the public' as married?" (Hebrew), 10 *Mehkerei Mishpat* (1993), 7, 14, 16. R. Henkin's definition is discussed in Frimer and Frimer, n. 84 above, n. 127.

141 Ellinson, n. 107 above, 93. And see Bleich, n. 107 above, 62–63.

142 *Responsa Mishpetei Uziel*, vol. 2, EH #54; *Responsa Heikhal Yitzhak*, EH 2:2, 33; 4 *PDR* 332, 335; 7 *PDR* 35, 43–44.

In certain cases, the determination as to whether a marriage was civil or religious is made by a rabbinical court; see RHC, case 4276/63, n. 128 above. For this reason, some have argued that non-observant Israelis should be allowed to marry civilly rather than be forced by civil law to undergo ostensibly-halakhic marriages; see R. Elijah Bakshi Doron, "The law of marriage and divorce: have the benefits of the law been lost?" (Hebrew), *Tehumin* 25 (2005), 99.

R. Rodner asked R. Uziel whether, at the time of a civil marriage, a husband's commitment to support his wife was analogous to the commitment made by an individual who undertakes an obligation to sustain a stranger.[143] In other words, was an express agreement or a civil law stipulating that one must maintain one's civilly-married spouse enforceable? Though no such duty follows from the *Shulhan Arukh*'s norms of family law (*Even Haezer*), would the duty follow from the *Shulhan Arukh*'s laws concerning monetary obligations (*Hoshen Mishpat*)? In principle, R. Uziel concurs that it would, though the efficacy of the formula used in undertaking the obligation would depend on its terms and provisions.[144]

R. Uziel was articulating the importance of correctly interpreting the language used by the obligor (*doreshin leshon hedyot*), which determines the legal effect of his words.[145] On the one hand, the imprecision of the language used in agreements is resolved by invoking the 'colloquial usage' (*leshon bnei adam*) principle.[146] However, at the time the agreement was made, the obligor may have attached a biblical or halakhic meaning to a term, and should this term later be disputed, we interpret it in accordance with this intent rather than in accordance with colloquial usage. Another problem that arises in connection with the language of agreements is vagueness. Courts have addressed this by adducing the biblical meaning of a given term.[147]

Clearly, obligating someone to maintain someone else raises many questions regarding the scope of the duty. Does 'maintenance' encompass clothing, lodging, and medical services? Decisors and rabbinical courts have long grappled with the meaning of terms such as 'maintenance,' 'livelihood' (*parnasa*), and 'food and drink.' For what period of time did the man commit himself to maintaining the

143 *Mishpetei Ishut*, n. 116 above, 140.

144 *Responsa Mishpetei Uziel*, EH #77. Given R. Uziel's position that civil marriage is an expression of a secular culture (see *Responsa Mishpetei Uziel*, n. 142 above), his willingness to recognize a maintenance obligation is somewhat surprising.

145 See Elon 1994, n. 82 above, 1:422–43; bNedarim 51b, 63a–b; bBaba Metzia 104b; bBaba Batra 143b; *Responsa Ribash*, #207; *SA*, HM 218:19.

146 R. David Hakohen (Corfu, 16th c.), *Responsa Radakh*, 28:2.

147 *Tosafot*, bPesahim 2a s.v. *detenan; Responsa Rivash*, #207, #304.

woman?[148] In a period of unanticipated spiraling inflation, is someone who is on a fixed income obliged to continue making maintenance payments?[149] R. Uziel's concern about the proper construction and formulation of the agreement is understandable.[150]

Whereas R. Uziel addresses the interpretive dilemma associated with agreements to maintain a civilly-married spouse, forty years later, R. Meir Issachar Mazuz, a Haifa rabbinical court judge, addresses the threshold issue of the actual validity of the agreement.[151] According to Maimonides,[152] maintenance is categorized as an 'undefined sum' (*davar sheino katzuv*), hence the agreement has no specific goal, and the husband cannot have firm resolve (*gmirut hadaat*), to undertake such an obligation.[153] The agreement should thus be invalidated. Some decisors contend that according to Maimonides, should the husband receive something in exchange for his obligation, it is transformed into a bilateral obligation that is legally effective even in the case of an undefined sum.[154] Adducing the talmudic dictum "in return for the benefit he receives . . . he resolves to undertake the obligation,"[155] a rabbinical court has, for instance, concluded that the benefit accrued by an adoptive parent in raising an adopted child constitutes an important element in establishing the obligation to maintain her.[156] Presumably, spousal maintenance is analogous: the husband's agreement to provide maintenance in exchange for her (civilly) marrying him is efficacious.

Most decisors, however, disagree with Maimonides, and assert that a maintenance agreement, despite the undefined sum of the monetary

148 *SA*, HM 60:3, *Rema* ad loc.; *Sema, SA*, HM 60:16; *SA*, EH 73:7, 114:12; *Rema, SA*, HM 212:1; *Shakh, SA*, HM 212:2; *Sema, SA*, HM 212:3; 3 *PDR* 170–75, 363; 4:374; 5:171; 10:145.

149 3 *PDR* 109, 121; 11:209, 213.

150 See *Pithei Hoshen*, Acquisitions, 455–67.

151 Meir Issachar Mazuz, n. 137 above, 257–58.

152 *Code*, Laws concerning Sales 11:16.

153 On the views of Maimonides and his predecessors, see Itamar Warhaftig, *Undertaking in Jewish Law* (Hebrew), (Jerusalem: 2001), 95, 98, 104–105.

154 R. Judah Rosanes, *Mishne Lamelekh*, Laws concerning Sales 11:16; R. Aryeh Leib Heller, *Ketzot Hahoshen*, HM 60:2; R. Jacob Lorberbaum, *Netivot Hamishpat*, HM 60:3.

155 bBaba Metzia 94a.

156 3 *PDR* 109, 120. See also *Shaarei Uziel*, 2, gate 39:1.

obligation being undertaken, is effective.[157] Even if the agreement is legally effective, the rules of legal interpretation apply to it, and these interpretive rules may determine that the scope and length of the maintenance obligation are open to question. Consequently, in cases where there is a spousal-maintenance exemption in secular law, R. Uziel concludes that a poorly-drafted spousal maintenance agreement does not establish such a duty.[158]

Aside from the intricacies of constructing a legally-efficacious agreement covering the varying exigencies that might arise, since, as some have argued, most cohabiting couples do not think of their relationship in contract terms[159] and consequently do not negotiate express agreements (oral or written), are there any other avenues for a wife's recovery of spousal support in a civil marriage? Some contemporary decisors have allowed recovery on the basis of an implied-in-fact contract theory. An implied-in-fact contract is an agreement that is inferred from the parties' reasonable expectations, as determined by examining their conduct, even though they may not have formulated an explicit agreement.

In our context, the primary difficulty with inferring a maintenance agreement from the provision of services for each other by a couple living together is that it may be unreasonable to infer an agreement to pay for the services rendered when the relationship of the parties makes it natural that the services were rendered gratuitously, with donative intent.[160] Personal services will frequently be rendered by two persons living together because they value each other's company or because they find it practical or rewarding.

Though various decisors have accepted this reasoning and deny restitution on the grounds that the benefit was conferred gratuitously, the majority award restitution in cases where the couple pooled their resources and concentrated their efforts. As the Rema put it: "If an individual undertakes an action or confers a benefit on a friend, the friend

157 *Shakh, SA,* HM 60:12; 3 *PDR* 109, 110–120, 363, 365–66; 4:193, 198, 289, 298–300; 11:240. Cf. 9 *PDR* 251; 11:252.

158 *Mishpetei Uziel*, n. 144 above.

159 See text at n. 35 above.

160 Sources for my discussion of implied contracts for services are taken primarily from Itamar Warhaftig, "Is there an obligation to compensate a friend for a benefit he conferred?" (Hebrew), *Tehumin* 10 (1988), 216.

cannot say that the action was carried out gratuitously, and claim 'I did not request it'; but rather, one must compensate him. . . . If one says to his friend 'dine with me,' [the latter] must pay him."[161]

R. Joseph Caro affirms this position.[162] R. Zalman N. Goldberg concurs that the 'this one derives a benefit and the other sustains a loss' (*ze nehene veze haser*) scenario that is implicit in the above rulings serves as the ground for mandating spousal maintenance in a civil marriage.[163] This conclusion, I contend, should also apply in the case of cohabiting partners.

Decisors have indeed awarded relief on the basis of an implied agreement.[164] In the context of civil marriage or cohabitation, the husband promises to care and provide for his wife for the rest of their lives. On the strength of his promises, she performs services of value to her husband, including housekeeping, cooking, entertaining his business associates, offering emotional support, and raising their children. Should the maintenance payments be withheld, these decisors have found that, in exchange for these contributions, the husband's mere promise to act in the customary fashion, that is, to provide maintenance, even though it was unaccompanied by a symbolic act of acquisition (*kinyan*), becomes a binding obligation. This is so even in situations where it is not customary to receive remuneration, for one is duty-bound to keep one's promise.

Another ground for awarding recovery for maintenance that has been adduced by rabbinical courts is the general rule that an individual must be compensated for doing his fellow a favor: "it is no different than an individual who performs an action for someone else without having discussed compensation, and nevertheless, the latter is obliged

161 *Rema, SA*, HM 264:4, 17. Though the Rema's subsequent codified ruling in HM 363:10 seems to contradict his earlier positions, nevertheless, three of the four ways in which the contradiction can be resolved reaffirm the right of recovery for services rendered; see Warhaftig, ibid., 221. For exceptions to the majority view, see *SA*, YD 253:5, *Rema* ad loc.; 8 *PDR* 325.

162 *SA*, HM 290:24. Rabbinical court judges have found that the mutual benefit derived from the relationship creates monetary obligations between the partners to a civil marriage, including but not limited to spousal maintenance. See, e.g., Petach-Tikva District Rabbinical Court, case 2084796–22-3 [30.9.2003].

163 In a personal communication with I. Warhaftig (September 2004).

164 bJebamot 106a; R. Asher b. Yehiel, *Piskei Rosh*, Jebamot 12:16; *Rema, SA*, HM 129:22; *Mishpetei Uziel*, n. 144 above, and 2nd edition, YD #60.

to pay."[165] The case of the civilly-married woman or cohabiting partner is analogous, and she may recover maintenance payments due her in exchange for the services she provided.[166]

There are thus several different grounds allowing recovery for maintenance.[167] These include an express written agreement, implied-in-fact agreements grounded in the 'this one benefitted while the other sustained a loss' rule, and the norm that favors are to be compensated for. Though invoking the various rationales may result in different outcomes with respect to the parameters and scope of the spousal maintenance obligation, it should be noted that with the exception of express written agreements, none of these grounds offer definitive guidelines for determining the amount of maintenance to be paid.

Addressing this concern, R. Zalman N. Goldberg suggests that custom (*minhag*) can provide the guidelines, as it does in other contexts. For example, though the Mishnah stipulates the hours of a workday, if custom dictates otherwise, custom prevails.[168] Scholars have pointed out that this is an instance where, de facto, custom nullifies the applicability of a halakhic norm.[169] In other words, though the law prescribes the hours of the workday, nevertheless, because private ordering is possible with regard to monetary matters, the law in question can be set aside. In effect, the prevailing custom is construed as an implied condition of any employment, and, preempting the halakhic norm, becomes the operative norm. Indeed, the 'custom abrogates law' (*minhag mevatel halakha*) rule is operative in all spheres of labor relations, including payment of wages.[170] Custom as an implied condition governing remuneration can thus serve to delineate the scope of the maintenance duty

165 9 *PDR* 16, 37–38. On the ramifications of this conclusion for the law of obligations, see Shilem Warhaftig, *Jewish Labour Law* (Hebrew), (Tel Aviv: 1989), 373–75; I. Warhaftig 2001, n. 153 above, 168–72.

166 See R. Z.N. Goldberg, "The maintenance obligation in civil marriages" (Hebrew), *Tehumin* 24 (2004), 188.

167 Yet another approach is to adduce secular law, in a jurisdiction where there are civil laws mandating spousal maintenance, as it can be presumed that the marriage is predicated on upholding the law of the land; see text below at n. 181.

168 mBaba Metzia 7:1; jBaba Metzia 7:1; Goldberg, n. 166 above, 188.

169 Berachyahu Lifshitz, "Custom abrogates law" (Hebrew), *Sinai* 86 (1980), 8, 11; David Henshke, "Custom abrogates law? (corroborating a theory)" (Hebrew), 17 *Dine Israel* (1993/4), 135–37.

170 See *Mishpatekha Leyaakov*, 1:166.

that arises from the various implied agreements vis-à-vis cohabitation and civil marriage. Hence even though financial relations between spouses are ordinarily predicated on a marital relationship (*ishut*), Jewish law does allow for implied (as well as express) agreements between spouses who are married civilly or living as cohabiting partners.

The implied agreements in question incorporate an implied condition regarding the scope of the husband's spousal maintenance obligation. To identify how much one must compensate his fellow for benefit derived from his labor, for a favor, or as reimbursement for a service provided, one must ascertain and match the prevailing customary fees for these activities. Moreover, on this line of reasoning, we can argue that custom itself constitutes an independent legal source that can serve as the basis for validating financial obligations between civilly-married and cohabiting couples. By dint of these living arrangements, the couples have an implied agreement in which they undertake to have their financial relations governed by the prevailing custom. This approach obviates the need to posit any other implied agreement.

In fact, relying on Maimonides' ruling, regarding financial relations between spouses, that "in all of these . . . matters, the custom of the land is a fundamental consideration, and must be followed, provided the custom has spread throughout the land,"[171] an Israeli rabbinical court allowed a divorcee to recover financial assets from the man to whom she had formerly been civilly married.[172]

But not all rabbinical court judges have concluded that a cohabiting woman is entitled to spousal maintenance on the strength of custom. R. Mazuz, for instance, has argued that custom can serve as a basis for validating financial ties between a couple only on the assumption that the couple's living together as husband and wife is based on matrimony prior to sexual intimacy (*kinyan ishut*).[173] It would be difficult to claim that this assumption can be made with regard to cohabiting couples. If so, on this view, custom does not, in fact, serve as a mechanism for inferring an implied agreement between cohabiting partners.

A close reading of the rabbinical court ruling in which R. Mazuz expressed his opinion, and the classic historical case that inspired it,

171 *Code*, Laws concerning Marriage 23:12.
172 5 *PDR* 124–25.
173 Mazuz, n. 137 above, 261–62. See also Dichovsky 2005, n. 205 below.

will shed light on the adequacy of utilizing custom as a basis for assuming implied agreements between civilly-married and cohabiting couples. The historical case dates back to the sixteenth century, and was the focus of discussion among the renowned decisors of the day:

> Gracia Mendes and her husband were married in Portugal when they were both Marranos [Jews living as Christians but still secretly faithful to Judaism]; and there "it was the custom, by authority of the king and the kingdom from ancient times . . . that when the husband dies, the widow takes half of all the property left by the husband." . . . The question arose: Could the husband's heirs prevail over the widow as to the half of the estate [claimed by her] and leave her with only the dowry she had brought to the marriage?
>
> Maharashdam ruled in favor of Gracia Mendes on the ground "that is known even to infants, that all matters pertaining to marriage are governed by the customs of the place of the marriage." Mabit also decided in favor of Gracia Mendes, but went even further and ruled that all provisions in contracts entered into by Marranos while they were in Spain and Portugal were valid even after they came to other countries and returned to the practice of Judaism. This is so, even though the law now being applied is Jewish law. . . . even if they have a second marriage ceremony in accordance with Jewish law and practice, so long as they do not expressly rescind the first agreement [which accompanied their marriage in the Christian religion], it is presumed that the second marriage is being entered into on the same understanding expressed in the original agreement.[174]

The controversy focuses on the claim submitted by Hannah Gracia Mendes for half of her husband's estate, pursuant to the "custom, by authority of the king and the kingdom." Custom, in this situation, served as a means of identifying a specific Portuguese estate law. The responsa in question establish that, Jewish inheritance law notwithstanding, Portuguese law has legal validity.[175] As Elon puts it: "custom serves . . . as a historical source of law, it merely develops the normative conduct to the point where it is ready to be accorded the force of law by virtue of legislation."[176]

174 Excerpted from Israeli Supreme Court Justice Simha Assaf's holding in *Miller v. Miller*, CA 100/49, 5 PD 1301, 1306 (1949), as translated by Elon 1994, n. 82 above, 3:1483–84 n. 93.

175 The opinion of the Mabit, R. Moses b. Joseph di Trani, is quoted in R. Joseph Caro, *Responsa Avkat Rokhel*, #80; R. Samuel di Medina, *Responsa Maharashdam*, HM #327.

176 Elon 1994, n. 82 above, 2:881.

Though this decision reflects various public policy considerations and a complex set of circumstances, an Israeli rabbinical court, in a case involving a Russian-Jewish couple that had immigrated to Israel, invoked it as a legal source for recognizing that upon divorce, common property should be divided in accordance with Russian law.[177] Invoking the 'everything in accordance with the custom of the country' (*hakol lefi minhag hamedina*) principle, the court assessed the parties' intent, and assumed that they desired to have their financial relations governed by Russian law. Adducing this rabbinical court ruling, R. Solomon Dichovsky argues that financial relations between Jews who were civilly married in the Diaspora and subsequently immigrated to Israel, are to be enforced in accordance with the laws of the locale where the marriage took place. Hence, a Jew who married in a civil ceremony in, say, the US or Canada, would be obligated to pay maintenance.[178] Here again, as in the Gracia Mendes case, the authority of custom is invoked by adducing the law of Diaspora countries.

The very fact that a couple married entails an implied agreement to comply with the governing secular law. R. Moses Feinstein made the following observation regarding an issue in American tenancy law:

> All of these halakhic rules are dependent on the custom of the country . . . it is not necessary that one follow a custom because Torah scholars so advise, nor is it even necessary that Jews do so. Even if it has been instituted by non-Jews . . . [it] is accorded the status of biblical law. . . . in a locale where there exists a custom, one follows the custom, and the reason is that ordinarily we presume that the parties made a condition that customs would be followed.[179]

177 5 *PDR* 124, 125–26.

178 R. Solomon Dichovsky, "Rabbinical and secular courts: spheres of contact" (Hebrew), *Tehumin* 25 (2005), 51, 68. However, R. Dichovsky does not extend the efficacy of custom to determination of the financial relations between cohabiting (as opposed to civilly-married) couples, see n. 205 below.

179 *Igrot Moshe*, HM 1:72. See also *Hazon Ish*, HM, Baba Kama 23:2; Likutim 16:1. It should not be inferred that R. Feinstein and R. Karelitz accept the line of reasoning developed in the text below at nn 186–91. Their position can be understood as recognition of a convention, based on common commercial practice, whereby certain commercial legal norms become an implied condition of any agreement; see *Hazon Ish*, HM, Likutim 16:5, 9. And see D. Frimer, "The influence of Israeli law on Jewish law" (Hebrew), *Jewish Studies* 39 (1999), 133, 138–41.

R. Feinstein's responsum seems to echo the words of R. Elijah Mizrahi, a fifteenth-century Turkish decisor, also in the context of a commercial matter: "we are witnesses (*anan sahedi*), that on the authority of the custom, the party acted. . . ."[180]

That is, we take judicial notice of the prevailing custom and construe the parties as intending to follow it. Both in the Diaspora and in Israel, contemporary decisors have applied this with respect to domestic partners' financial relations, and have inferred the parties' intent to have these arrangements governed, as is customary, by secular law.[181]

This conclusion would seem to have serious ramifications, and to ignore the prohibition against recourse to non-Jewish courts (*arkhaot*). As R. J. David Bleich notes,

> Recourse to a gentile forum is tantamount to a declaration by the litigant that he is amenable to allowing an alien code of law to supersede the law of the Torah. Such conduct constitutes renunciation of the law of Moses. . . . recourse to a gentile court to administer laws recorded in *Hoshen Mishpat* . . . is forbidden because . . . it enhances the status of an alien legal system. . . . The litigant appears before the gentile courts because he accepts their authority, and if they administer the law of Moses he accepts that law, not because he regards it as binding upon him by virtue of having been commanded by God, but because it has been endorsed and adopted by gentiles.
>
> The prohibition . . . is not limited to bringing a suit before a gentile court. The prohibition includes any judicial proceeding that negates the law of Moses. A judicial body composed entirely of judges who happen to be members of the Jewish community but who administer an alien system of law, is undoubtedly to be classified as within the halakhic category of *arka'ot shel akum* for the simple reason that the laws such a court administers are not those of the Torah.
>
> Since . . . acquiescence by both litigants does not serve to mitigate the prohibition . . . and since the prohibition applies even when the judges themselves are Jews, it follows that the parties are not entitled to accept the

180 *Responsa Reem*, #16.

181 18 *PDR* 319, 322; *Rulings of the Chief Rabbinate's Rabbinical Court for Monetary Matters*, 1:87; R. Sternbuch, *Teshuvot Vehanhagot*, 3:455; Solomon Dichovsky, "The community property system: does one follow the law of the land?" (Hebrew), *Tehumin* 18 (1998), 28; Warburg 2001, n. 89 above, 137; Yona Reiss, "Contracting out of a law written in the Torah in monetary matters" (Hebrew), *Shaarei Tzedek* 4 (2003), 288, 294–95. Cf. R. Z.N. Goldberg, "The validity of a memorandum (*zikhron dvarim*) asserting an undertaking to sell something" (Hebrew), *Tehumin* 12 (1991), 279, 290, which argues that custom grounded in civil legislation has no validity.

> authority of a rabbinic court . . . but stipulate that the beth din shall apply the law of a secular state. Accordingly, if two parties . . . enter into a contract and stipulate that any dispute with regard to fulfillment of the terms of the contract is to be resolved by a rabbinic court in accordance with, for example, the laws of the State of Delaware, the stipulation is void by virtue of being inconsistent with biblical law (*matneh al mah she-katuv ba-Torah*).[182]

Other contemporary decisors, such as R. Zvi Spitz[183] and R. Zvi Gartner,[184] concur, and prohibit private ordering that turns to a foreign legal system for the creation, revision, or termination of a legal arrangement.

Though such recourse to secular law has met with trenchant criticism, there are contexts in which private ordering is deemed halakhically acceptable. Private arrangements concerning the disposition of property which are undertaken and executed in accordance with the formal requirements of the halakha are valid. In the context of monetary affairs, the operative rule is that 'one's stipulation is valid,' and one may even make stipulations that are contrary to Torah law.[185] With respect to monetary matters, the system, rather than taking the halakhic norms to be inviolate, views them as default rules, and allows for contractual variation and even opting out of the default rule entirely.

What is Jewish law's underlying rationale for allowing private ordering? Upon establishing an express agreement that is contrary to the default rule, has one negated the presumption created by the default rule? Is an agreement whereby the financial relations between partners to a civil marriage or cohabitation union will be adjudicated by a rabbinical court pursuant to secular law tantamount to rejecting the authority of the halakhic legal system in general, and the monetary obligations ensuing from marital status in particular? One approach is that once an individual opts out of a privilege accorded by the Torah, the privilege has indeed been nullified. Others contend that an individual cannot uproot monetary provisions by means of stipulation,

182 J. David Bleich, "Litigation and arbitration before non-Jews," *Tradition* 34 (2000), 58, 65–7; idem, *Bintivot Hahalakha*, 2:170–71.

183 R. Zvi Spitz, *Responsa Minhat Zvi*, Laws of Neighbors, #16.

184 R. Zvi Gartner, "On *arkhaot*" (Hebrew), *Yeshurun* 11 (2002), 698–701. See also R. Abraham Sherman, "The community property system is not anchored in Jewish law" (Hebrew), *Tehumin* 19 (1999), 205, 212.

185 bKidushin 19b; bKetubot 56a; bBaba Metzia 94a.

but individuals may make stipulations that waive a right (*mehila*), and establish norms at variance with those of the Torah.[186]

One of the most frequently cited responsa on the prohibition against recourse to Gentile courts in general, and in particular, doing so to nullify normative monetary arrangements, was authored by R. Solomon B. Aderet (Rashba), a thirteenth-century Spanish halakhic authority.[187] A close reading of the responsum, however, provides a firm foundation for validating these arrangements.

> A certain Reuben gave his daughter Leah in marriage to a certain Shimon. From this marriage a daughter was born. After a short time Leah died, and later on her daughter died as well. Reuben, who had given Leah a large dowry, now claimed it back. Although according to the Jewish law of inheritance the husband had a claim to the dowry, as he inherited the estate of his wife as well as that of his daughter, Reuben maintained that in this case the Jewish law of inheritance did not apply, as it was superseded by the law of the land. According to that law, the dowry had to be returned to the father in the circumstances prevailing, and Reuben held that any marriage entered into by residents of the country, whether Jewish or non-Jewish, was subject by custom to the law of the land, a fact which must have been known to all concerned when the marriage contract was effected.[188]

Quite apart from the issue of the applicability of the principle that 'the law of the land is the law' (*dina demalkhuta dina*), the Rashba invalidates the alleged implied agreement, arguing that the father, Reuben, was desirous of imitating the ways of the non-Jews (*meyaker hukot goyim*) by invoking a secular law of inheritance and even turning to a non-Jewish court to adjudicate his claim. In other words, according to the Rashba, one's motivation for incorporating a secular law into one's agreement determines whether it is deemed valid.[189] If the

186 See Shochetman 1981, n. 105 above, 180–81; B. Lifshitz, "*Situmta*: between acquisition and contract" (Hebrew), in M. Corinaldi et al. (eds.), *Studies in Memory of Professor Ze'ev Falk* (Jerusalem: 2005), 59.

187 *Responsa Rashba*, 6:254, cited in *Tur*, HM 26; *Rema, SA*, HM 369:11.

188 Quoted in R. I. Grunfeld, *The Jewish Law of Inheritance* (NY: 1987), 24–25.

189 My reading of the Rashba's position is supported by the interpretation offered in R. Z.N. Goldberg, "Responsum and suggestion regarding recourse to civil courts" (Hebrew), *Yeshurun* 11 (2002), 702; 18 *PDR* 319, 324. Similar readings are found in G. Blidstein, "The Israeli legal system as viewed by contemporary halakhic authorities" (Hebrew), 13–14 *Dine Israel* (1986/88), 21, 42; E. Shochetman, "The halakha's recognition of the laws of the State of Israel" (Hebrew), 16–17 *Shenaton Hamishpat Haivri* (1991), 417, 456–57.

purpose of the private ordering is to negate or modify a Jewish legal institution or provision, the arrangement is null and void. But if the individuals entering into this agreement are merely withdrawing from a privilege granted by the halakhic legal system, their agreement is binding.[190] Applying this principle to civil marriage, in 1990 a rabbinical court handed down a decision that, relying on the secular law in effect at the time the couple married, or in other words, on the implied agreement between them, mandated maintenance payments in a case of a civil marriage between a Jewish man and a non-Jewish woman.[191]

Ought maintenance be awarded to a cohabiting partner? As we saw above, from a halakhic perspective, cohabitation is equivalent to civil marriage. Addressing this issue, R. Solomon Dichovsky argued that, given that such a union lacks both solemnization and contractual ties under Israeli law,[192] there are no grounds for awarding such payments. On this reasoning, under legal systems that have assimilated informal unions into the legal framework of marriage by awarding property rights and benefits such as health insurance and pensions, maintenance awards should be forthcoming. In the United States, as we saw, in many jurisdictions the legal recognition of express and implied agreements between cohabiting partners would mandate maintenance payments. Were an American rabbinical court to adjudicate a claim for maintenance by a cohabiter residing in a jurisdiction where such payments are made, an implied agreement to follow the custom of the locale — civil law — could be inferred, and an award might be made.[193]

190 See *Responsa Minhat Yitzhak*, 9:112; R. Ezra Batzri, *Dinei Mamonot*, 3:197; R. Z.N. Goldberg, "Acquisition in the sale of kidneys" (Hebrew), *Ateret Shlomo* 4 (1997), 49, 52; idem, *Lev Mishpat*, 1:286; Shochetman 1981, n. 105 above, 180–218; D. Malka, "Litigation in rabbinical courts pursuant to secular law" (Hebrew), 8 *Shurat Hadin* 86 (2003); A. Weiss, *Kovetz Darkhei Horaa* 6:111 (2007). For antecedents to this approach, see *Sema*, *SA*, HM 26:11; 61:14; *Netivot Hamishpat* 26:11; R. Haim Halberstam, *Responsa Divrei Haim*, HM 2:30.

191 18 *PDR* 319, 324. This conclusion is in line with the view expressed in R. Jacob Reischer, *Responsa Shvut Yaakov*, 1:20, though the argument there differs.

192 Dichovsky 1998, n. 181 above, 69–70.

193 But see text at n. 211 below.

3. Comparison of the approaches of American law and Jewish law

What role is played by the notion of contract in the approaches to the enforcement of spousal maintenance adopted by these two diverse legal systems? On the surface, both systems seem to have addressed the issue of the financial responsibilities of cohabiters in a similar fashion. Both systems have utilized contractual techniques such as express (written or oral) and implied agreements to resolve this issue. However, on closer analysis, the resolution suggested by Jewish law can be seen to diverge from that of the American legal tradition.

As we saw, in American law, contractual ordering of intimate non-marital relationships was, until recently, barred by public policy interests because of the illegality of the sexual relations that were an element of the living arrangements in question. These relations were construed as consideration in the cohabiting couples' contractual transactions.[194] While many courts invalidated agreements in their entirety on the basis of this illegal consideration doctrine, *Marvin* and other seminal cases demonstrated willingness to view the sexual relations as merely a minor or collateral element in an agreement, and therefore severable, enabling these courts to uphold the legal aspects of the couples' contracts.[195]

There is, however, much disagreement as to whether it is realistic to apply the concept of severability to cohabitation agreements and express and implied contracts. The judicial consensus is that a contract that rests explicitly on consideration for meretricious sexual services is an illegal contract that contravenes public policy.[196] Though it is doubtful that cohabiters expect a weekly check for their domestic services, it is equally obvious that some benefit, other than emotional satisfaction, is almost certainly envisioned by both partners in exchange for their services. Clearly, this type of agreement is inextricably intertwined with the illicit sexual relationship. In such cases, the dictum "*in pari delicto melior est conditio possidentis*" — if two parties are equally at fault, the party in possession is in a better position — is applicable. In other words, the court will not enforce the agreement; it is null and void.

194 Bruch, n. 18 above, 106–109.

195 See text at n. 76 above

196 See text above at n. 19, and see Prince, n. 29 above, 207.

How does Jewish law view this type of agreement? R. Moses Sofer notes that an illicit union ought to impact the legal validity of any contract between the parties.[197] However, adducing various talmudic dicta,[198] he also argues that a prostitute hired by a close relative, who thus commits incest in providing her services, can nonetheless submit a claim for payment to the court. In other words, though such a contract ought to be null and void, R. Sofer concludes that it is an exception to the general rule that prohibited acts invalidate contracts related to the acts in question.

Shochetman has argued that in construing such a contract as illegal, R. Moses Sofer is voicing a minority view.[199] An agreement to pay for prostitution involves undertaking a personal obligation, accompanied by a formal act of acquisition (*kinyan*), to pay for a service. Undertaking the obligation is not in itself commission of a prohibited act. The agreement between the prostitute and her client is contractual in nature, it is a personal undertaking to fulfill a certain duty, a duty that is legally enforceable even though the service provided (incestuous intercourse) is not only prohibited, but a capital offense.[200] The prostitute's engaging in relations with a close relative is indeed prohibited, but her compliance with the conditions of the agreement she made with the client does not constitute violation of a prohibition. That is, the illegality is not in the agreement to pay for sexual services itself. Generally speaking, an illegal agreement is unenforceable if its enforcement results in the contravention of a prohibition. If it meets the requirements of the law of obligations, a 'remuneration for services' agreement can be enforced if it does not result in the contravention of prohibitions. Thus, in theory, such an agreement creates a debt that can be submitted to a court for enforcement.

197 *Responsa Hatam Sofer*, HM #27.

198 bBaba Kama 70b; bBaba Metzia 91a, bAvoda Zara 63a.

199 Shochetman 1981, n. 105 above, 218–19, 224 n. 246; *Taz, SA*, HM 208:2; Shakh, *SA*, HM 208:2; R. Moses Amiel, *Hamidot Leheker Hahalakha*, vol. 2, 14:24–25. Some argue that the illegality does not invalidate the agreement since voiding the agreement will not remedy the violation; see *Responsa Sridei Esh* 1, Hidushim, 258; *Responsa Tzitz Eliezer*, 4:3:13.

200 Shochetman, ibid., 122–24, 217. Cf. Berachyahu Lifshitz, *Kim Lei Bederaba Minei* (PhD dissertation, Hebrew University of Jerusalem, 1979), 168, which challenges the logic of this distinction.

However, in the case of incestuous intercourse, which is a capital offense, we invoke the rule that one who has committed both a capital and a monetary offense, is liable only for the capital offense (*kim lei bederaba minei*), and exempt from the monetary.[201] But the exemption from civil liability (though liability by the laws of heaven remains) does not cancel the monetary obligation.[202] Relying on the agreement, prior to the sexual act, the prostitute has acquired that which the client obligated himself to pay her. As a rabbinical court noted, "the entire obligation stems from the laws of hiring. . . . therefore payment must be mandated . . . pursuant to the value of the work that was done and according to its market value."[203]

Although the *kim lei* rule precludes civil liability for any outstanding nonpayment for services provided, one's duty vis-à-vis heaven must also be discharged.[204] Hence, the prostitute's client remains obligated to make payment. Consequently, should the prostitute seize the object promised as payment, any attempt by the owner to recover it in a court proceeding will be dismissed. Here again, the fact of the prohibited intercourse does not enter into the discussion. In cases of a union which, though illicit, does not involve a capital offense, or the evidentiary requirements for conviction for a capital offense have not been met, civil liability for the debt remains.

The absence of any debate over the impact of the prohibited sexual intercourse on the subsequent legal validity of the 'service contract' is by no means limited to the case of the prostitute. In general, the absence of such discussions highlights the halakha's rejection of the notion that the impropriety of a couple's living arrangement, be it civil marriage or cohabitation, should affect the validity of their financial agreements. Since the system's policy is to refrain from offering benefits to cohabiting partners lest this be construed as sanctioning non-marital unions, there is little discussion of possible grounds for mandating spousal

201 Lifshitz, ibid., 168–98.

202 Cf. R. Arye b. Asher, *Turei Even, Avnei Shoham*, bHagiga 10a.

203 9 *PDR* 16, 37.

204 On liability by the laws of heaven, see Aaron Kirschenbaum, *Equity in Jewish Law* (NY: 1991), 136–77; R. Z.N. Goldberg, "The nature of the prohibition against doing damage, and liability for *gerama* according to the laws of heaven" (Hebrew), *Shaarei Tzedek* 1 (2005).

maintenance.[205] Refusal to engage in such discussions is not a new phenomenon. In the nineteenth century, R. Elijah Hazan of Alexandria was initially opposed to concubinage, which he viewed as lacking in propriety and endorsed only by "rabbis who lack schooling."[206] However, he changed his mind fourteen years later, allowing it under certain prescribed conditions.[207] Concerned about the plight of concubines abandoned by their partners, R. Hazan recommends the drafting of an agreement that would provide concubines, should they be abandoned, with financial support. In other words, he suggested execution of a contract that could be construed as encouraging women to enter into concubinage.[208]

Although R. Hazan, in the cited responsa, offers a detailed analysis of the legitimacy of the institution of concubinage, his suggestion about drafting a cohabitation agreement to protect the concubine's rights is not accompanied by prooftexts or argumentation. Nevertheless, this case provides another example of how the system distinguishes between commission of a prohibited or objectionable act, and the undertaking of an agreement.

> We see clearly that Jewish law does not establish a causal connection between the commission of an offense and the voiding of a civil contract. . . . The violation of the law or of morality is one thing, and the legal validity

205 This explains R. Dichovsky's reluctance, both in theory and in his rulings, to accept arguments for recognition of a spousal maintenance duty in relationships other than halakhic marriage, and arguments for applying the community property regime (*hilkhat shituf*) to domestic partnership. See Solomon Dichovsky, "Rabbinical courts and civil courts: thoughts on their overlapping boundaries in the sphere of family matters" (Hebrew), 4 *Moznei Mishpat* (2005), 290–91; *Plonit v. Almoni*, RHC, case 1–24–2201 [22.3.2004].

206 *Responsa Taalumot Lev*, 1:5. See also *Responsa Rashba Attributed to Nahmanides*, #284; *Responsa Radbaz*, 4:225.

207 *Responsa Taalumot Lev*, 3:32.

208 R. Hazan died in 1908. More than half a millennium earlier, Spanish halakhic authorities had also considered questions concerning concubinage. On contrasting public-policy responses to concubinage, see S. Shtober, "On two questions posed to R. Abraham b. Maimonides (concerning servant-concubines)" (Hebrew), 6–7 *Shenaton Hamishpat Haivri* (1979/80), 339; Yom Tov Assis, "Sexual behavior in medieval Hispano-Jewish society," in A. Rapoport-Albert and S. Zipperstein (eds.), *Jewish History: Essays in Honor of Chimen Abramsky* (Jerusalem: 1988), 36.

> of the contract is another — to the extent that the fulfilling of the contract itself does not activate the offense. . . . Precisely because Jewish law does not distinguish between law and morality, and practically every performance of an obligation is at the same time a fulfillment of a religio-moral commandment — as [in the case of] 'the commandment' of repaying a debt of monetary obligation — the non-fulfillment of a contract entered into through a violation of law will only turn out to be an additional offense to supplement the original one committed by the transgressor.[209]

The notion expressed in the dictum of the talmudic Sage R. Papa, "the payment of a debt is a religious obligation"[210] is implicit here. Despite transgression — failure to live up to the prescribed halakhic directives regarding marital arrangements — agreements that are premised on illicit unions must, on the strength of the obligation to comply with one's contractual agreements, be enforced. Yet though the system upholds contractual agreements between cohabiting couples, it continues to deem the parties' conduct — in rejecting marriage — reprehensible. Consequently, should it be the case that, in a particular context, validating these agreements would serve to promote and legitimize non-marital relationships, decisors are empowered to declare the non-enforceability of these agreements in order to safeguard the law (*lemigdar milta*).[211]

209 Moshe Silberg, *Talmudic Law and the Modern State* (NY: 1973), 82. This doctrine of severability also explains the binding nature, even in the case of a prohibited marriage, of additional amounts specified in the marriage contract (*tosefet ketuba*), see text at nn 110–13 above. On rationales for the doctrine of severability, see Shochetman 1981, n. 105 above, 263–64.

210 bKetubot 86a; bBaba Batra 174a; bArakhin 22a.

211 *Responsa Radbaz*, 1:517, 4:225; *Responsa Shvut Yaakov*, 1:145, 2:136; R. Judah Haim Maslaton, *Responsa Vezot Liyehuda*, EH #7; *Responsa Maarkhei Lev*, n. 134 above, #113. In a case where a child was born from a cohabitation relationship, the rabbinical court mandated maintenance payments precisely due to the impropriety of man's conduct, see 9 *PDR* 307, 323. In other words, disapproval of the relationship may be expressed by obligating the man to pay maintenance. This policy is evident in other contexts as well, see my *Rabbinic Authority: The Vision and the Reality* (Jerusalem: 2013), 111–80. On the other hand, in a recent decision, a rabbinical court denied monetary rights to the wife in a common-law marriage, arguing that any monetary award would undermine the institution of halakhic marriage, see *Plonit v. Ploni*, Tel Aviv-Jaffa Rabbinical Court, case 344858/3 [1.6.2011].

In American law, some jurisdictions have held that contracts between parties to a non-marital union involve immoral consideration and are therefore against public policy and hence unenforceable. Others have adopted the doctrine of severability and upheld contracts for continued support or property division, in the wake of the decriminalization, in numerous states, of sexual relationships between unmarried consenting adults; recognition of constitutional guarantees of individual privacy; and societal acceptance of cohabitation. The severability doctrine, in effect, removes from judicial consideration the moral question of whether a relationship is so objectionable that the state should decline to enforce contracts related to it.[212] The increasing acceptability of these arrangements in American family law in recent decades can be understood as reflecting "a diminution of the law's discourse in moral terms about the relations between family members, and the transfer of many moral decisions from the law to the people the law once regulated."[213]

> What has diminished, over time and variously across sub-domains of family law, is a view that the family has certain characteristics and functions, universal at least within our culture, against which the goodness of behavior and rules can be measured.[214]

Whereas *Hewitt* and its progeny continue to promote conventional marriage, *Marvin* and its progeny adopt a morally-neutral stance on alternative lifestyles, and promote a 'hybrid model,' whereby a married couple is governed by a status-oriented approach and cohabitation arrangements are based on a contractual construct.[215] The legalization of various marital models competing among themselves for state recognition will, it has been argued, eventually lead to the privatization of marriage, allowing "different conceptions of marriage to flourish side-by-side."[216]

212 Hunter, n. 30 above, 1091.

213 Carl Schneider, "Moral discourse and the transformation of American family law," 83 *Michigan Law Review* (1984/85), 1803, 1807–808

214 Lee Teitelbaum, "Moral discourse and family law," 84 *Michigan Law Review* (1985/86), 430, 434.

215 See text above at nn 73–80.

216 Edward Zelinsky, "Deregulating marriage: the pro-marriage case for abolishing civil marriage," 27 *Cardozo Law Review* (2006), 1161. On potential pitfalls of privatization, see Charles Reid Jr., "And the State makes three:

Jewish law continues to be based on a traditional family-based model. Nevertheless, the system addresses the emergence of varying living arrangements in accordance with its inner logic, on its own terms, and on the basis of its own decision-making process.[217] Adjudicators working within the Jewish legal system, like those working within a secular legal system, are bound to interpret its provisions so as to affirm the integrity of its norms and decision-making process. In Jewish law, the illegality of a relationship is not an impediment to enforcing cohabitation agreements. But given that, in the final analysis, Jewish law is by definition a religious legal system, its decisors may, out of policy concerns, choose to consider these contracts unenforceable so as to assure the integrity of Jewish law and sustain the nuclear family as its paradigm.

should the State retain a role in recognizing marriage?" 27 *Cardozo Law Review* (2006), 1277, 1302; Robin Wilson, "The overlooked costs of religious deference," 64 *Washington and Lee Law Review* (2007), 1363.

217 See I. Englard, "Research in Jewish law: its nature and function," in B. Jackson (ed.), *Modern Research in Jewish Law* (Leiden: 1980), 21, 25.

Yuval Sinai, *Application of Jewish Law in the Israeli Courts* (Hebrew), Israel Bar Publishing House, Tel Aviv-Yaffo, 2009, 655 pp.

Steven F. Friedell*

This book has three parts. The first part provides statistics on the use of Jewish law in Israel's courts from 1994 through 2006. The second and longest part contains advice on Jewish law tendered to judges during that period by the Center for the Application of Jewish Law (ISMA) at Netanya Academic College. The final section comments on invocations of Jewish law in various Israeli Supreme Court opinions.

One of the book's contributions is documentation of the number of times Israel's judges have drawn on Jewish law. Although the rates of citation are low, they are not insignificant. In the years 1978 through 2006, between 1% and 16% of the cases heard by Israel's Supreme Court adduced Jewish law. The percentage of lower court cases that adduced Jewish law is smaller, but in light of the fact that there are many more lower court cases, the number of instances where these courts adduced Jewish law is greater. Most of the cases addressed in the book are the lower court cases. These cases cover a wide range of subjects, including: medicine, criminal law, torts, commercial law, contracts, family law, employment, evidence, and civil rights. The second part of the book is arranged by areas of practice. For each area, several cases regarding which ISMA was asked for its opinion are presented. Both the factual background and the legal issue in question are presented for each case, along with the ISMA opinion, which generally discusses various halakhic sources and suggests an analysis of the matter, followed in most instances by a quotation from an Israeli court ruling where Jewish law is adduced. The depth of the explorations of the issues in question is impressive, and each chapter provides a wealth of material and source citations that will be helpful to any researcher.

How should Jewish law be applied in Israel's civil courts? This is not a simple question. It is not merely a matter of identifying the

* Rutgers School of Law–Camden

pertinent halakhic rule or tracing its development from the Talmud to the modern era. Delicate judgment is often required to distill from the often-conflicting halakhic sources a rule that will fit into the framework of existing Israeli law so as to advance a policy that supports the interests of Israeli society.

Jewish law consists of several interrelated regimes. One is the formal system of law, consisting of rabbinical interpretations of Torah law. A second system is that of the king's law. This system, derived from the inherent power of the Jewish king to set rules for an ordered society, allows Jewish communities to establish their own rules. Supplementing these systems, rabbinical courts possess the power to 'make a fence around the Torah' by imposing rules that can protect society during an emergency situation. Moreover, the rabbis recognized the power of custom to change the law, as well their own authority to 'borrow,' as it were, from the laws of the surrounding non-Jewish society. Jewish law also recognizes that obligations to heaven may transcend obligations to earthly lawmakers.[1]

Complicating the picture, there are frequently debates over the scope and interpretation of particular rules drawn from each of these spheres. The law relating to liability for indirect damage is a good example.[2] Some maintain that the rules imposing liability for a certain type of damages, known as *garmi*, are derived from the formal law; others maintain that these rules reflect only the rabbinical authority to levy fines. As a result, there is disagreement over whether liability applies only in the case of intentional torts or also extends to unintentional injuries. It is hard enough to map these developments and understand how they are to be applied to future cases. It is harder still to decide which of them an Israeli civil court should apply.

The book demonstrates the difficulty of determining what it means to 'apply Jewish law,' especially when the halakhic sources support multiple interpretations or when there is no direct precedent. One approach would be to try to apply the view that is dominant among the most recent halakhic authorities. Short of that, one might seek to

1 *Application of Jewish Law in the Israeli Courts* (henceforth, *Application*) discusses four of these systems: the formal law, the king's law, emergency powers, and heavenly law (165–73). It also remarks on the power of custom (281) and the principle that "the law of the kingdom is the law" (519).

2 E.g., *Application*, 263.

determine how a contemporary rabbinical court would resolve the issue. One might also try to extrapolate a rule from an earlier doctrine or set of doctrines. Yet another approach would be to take whichever view appears best suited to the needs of the time. A more liberal approach might evince willingness to take a halakhic rule out of context if this would support a result that was deemed wise. An even more liberal approach would be to use a concept from the Torah or rabbinical literature even if it was not a halakhic legal rule.

Recourse to a range of approaches can be traced to medieval times. Medieval responsa sometimes closely adhere to talmudic rules, and at other times depart from them, applying general principles derived from biblical injunctions. This flexibility affords the court a wide range of possibilities for tying a decision to the Jewish tradition. It does so, however, at substantial cost. If, regardless of how a court may decide a case, it is able to find support in the Jewish tradition, then the worth of citing the tradition is obviously diminished. The constant refrain of, "There is a baraita that supports you, there is a baraita that supports you" can be distressing.[3] Nonetheless, precedent can be valuable in limiting the range of options available to the court, and if the court's decision meets the needs of the time, adducing a precedent from the Jewish tradition will strengthen the decision by grounding it in accepted societal values.

A larger problem is that the formal law has religious goals that may not be 'translatable' into a secular legal system. For example, repentance and atonement are goals of Jewish tort law and Jewish criminal law, goals that are not fully captured by the secular goals of deterrence and rehabilitation. The formal halakhic remedies for tort and crimes often seem lenient, apparently with a view to encouraging the wrongdoer to repent, or at least not discouraging him from repenting. An ordered society, however, requires stricter penalties, and Jewish law provides them through the king's law and the courts' emergency powers. Jewish law is at its weakest when it resorts to using these latter sources of law to support a decision.[4] Although medieval rabbinical authorities and communities had recourse to these sources for the purpose of adopting specific measures they deemed appropriate for social ordering, reliance on that precedent is either unnecessary or inappropriate. It is unnecessary to the extent it affirms the obvious

3 See bBaba Metzia 84a.
4 *Application*, 198–99.

point that Israel's courts and legislature have the power to make rules necessary for the orderly governance of society. It is inappropriate because the rabbinical authorities and community leadership have certain powers that a contemporary civil court cannot legitimately employ, such as the authority to depart from the law in a particular case if this is deemed appropriate.[5]

Some features of the legal regimes worked out by Jewish communities, such as permanent or temporary exile,[6] infliction of corporal punishment,[7] and forgoing the institution of bail,[8] are inappropriate today. Others, such as house arrest,[9] are appropriate. Jewish law does not provide the criteria for choosing which precedents are appropriate. The court makes that determination by applying a set of values that it derives independently of the halakha.

The book discusses many disputes that arose among the Jewish legal authorities. Some of these disputes involve legal doctrines that were undeveloped for most of Jewish history. How is a civil court to choose which position to adopt when the law in question is the subject of halakhic controversy? An example of a question regarding which there is, beyond the Bible, little or no precedent in the sources of Jewish law, is that of whether collective punishment in wartime is permitted.[10] Should we be motivated by the ideal that an offender should be put to death only "for his own sin" (2 Kings 14:6)? Or are we

5 E.g., bBaba Kama 96b (imposing liability contrary to the law in order to fine a notorious robber); R. Nissim b. Reuven Gerondi (Spain, c. 1310–1375), *Responsa Ran*, #41 (communal leaders can fine a creditor who lent money on interest even though under the formal law the court can only disallow the collection of interest); R. Israel b. Petahiah Isserlein (Germany, 1390–1460), *Trumat Hadeshen*, 1:307 (Shimon slandered Reuben, causing Reuben to lose his position as prayer leader. Even though Shimon is not obligated, as a matter of strict law, to compensate Reuben, the court may fine him in order to try and limit such acts). See *SA*, HM 2:1.

6 See Jacob Bazak, "The laws of manslaughter in the responsa literature" (Hebrew), *Sinai* 68 (1970/71), 275, 279–80, 286.

7 See Jacob Bazak, *Punishment: Principles and Application in Israel and in Jewish Law* (Hebrew), (Jerusalem: 1981), 51–53.

8 *Respona Rivash*, #336, quoted in *Application*, 151–52.

9 See *Application*, 153.

10 Ibid., 440–45.

to follow examples that depart from this ideal?[11] The answer cannot be arrived at by biblical scholarship or interpretive analysis.[12] One might bolster a decision by adducing these precedents, but at the end of the day, the halakhic tradition offers little direct guidance regarding such questions.

In other areas, Jewish law has developed only recently, largely in reaction to developments in the law of the surrounding cultures. Examples include intellectual property law,[13] corporate law,[14] and statutes of limitation.[15] The book's discussion of these topics tends to demonstrate how Jewish law has assimilated these doctrines rather than to show how Jewish law itself might be applied to these new spheres.

In some areas, like regulation of monopolies and competition,[16] the social and economic conditions have changed so much that earlier precedent is useful only with respect to the question of the community's regulatory power. Specific regulations, obviously, have little contemporary applicability.

What, then, is the purpose of adducing Jewish law in the context of opinions rendered by Israel's civil courts? To some extent the purpose is simply "to enlarge the Torah in utmost beauty" (*lehagdil tora ulehaadira*).[17] That is, adducing and citing Jewish law, even in support of decisions reached on other grounds, attests to its relevance and applicability.[18] Invoking Jewish law is, therefore, in that sense somewhat apologetic.

11 E.g., Genesis 36:25 (the massacre at Shechem); Deuteronomy 13:16–17 (directive to destroy a city that has worshipped other gods); Judges 21:10–11 (massacre of inhabitants of Jabesh-Gilead for failure to fight the Benjaminites); 2 Samuel 21:6–9 (handing over seven of Saul's descendants to the Gibeonites to be killed in revenge for Saul's killing Gibeonites).

12 In addition to the sources cited in *Application*, 444 n. 19, see M. Greenberg, "Some postulates of biblical criminal law," in Menahem Haran (ed.), *Studies in Bible and Jewish Religion: Yehezkel Kaufmann Jubilee Volume* (Jerusalem: 1960), 5, 20–27 (only crimes against God are subject to collective punishment).

13 *Application*, 513–20.

14 Ibid., 261–62.

15 Ibid., 281.

16 Ibid., 243–57.

17 See David De Sola Pool, *Book of Prayers according to the Custom of the Spanish and Portuguese Jews* (NY: 2001), 228.

18 E.g., *Application*, 258–69 (piercing the corporate veil).

Sometimes a judge seeks to use Jewish law to justify the court's judgment to the losing party who happens to be an observant Jew. This has occurred in cases of child and spousal abuse, for example, where the abuser based his defense on his own understanding of Jewish tradition.[19] Although not stated, adducing halakhic sources in these opinions also seem intended to demonstrate to the secular public that Jewish law does not condone immoral behavior.

In other instances, Israeli courts refer to Jewish law in the course of explaining the historical development of a legal tradition. Use of Jewish law in this manner helps to anchor the court's ruling, showing that it is based on a long-standing tradition or expresses a cultural value. It is here that the use of Jewish law may have its greatest impact in helping to define and reinforce a sense of national identity. And it is here that the book under review makes the greatest contribution.

19 Ibid., 124, 179.

STYLE SHEET

STYLE SHEET

In preparing your manuscript, please conform to the following guidelines. Manuscripts not so prepared will be edited by JLA staff or returned for revision.

1 Please provide a line or two of information about yourself, such as an institutional affiliation, before the first footnote.
2 Manuscripts should be submitted electronically, in WORD 2010 or lower, and should be double-spaced (text and footnotes).
3 The file should not contain any tracked changes, comments, electronically linked cross-references, highlighting, underlining, different font colors, or other markings. 12 pt. font, preferably Times New Roman, should be used throughout, including the notes.
4 All references must conform to the *Jewish Law Annual* house style specified below.
5 All references containing titles originally in Hebrew should provide both the original title of the work in transliteration, and the official title in English if it is given in the book or appears in an English table of contents (often found at the end of the volume). If no English title is given, please suggest a translation, indicating that it is your own.
7 Authorized Version abbreviations for books of the Bible, listed in dictionaries and style guides such as the *Chicago Manual of Style*, should be used. In referring to the Talmud, tractate names should not be abbreviated. m, b, j, or t should be prefixed to the tractate name to indicate whether the Mishnah, the Babylonian Talmud, Jerusalem Talmud or Tosefta is being referred to.

CITATION STYLE

Halakhic literature

Beit Yosef, Tur, HM 362:57
Kli Hemda, Torah portion 'Pinhas,' at the beginning
Maimonides, *Code*, Laws concerning Robbery and Lost Property 11:1
R. Jacob Castro (Maharikash), *Erekh Lehem*, EH 143
Perisha, HM 201:1 (at the end)
Rashi, bBaba Kama 27a s.v. *lemikah umimkar*
Responsa Beit Shlomo, OH #57

Responsa Igrot Moshe, YD 2:174
Responsa Mabit, #37
Responsa Tzitz Eliezer, 9:28:3
Sefer Hasidim, §723
Sefer Mitzvot Katan, #265 (Rosenberg edition, 2:371)
Shulhan Shlomo, 2:14–16

Books

W.C. Kaiser, *Toward Old Testament Ethics* (Grand Rapids MI: 1978), 99.
E.E. Urbach, *The Sages: Their Concepts and Beliefs*, trans. I. Abrahams (Jerusalem: 1987), 1:343.

Journal articles

R. Kleinman, "Early interpretations of the Bible and Talmud as a reflection of medieval legal realia," 16 *Jewish Law Annual* (2006), 25–50.
Joseph Raz, "Legal principles and the limits of law," 81 *Yale L.J.* (1972), 823, 830.
A. Shaffer, "Cuneiform tablets from Palestine I: the letter from Shechem" (Hebrew), *Beer-Sheva* 3 (1988), 163–69.

Articles in edited volumes

B.S. Jackson, "Legalism and spirituality," in E.B. Firmage, B.G. Weiss and J.W. Welch (eds.), *Religion and Laws: Biblical, Judaic and Islamic Perspectives* (Winona Lake IN: 1990), 243–61.
D. Sinclair, "Defending the lives of the mortally ill, the embryo, and the non-Jew" (Hebrew), in G. Frishtick (ed.), *Human Rights in Judaism* (Hebrew), (Jerusalem: 1992), 37 n. 19.

Cross-references in notes

22 S. Assaf, *The Courts and Their Procedures after the Finalization of the Talmud* (Hebrew), (Jerusalem: 1924), 38–41.
23 D. Sperber, *Material Culture in Eretz-Israel during the Talmudic Period* (Hebrew), vol. 1 (Jerusalem: 1993), vol. 2 (Jerusalem: 2006).
24 See Assaf 1924, n. 22 above, 67.
25 Ibid., 121.
26 Sperber, n. 23 above, 2:126–33.

TRANSLITERATION

Wherever possible, essential Hebrew is to be transliterated into English rather than word-processed in Hebrew characters, as follows:

alef	a	lamed	l
bet	b	mem	m
vet	v	nun	n
gimel	g	samekh	s
dalet	d	ayin	a
hei (pronounced)	h	pei	p
vav	v	fei	f
zayin	z	tzadi	tz
het	h	kuf	k
tet	t	reish	r
yod	y	shin	sh
kaf	k	sin	s
khaf	kh	tav	t

patah; kamatz	a
hirik	i
shva (pronounced)	e
segol	e
shuruk; kubutz	u
holam	o
tzeire	ei

No diacriticals, apostrophes, hyphens, doubling of consonants or capitalization should be used as elements of the transliteration or to indicate prefixes and the definite article.

These transliteration guidelines are not intended to apply to papers addressing linguistic or philological issues.